ABSTRACTS

OF

WESTMORELAND COUNTY, PENNSYLVANIA

TAX RECORDS

1815

Amy E. K. Arner

HERITAGE BOOKS
2014

HERITAGE BOOKS

AN IMPRINT OF HERITAGE BOOKS, INC.

Books, CDs, and more—Worldwide

For our listing of thousands of titles see our website
at
www.HeritageBooks.com

Published 2014 by
HERITAGE BOOKS, INC.
Publishing Division
5810 Ruatan Street
Berwyn Heights, Md. 20740

International Standard Book Numbers
Paperbound: 978-0-7884-5587-2
Clothbound: 978-0-7884-6021-0

Abstracts of Westmoreland County, Pennsylvania,
Tax Records 1815

Contents

Abstracts of Westmoreland County, Pennsylvania,
Tax Records 1815

Abstracts of Westmoreland County, Pennsylvania, Tax Records 1815

Introduction

This is a book of abstracts of tax records. The original records are arranged by township and within each township alphabetically by the first letter of the surname. I followed the same arrangement. For each entry, I included the name of the taxpayer, the types of taxable property, and the tax paid. When an occupation or marital status is given, I included it. Any notes written in the entries or margins are included. I did not include the tax rates for the various types of property. For this information, please consult the original records. These records are held by the Westmoreland County Records Management Office in Greensburg. The Westmoreland County Historical Society has photocopies of some of the records. As of this writing, the records have not been microfilmed nor digitized.

Each tax collector formatted his records in his own way. Some included single men on the main list; others put single men on a separate list. Some wrote a list of poor children at the end of their records. I included all of the lists of poor children. Some included unseated land on the main list; others put unseated land on a separate list. Unseated land is "land which, though owned by a private person, has not been reclaimed, cultivated, improved, occupied, or made a place of residence." [1]

The available records for Fairfield and Washington townships do not list the taxable property—only the name of the tax payer and the tax.

---

[1] Henry Campbell Black, *A Dictionary of Law* (1891), image reprint, CD-ROM, *A Dictionary of Law* (Columbia, Maryland: Archive CD Books USA, 2006), 1203, "unseated land."

Abstracts of Westmoreland County, Pennsylvania, Tax Records 1815

Conventions Used
- Some entries in the records were crossed out. This could be entire entries, part of a name, or just some of the property. In these cases, I used strikethrough over the text.
- The number for a type of livestock may have been written over a different number. In these cases, what I interpreted to be the final number is listed and the number that was written over is included as text with a strikethrough.
- Any text in square brackets represents additions I made to the records.
- Any text in quotation marks appears exactly that way in the original records.
- There are some entries that had superscript text. The superscript is included as it was in the original.
- In some cases an occupation was listed as an abbreviation. When I was certain what the occupation was, I expanded it to the full word. I did not use square brackets in these cases.
- In all cases I expanded the abbreviation SM to single man. I did not use square brackets in these cases.
- The tax collectors in some townships had tax amounts in two columns. In these cases, I included the amount in the column on the left. If there were two numbers in the same column, I included the number on top.

I would like to thank the Westmoreland County Historical Society, in particular Lisa Hays and Joanna Moyar, for their help with this project. I also thank my friend and colleague Harold Henderson for his valuable feedback on the introduction.

AEKA
September 2014

Abstracts of Westmoreland County, Pennsylvania, Tax Records 1815

Derry Township Name of Person and Taxable Property	Tax
Thomas Anderson, Senior	$4.34
300 acres, 1 horse	
"the Land to John M Hillip"	
Andrew Armstrong, "B man"	$0.06
2 cows, 1 horse	
James Alexander	$0.07
2 horses, 2 cows	
Thomas Anderson, Junior	$2.26
250 acres, 2 horses, 2 cows	
John Anderson, Senior	$1.72
130 acres, 100 acres, 2 horses, 2 cows	
John Anderson, "point"	$0.67
100 acres, 2 horses, 2 cows	
John Anderson, Junior	$2.27
155.5 acres, 4 horses, 3 cows	
Abraham Adams, forgeman	$0.14
2 cows	
Andrew Aalison	$10.20
80 acres, 80 acres in trust, 4 horses, 3 cows	
Thomas Aaron, single man	$0.50
John Andrew, single man	$0.50
Michael Anderson, single man	$0.50
Joseph Andrew, single man	$0.50
John Bollman	$1.00
73 acres, 1 horse, 1 cow	
James Bell, taylor	$0.37
1 house and lot in "Den Town," 1 cow	
"House and lot to John Collins"	
William Baird, Senior	$1.24
~~150 acres~~, 1 horse, 1 cow, 156 acres	
"150 acres of the land to Andrew Dushane"	
"Mr Ass^r at the appeal entre whether Baird W$_m$	
Senr is taxed fro any land or how much"	
Samuel Baird, single man	$0.50

1

Abstracts of Westmoreland County, Pennsylvania, Tax Records 1815

Derry Township Name of Person and Taxable Property	Tax
~~John Baird, single man~~	$0.50
William Baird, Junior	$0.13
2 horses, 1 cow, 100 acres	
James Baird, Senior	$6.66
192 acres, 275 acres, 100 acres, 3 horses, 4 cows	
100 acres "to Wᵐ Baird Junʳ"	
Charles Baird	$2.26
244 acres, 3 horses, 4 cows	
~~Thomas Baird~~	$0.15
2 horses, 2 cows	
Joseph Barns	$1.22
150 acres, 1 sawmill, 2 horses, 2 cows	
David Beatty, wheelwright	$0.14
1 horse, 2 cows	
Samuel Bell, weaver	$0.16
3 horses, 4 cows	
~~Dennis Brojan, single man~~	$0.50
William Bell	$2.30
130 acres, 2 ~~3~~ horses, 4 cows	
Robert Bell, tanner	$0.29
John Bell, ~~single man~~	$0.07
1 horse, 90 acres	
John Bell, Junior, single man	$2.12
130 acres, 4 horses, 4 ~~2~~ cows	
~~young mans tax~~	
~~John Bell, Junior, single man~~	$0.06
Robert Barr	$1.70
100 acres, ~~2 horses~~, 2 cows	
Elizabeth Barr, widow	$0.70
63 acres, 2 horses, 2 cows	
Charles Brogan, weaver	$0.37
20 acres, 2 cows	
Nathaniel Burns	$0.00
1 cow, 1 horse	
James Blair	$0.48
100 acres, 2 horses, 1 cow	

Abstracts of Westmoreland County, Pennsylvania, Tax Records 1815

Derry Township Name of Person and Taxable Property	Tax
~~Robert Baird~~	$1.50
300 acres	
"Land to Jonathan Staut"	
John Bigham	$1.04
100 acres, 3 horses, 2 cows	
John Bell	$0.06
1 horse, 1 cow	
Peter Bellows	$1.96
260 acres, 2 horses, 2 cows	
Giles Butterfield, shoemaker	$0.23
1 acre, 1 horse, 1 cow, 30 acres	
~~Mathias~~ Mary Bridge, widow	$0.56
100 acres, 1 horse, 2 ~~1~~ cows	
Henry Bridge	$0.28
50 acres,1 ~~2~~ horse, 1 cow	
Thomas Boyd	$0.47
50 acres, 2 ~~1~~ horses, 2 cows	
John Berry	$0.85
150 acres, 1 horse	
Andrew Bell	$1.43
93 acres, 1 horse, 2 cows, 1 horse	
William Beatty	$1.23
200 acres, 2 horses, 1 cow	
Henry Buckholder	$1.75
200 acres, 2 horses, 4 cows, ~~1 cow~~	
~~Daniel Bates~~	$0.06
1 horse	
John Braden	$1.95
216 acres, 2 horses, 2 cows, 1 cow	
Joseph Baldridge	$7.94
450 acres, 1 gristmill, 1 sawmill, 1 distillery 4 horses, 6 cows	
"134 Acres of land to Joseph Smith"	
Edward Braden	$4.83
203 acres, 231 acres, 200 acres, 3 horses, 3 cows	
"203 acres of land to James McGee"	

Derry Township Name of Person and Taxable Property	Tax
William Braden	$4.77
~~300~~ 150 acres, 100 acres, 2 horses, 2 cows	
"450 acres of the land to James Breaden"	
George Beer, gunsmith	$0.14
1 horse, 1 ~~2~~ cow	
~~Daniel Brine, weaver~~	~~$0.06~~
John Barnett, Esquire	$2.91
343 acres, 3 horses, 4 ~~5~~ cows	
Samuel Barnett, single man	$0.50
William Barnett	$0.14
1 ~~2~~ horse, 3 cows	
Thomas Beaty	$0.00
22 acres, 1 horse, 1 cow	
Jacob Barlein, blacksmith	$0.16
1 cow	
James Breaden	$0.00
150 acres, 100 acres, 1 horse, 1 cow	
Joseph Culbertson	$0.00
2 horses, 3 cows	
William Caruthers	$0.09
1 horse, 2 cows	
Samuel Caskey	$4.16
300 acres, 2 horses, 2 cows	
Michael Crate, single man	$0.00
John Cavett	$0.06
1 cow	
John Campbell, Senior	$0.70
100 acres, 2 horses, 2 cows	
John Campbell, single man	$0.50
Andrew Campbell, ~~single man~~	$0.55
2 ~~1~~ horses, 4 cows	
James Samuel Culbertson	$5.22
382 acres, 4 ~~5~~ horses, 4 cows	
"200 acres of land to ~~James~~ Hugh & Alexander Culbertson"	
~~James~~ Alexander Culbertson, single man	$0.79

Abstracts of Westmoreland County, Pennsylvania, Tax Records 1815

Derry Township Name of Person and Taxable Property	**Tax**
100 acres, 1 distillery, 1 ~~2~~ horse, 1 cow	
"There is no single mans tax charged to Alex^r Culbertson put it on at the appeal if he is not married yet Mr Ass^r & "	
James Culbertson, single man	$0.50
Hugh Culbertson	$0.37
100 acres, 1 distillery, 2 horses, 3 cows	
Jane Crow, widow	$0.59
100 acres, 2 cows	
Samuel Crow, ~~single man~~	$0.50
1 horse, 1 cow	
~~James Craig~~	~~$0.06~~
~~1 cow~~	
Nicholas Chapman	$3.76
246 acres, 3 horses, 5 cows	
Daniel Carty	$0.09
2 horses, 1 cow	
Robert Charleton	$0.98
200 acres, 1 horse, 1 cow	
Robert Cooper, ~~carpenter~~	$0.06
1 cow	
~~Barney Cline, Junior~~	~~$0.37~~
~~72 acres, 1 horse, 2 cows~~	
"the land to John Eggen"	
Barnabas Cline, Senior	$0.88
150 acres, 1 ~~2~~ horse, 2 cows	
Peter Cline	$0.06
1 cow	
Joseph Canan	$0.79
129 acres, 1 ~~2~~ horse, 4 ~~3~~ cows	
Jonathan Canaan, ~~single man~~	$0.50
1 horse	
James Caldwell, blacksmith, ~~single man~~	$0.50
James Caldwell, Senior	$0.73
100 acres, 1 cow, 1 horse	
Benjamin Caldwell	$0.06

Derry Township Name of Person and Taxable Property	Tax
1 horse	
Richard Canaan	$0.10
2 horses, 3 2 cows, 100 acres	
William Carson	$0.06
1 cow, 1 horse	
John Craig	$0.06
1 cow, ~~1 horse~~	
James Campbell, shoemaker	$0.00
1 cow	
James Carson, single man	$0.56
1 horse	
~~Richard Conden~~	~~$1.21~~
162 acres, ~~3 horses, 3 cows~~	
"the land to John Flowers"	
James Cochran	$0.57
90 acres, 1 2 horse, 2 cows	
Christopher Cribbs	$0.10
2 horses, 1 2 cow, 100 acres	
Daniel Crate	$0.92
153 acres, 2 horses, 2 cows	
Benjamin Crozan, ~~single man~~	$0.50
1 horse, 1 cow	
Nancy Craig, widow	$0.00
60 acres, 1 cow	
Garret Crossan	$0.40
200 acres, 2 horses, 4 cows	
John Carson, Junior	$0.80
100 acres, 2 horses, 1 cow	
~~William or John~~ Matthews Craig	$0.52
100 acres, 1 cow, 1 horse	
Joseph Carson	$0.47
75 acres, 1 2 horse, 2 cows	
Paine Carson, blacksmith	$0.13
~~1 horse~~	
John Carson, Senior, taylor	$0.17
2 cows	

Abstracts of Westmoreland County, Pennsylvania, Tax Records 1815

Derry Township Name of Person and Taxable Property	Tax
Jesse Cable, shoemaker	$0.16
1 cow	
Joseph Case	$0.26
45 acres, 1 horse, 1 ~~2~~ cow	
Timothy Connor	$2.15
260 acres, 3 horses, 4 cows	
Dennes Connor	$0.10
2 horses, 2 cows	
~~John~~ Jesse Cogan, shoemaker	$0.06
1 cow, 2 horses	
Robert Cochran	$0.06
1 horse, 1 cow	
William Cochran, single man	$0.50
John Cannon, ~~taylor~~	$0.36
42 acres, ~~1 horse, 1 cow~~	
John Cummins	$0.41
58 acres, ~~1 horse~~, 1 ~~3~~ cow	
Alexander Cannon	$1.53
301 acres, 2 horses, 2 ~~3~~ cows	
Michael Churn	$0.47
100 acres, 2 horses, 3 cows	
John Cochran	$2.78
230 acres, 4 ~~3~~ horses, 5 ~~3~~ cows	
Samuel Cochran	$2.72
220 acres, 1 tanyard, 2 horses, 4 cows	
Andrew Craig	$3.28
125 acres, 1/2 a gristmill, 1/2 a sawmill, 2 ~~3~~ horses, 5 cows	
~~James Coutler~~	~~$0.68~~
~~5 horses~~	
Joseph Craig	$3.28
125 acres, 1/2 a gristmill, 1/2 a sawmill, 3 horses, 5 cows	
James Coulter, ~~Senior~~ Junior	$2.35
394 acres, 4 ~~2~~ horses, 1 cow	
Robert Coulter	$0.16

Abstracts of Westmoreland County, Pennsylvania, Tax Records 1815

Derry Township Name of Person and Taxable Property	Tax
2 4 horses, 1 cow	
Thomas Culbertson, Esquire	$2.63
240 acres, 2 4 horses, 3 6 cows, wheelwright manufactory	
Henry Clever	$0.06
1 horse, 1 cow	
Cornelius Casally	$0.00
90 acres, 3 horses, 3 cows	
Thomas Culbertson, single man	$0.00
John Connor, single man	$0.00
Frederick Deemer	$0.00
1 cow	
Nicholas Day, postmaster	$9.26
160 acres, 4 acres and house, 10 acres, 1 tanyard, 1 gristmill, 1 sawmill, 9 5 horses, 4 cows, 1 house and lot	
John Donnelly	$0.19
45 acres, 2 1 horses, 2 cows	
~~Truman Donnelly, single man~~	~~$0.54~~
~~1 horse~~	
Levi Doty	$0.70
100 acres, 2 horses, 2 cows	
Samuel Denniston	$1.32
1 house and lot, 2 horses, 2 cows	
~~Stephen Drury~~	~~$0.90~~
~~1 house and lot in Der Town, 1 horse, 3 cows~~	
"the House and lot to Nicholas Day & Timothy Janes"	
David Dixen, weaver	$1.65
130 acres, 1 horse, 3 cows	
Francis Donald	$0.49
200 acres, 1 horse, 2 cows	
Nathaniel Doty, ~~single man~~	$0.57
1 horse, 2 cows	
Zebulon Doty	$2.24
234 acres, 2 3 horses, 5 cows	

Abstracts of Westmoreland County, Pennsylvania,
Tax Records 1815

Derry Township Name of Person and Taxable Property	Tax
John Doty, single man	$0.00
1 horse	
James Duncan	$0.62
100 acres, 2 horses, 1 2 cow	
Robert Duncan	$0.64
100 acres, 2 horses, 2 cows	
Thomas Dunlap	$4.28
399 462 acres, 59 acres, 6 horses, 4 2 cows	
the 59 acres was "to Daniel Vanleer"	
James Donaughy	$0.06
1 horse, 1 cow	
Joseph Dixon	$3.28
282 acres, 1 horse, 1 cow	
Israel Doty	$0.10
1 horse, 2 cows	
Nathaniel Doty, Senior	$1.88
120 acres, 164 acres, 3 5 horses, 3 5 cows	
James Donald, tanner	$0.80
108 acres, 1 tanyard, 1 horse, 1 cow	
"Land to Dr. Talmage"	
William Dunlap, single man	$0.57
1 horse	
Jonathan Doty, Junior	$1.03
195 150 acres, 2 horses, 1 cows	
William Dunlap, Senior	$1.80
150 acres, 1 horse, 2 cows	
John Dunlap	$0.07
3 1 horses, 1 cow	
Jonathan Doty, Senior	$2.95
112 acres, 104 acres, 4 2 horses, 2 3 cows	
William Davis	$0.06
1 horse, 3 cows	
William Denniston	$6.10
480 acres, 1 distillery, 1 slave, 4 horses, 7 cows	
James Dunlap	$0.00
1 cow	

Abstracts of Westmoreland County, Pennsylvania, Tax Records 1815

Derry Township Name of Person and Taxable Property	Tax
Thomas Donald	$0.00
1 horse, 1 cow	
Jonathan B. Doty, single man	$0.00
Jonathan Doty, single man	$0.00
~~John Doty~~	$0.00
Robert Elder	$4.70
300 acres, 1 distillery, 5 horses, 5 cows	
Samuel Eckels, constable	$0.49
100 acres, 2 horses, 1 cow	
James Eaton	$1.00
100 acres, ~~1 horse~~	
Joseph Eckels	$0.73
86 acres, 3 horses, 3 cows	
"land to James Read"	
~~Andrew Ellison~~	~~$1.46~~
~~80 acres, 80 acres, 4 horses, 4 cows~~	
John Eggen	$0.06
~~1 horse,~~ 1 cow, 72 acres	
~~John Eykes~~	$0.00
Thomas Elder	$0.06
1 ~~2~~ horse	
~~John Fenton, saddler~~	~~$0.36~~
~~1 horse~~	
Elijah Fells, single man	$0.50
Albert Ferguson	$1.55
199 acres, ~~2 horses, 3 cows~~	
~~William Frame, single man~~	~~$0.50~~
William Ferguson	$0.12 1/2
2 horses, 1 ~~2~~ cow	
James Fleming	$0.09
2 horses, 1 ~~2~~ cow	
James Fulton, Senior	$4.16
430 acres, 3 horses, 3 cows	
~~James Fulton, single man~~	~~$0.50~~
Abraham Fulton, Junior	$0.06
1 horse, 1 cow	

Abstracts of Westmoreland County, Pennsylvania,
Tax Records 1815

Derry Township Name of Person and Taxable Property	**Tax**
~~James Ferguson~~	~~$2.17~~
~~180 acres, 2 horses, 2 cows~~	
"The land to Peter Hinckle"	
Abraham Fulton, Senior	$2.78
300 acres, 1 distillery, 4 ~~3~~ horses, 6 cows	
Joseph Fulton, single man	$0.56
~~1 horse~~	
James George	$1.96
200 acres, 4 ~~2~~ horses, 3 ~~5~~ cows	
Robert Guthrie	$1.40
230 acres, 1 ~~2~~ horse, 1 cow	
~~John Guinn, single man~~	~~$0.50~~
Eleanor Gilchrist, widow	$0.14
1 house and lot in Den Town	
~~Aaron Gamble~~	~~$0.10~~
~~2 horses, 2 cows~~	
Israel Gray	$0.06
1 horse, 1 cow	
Mathew George	$1.56
200 acres, 3 ~~2~~ horses, 2 ~~3~~ cows	
William George	$0.09
1 horse, 1 ~~2~~ cow	
John George	$1.26
36 acres, ~~2 horses, 2 cows,~~ 300 acres in trust the 300 acres were "to Robert McCanoughy"	
James Guthrie, single man	$2.06
112 acres, 1 horse, 3 ~~2~~ cows	
Joseph Guthrie	$4.99
100 ~~380~~ acres, 1 horse, 2 cows "280 acres of the land to David Spedman"	
Thomas Gallaher	$1.73
196 acres, 1 horse, 1 cow	
John Gallaher	$1.50
142 acres, 1 sawmill, 2 horses, 4 ~~5~~ cows	
David Gilson	$2.28
172.5 acres, 2 horses, 1 ~~2~~ cow	

Derry Township Name of Person and Taxable Property	Tax
John Garland, shoemaker	$0.06
1 cow	
John Gourley, single man, clerk	$0.64
Moses Gillespie, single man, forgeman	$0.07
~~George Gray, carpenter~~	~~$0.13~~
~~1 horse, 1 cow~~	
John Gilson	$2.32
172.5 acres, 2 horses, ~~1 cow~~	
James Gibson	$0.30
2 5 horses, 2 cows	
John Guier, single man	$0.00
Morten Geary	$0.00
3 horses, 2 cows	
John Geary	$0.00
1 cow	
William Hamilton	$1.62
183 acres, 6 horses, 2 4 cows	
Joseph Hill	$2.78
290 acres, 5 horses, 4 5 cows, 21 acres	
Joshua Hill, single man	$0.50
~~David~~ Anna Henon, widow	$1.10
180 acres, 1 horse, 1 2 cow	
Edward Harkins	$1.10
250 acres, 300 acres, 200 acres, ~~2 horses, 1 cow~~	
Neal Harkins	$0.06
1 cow	
Richard Hill	$2.64
250 acres, 2 horses, 2 3 cows	
Abraham Hill, single man	$0.57
1 horse	
James Henry, single man	$1.43
200 acres, 2 horses, 1 cow	
~~Robert Henry, single man~~	~~$0.57~~
~~1 horse~~	
John Housholder	$0.94
119 ~~150~~ acres, 2 horses, 2 cows	

Abstracts of Westmoreland County, Pennsylvania, Tax Records 1815

Derry Township Name of Person and Taxable Property	Tax
Jonathan Housholder, single man	$0.50
John Harshman ~~Harsman or~~ 40 acres, 2 cows	$0.14
Robert Hartley, saddler 160 acres, 3 ~~2~~ horses, 4 ~~2~~ cows	$1.26
John Hainey 60 acres, 1 horse, 1 ~~2~~ cow	$0.59
James Henderson 124 acres, 2 horses, 2 cows	$0.44
~~James Holliday, shoemaker~~	~~$0.06~~
James Hainey, single man 1 horse	$0.50
John Horrel, hatter 5 acres, 1 horse, 2 cows	$0.67
Edward Hill, single man	$0.00
Mathias Holston 130 acres, 2 horses, 3 cows	$0.77
Isaac Hews 200 acres, 95 acres, 2 horses, 1 ~~3~~ cow	$1.67
William Hews, Junior 130 acres, 1 ~~2~~ horses, 3 cows	$1.66
John Hare 2 horses, 1 cow	$0.06
William Hews, Senior 137 acres, 2 horses, 3 cows	$1.70
George Harshman ~~Marchman~~, single man	$0.00
Peter Hoontsbarger, blacksmith 1 horse, 2 cows	$0.00
Peter Hinckle 180 acres, 6 horses, 4 cows	$0.00
Andrew Irwin, tanner ~~1 cow~~	$0.30
Timothy Jaynes, carpenter 100 acres, 2 horses, 3 cows	$1.02
Robert Jellison, Senior 126 acres, 3 horses, 5 cows	$0.92

Abstracts of Westmoreland County, Pennsylvania, Tax Records 1815

Derry Township Name of Person and Taxable Property	Tax
Robert Jellison, Junior	$0.60
100 acres, 2 horses, 2 cows	
Hugh Irwin	$1.28
121 acres, 1 horse, 2 cows	
Samuel Irwin	$1.24
121 acres, 3 2 cows, 1 horse	
James Ingles	$0.10
2 horses, 2 cows	
Ephraim Jellison	$1.30
100 acres, 100 acres, 2 horses, 4 cows	
Thomas Jordan	$0.77
100 acres, 1 horse, 1 cow	
~~Robert Johnston, fuller~~	~~$0.37~~
~~1 horse, 1 2 cow~~	
~~George Johnston, fuller~~	~~$0.30~~
~~1 horse, 1 cow~~	
Samuel Jordan	$0.62
66 acres, 1 horse, 1 cow	
David Jordan, single man	$1.81
134 acres, 3 horses, 3 2 cows	
~~William Joice, single man~~	~~$0.50~~
John Jordan, single man	$0.00
James Johnston	$0.72
86 acres, 2 horses, 1 cow	
Ephraim Johnston	$0.32
90 acres, 2 horses, 1 cow	
William Johnston	$5.96
188 acres, 159 acres, 1 gristmill, 1 sawmill, 1 distillery, 6 5 horses, 6 5 cows	
~~William Johnston, Junior~~ Alexander Johnston	$8.56
1 forge, 1 sawmill, 2000 acres, 11 horses, 4 cows	
~~Thomas Jones~~	$1.53
~~200 acres, 2 horses, 2 cows~~	
[either the land or the horses] "to Elizabeth Craig"	
Arthur Kiskaddin	~~$0.49~~

Abstracts of Westmoreland County, Pennsylvania, Tax Records 1815

Derry Township Name of Person and Taxable Property	Tax
50 acres, ~~1 horse, 2 cows~~	
Francis Kilday	$0.46
119 acres, 2 horses, 2 ~~4~~ cows	
John King	$0.06
1 horse, 1 cow	
John Kincaid, single man	$0.50
1 horse	
~~James Kiskaddin~~	~~$1.22~~
~~202 acres, 1 horse, 2 cows~~	
"the land to Andrew Harps"	
Andrew Kincaid, Esquire	$1.19
188 acres, 4 ~~3~~ horses, 4 ~~2~~ cows	
George Kincaid	$0.48
175 acres, 1 ~~2~~ horse, 2 cows	
Henry Kerns	$3.91
300 acres, 1 horse, 1 cow	
~~Daniel Keely, mason~~	~~$0.10~~
~~1 horse, 1 cow~~	
John Kirkpatrick	$0.22
100 acres	
Wilson Knott	$0.07
2 ~~1~~ horses, 1 cow	
John Knight	$0.75
126 acres, 2 horses, 3 ~~2~~ cows	
~~John Keely, mason~~	~~$0.06~~
~~1 horse~~	
Andrew Kincaid	$0.00
1 horse	
Henry Livingood	$0.39
111 acres, 1 horse, 2 cows	
Adam Lenhard	$0.63
80 acres, 1 gristmill, 2 horses, 3 cows	
"20 acres of the land to Margaret Ferguson"	
~~James~~ Sarah Little, widow	$0.60
150 acres, 1 horse, 1 cow	
William Lemmon, weaver	$0.14

Abstracts of Westmoreland County, Pennsylvania, Tax Records 1815

Derry Township Name of Person and Taxable Property	Tax
1 house and lot in Den Town "1/2 house and lot to John Collins" Robert Lee, "Zev^d"	$1.22
195 ~~190~~ acres, 2 horses, 1 cow William Lattimore	$2.02
280 acres, 3 horses, 3 ~~2~~ cows Robert Lattimore, tanner	$0.35
~~1 horse~~ James Long	$1.46
194 acres, 3 horses, 2 ~~4~~ cows ~~John Long~~	~~$0.26~~
~~4 horses~~ Solomon Lightcap, single man	$0.50
William Latta	~~$2.64~~
276 acres, ~~4 horses, 3 cows~~ ~~Solomon Lightcap, single man~~	~~$0.00~~
James Lemmon	$2.30
250 acres, 1 ~~2~~ horse, 4 cows John Lee	$1.38
103.5 acres, 1 horse, 1 cow Alexander Lemmon, Senior	$1.85
300 acres, 2 ~~3~~ horses, 2 ~~4~~ cows Samuel Lightcap	$1.17
150 acres, 2 ~~6~~ horses, 2 ~~4~~ cows James Langllen, blacksmith	$1.07
100 acres, ~~1 horse,~~ 1 ~~2~~ cow John Laird, single man	$0.50
William Laird	$1.54
112 acres, 4 horses, 2 cows Alexander Lemmon, Junior	$0.00
1 horse, 1 cow John Little, single man	$0.00
Robert McClure, single man	$0.00
Peter Morgan	$0.06
1 cow John Moore	$0.06

Abstracts of Westmoreland County, Pennsylvania, Tax Records 1815

Derry Township Name of Person and Taxable Property	Tax
1 cow	
Joseph Musgrave, taylor	$0.45
1 house and lot in D. Town, 1 cow	
"house and lot to John Porter"	
John McMaken, weaver	$0.39
1 house and lot, 1 2 cow	
Edward McDonald, carpenter	$0.06
1 horse	
Anna McQuinton, widow	$0.81
94 acres, 1 horse, 2 cows	
Daniel Murray	$1.00
28 acres, 150 acres, 1 horse, 1 cow	
David McQuiston	$0.84
80 acres, 1 2 horse, 2 cows	
William McQuiston	$1.24
149 acres, 1 horse, 1 2 cow	
James McQuiston, Junior	$0.06
1 2 horse, 1 cow	
William McMullen, single man	$0.50
Thomas McCartney	$4.04
379 acres, 1 gristmill, 1 mare, 1 cow	
Smith McMullen, single man, taylor	$0.22
1 horse	
Josiah Moorhead	$2.00
129 acres, 156 acres, 6 horses, 3 cows	
"the land to James George Mulholland and Wm Baird"	
John McKinley	$0.67
67.5 acres, 1 horse, 1 cow	
James McQuiston, Senior	$0.37
44 acres, 1 horse, 2 cows	
Robert McConaughy	$3.48
350 acres, 4 horses, 4 cows, 300 acres in trust	
Wm MacLauren, blacksmith	$0.28
8 acres, 1 "B. mare," 1 cow	
Robert McGenley	$4.76

Abstracts of Westmoreland County, Pennsylvania, Tax Records 1815

Derry Township Name of Person and Taxable Property	Tax
298 acres, 1 distillery, 4 horses, 4 cows	
Matthew Maclauren	$2.52
250 acres, 2 horses, 4 cows	
John McCormick	$0.06
1 horse, 2 cows	
~~Reverend Thomas Moore~~	$1.14
~~100 acres, 4 horses, 3 cows~~	
"Land to Richard Canaan"	
~~John Moorhead~~	$2.20
~~195 acres, 3 horses, 5 cows~~	
"the land to Revd Robt Lee"	
James McClure	$2.73
175 acres, 3 horses, 5 cows	
Samuel Moorhead	$11.14
30 acres, 250 acres, 250 acres, 100 acres, 70 acres, 200 acres, 200 acres, 1 tanyard, 3 horses, 10 cows	
Daniel McCullen, taylor	$0.20
1 horse, 2 cows	
James McClelland	$0.09
2 ~~1~~ horses, 4 ~~2~~ cows	
Laurence McQuown	$0.06
1 cow	
Robert McMullen	$1.35
110 acres, 2 horses, 4 ~~2~~ cows	
William McMullen	$1.32
150 acres, 2 horses, 3 ~~2~~ cows	
James MaGill	$0.86
100 acres, 1 horse, 2 cows	
Thomas McGaughey, Senior	$0.66
100 acres, 1 cow	
Samuel McGaughey, single man	$0.56
1 horse	
~~James McGaughey, single man~~	~~$0.50~~
Archibald McGaughey, single man	$0.50
William McGaughey, ~~single man~~	$0.06

Abstracts of Westmoreland County, Pennsylvania, Tax Records 1815

Derry Township Name of Person and Taxable Property	Tax
1 horse	
John McGaughey	$1.17
150 acres, 1 ~~2~~ horse, 2 cows	
Robert McNutt	$2.08
200 acres, 2 horses, 3 cows	
Thomas McGaughey, Junior	$2.11
254 acres, 2 horses, 2 cows	
John McIntyre	$1.45
327 acres, 2 horses, 2 cows	
William McMaster	$1.28
150 acres, 2 horses, 2 cows	
~~Alexander Maclean~~	$1.57
~~200 acres, 3 horses, 2 cows~~	
"land to ~~John Anderson~~ David Anderson"	
Thomas McKee	$2.74
300 acres, ~~3 horses, 3 cows~~	
Andrew McBraem, single man	$0.50
William McKee	$0.96
140 acres, 2 ~~3~~ horses, 2 cows	
David McGinley	$0.14
2 horses, 2 cows	
William Martin	$0.08
~~1 horse~~, 1 ~~2~~ cow	
Archibald McCallister, taylor	$0.06
Barney McGuire	$0.06
1 cow	
~~John~~ McGuire, ~~Senior~~ Mary, widow	$1.32
160 acres, 2 ~~3~~ horses, ~~3 cows~~	
~~Wm McGuire, single man, chairmaker~~	~~$0.57~~
Uriah Matson	$3.07
207 acres, 4 ~~2~~ horses, 4 cows	
Samuel Matson, single man	$0.50
1 horse	
John McIntyre, Senior	$0.06
1 horse, 1 cow	
Robert Marshal, blacksmith	$0.14

Abstracts of Westmoreland County, Pennsylvania, Tax Records 1815

Derry Township Name of Person and Taxable Property	Tax
John Montgomery, single man	$0.50
David Mears, single man	$0.50
John Mears	$0.09
2 horses, 1 cow	
John McGuire	$0.13
1 small still, 1 2 horse, 1 cow	
~~Benjamin McFarland~~	~~$0.06~~
~~1 cow~~	
Nicholas Miller	$0.06
2 cows, 1 horse	
~~Wm McCroskey, carpenter~~	~~$0.19~~
~~1 horse~~	
Wm McClelland, ~~single man~~, miller	$0.66
3 4 cows, 1 horse	
Alexr Maclean	$0.06
1 cow, 1 horse	
James McCletchy	$0.06
1 cow	
James McGee	$0.00
203 acres, 2 horses	
Samuel McKee, tanner	$0.00
1 horse, 1 cow	
William McFarland, single man, taylor	$0.00
John Moorhead, single man	$0.00
Jane Nixon, widow	$1.73
200 300 acres, 1 cow	
"100 acres of the land to George Mulholland"	
Robert Nicholson	$0.09
1 horse, 1 cow	
Samuel Neel	$0.87
150 acres, 1 cow	
Simon Nixon, single man	$0.00
2 horses	
Michael Osburn	$0.06
1 cow	
~~Robert Pearson, nailor~~	~~$0.24~~

Abstracts of Westmoreland County, Pennsylvania, Tax Records 1815

Derry Township Name of Person and Taxable Property	Tax
~~2 cows~~	
Benjamin Parr	$0.79
1 house and lot in Den Town, 1 horse, 1 cow	
James Patterson, ~~single man~~	$1.69
150 acres, 1 ~~2~~ horse, 1 ~~2~~ cow	
Thomas Patterson, Junior	$1.00
170 acres, 2 ~~1~~ horses, 2 cows	
Isaac Parr, Senior	$5.27
300 acres, 146 acres in trust and unseated, 4 horses, 4 cows	
John Pumroy	$1.56
100 acres, 2 horses, 2 ~~3~~ cows	
Thomas Pumroy	$1.64
100 acres, 3 ~~4~~ horses, 1 ~~3~~ cow	
George Pumroy	$3.07
181 acres, 111 acres, 1 gristmill, 1 fulling mill, 2 horses, 3 ~~4~~ cows	
Isaac Parr, Junior	$3.80
300 acres, 5 ~~3~~ horses, 2 cows	
~~Thomas Patrick~~	~~$0.72~~
~~100 acres, 2 horses, 3 cows~~	
"the land to Valenitne Flowers"	
James Patterson, Senior	$0.00
1 horse	
Samuel Patterson	$0.80
100 acres, 2 ~~3~~ horses, 3 ~~2~~ cows	
James Patrick, single man	$0.50
Thomas Patterson, Senior	$1.27
200 acres, 2 horses, 3 ~~4~~ cows	
Robert Patterson	$0.77
109 acres, 1 ~~2~~ horse, 1 ~~3~~ cow	
Peterson's Heirs	$0.22
100 acres of unseated land	
Stephen Pounds	$0.38
71 acres, 2 horses, 1 cow	
B James Parr, hatter	$0.00

Derry Township Name of Person and Taxable Property	Tax
Joseph Pounds	$0.37
50 acres, 2 horses, 2 cows	
James Patton	$1.93
200 acres, 200 acres, 3 horses, 2 ~~3~~ cows	
Joseph Porter	$0.09
~~1 horse,~~ 1 cow	
~~John Senoir~~ William Patrick, single man	$1.17
200 acres, 3 horses, 2 ~~3~~ cows	
Francis Pumroy	$2.18
150 acres, 2 horses, 2 cows	
~~Martin Peaghth~~	~~$0.06~~
~~1 horse, 1 cow~~	
Daniel Pershian	$1.56
103.5 acres, 2 horses, 4 ~~5~~ cows	
~~Benjamin Purnel~~	~~$1.82~~
~~270 acres, 1 horse, 2 cows~~	
"land to Walter Ferguson"	
James Porter	$0.07
3 old mares, 2 cows	
Isaac Pierce	$1.12
100 acres, 4 ~~3~~ horses, 3 cows	
Jacob Porter, single man	$0.00
Martin Pehil	$0.00
2 horses, 2 cows	
Christianna Pehil, widow	$0.00
40 acres, 1 cow	
Samuel Patterson, Junior	$0.00
1 horse	
John Porter	$0.0
1 house and lot, 1 horse, 1 cow	
John Raynold, single man, blacksmith	$0.00
Ephraim Robertson, single man	$0.57
~~1 horse~~	
James Reed	$0.73
2 houses and lots, 2 horses, 2 cows	
George Reynolds	$0.73

Derry Township Name of Person and Taxable Property	Tax
1 house and lot, ~~1 cow~~	
John Rainey	$1.80
146 acres, 3 horses, 2 ~~3~~ cows	
James ~~Samuel collr of revenue~~ Reed	$5.86
2 houses and lots in Den T, 2 horses, 2 cows	
~~Rebecca~~ John Robertson	$1.39
300 acres, 1 ~~2~~ horse, 1 ~~3~~ cow	
David Rankin	$0.53
150 acres, 2 horses, 2 ~~3~~ cows	
James Russel	$1.36
123 acres, 2 horses, 3 cows	
John ~~Agnes widow~~ Russel	$1.20
226 acres, 2 ~~1~~ horses, 2 cows	
"to John Russel"	
~~John Russel, single man~~	~~$0.55~~
~~1 horse~~	
Caleb Russel, single man	$0.57
~~1 horse~~	
James Russel, Senior	$1.79
166 acres, 2 horses, 3 cows	
David Russel, ~~single man~~	$0.50
1 horse	
William Rider	$0.66
140 acres, ~~2 horses, 4 cows~~	
John Reynolds	$3.21
125 acres, 130 acres in trust,2 horses, 2 ~~[illegible number]~~ cows	
"There is some mistake in this return M ass[r] put it right"	
Samuel Reynolds	$0.12
2 horses, 1 ~~2~~ cow, 75 acres	
Robert Reynolds, single man, blacksmith	$0.14
William Reed	$1.52
100 acres, 1 horse, 1 ~~2~~ cow	
James Reed	$1.14
100 acres	

Derry Township Name of Person and Taxable Property	Tax
~~Joseph Ross, taylor~~	~~$0.14~~
Henry Rensel	$0.86
132 acres, 2 horses, 1 cow	
Matthew Rankin, tanner	$0.19
1 horse	
Henry Richard	$0.80
116 acres, 2 horses, 3 cows	
~~Robert Richard~~	~~$0.30~~
~~1 carding machine, 1 cow~~	
~~Robert Rainey~~	~~$2.33~~
~~146 acres, 1 distillery, 5 cows, 4 cows~~	
"to Andrew Sterret"	
George Rensel	$0.00
1 horse, 1 cow	
Henry Ransel, single man	$0.00
Jacob Roof, shoemaker	$0.00
50 acres, 2 horses, 2 cows	
Matthew Stephenson	$0.44
1 house and lot, 1 cow, 1 horse	
William Snodgrass's administrator	$1.40
200 acres, ~~3 horses, 4 cows~~	
Isaac Shinniman	$0.66
60 acres, 400 acres, ~~5 horses, 3 cows~~	
Jacob Steefer	$0.06
1 cow, 1 horse	
Anna Speck, widow	$0.47
329 acres	
Peter Stimmel	$0.10
1 ~~2~~ horse, 1 cow	
~~George Singley, Senior~~	~~$0.43~~
~~21 acres, 2 horses, 2 cows~~	
"the land to Joseph Hill"	
Peter Singley, single man	$0.50
John Snider, shoemaker	$0.06
1 cow	
Joseph Sutton	$0.33

Abstracts of Westmoreland County, Pennsylvania, Tax Records 1815

Derry Township Name of Person and Taxable Property	Tax
60 acres, 1 horse, 1 cow	
John Scott, shoemaker	$0.17
2 ~~1~~ horses, 1 cow	
William Stirling	$2.38
280 acres, 90 acres, 3 horses, 3 cows	
George Steefer	$0.06
1 horse, 1 cow	
Adam Stump	$0.91
170 acres, 1 horse, 2 cows	
Abraham Stout	$0.06
2 cows	
Jonathan Stout	$0.12
2 horses, 1 ~~2~~ cow, 300 acres	
Frederick Schaeffer, weaver	$0.12
1 horse, 1 cow	
~~Church Smith~~	~~$0.17~~
~~1 stud horse, 2 cows~~	
William Shields	$0.00
2 horses	
Conrad Steefer	$0.90
174 acres, 3 horses, 3 cows	
Henry Shoup	$1.70
200 acres, 4 horses, 3 cows	
John Shoemaker	$1.33
246 ~~150~~ acres, 4 ~~6~~ horses, 2 ~~3~~ cows	
~~William Stosy~~	~~$0.12~~
~~2 horses, 2 cows~~	
~~Philip Shoemaker~~	~~$0.44~~
~~50 acres, 2 horses, 2 cows~~	
"the land to John Shoemaker"	
Robert Story	$0.06
1 horse, 1 cow	
Joseph Smith	$0.64
100 acres, 2 horses, 2 cows, 134 acres	
"the land to Christopher Cribs"	
Michael Shull, carpenter	$0.75

Derry Township Name of Person and Taxable Property	Tax
111 acres, 1 ~~2~~ horse, ~~1 stud horse, 3 horses~~, 2 ~~3~~ cows	
John Sloan, Esquire	$4.44
300 acres, 1 stud horse, 3 horses, 4 cows	
George Selders, blacksmith	$0.14
William Smith	$1.95
217 acres, 2 horses, 2 ~~1~~ cows	
Christian Saxman, Junior	$0.98
133 acres, 1 horse, 1 cow	
Christian Saxman, Senior	$1.54
134 acres, 1 gristmill, 1 sawmill, 2 horses, 3 cows	
Mathias Saxman	$1.13
133 acres, 3 horses, 4 ~~5~~ cows	
John Shannon	$0.80
100 acres, 2 horses, 2 cows	
Robert Shannon, single man	$0.50
Jacob Snider, shoemaker	$0.06
David Speelman	$0.00
280 acres, 3 horses, 2 cows	
Harman Skiles, single man	$0.00
2 horses	
~~John Speelman~~ Andrew Sterrett	$0.00
146 acres, 1 distillery, 5 horses, 4 cows	
John Tweedy	$0.22
45 acres, 1 horse, 2 cows	
Jacob Tallman, ~~miller~~	$0.23
1 horse, 2 ~~1~~ cows	
~~Robert Thompson~~	~~$0.07~~
~~1 horse, 2 cows~~	
Isaac Taze, single man	$0.56
1 horse	
Robert Taylor	$1.54
200 acres, 2 horses, 2 ~~3~~ cows	
Samuel Talmadge	$0.19
1 horse, 1 cow, 108 acres	
Isaac Taylor	$0.70

Abstracts of Westmoreland County, Pennsylvania,
Tax Records 1815

Derry Township Name of Person and Taxable Property	**Tax**
100 acres, 1 ~~2~~ horse, 2 cows	
Alexander Trimble, single man	$0.85
150 acres, 2 horses, 2 ~~3~~ cows	
James Trimble	$0.06
~~1 horse~~, 2 cows	
William Trimble, carpenter	$0.22
1 horse, 1 cow	
Robert Thompson	$1.75
124 acres, 2 horses, 2 cows	
Elizabeth Thompson	$0.30
60 acres, 2 horses, 2 cows	
John Thompson, single man	$0.50
Andrew Taylor, cooper	$0.16
1 acre, 1 cow	
Daniel Thompson	$0.86
600 acres	
James Trimble, Senior	$0.00
50 acres, 1 cow	
George Unkafair	$2.35
267 acres, 1 distillery, 3 horses, 4 cows	
Daniel Vanlier	$0.00
59 acres	
~~Anthony Walker, single man~~	~~$0.50~~
~~William Walker, hatter~~	~~$0.22~~
Samuel Wilson	$1.84
197.5 acres, 1 ~~3~~ horse, 1 ~~3~~ cow	
Peter Wallace, Esquire	$6.75
450 acres, 311 acres, 1 gristmill, 4 horses, 4 cows	
John Waggoner	$1.67
150 acres, 3 horses, 3 ~~4~~ cows	
James Wilson, Junior	$0.06
1 horse, 1 cow	
~~Doe Wilhifrd~~	~~$0.22~~
~~1 horse~~	
~~Joseph Welsh, blacksmith~~	~~$0.90~~
~~90 acres, 2 horses, 2 cows~~	

Abstracts of Westmoreland County, Pennsylvania, Tax Records 1815

Derry Township Name of Person and Taxable Property	Tax
"Land to Cornelius Casally"	
Hannah Winnings	$0.62
130 acres, ~~1 horse~~, 2 cows	
William White	$0.66
75 acres, 1 stud horse, ~~2 horses~~, 2 cows	
James Waddel	$0.51
87 acres, 4 horses, 2 cows	
James Wilson, Senior	$5.94
400 acres, 1 slave, 4 horses, 4 cows	
Anthony Woodruff	$0.12
50 acres, 1 horse, 1 cow	
Isaac Woviel, shoemaker	$0.14
2 horses, ~~1 cow~~	
John Welsh, blacksmith	$0.90
90 acres, 2 horses, 2 cows	
Hannah White	$1.38
103.5 acres, 1 horse, 1 cow	
James White, single man	$0.54
1 horse	
Michael Windland	$0.43
50 acres, 1 horse, 3 cows	
Michael Waugh	$0.06
1 cow	
John Whitman, saddler, single man	$0.56
Frederick Weaver	$0.00
225 acres, 3 horses, 2 cows	
James Young	$0.50
1 horse	
David Anderson	$1.49
200 acres, 1 horse, 1 cow	
Samuel Boyles	$0.07
2 horses, 1 cow	
Elizabeth Craig, widow	$1.47
200 acres, 1 horse, 1 cow	
Philip Cline, blacksmith	$0.09
3 cows	

Abstracts of Westmoreland County, Pennsylvania,
Tax Records 1815

Derry Township Name of Person and Taxable Property	Tax
"Cleric P1/2"	
Robert Crozan, single man	$0.50
John Crozan, single man	$0.50
Edward Carlton, single man	$0.50
John Caskey	$0.10
2 horses, 1 cow	
John Collins, saddler	$0.44
1 house and lot, 1/2 house and lot, 1 cow	
Andrew Dushane	$1.26
150 acres, 1 horse, 3 cows	
John Hartley	$0.00
1 horse	
Valentine Flowers	$0.67
100 acres, 2 horses, 1 cow	
John Flowers	$1.33
160 acres, 4 horses, 4 cows	
Margaret Ferguson, widow	$0.10
20 acres, 1 horse, 1 cow	
John Fulton, single man	$0.50
Cochran Fulton, single man	$0.50
Robert Fulton	$0.08
1 horse, 2 cows	
Walter Ferguson	$1.85
270 acres, 2 horses, 2 cows	
Daniel Flack	$0.06
1 cow	
John Hartley	$0.06
1 horse, 1 cow	
Samuel Holstein, single man	$0.50
Andrew Harps	$1.17
202 acres, 1 cow	
William Hilborn, single man	$0.50
John Hilborn, single man	$0.50
William Henry, single man	$0.50
John Huster, single man	$0.50
Andrew Hawk	$0.06

Abstracts of Westmoreland County, Pennsylvania, Tax Records 1815

Derry Township Name of Person and Taxable Property	Tax
1 horse, 1 cow	
Robert Johnston, single man	$0.50
James Ingles, Senior	$0.06
1 horse, 1 cow	
Joseph Ingles	$0.08
1 horse, 2 cows	
John Latimore, single man	$0.50
John Miller, nailer	$0.21
James McConnoughy, single man	$0.50
John McKellep	$4.40
300 acres, 2 horses, 2 cows	
Andrew McCurdy	$0.06
1 cow	
John McJunkins	$0.06
2 horses, 1 cow	
Robert McGuire, single man	$0.50
Samuel McQuiston	$0.06
2 horses, 1 cow	
George Mulholland	$1.35
122 acres, 100 acres	
James Pounds, single man	$0.50
Andrew Roulston	$0.07
1 horse	
Hugh Robison	$0.06
1 cow	
William Scott	$0.06
1 cow	
James Sweeney	$0.06
2 cows	
John Shoup, single man	$0.50
Joseph Whetmore	$0.06
1 cow	
Peter White	$0.06
1 cow	
James Wilson, Junior	$0.06
1 horse, 1 cow	

Abstracts of Westmoreland County, Pennsylvania, Tax Records 1815

Derry Township Name of Person and Taxable Property	Tax
Benjamin Wright 500 acres	$0.07

*Abstracts of Westmoreland County, Pennsylvania,
Tax Records 1815*

Abstracts of Westmoreland County, Pennsylvania, Tax Records 1815

East Huntingdon Township Name of Person and Taxable Property	Tax
George Auble	$0.47
50 acres, 2 horses, 2 cows	
Michael Altman	$0.95
122 acres, 2 horses, 2 cows	
"1 cow more"	
John Andrew	$0.84
66 acres, 1 horse, 1 cow, 2 stills	
Philip Brake	$0.83
70 acres, 2 horses, 2 cows	
Christian Black	$0.07
7 acres	
"out of Township"	
Peter Bunison	$0.13
2 horses, 2 cows	
David Brenneman	$4.12
280 acres, 3 horses, 1 stud horse, 4 cows	
"1 cow Less"	
William Bachelor	$0.13
2 horses, 2 cows	
"1 cow Less 1 horse Less"	
David Bare	$0.07
1 horse, 1 cow	
"1 cow more"	
Henry Bare	$1.50
135 acres, 2 horses, 3 cows	
Adam Brown	$1.60
160 acres	
"Land to Hugh Daugherty"	
Christian Bare	$0.13
2 horses, 2 cows	
"2 cows Less"	
James Beverlin	$1.34
94 acres, 1 horse, 2 cows	
Michael Brenison	$1.60
145 acres, 2 horse, 3 cows	

Abstracts of Westmoreland County, Pennsylvania, Tax Records 1815

East Huntingdon Township Name of Person and Taxable Property	Tax
"1 horse Less"	
Oliver Bovard	$1.47
100 acres, 2 horses, 2 cows	
"1 cow more"	
John Berkey	$0.35
24 acres, 2 cows	
Philip Bare	$0.23
4 horses, 2 cows	
"out of Township"	
Jacob Bauder	$1.96
174 acres, 2 horses, 4 cows	
"1 cow more"	
John Brandon	$0.06
1 cow	
Abraham Black, single man	$0.52
1 cow	
"out of Township"	
Jacob Butler	$0.06
2 cows	
"1 cow Less"	
William Boyd	$5.00
300 acres, 2 horses, 3 cows	
John Cochran	$0.67
100 acres	
Jacob Conrad	$2.35
120 acres, 2 horses, 1 cow, 2 stills	
George Collins	$0.06
1 cow	
"out of Township"	
John Cummins	$0.62
70 acres, 2 horses, 3 cows	
Henry Coller	$0.07
1 horse, 1 cow	
"out of Township"	
~~Elizabeth~~ John Cunning	$3.47
180 acres, 6 horses, 5 cows, 1 tanyard	

34

Abstracts of Westmoreland County, Pennsylvania,
Tax Records 1815

East Huntingdon Township Name of Person and Taxable Property	Tax
"2 horses Less 2 cows Less"	
Widow Duggin	$0.63
50 acres, 2 horses, 2 cows	
Jacob Durstine	$2.77
180 acres, 6 horses, 4 cows	
"1 cow Less"	
Philip Davis	$0.10
1 horse, 3 cows	
"out of Township"	
James Foster	$0.00
110 acres, 4 horses, 3 cows	
John Frest, single man	$1.49
94 acres, 1 horse, 1 cow	
"if he is not married he ought to be $1.50 of tax	
Mr Ass^r"	
Martin Fry	$0.13
2 horses, 2 cows	
"1 horse Less"	
Christian Frets	$1.15
76 acres, 2 horses, 2 cows	
David Funk	$2.26
150 acres, 4 horses, 1 cow, 1 still, 47 acres	
"1 cow more"	
John Funk	$0.15
2 horses, 3 cows	
Jacob Fultz	$2.15
125 acres, 1 horse, 1 cow	
Henry Frets	$2.15
150 acres, 2 horses, 3 cows	
"1 cow Less 1 horse more"	
Jacob Felger	$0.00
180 acres, 3 horses, 3 cows	
Jacob Gardner	$1.60
100 acres, 4 horses, 3 cows	
John Gowdy	$1.08
100 acres, 1 horse, 2 cows	

Abstracts of Westmoreland County, Pennsylvania, Tax Records 1815

East Huntingdon Township Name of Person and Taxable Property	Tax
John Galloway 2.75 acres, 2 cows "1 horse more"	$0.07
Matthew Gault, Esquire 80 acres	$0.60
Abraham Gross 37 acres, 1 horse, 2 cows "1 horse more"	$0.45
John Gault 5 horses, 5 cows "1 cow Less"	$0.33
Michael Gilmore 25 acres	$0.17
John Graham 29 acres, 1 cow	$0.31
John Gerby 2 horses, 1 cow "out of Township"	$0.12
James Henry 1 horse "out of Township"	$0.06
Robert Hunter 60 acres, 1 horse, 2 cows "1 cow Less"	$0.68
William Husband 123 acres, 1 horse, 3 cows "2 cows Less"	$1.33
Paul Hough 243 acres, 3 horses, 3 cows, 2 stills, 1 gristmill, 1 sawmill	$4.61
John Hutcheson 90 acres, 2 horses, 2 cows "Land Sold to John Hendricks"	$1.03
Daniel Hepler 3 acres, 1 horse "2 Cows more"	$0.09

Abstracts of Westmoreland County, Pennsylvania, Tax Records 1815

East Huntingdon Township Name of Person and Taxable Property	Tax
David Hunter	$2.00
141 acres, 2 horses, 2 cows	
David Hunter, Junior	$0.08
1 horse, 2 cows	
Solomon Hough	$0.06
1 cow	
Henry Irwin, Esquire	$1.77
150 acres, 2 horses, 3 cows, 2 stills	
"1 Cow Less"	
James Johnston	$0.07
1 horse, 1 cow	
"1 horse Less"	
Ambrose Irwin	$0.08
1 horse, 2 cows	
"1 cow Less 1 horse more"	
William Kinard	$0.07
1 horse, 2 cows	
"1 horse more 1 cow Less"	
Jacob Keister	$0.64
76 acres, 2 horses, 2 cows	
John Kerr	$0.08
1 horse, 2 cows	
"no Taxable property"	
Alexander Kelly	$0.13
2 horses, 2 cows	
Matthias Kamp	$2.92
4 horses, 199 acres, 3 cows	
"1 cow more"	
M Kerr, widow	$0.73
100 acres, 1 horse, 1 cow	
P Kerr, widow	$0.36
44 acres, 1 horse, 1 cow	
"Land Sold to Jacob Delinger"	
"no horse nor Cow"	
John Knight	$0.08
1 horse, 2 cows	

Abstracts of Westmoreland County, Pennsylvania, Tax Records 1815

East Huntingdon Township Name of Person and Taxable Property	Tax
"out of Township"	
James Kerr, deceased	$1.50
150 acres, 1 horse, 1 cow	
Henry Low	$4.10
380 acres, 3 horses, 4 cows, 2 stills	
Abraham Luchins	$1.52
110 acres, 3 cows	
"Land to James Robenson"	
Marks Lightly	$1.18
100 acres, 2 horses, 2 cows, 1 oil mill	
Peter Loucks	$3.50
250 acres, 2 horses, 4 cows	
"1 cow more 1 horse more"	
Jacob Leedy	$0.12
2 horses, 1 cows	
"1 Cow more 1 horse Less"	
John Macfadden	$0.44
61 acres, 2 cows	
"2 horses more"	
Henry Miller	$0.18
5 acres, 2 horses, 1 cow	
"Land to James Collin"	
Andrew Mumma	$0.15
2 horses, 3 cows	
John Morgan	$0.08
1 horse, 2 cows	
"1 horse more"	
Hugh Martin, single man	$0.06
1 horse	
Dr. Matthew McClinahen	$2.37
130 acres, 3 horses, 3 cows	
"land to Mr Robt Brown	
"Land to Jacob Stem"	
"no horse nor cows"	
Jacob Moyer	$1.43
140 acres, 1 horse, 1 cow	

Abstracts of Westmoreland County, Pennsylvania, Tax Records 1815

East Huntingdon Township Name of Person and Taxable Property	Tax
"1 horse more"	
James Martin	$0.15
10 acres, 1 cow	
"1 horse more"	
Francis Mawhias	$0.20
17 acres, 1 horse, 2 cows	
"1 horse and one cow Less"	
Samuel Montgomery	$3.47
250 acres, 2 horses, 2 cows	
"1 cow Less"	
James McKean	$5.30
250 acres, 150 acres, 4 horses, 3 cows, 1 still, 1 tanyard	
William Martin	$0.06
1 cow	
"out of township"	
William McKinley	$1.12
100 acres, 1 horse, 1 cow, 1 still	
"1 Cow more"	
Gilbert McMaster	$2.33
100 acres, 2 horses, 4 cows, 1 negro slave	
"1 horse more"	
James Martin, shoemaker	$0.12
15 acres, 1 cow	
"Land to John Dilon"	
"15 acres of Land Less"	
David Mumma	$2.85
205 acres, 1 horse, 4 cows	
"1 horse more 1 cow Less"	
George Mumma, Senior	$2.38
170 acres, 1 horse, 4 cows	
George Mumma, Junior	$1.45
94 acres, 3 horses, 3 cows	
John Moyer	$0.88
55 acres, 2 horses, 3 cows	
"1 horse more"	

Abstracts of Westmoreland County, Pennsylvania, Tax Records 1815

East Huntingdon Township Name of Person and Taxable Property	Tax
Joseph Miller, deceased 200 acres, 3 horses, 3 cows "1 Cow Less"	$3.53
Abraham Myers 151 acres, 2 horses, 4 cows "1 cow Less"	$2.18
William Miller 100 acres, 1 horse, 1 cow	$1.42
Isaac Mearson, Esquire 270 acres	$3.33
Charles McFadden 150 acres, 2 horses, 2 cows, 2 stills "Land Sold to Jacob Longeneker" "no horses nor cows nor stills" "this land ought to be charged to some other but I don't know who"	$2.25
John McCammont 51 acres, 2 horses, 1 cow "See page 20 at the far Side" "Land Sold to Wᵐ Flinn"	$0.76
David Myers 300 acres, 1 horse, 2 cows "Land to Robert Reed"	$4.08
Malcom or Joshua McHenry 50 acres, 1 cow "1 cow more"	$0.35
Isabella McHenry 200 acres, 1 cow	$1.33
John Neel, Senior 300 acres, 4 horses, 4 cows, 2 stills	$4.41
Peter Newcomer 200 acres, 1 horse, 1 cow "1 cow more"	$3.40
Jacob Newcomer 3 horses, 5 cows "1 horse more"	$0.23

Abstracts of Westmoreland County, Pennsylvania, Tax Records 1815

East Huntingdon Township Name of Person and Taxable Property	Tax
Samuel Neel	$0.07
1 horse, 1 cow	
Christian Newcomer	$0.08
1 horse, 2 cows	
"out of township"	
Thomas Norris	$0.06
1 cow	
"out of township"	
David Newcomer	$0.06
1 cow	
"1 cow more 1 horse more"	
Jacob Overholt	$1.97
108 acres, 2 horses, 4 cows	
Christian Overholt	$1.50
100 acres, 2 horses, 4 cows	
Abraham Overholt	$4.49
230 acres, 5 horses, 6 cows, 1 stud horse, 2 stills	
Martin Overholt	$2.83
160 acres, 2 horses, 4 cows	
"1 cow more"	
Peter Pool	$1.35
120 acres, 2 horses, 3 cows	
John Parker	$5.08
370 acres, 2 horses, 3 cows,	
"2 cows Less"	
Samuel Peeples	$0.12
2 horses, 1 cow	
"1 horse Less"	
James Richey, Junior	$0.07
1 horse, 1 cow	
"1 horse more"	
Allen Rose	$7.08
270 acres, 180 acres, 3 horses, 2 cows	
Daniel Rudy	$0.25
35 acres, 1 horse, 1 cow	
"out of Township"	

Abstracts of Westmoreland County, Pennsylvania,
Tax Records 1815

East Huntingdon Township Name of Person and Taxable Property	Tax
Tilman Rosenberger, deceased	$1.06
94 acres, 2 horses, 1 cow	
"2 horses and 1 cow Less"	
Samuel Rhodes	$0.07
1 horse, 1 cow	
Henry Rosenberger	$1.36
128 acres, 1 horse, 2 cows	
"1 cow Less"	
Philip Reagan	$0.43
25 acres, 1 horse, 3 cows	
"1 Cow Less"	
John Rodgers	$0.06
2 cows	
"out of township"	
Abraham Ruth	$1.50
135 acres, 2 horses, 2 cows	
"1 horse more"	
Samuel Richey	$0.06
1 cow	
Matthew Ray	$3.17
238 acres	
Weldon Reagan	$0.06
1 cow	
"out of Township"	
Collin Reagan	$0.42
25 acres, 1 horse, 2 cows	
Asher Story	$0.06
4 acres, 1 cow, 3 horses	
"1 cow more"	
"Land Sold to Joseph Tinstman"	
Charles Stockslager	$0.08
1 horse, 2 cows	
"out of County"	
Valentine Sandal	$0.07
1 horse, 1 cow	
"1 horse Less 1 cow more"	

Abstracts of Westmoreland County, Pennsylvania, Tax Records 1815

East Huntingdon Township Name of Person and Taxable Property	Tax
James Stephenson	$1.13
100 acres, 2 horses, 2 cows	
Peter Showalter	$1.47
130 acres, 2 horses, 4 cows	
"1 cows [*sic*] Less"	
Joseph Suter	$3.38
100 acres, 180 acres, 4 horses, 3 cows	
Widow Shevler	$0.43
50 acres, 1 horse, 3 cows	
"no horse nor cows"	
Lennox Shepherd	$~~0.80~~
1 horse, 2 cows	
Jacob Shupe	$2.08
150 acres, 1 horse, 2 cows	
"no cows"	
William Smith	$2.12
144 acres, 3 horses, 3 cows	
Moses Sterret	$2.45
169 acres, 3 horses, 3 cows	
Jacob Snyder	$0.07
1 horse, 1 cow	
"1 horse more"	
John Snyder, Junior	$3.82
10 acres, 15 acres, 1 gristmill, 1 sawmill, 1 horse, 2 cows	
"1 Cow more"	
John Sandals	$0.08
1 horse, 2 cows	
"out of Township"	
Jacob Showalter	$0.13
2 horses, 2 cows	
"out of township"	
Henry Stouffer	$4.30
300 acres, 3 horses, 2 cows, 2 stills	
"1 horse and 3 Cows more"	
"128 acres of Land more"	

Abstracts of Westmoreland County, Pennsylvania, Tax Records 1815

East Huntingdon Township Name of Person and Taxable Property	Tax
Conrad Spring 150 acres, 2 horses, 2 cows "50 acres of Land Less"	$1.13
Abraham Stoner 113 acres, 2 horses, 3 cows	$1.66
John Stoner 113 acres, 2 horses, 3 cows "1 cow Less"	$1.66
Peter Stocklager 3 horses, 2 cows "1 cow Less"	$0.18
Philip Stut 1 horse, 3 cows "1 Cow Less"	$0.10
Christian Stouffer 212 acres, 2 horses, 3 cows "1 horse more"	$2.98
Joseph Sharg 113 acres, 3 horses, 4 cows	$1.72
Jacob Stouffer 150 acres, 4 horses, 1 cow "land to Sludebech Jacob" "3 horses Less 2 cows more"	$2.22
John Snyder, Senior 150 acres, 2 horses, 3 cows "no horses nor cows"	$2.15
Laurence Shupe 150 acres, 2 horses, 3 cows	$2.15
Jacob Swab 2 horses, 1 cow "out of Township"	$0.12
Robert Slemmons widow 50 acres, 1 horse, 1 cow	$0.40
Joseph Showalter 1 horse, 2 cows "1 horse more"	$0.08

Abstracts of Westmoreland County, Pennsylvania, Tax Records 1815

East Huntingdon Township Name of Person and Taxable Property	Tax
George Smith 136 acres, 4 horses, 1 cow "1 cow more"	$1.41
Timothy Shepherd 2 cows "1 horse more"	$0.06
Nicholas Swope, Esquire 175 acres, 1 horse, 1 cow "47 acres of land to David Frunk" "128 acres to Henry Soffer"	$2.40
Christian Stoner, deceased 226 acres, 2 horses, 5 cows	$3.20
John Shupe 1 horse, 1 cow	$0.07
George Sickesfoos 1 horse, 1 cow "out of Township"	$0.07
Conrad Stem 145 acres, 4 horses, 4 cows	$2.20
Melchar Sherbandy 220 acres, 3 horses, 4 cows, 2 stills	$3.29
John Selby 109 acres, 2 horses, 2 cows "1 horse Less"	$1.59
John Suter 10 acres, 2 cows, 1 horse	$0.17
Henry Suter 14 acres, 1 horse, 2 cows, 1 gristmill, 1 sawmill, 2 stills, 50 acres "1 horse more"	$2.09
John Slemmons 1 horse, 1 cow	$0.07
Samuel Summony 141 acres, 2 horses, 3 cows "To Jacob Long"	$1.56
Jacob Swope	$0.07

Abstracts of Westmoreland County, Pennsylvania, Tax Records 1815

East Huntingdon Township Name of Person and Taxable Property	Tax
1 horse, 1 cow	
"out of Township"	
Henry Showalter	$0.08
1 horse, 2 cows	
"1 horse more 1 cow more"	
Samuel Springer	$0.08
1 horse, 2 cows	
"out of county"	
Widow Shepherd	$0.68
100 acres, 1 cow	
John Sherbandy	$0.07
1 horse, 1 cow	
Joseph Trimble	$2.53
86 acres, 189 acres, 1 horse, 1 cow	
"1 Cow Less also 1 horse more"	
Matthias Tinstman	$2.37
165 acres, 2 horses, 3 cows	
Jacob Tinstman, Esquire	$0.94
54 acres, 3 horses, 4 cows	
"1 horse more 1 cow more"	
John Troxel	$5.23
300 acres, 4 horses, 2 cows	
"2 cows more"	
Henry Tinstman	$1.22
94 acres, 5 horses, 2 cows	
"Jacob Markle Bought the Land"	
"2 horses Less"	
Daniel Tarr	$1.42
100 acres, 1 horse, 2 cows	
"2 horses more"	
Frederich Tallhamer	$0.31
37 acres, 1 horse, 1 cow	
"one Horse Less"	
Gasper Tarr, Esquire	$2.12
172 acres, 66 acres, 2 horses, 4 cows	
[illegible line struck out]	

East Huntingdon Township Name of Person and Taxable Property	Tax
"2 Horses More"	
Abraham Tinstman	$0.59
37 acres, 1 horse, 3 cows	
"1 horse more, 1 cow ~~more~~ Less"	
John Tinstman	$2.78
180 acres, 4 horses, 3 cows, 2 stills	
"1 cow more"	
John Thompson, single man	$2.70
330 acres, 1 horse	
"the single mans tax is not added"	
Michael Trout, single man	$4.74
300 acres, 2 horses, 5 cows, 1 still	
"1 horse Less 1 cow Less"	
"the sm's [single man's] tax is not charged is he married Mr Assr or not say"	
Joseph Tinstman	$0.07
1 horse, 1 cow, 4 acres	
Jacob Tooman	$1.13
100 acres, 2 horses, 2 cows	
"1 horse Less"	
"Land to William Willson page 20"	
John Thompson	$0.44
37 acres 1 horse, 1 cow	
"2 cows more"	
John Vance	$1.53
100 acres, 1 horse, 2 cows, 2 stills	
"30 Acres Land more"	
William Vance	$0.87
50 acres, 1 horse, 2 cows, 2 stills	
"1 horse more"	
Francis Vance	$0.75
50 acres, 1 horse, 2 cows	
"6 acres of Land Less 1 cow more"	
John Wertz, Junior	$3.09
222 acres, 2 horses, 1 cow	
"1 cow more"	

Abstracts of Westmoreland County, Pennsylvania,
Tax Records 1815

East Huntingdon Township Name of Person and Taxable Property	Tax
John Wertz, Senior	$4.38
309 acres, 4 horses, 4 cows, 1 still	
Peter Williams	$0.67
90 acres, 1 horse, 1 cow	
"no cow"	
Jacob Welshons	$0.06
1 horse, 2 ɫ cows	
Samuel Wenter	$1.47
100 acres, 2 horses, 2 cows	
"1 horse more"	
John Whann	$0.06
1 horse	
"out of Towns"	
John Walter	$0.13
2 horses, 2 cows	
"out of County"	
John Wyandt, Senior	$1.17
180 acres, 4 horses, 6 cows, 1 still	
"no horse no Still 2 cows Less"	
Samuel Warden, deceased	$4.82
339 acres, 3 horses, 7 cows, 1 malt house	
"2 Cows Less 1 horse more"	
James White	$1.13
100 acres, 2 cows, 2 horses	
Robert Wallace	$0.06
1 cow	
Laurence Yaw	$0.13
5 acres, 1 horse, 2 cows	
"1 horse Less 1 cow Less"	

East Huntingdon Township Newcomers in 1815	Tax
Alexander Campbelle	$0.12
2 horses, 1 cow	
James Boreland	$0.06

1 horse
John Dilon $0.15
15 acres, 1 horse
John Coughinower $0.06
1 cow
Paoly Shepperd $0.06
1 cow
Barbary Harbst $0.06
1 cow
Conrad Low $0.06
1 cow
Christena Snyder $0.06
1 cow
B Love, Widow $0.06
2 cows
Thomas Trinton $0.06
1 cow
Ephriem McCardy $0.06
1 cow
Peter Smith $0.06
1 horse
James Ray, single man $0.06
1 horse
"Should not he be charged with a young mans tax
Mr Ass^r"

East Huntingdon Township Single Free Men	Tax
~~John Amberson~~	~~$0.50~~
Peter Brow	$0.50
Henry Bechtle	$0.50
Abraham Bechtle	$0.50
Joshua Black	$0.50
Abraham Black	$0.52
1 cow	
John Coyle	$0.50
~~Michael Crotzy~~	~~$0.50~~

Abstracts of Westmoreland County, Pennsylvania, Tax Records 1815

East Huntingdon Township Single Free Men	Tax
~~Robert Gowdy~~	~~$0.50~~
William Gault	$0.50
William Jack	$0.50
Henry Kamp	$0.50
1 horse	
Henry Low	$0.50
Adam Low	$0.50
~~Conrad Low~~	~~$0.50~~
Samuel Martin	~~$0.50~~
James Martin	$0.56
1 horse	
Isaac McCommont	$0.50
1 horse	
James McKean	$0.50
1 horse	
Thomas McKean	$0.50
Thomas Montgomery	$0.56
1 horse	
"no horse"	
William McMaster	$0.50
Alexander Miller	$0.50
John Neel	$0.50
Alexander Reagan	$0.50
1 horse	
~~Pheobe Shepherd~~	$0.50
John Scott	$0.50
1 horse	
~~Henry Sndyer~~ deceased	$0.50
~~Samuel Selby~~	$0.56
1 horse	
William Smith	$0.50
Henry Shevelar	$0.50
Abraham Suter	$0.50
George Swope	$0.50
Henry Swope	$0.56
1 horse	

Abstracts of Westmoreland County, Pennsylvania, Tax Records 1815

East Huntingdon Township Single Free Men	Tax
~~Solomon Suter~~	$0.56
1 horse	
~~John Showalter~~	$0.50
~~George Sherbandy~~	$0.56
1 horse	
Thomas Thompson	$0.50
~~Daniel Wyandt~~	$0.50
Jacob Wyandt	$0.50
1 horse	
Samuel Warden	$0.50
Paul Warden	$0.50
John Winter	$0.50
Stephen White	$0.50
David Wyandt	$0.50
1 horse	
George Trout	$0.00
John Carnahan	$0.00
William Tallhammar	$0.00
Philip Hough	$0.00
Mathias Camps	$0.00
George Robenson	$0.00
Christian Stoner	$0.00
George Tomen	$0.00
Samuel Ray	$0.00
David Ray	$0.00
Martin Hugh	$0.00
Michael Crotzy	$0.00
"Back"	
"mistake on the first Tax Returnd"	
Samuel Frances, single man	$0.00
John Brown, single man	$0.00
Isaac Hileman, single man	$0.00
Isaac Gault, single man	$0.00
Frederick Tarr, single man	$0.00
Nathan Garner	$0.00
John Gardner	$0.00

East Huntingdon Township Single Free Men	Tax
John McFadden	$0.00

East Huntingdon Township A List of Newcomers and What Mistake [sic] Was Made	Tax
Henry Fox	$3.04
280 acres, 1 horse, 2 cows	
Christian Fox	$0.15
2 horses, 3 cows	
Nancy Miller, widow	$0.06
1 horse, 1 cow	
James Collins	$0.08
5 acres, 1 cow	
Philip Reasman	$0.06
1 cow	
Christopher Sondels	$0.12
2 horses, 1 cow	
Jane McFadden, widow	$0.06
2 cows	
Robert Francis	$0.23
4 horses, 2 cows	
William Willson	$1.00
100 acres	
Peter Weaver	$0.12
2 horses, 1 cow	
William Flinn	$1.00
75 acres	

East Huntingdon Township List of Poor Children	Age
James Marten, shoemaker	
1 Child Nancy	10
Susen Blackston, widow	
Susen	9
Hanah	7
Barbara	5

East Huntingdon Township List of Poor Children	**Age**
Nancy Miller, widow	
James	9
John	5

Abstracts of Westmoreland County, Pennsylvania, Tax Records 1815

Abstracts of Westmoreland County, Pennsylvania, Tax Records 1815

Fairfield Township Name of Person and Taxable Property	Tax
Henry Ambrose	$1.84
John Anderson, single man	
Joseph Anderson	$0.18
John Adams, teacher	
Thomas Atcheson	$0.07
Thomas Anderson, single man	
Alexander & Martin	$1.71
"Cal on John Peoples for the above"	
Nicholas Bennet, single man	$0.50
David Bennet, single man	$0.50
Robert Boyd, Esquire	$0.07
John Bennet	$0.80
Allanson Bills, blacksmith	
William Boyd	$0.40
David Brown	$1.63
Brady's Heirs	$0.21
James Black	
Daniel Burris	$0.33
David Brown, wheelwright	$0.28
Philip Bier	
Robert Brown	$0.38
"Tub mill"	
William Brown, single man	$0.56
Jacob Beck	$0.25
John Blair	$2.04
William Blair	$1.10
John Beach	$0.19
Alexander Blair	$2.03
John Brady	$1.09
Jane Brady, widow	$0.66
David Brown	
"Cone"	
Robert Brown	$0.73
William Bennet, Junior	$0.74
Matthew Brown	$0.99

Fairfield Township Name of Person and Taxable Property	Tax
James Brown, millwright	$1.39
William Brown, Senior	$0.06
William Brown	$0.12
Charles Black	$0.38
Abraham Bennet	$0.06
Henry Beam	$0.12
James Brady	
John Brown, weaver	$0.54
Jeremiah Bradley	$0.06
John Benninger	$0.06
Abraham Brant	$0.07
William Bennet, Senior	
Robert Brown	$0.06
William Barns, taylor, single man	$0.53
Joseph Baird, single man	$0.50
James Brown, single man	$0.54
Robert Black	$0.06
Carlton[']s Administrators	$0.28
John Cross, single man	
Henry Clark, single man	$0.58
Samuel Cochran	$0.25
James Clark	$2.43
"Conemaugh"	
Michael Coup	
Paul Clark, single man	$0.56
William Clark, single man	$0.56
Cornelius Clawson	$0.74
John Craven	$0.92
John Caldwell	$0.84
"& for Barrens"	
John Cauffield, ~~single man~~	$0.11
Mary Clifford	$0.52
James Clerk	$4.27
"Mill creek"	
William Clerk, miller	$0.10
John Clerk	$0.64

*Abstracts of Westmoreland County, Pennsylvania,
Tax Records 1815*

Fairfield Township Name of Person and Taxable Property	Tax
James Clerk, wheelwright	$0.10
Charles Clifford, Senior	$1.56
Thomas Clifford	$0.97
Philip Coyle	$0.96
Charles Clifford, Junior	$1.10
Joseph Clifford	$1.30
William Campbell, miller	$0.06
Samuel Caldwell	$0.11
Henry Caldwell	$0.14
Jacob Cavode	$1.94
Herman Cammon, single man "at Hermitage"	$0.50
Henry Caldwell	$0.06
James Donaldson, single man	$0.53
Sarah Davis	$1.19
Job Deckart	$0.19
John Deckart	$0.34
John Duncan	$0.92
Isaiah Davis	$0.72
James Donaldson	$0.60
Caleb Davis, single man	$0.59
Daniel Deckart	$0.17
Ebenezer Deckart	$0.60
John Douglas	$0.23
Andrew Dougherty	$0.06
Andrew Dushane	$0.00
Hugh Dever, miller	$0.10
Christopher Dumars	$0.57
Isaac Dushane	$0.63
William Drips, joiner	$0.06
Isaac Deckart	$0.06
Samuel Elder	$0.24
John Elliott, Senior	$0.30
Thomas Elliott	$0.45
William Elliott	$1.69
John Elliott, single man	$1.70

Fairfield Township Name of Person and Taxable Property	Tax
William Elder	$0.50
Abraham Eickart, taylor	
Abraham Eickart, shoemaker	
James Enos	$0.06
A Irwin Elliott	$3.79
Thomas Enos	$0.06
Godfrey Eickleberger	$0.87
John Finley	$0.50
John Falloon, Senior	$0.50
John Falloon, Junior	$0.06
James Flack	$2.62
David Falloon, single man	$0.53
Mary Finley	
John Flack	$0.67
George Fruman	
Peter Fry	$0.26
Christopher Gillespie	$0.06
James Galbreath	$0.06
Robert Graham	$1.52
James Gilmore	$0.50
John Gilmore	$0.90
~~Hugh Gillespie~~	
George Gardner	$0.06
James Gageby	$1.00
John Gageby, single man	$0.50
Thomas Gray	$0.06
Guthre "on Cover land"	$2.14
Michael Hartman	$0.06
Abraham Hendricks, Esquire	$2.40
Abraham Hendricks, Junior	$1.08
Andrew Haslet	$0.70
William Hashberger	$0.34
Gasper Hill	$2.36
Peter Howard	$0.14
John Harkins	$1.13
James Huston	$0.77

Abstracts of Westmoreland County, Pennsylvania, Tax Records 1815

Fairfield Township Name of Person and Taxable Property	Tax
Robert Howel, single man	$0.50
William Halferty, ~~single man~~	$0.09
John Halferty	$0.06
Colonel Edward Halferty	$6.93
Samuel Henderson	$0.06
John Huston, ~~single man~~	$0.10
Daniel Hendricks, Junior	$2.17
Daniel Hendricks, Senior	$1.36
Samuel Henderson	$0.06
Thomas Hendricks, single man	$0.54
Robert Huston	$2.24
Andrew Henderson	$0.10
Charles Henderson, Junior	$0.36
Samuel Henderson, single man	$0.50
William Haslet	$0.06
Alexander Henderson	$0.56
Thomas Henderson	$0.31
Colonel Thomas Hendricks	$1.03
Catrine Heney	$1.36
Samuel Henderson, Senior	$0.62
Jamieson Hendricks	$0.14
John Hare	$0.09
Charles Henderson, Senior	$0.63
Joseph Howell	$1.23
Hugh Hammil, Esquire	$1.96
Robert Hammil	$2.43
John Henderson	$0.27
Jacob Hartman, single man	$2.24
Orange Hill	$0.33
John Hills	$0.70
"river"	
James Hamilton	$0.09
James Huston, single man	$0.50
Irwin Hurl, hatter	$0.54
Robert Haslet	$1.04
Reverend George Hill	$5.13

Abstracts of Westmoreland County, Pennsylvania, Tax Records 1815

Fairfield Township Name of Person and Taxable Property	Tax
Daniel Hendricks, single man	$0.50
Solomon Humbard	$0.10
William Hanlon, single man	$1.36
James Hill, single man	$0.50
Captain John Hill	$1.41
James Hurl, hatter	$0.09
Robert Halferty	$0.81
James Henderson	$0.06
Joseph Hulen	$0.06
Henry Hooller	$2.97
H. John Hopkins, single man	$9.73
Henry Hise	$0.10
Archibald Huston	$1.14
Samuel Henderson "Tub mill"	$0.06
Henry Johnston	$0.06
Margret Jamieson	$0.49
Robert Johnston	$0.13
Alexander Johnston, Esquire	$1.71
Samuel Johnston	$0.72
Edward Irwin	$1.21
Daniel Jones	$0.61
Benjamin Johnston	$3.05
Thomas Jamieson, single man	$1.87
James Jones, single man	$0.50
Boyle Irwin	$4.83
Alexander Johnston	$1.64
William Jenkins	$0.22
Jacob Kuhns & John Schaefer	$3.70
Samuel Kennedy	$0.46
William Kerns	$0.11
Samuel Knox	$0.06
Robert Knox	$1.80
Nathaniel Kirkwood	$1.49
William Lemmon	$0.73
Captain James Lawson	$0.06

Abstracts of Westmoreland County, Pennsylvania, Tax Records 1815

Fairfield Township Name of Person and Taxable Property	Tax
William Little	$0.97
Thomas Lemmon	$0.63
James Lawson	$3.84
~~Alexander Love~~	
James Lemmon	$1.07
Robert Larimer	$0.18
Jean Little	$0.91
James Lessley, single man	$0.50
John Long's executors	$1.14
David Louther	$1.57
Sarah Lilley	$0.11
George Lules	$0.06
James Louther	$1.56
Joseph Lawson, single man	$0.50
Hugh Lawson, single man	$0.50
John Lemmon	$0.81
Jonathan Louther, single man	$0.50
Jacob Lup	$0.60
Bernard McFeely	$0.06
William Myler, merchant	$1.95
Thomas Myler, single man	$0.56
William McCullough	$0.87
Thomas McFarlen	$0.38
James Maxwell	$1.47
James McKelvey	$1.36
Lewis McKelvey	$0.27
William Matthews	$2.41
Abraham Moyers	$0.96
Elizabeth McGriff	$0.20
~~James McGriff, single man~~	
William McDowel, Junior	$0.22
Robert McCreary, single man	$0.50
~~James Murphy, single man~~	
Philip Milliron	$2.93
James Matthews, single man	$3.60
John McCoy	$1.53

Abstracts of Westmoreland County, Pennsylvania, Tax Records 1815

Fairfield Township Name of Person and Taxable Property	Tax
Robert Murphy, single man	$0.50
Robert McNair	$0.06
John McCurdy	$0.46
John McDowel	$0.07
John McNoher	$2.06
William McCreary	$0.91
Doctor David Marchant	$0.57
John McKelvey, sickle maker	$0.21
Charles McCreary	$0.91
John Murphy, Senior	$1.22
John McAbee	$1.22
John Murphy, shoemaker	$0.06
James McKelvey, single man	$0.95
Robert McDowel, single man	$0.50
Joseph McBay	$0.49
James McCurdy "river"	$0.83
John McKinley	$0.84
Daniel McCoy	$2.17
Daniel Mattocks	$0.06
Barbara Matthews	$1.27
William Murphy	$0.83
Elizabeth McCurdy	$1.49
William McCurdy	$1.59
Robert McKelvey	$0.84
John McKelvey	$0.79
William McWhorter, Senior	$0.83
Henry McDowel	$0.07
Samuel McDowel	$0.54
Robert McConkey	$1.34
Alexander McElroy, single man	$0.30
James McConaughy, Junior	$0.09
James McCurdy, Senior	$2.03
Joseph McManus	$1.23
Martha Moore	$0.90
Richard McCracken, single man	$0.54

Fairfield Township Name of Person and Taxable Property	Tax
Colonel William McDowel	$0.97
John Martin	$1.27
James McConaughy, Senior	$2.22
John McConaughy, shoemaker	$0.10
Robert McCurdy	$1.77
James McKelvey, joiner	$0.06
James McCurdy, single man	$0.54
William McKonkey	$0.07
John McElroy, shoemaker	$0.07
~~Neal McGlonehy, single man~~	
George Mabyben	$0.86
William McClellan	$0.65
David McClellan	$0.06
Joseph Musgrove	$0.29
Samuel Macdonald	$1.33
Robert McDowel, Senior	$2.33
Archibald McClellan	$0.46
John Matthews, single man	$0.56
John McCurdy, single man	$0.50
William McIlwain	$0.06
George McKinley, single man	$0.50
Robert McConaughy	$0.06
Christian Moyers	$2.31
Frederick Moyers	$0.14
John Nesbet	$0.72
William Nesbet	$0.06
Joseph Nelson	$0.06
Joseph Ogden	$2.50
James Ogden	$0.68
John Ogden	$1.81
Peter Over	$3.34
Hugh Peoples	$0.11
James Peoples	$2.39
Robert Peoples	$1.74
Joseph Peoples	$1.74
Samuel Peoples	$0.06

Abstracts of Westmoreland County, Pennsylvania, Tax Records 1815

Fairfield Township Name of Person and Taxable Property	Tax
~~Samuel Phipps~~	
John Peoples	$0.06
Catrine Peoples	$1.60
John Piper	$1.10
Robert Piper, Esquire	$2.85
William Piper	$0.70
Thomas Patterson	$0.12
Thomas Pollock, Esquire	$2.00
John Pollock	$2.32
Robert Phipps	$0.06
Hugh Peoples administrator	$1.72
John Parks	$3.00
Patrick Quig	$0.44
Thomas Reeves	$0.09
John Ramsay	$1.23
Charles Rodgers	$0.06
Robert Reed	$1.30
George Richeson	$2.74
Michael Row, single man	$0.50
Peter Reed	$0.12
Colonel John Ramsay	$5.43
John Robison	$0.07
Jacob Reiger	$0.10
John Rodgers	$0.50
William Riddel	$1.54
George Robison	$1.26
William Russel, single man	$0.50
Babara Schaeffer	$0.51
Alexander Stewart	$0.20
Charles Stewart	$0.39
David Shrum, single man	$1.36
George Shrum	$4.36
Samuel Shannon	$1.50
George Shrum, single man	$0.50
George Steel	$3.22
James Steel	$0.14

Abstracts of Westmoreland County, Pennsylvania,
Tax Records 1815

Fairfield Township Name of Person and Taxable Property	Tax
William Steel, single man	$0.57
Robert Smith	$0.54
Joseph Seaburd	$2.71
Henry Symonds	$0.10
Nicholas Snyder	$1.47
Jacob Stewart	$1.29
Joseph Snodgrass, single man	$0.59
~~Richard Snodgrass, single man~~	
John Snodgrass, single man	$0.50
Moore Selders	$0.06
Mary Snodgrass	$0.64
Adam Snyder	$0.77
John Smith	$0.86
Randles Stephen	$0.35
John Seaton, single man	$0.50
George Seaton	$0.60
James Smith	$1.02
John Shields	$0.28
Thomas Smith, Senior	$2.12
Thomas Smith, Junior	$1.14
James Seaton	$0.07
Alexander Seaton, single man	$1.36
Thomas Seaton, Senior	$3.92
John Murray St. Clair	$3.63
Mathias States, Senior	$0.74
M. Hugh Skiles	$1.19
Michael Shank	$0.43
William Story	$0.06
Hugh Shields	$0.06
Daniel Shrum, single man	$0.50
George Seaton	$0.29
"for Jno McWhorter"	
George Taylor	$2.57
Thomas Taylor	$0.06
Thomas Trimble	$0.90
James Trimble	$0.79

Fairfield Township Name of Person and Taxable Property	Tax
Jacob Task	$1.09
Henry Talbot	$1.39
Henry Tash	$2.56
John Tash, single man	$0.56
Peter Tash	$0.20
William Trindle	$0.87
Eli Updegraff	$2.76
James Updegraff	$1.14
Daniel Wallace	$0.53
Hugh Wallace	$0.46
William Wallace	$0.58
John Woods	$0.33
William Wylie, single man	$0.50
James Wylie	$1.35
James Wilson	$0.69
Thomas Wilson	$0.70
~~Robert Williams~~	
Jacob Welshunts	$0.51
Henry Welshunts	$0.79
Annanias Wismer	$0.30
John Wilson	$1.31
Joseph Williams, single man	$0.50
James White	$0.06
Jacob Walker, single man	$0.50
John Weimer	$0.06
John Wallace, single man	$0.50
William Wisner, single man	$0.50

Fairfield Township Unseated Lands Warrantee Names	Tax
Terrence Campbell	$1.43
Daniel Thompson	$0.86
George Hettick	$0.28
B. Regee	$0.86
Bonar Jacob	$0.43

Abstracts of Westmoreland County, Pennsylvania,
Tax Records 1815

Fairfield Township Unseated Lands Warrantee Names	Tax
Penrose	$0.57
John Young, Esquire	$0.49
Samuel M. Fox	$2.63
Philip Bier	$0.43
Barington	$0.86

*Abstracts of Westmoreland County, Pennsylvania,
Tax Records 1815*

Abstracts of Westmoreland County, Pennsylvania, Tax Records 1815

Franklin Township Name of Person and Taxable Property	Tax
Archibald Adair, farmer	$0.97
100 acres, 1 horse, 2 cows	
George Amond, Senior, farmer	$2.56
250 acres, 2 horses, 3 cows, 1 gristmill	
Daniel Amalong, single man, laborer	$0.50
Catrine Amalong	$0.23
57 acres, 1 cow	
William Anderson, farmer	$1.27
300 acres, 2 horses, 2 cows	
"agness" [written above William]	
David Abers, farmer	$1.25
220 acres, 1 horse, 3 cows, 2 oxen	
James Anderson, sicklemaker	$0.46
70 acres, ~~1 horse~~, 1 cow, 100 acres	
John Anderson, farmer	$0.18
2 horses, 1 cow	
George Amond, Junior, farmer	$0.08
2 horses, 1 cow	
George Anthony, farmer	$0.90
"Left the County"	
100 acres, 2 horses, 2 cows	
"~~who is their land charged~~"	
"Ass^r who is taxed for this land"	
John Anthony, farmer	$0.06
1 cow	
"Left the County	
Samuel Anthony, farmer	$0.06
1 cow	
"Left the County	
Anthony Amond, cooper	$0.07
1 horse, 1 cow	
John Altman, "Jober" [?]	$0.06
1 horse, 1 cow	
James Anderson, single man	$0.50
Wm Alexander, farmer	$0.00

Abstracts of Westmoreland County, Pennsylvania, Tax Records 1815

Franklin Township Name of Person and Taxable Property	Tax
1 horse, 1 cow	
Christian Bush, farmer	$0.00
64 acres, 1 horse, 2 cows	
Robert Baxter, taylor	$1.01
130 acres, 2 ~~3~~ horses, 4 ~~3~~ cows, 1 distillery	
Alexander Baxter, single man, stiller	$0.50
1 horse	
John Borland, single man	$0.00
1 horse	
Peter Briney, ~~single man~~, "Joller"	$0.56
1 cow	
Michael Briney, farmer	$0.45
100 acres, 1 horse, 1 ~~2~~ cow	
~~Thomas Blair, farmer~~	$0.60
~~100 acres, 1 horse, 2 cows~~	
"Deceased"	
"land to James Anderson"	
John Borland, farmer	$3.17
300 acres, 2 horses, 4 cows	
Jacob Barlin, Senior	$0.06
1 horse	
Jacob Barten, taylor	$0.63
50 acres, 2 horses, 2 cows	
Samuel Barber	$0.00
83 acres	
Israel Bigelow, doctor	$0.19
2 horses, 2 cows	
Lydia Borland	$3.82
300 acres, 1 horse, 1 cow	
John Borland, single man	$0.50
100 acres	
Barnabas Bloss, wagon maker	$0.09
2 cows	
George Bloss, farmer	$2.42
176 acres, 3 horses, 3 cows	
Jacob Brinker, farmer	$5.78

Abstracts of Westmoreland County, Pennsylvania, Tax Records 1815

Franklin Township Name of Person and Taxable Property	Tax
400 acres, 4 horses, 4 cows, 200 acres	
Christiana Boch	$0.00
100 acres	
"Transfered [*sic*] to Wm Edwards"	
John Beacorn, Junior, farmer	$1.78
170 acres, 1 horse, 1 cow	
"Left the County"	
"and who pays the tax tell that M^r ass^r To	
John Morrow"	
Robert Beacorn	$1.75
160 acres, 2 horses, 3 cows, 50 acres	
John Beacom, Senior, farmer	$1.44
200 acres, 1 horse, 4 cows	
John Beamer, farmer	$1.74
200 acres, 2 horses, 4 cows, 2 oxen	
Henry Brantheiffer	$0.13
2 horses, 1 cow	
~~Richard Borland~~ [?]	
Mathew Borland, single man	$0.00
Benjamin Buel, doctor	$0.00
150 acres, 1 horse	
John Barlin	$0.00
1 cow	
Thomas Blair, "fa" "[farmer?], single man	$0.00
Frederick Barlin, single man	$0.00
Jacob Barlin, farmer	$2.71
185 acres, 2 horses, 2 cows, 1 distillery	
"Look for the rate in the original Duplicate"	
James Clark, farmer	$1.12
130 acres, 1 horses, 2 cows, 12 acres	
~~Joseph Carlean, Junior, farmer~~	$0.08
~~1 horse, 1 cow~~	
"Sent to the penitentiary"	
William Christy, schoolmaster	$0.66
72 acres, 2 horses, 3 cows	
Peter Coons, farmer	$0.10

Franklin Township Name of Person and Taxable Property	**Tax**
1 horse, 2 cows	
"Left the Township"	
Joseph Carleen, Senior	$1.22
Eliza [written above Joseph]	
~~150 acres~~, 1 horse, 2 cows	
"land to Agness Anderson not worthwhile to tax her"	
John Cratty, farmer	$1.38
165 acres, 3 horses, 3 cows, 1 distillery	
David Crookshank, farmer	$1.95
177 acres, 2 horses, 4 ~~3~~ cows	
"There seems to be a mestake [*sic*] in this calculation for 177 acres of land at 4$ will make 708 instead of 408"	
Moses Cunningham, innkeeper	$0.11
~~3 horses~~, 1 cow	
John Coy, farmer	$0.97
75 acres, 1 horse, ~~1 cow~~	
Dewalt Coy, farmer	$0.08
1 horse, 1 cow	
John Cachran, "Jobber"	$0.08
1 horse, 1 cow	
Adam Camray, farmer	$1.79
130 acres, 3 horses, 3 cows	
Jacob Clint, farmer	$0.60
~~100 acres~~, 1 ~~2~~ horse, 2 cows	
Joseph Collins' heirs	$1.19
100 acres, ~~1 stud horse~~, 3 horses, 1 ~~3~~ cow, 1 distillery	
Asa Cook	$0.41
47 acres, 1 horse	
"Left the County"	
William Campbell, weaver	$0.21
60 acres, ~~1 horse~~, 1 cow	
Moses Clark, farmer	$1.03
112 acres, 2 horses, 2 cows	

Abstracts of Westmoreland County, Pennsylvania, Tax Records 1815

Franklin Township Name of Person and Taxable Property	Tax
Michael Cline, weaver	$0.06
1 cow	
Wm Clarke	$0.00
1 horse, 1 cow	
Jacob Cline, Senior, farmer	$1.37
150 acres, 3 horses, 3 cows, 1 bull	
John Cline, farmer	$0.06
1 cow	
Jacob Cline, Junior, farmer	$0.06
1 cow	
James Collins, single man	$0.50
Adam Close, shoemaker	$0.06
John Carpenter, single man	$0.00
130 acres, 1 gristmill, 1 sawmill, 1 horse	
"Plaing up poor Mill"	
William Cook, saddler	$0.00
1 horse	
James Coo	$0.00
275 acres, 1 horse, 1 cow	
James Duff, hatter, single man	$0.06
"Left the township"	
William Darragh, Junior, farmer	$0.20
50 acres, 1 2 cow, 2 horses	
Alexander Duff, farmer	$0.08
1 horse, 1 cow	
John Duff, Senior, farmer	$3.63
330 acres, 2 horses, 2 cows, 1 sawmill, 1 distillery	
John Duff, Junior, farmer	$0.06
1 horse, 1 cow	
Philip Drum, farmer	$1.69
200 acres, 3 4 horses, 2 cows	
Simon Drum, farmer	$0.06
1 cow	
"Sent to the Pennetentray [sic]"	
John Darragh, farmer	$1.28

Abstracts of Westmoreland County, Pennsylvania, Tax Records 1815

Franklin Township Name of Person and Taxable Property	Tax
2 horses, 1 cow, 133 acres	
William Darragh, Senior, farmer	$6.72
100 ~~133~~ acres, 2 cows, 1 horse	
John Drum, farmer	$0.53
81 acres, 1 cow	
"left the County"	
"and who pays the tax say M^r ass^r"	
Samuel Dunbar, innkeeper	$0.18
2 horses, 1 cow	
"Left the Township"	
Jacob Dible, farmer	$0.72
100 acres, 1 horse, 3 cows	
Ephraim Dougherty, carpenter	$0.08
1 cow	
John Davis, farmer	$0.06
2 horses	
Fredrick Dibler, "Jober"	$0.00
1 cow	
Wm David, single man	$0.00
Robert Duff, single man	$0.00
Jacob Double, farmer	$0.00
300 acres, 1 horse	
"I suppose it should be 300 acres of land M^r ass"	
George Elwood, farmer	$0.11
2 horses, 2 cows	
?oisard [?] Edmam, single man	$0.00
Thomas Elwood, farmer	$1.00
100 acres, 2 horses, 2 cows	
Christian Enders, Senior, farmer	$0.43
100 acres 1 horse, 2 cows	
William Elwood, Senior, farmer	$1.08
150 acres, 2 horses, 2 cows	
Robert Ellwood, single man, farmer	$0.56
1 horse	
William Elwood, Junior, farmer	$0.58

Franklin Township Name of Person and Taxable Property	**Tax**
100 acres, 1 horse, 1 cow	
John Elliot, farmer	$0.93
150 acres, 2 horses, 2 cows, 1 distillery	
"Left the County"	
"land to Ja Murry"	
William Edwards, farmer	$0.58
100 acres, 4 ~~2~~ horses, 2 cows, 100 [type of property not specified]	
James Erwin, farmer	$0.65
100 acres, 2 horses, 2 cows	
Christian Everheart, farmer	$1.99
740 acres, 3 horses, 5 cows	
James Elwood, single man, "far" [farmer?]	$0.50
John Ervin, single man	$0.50
Jairas Elliss, single man	$0.00
"student in frkini [?]"	
1 horse	
Henry Edwards, single man	$0.00
1 horse	
Joshua Fluharty, farmer	$0.70
120 acres, 2 horses, 1 cow	
Joseph Frier, shoemaker	$0.13
1 horse, 1 cow	
"not to be found"	
Michael Fink, blacksmith	$0.65
50 acres, 1 horse, 3 cows	
Jacob Fink, blacksmith	$0.83
75 acres, 2 horses, 2 cows	
Charles Flanigan, farmer	$2.68
200 acres, 3 horses, 1 cow	
Jacob Friedt, farmer	$0.06
"Left the township"	
Abraham Friedt, farmer	$1.56
118 acres, 1 horse, 1 cow	
"left the Township"	
"and to whom is the land taxed say M^r ass^r"	

Abstracts of Westmoreland County, Pennsylvania, Tax Records 1815

Franklin Township Name of Person and Taxable Property	Tax
William Fletcher, farmer	$0.08
1 horse, 2 cows	
James Fletcher, farmer	$0.06
"Left the County"	
Bastian Fink, cabinetmaker	$0.11
1 horse, 1 cow	
Joseph Fry	$0.00
200 acres	
"Unseated"	
Robert Gibb, farmer	$0.60
81 acres, 1 2 horse, 2 cows	
Joseph Giger	$0.10
1 horse, 2 cows	
John Giger, farmer	$1.75
186 acres, 2 3 horses, 1 cow	
William Gillespie, farmer	$0.72
84 acres, 3 horses, 4 cows	
Samuel Gordon, single man, farmer	$2.40
150 acres, 3 horses, 2 3 cows	
William Gordon, single man, hatter	$0.56
"Left the Township"	
John Gordon, farmer	$0.71
100 acres, 2 horses, 2 3 cows	
James Gibson	$0.46
101 acres, 1 cow	
"Deceased"	
"and who pays the tax for the land say M^r ass^r"	
John Gibson	$0.46
1 cow, 101 acres	
Henry George, weaver	$0.29
40 acres, 1 horse, 1 cow	
Abraham Gray, farmer	$4.46
300 acres, 2 horses, 2 cows	
"100 acres of this charged to Squire Murray & 200 acres to Jacob Brinker"	

Abstracts of Westmoreland County, Pennsylvania,
Tax Records 1815

Franklin Township Name of Person and Taxable Property	Tax
Widow Gibson	$1.13
~~170 acres~~, 1 horse, 1 cow	
"no tax on a poor widow but who pays tax for the land M^r ass^r"	
Laurence Good, farmer	~~$2.04~~
~~159 acres~~, 2 cows, 1 horse	
Jacob Gilbert, carpenter	$0.69
96 acres, 1 horse, 2 cows	
Mathew Gordon "his heirs ~~heirs John Gordon~~"	$0.00
150 acres	
John Gibson, single man, farmer	$0.00
Charles Hercles, single man	$0.00
1 horse	
~~John Hamilton, Esquire~~	~~$1.31~~
~~200 acres, 1 stud horse, 2 horses, 3 cows~~	
"Deceased"	
"and who pays the tax for the land M^r ass^r"	
Mathew Hamilton, farmer	$0.06
"Left the Township"	
Thomas Hamilton, farmer	$0.06
~~2 horses~~	
"Left the County"	
Philip Heckman, farmer	$0.95
125 acres, 2 ~~1~~ horses, 3 cows	
Jacob Hill	$1.94
225 acres, 2 horses, 1 cow, 1 distillery	
Peter Hill, ~~single man~~, farmer	$0.56
1 horse, 1 cow	
Katrine Hill	$1.94
250 acres, 3 cows	
William Hays, farmer	$1.16
160 acres, 2 horses, 3 cows	
Samuel Hays, "Jobber"	$0.06
1 cow	
Charles Hartless, farmer	$0.62

Abstracts of Westmoreland County, Pennsylvania, Tax Records 1815

Franklin Township Name of Person and Taxable Property	Tax
134 acres, 1 horse, 1 cow	
Elizabeth Hartless	$0.61
138 acres, 1 horse, 1 cow	
Jebus Hartless, "Jobber"	$0.06
"Left the Township"	
Jacob Haymaker, farmer	$0.34
3 horses, 4 cows, 2 oxen	
John Hamilton, farmer	$1.42
200 acres, 2 horses, 3 2 cows	
John Hill, farmer	$1.32
264 acres, 2 horses, 4 3 cows	
Daniel Hankey, farmer	$1.97
250 acres, 2 horses 2 cows	
George Hayley, blacksmith farmer	$0.06
John Humes, farmer	$1.10
120 acres, 3 horses, 1 3 cow, 1 distillery, 1 malt house	
William Hooker, shoemaker	$0.11
1 horse, 1 cow	
Jacob Hartman, shoemaker	$0.10
2 cows	
George Huffman, farmer	$0.06
1 cow, 1 horse	
James Hay, farmer	$0.07
3 cows	
John Henderson, carpenter	$0.06
Leonard Heasley, farmer	$2.72
170 acres, 3 cows, 1 horse	
Henry Heasley, farmer	$0.15
2 horses, 2 cows	
Michael Heasley, farmer	$0.18
1 horse, 1 2 cow, 1 distillery	
Samuel Hay, Senior, shoemaker	$1.67
286 acres, 3 horses, 4 cows	
"Deceased"	
"and who is this land charger to M^r ass^r"	

Abstracts of Westmoreland County, Pennsylvania,
Tax Records 1815

Franklin Township Name of Person and Taxable Property	Tax
"To James and Ann Hay"	
William Hodge, farmer	$1.39
175 acres, 1 ~~2~~ horse, 1 cow	
John Hodge, single man, farmer	$0.50
~~2 horses~~	
Josiah Harvey, fuller	$0.70
2 horses, 2 ~~1~~ cows, 1 fulling mill	
James Hutcheson, ~~innkeeper~~ farmer	$0.18
2 horses, 2 cows	
Richard Hutcheson, farmer	$0.16
17 acres, ~~1 horse~~, 2 cows	
John Hutcheson, farmer	$0.06
1 horse, 1 cow	
"Left the County"	
James Hutcheson, Senior's Executors	$0.00
309 acres, 1 horse, 1 cow	
"assessor set down the rest"	
John Hedinger, baker	$0.12
1 horse, 1 cow	
John Holser, farmer	$1.56
113 acres, 2 horses, 2 cows	
John Henen, laborer	$0.06
1 cow	
Josiah Hervy, single man, fuller	$0.56
Ann Hoy	$0.80
143 acres, 1 horse, 2 cows	
James Hoy, farmer	$0.83
145 acres, 1 horse, 3 cows	
Henry Johnston, single man	$0.50
Thomas Jones, "Jober"	$0.00
Barnabas Kerns, farmer	$0.79
100 acres, 2 ~~1~~ horses, 3 cows	
Conrad Knapinberger, farmer	$3.06
180 acres, 3 horses, 4 cows, 1 sawmill	
John Knapinberger, farmer	$2.09
128 acres, 2 ~~3~~ horses, 3 cows	

Franklin Township Name of Person and Taxable Property	Tax
Christian Keppel, single man, farmer	$1.23
108 acres, 1 horse	
Andrew Keppel, farmer	$2.00
293 acres, 2 cows	
George Keppel, farmer	$0.17
2 horses, 3 cows	
Andrew Keppel, Junior, farmer	$0.17
2 horses, 2 cows	
Philip Knapinberger, gunsmith	$0.08
1 cow	
"See the last of the Ks in this"	
John Kister, farmer	$0.95
160 acres, 1 2 horse, 2 cow	
Philip Kister, farmer	$2.41
290 acres, 3 horses, 4 cows	
Daniel Kister, single man, farmer	$0.50
Michael Kister, single man, hatter	$0.56
"Left the County"	
Philip Kister, Junior, farmer	$1.06
1 horse, 2 cows	
Samuel Kistler, farmer	$2.99
193 acres, 2 ± horses, 2 cows	
Mathew Kerr, farmer	$0.89
125 acres, 1 horse, 3 cows	
Gilbert Kirker, farmer	$1.60
200 acres, 3 horses, 3 cows	
Philip Knapinbarger, "Bs" [blacksmith?]	$0.00
1 horse, 1 cow	
Adam Long, cooper	$0.06
Gabriel Lang, Senior, weaver	$0.58
1 cow	
Tobias Lang, single man, "J obber"	$0.50
Robert Luch, farmer	$0.16
Widow	
2 horses, 3 cows	

Abstracts of Westmoreland County, Pennsylvania, Tax Records 1815

Franklin Township Name of Person and Taxable Property	Tax
Conrad Ludwich, farmer	$4.52
300 acres, 400 acres, 3 horses, 2 cows, 1 sawmill	
George Ludwich, single man	$0.63
1 horse, ~~1 cow~~, 1 horse	
John Ludwich, farmer	$0.06
1 horse	
"say is he a single man yes"	
Philip Long, farmer	$1.33
160 acres, 2 horses, 1 cow	
Philip Leavely, farmer	$0.10
1 horse, 1 ~~2~~ cow	
Francis Laird, reverend	$2.51
181 acres, 3 horses, 4 ~~5~~ cows	
Henry Lang, farmer	$0.92
95 acres, 2 ~~3~~ horses, 4 ~~3~~ cows	
John Laffer, farmer	$1.32
120 acres, 1 ~~2~~ horse, 3 cows	
James Larimer, farmer	$0.87
150 acres, 2 horses, 1 ~~2~~ cow	
Conrad Leninger, blacksmith	$0.08
1 cow	
"Left the Township"	
John Lang, farmer	$0.91
180 acres, 1 cow	
George Leightley, farmer	$2.28
~~300 acres~~, 1 cow	
"and what is $ gone with the land To Jacob Double"	
Jonathan Lewis, farmer	$0.31
1 ~~2~~ horse, 4 cows, 1 distillery	
Joseph Lewis	$0.51
100 acres, 1 horse	
Jacob Long, farmer	$0.06
Henry Lapher, farmer	$0.00
113 acres	

Abstracts of Westmoreland County, Pennsylvania,
Tax Records 1815

Franklin Township Name of Person and Taxable Property	Tax
Philip Leavly, single man	$0.55
1 horse	
John Leavly, single man	$0.50
Hugh Miskelly, cabinetmaker	$0.56
"say is he a single m[an] yes"	
William McLeese, single man	$0.50
Jeremiah Murry, Esquire	$2.16
100 acres, 150 acres	
James McWilliams, single man	$0.50
Josias Meanoro, single man, tanner	$1.55
100 acres, 1 horse, 1 tanyard	
Sarah Moots	$1.01
162 acres	
"now married to Jas Neisbet"	
James McKean, gunsmith	$1.68
200 acres, 2 horses, 2 cows, 2 cows	
William McKean, single man	$0.56
~~1 horse~~	
James McGranahen, farmer	$2.02
300 acres, 2 horses, 2 cows	
Alexʳ McCutchen, farmer	$0.77
200 acres, 2 horses, 2 cows	
David McClean, wheel iron	$0.84
~~90 acres~~, 1 horse, 1 ~~2~~ cow, ~~1 gristmill, 1 sawmill~~	
William Masters, Senior	$0.13
2 horses, 2 cows	
Manus McCloskey heirs	$0.26
75 acres, ~~1 horse, 1 cow~~	
John McConnel, farmer	$2.65
400 acres, 2 horses, 2 cows	
Patrick McQuead, farmer	$0.92
100 acres, 2 horses, 3 cows, 1 distillery	
Samuel McMehan, farmer	$0.97
100 acres, 3 ~~4~~ horses, 3 cows	
Nicholas Martz, "Jobber"	$0.06

Abstracts of Westmoreland County, Pennsylvania, Tax Records 1815

Franklin Township Name of Person and Taxable Property	Tax
1 cow	
John McCreary, farmer	$0.70
96 acres, 2 horses, 2 cows	
Isaac Moore, farmer	$2.84
350 acres, 2 horses, 2 ~~3~~ cows	
Michael McCloskey, farmer	$0.31
75 acres, 1 horse, 1 ~~2~~ cow	
Matthew McKever, farmer	$1.10
150 acres, 2 horses, 3 cows	
Joseph McLees, farmer	$2.05
150 acres, 2 horses, 1 cow	
John Miskelly, farmer	$0.13
2 horses, 1 cow	
"Left the township"	
John McCall, farmer	$3.38
239 acres, 1 ~~2~~ horse, 2 cows	
Richard McCalt, farmer	$0.56
1 horse	
"is he a Single man yes"	
David McCall, farmer	$0.06
1 horse	
Samuel Milligan, schoolmaster	$0.06
1 horse	
Alexander McKeain, farmer	$0.30
100 acres 1 cow	
Eleanor McKeever, tenant	$0.11
83 acres, 2 cows, 1 horse	
William McKeever, single man, laborer	$0.50
Abraham Myers, "jobber"	$0.08
1 horse, 1 cow	
"not to be found"	
Samuel McGuire, farmer	$1.60
~~200 acres~~, 1 horse, 2 cows	
"what is gone with the land ~~to Thomas Snyder~~ Joseph McLeese"	
Thomas McGuire, farmer	$1.74

Abstracts of Westmoreland County, Pennsylvania, Tax Records 1815

Franklin Township Name of Person and Taxable Property	Tax
270 acres, 1 horse	
William McKean, schoolmaster	$0.07
1 horse, 2 ~~1~~ cows	
Robert McCrea, farmer	$0.06
1 cow	
John McIlvain, ~~single man~~	$0.50
2 horses	
Andrew McIlvain, farmer	$1.70
175 acres, 2 horses, 3 cows	
Jeremiah Murray, Esquire, merchant	$4.36
150 acres, 1 gristmill, 1 sawmill, 600 acres, 4 horses, 5 cows	
General James Murray, single man, "D. S."	$1.76
55 acres, 1 horse	
John Mitchel, single man, auger maker	$0.56
"Left the township"	
William McWilliams, farmer	$1.80
200 acres, 2 horses, 2 cows, 1 distillery	
John Moore, single man	$0.50
"Lef the Township"	
Andrew McWilliams, farmer	$2.84
300 acres, 2 ~~3~~ horses, 2 cows	
James McWilliams	$0.12
10 acres, 1 horse, 1 cow	
George McWilliams, single man	$0.56
~~1 horse~~	
Robert McWilliams, single man	$0.50
"~~Left the Township~~"	
James McWilliams, single man, shoemaker	$0.56
"Dead"	
William McQuaid, single man	$0.50
William Masters, ~~single man~~	$1.63
100 acres, 1 distillery, 1 cow	
William Morris, innkeeper	$0.00
Sam¹ McConnel, single man, farmer	$0.50
John McConnel, single man	$0.50

Abstracts of Westmoreland County, Pennsylvania, Tax Records 1815

Franklin Township Name of Person and Taxable Property	Tax
Daniel McQuaid, single man	$0.50
Christian March, farmer	$0.00
2 horses, 1 cow	
David Masters, single man	$0.00
Isaac Masters, single man	$0.00
Samuel Morehead	$0.00
140 acres	
John Morrow, farmer	$0.00
120 acres, 1 horse, 170 acres	
James Nesbit, laborer	$0.73
150 acres, 2 horses, 2 cows	
Paul Nealy, farmer	$3.34
200 acres, 3 2 horses, 4 cows, 1 distillery	
Martin Nealy, farmer	$1.33
100 acres, 1 horse, 2 1 cows	
Philip Nealy, farmer	$1.45
100 acres, 1 horse, 1 cow	
Paul Nealy, Junior, single man, potter	$0.00
170 acres, 2 horses	
Frederich Nealy, farmer	$1.87
100 acres, 1 horse, 3 cows, 100 acres	
Henry Nealy, farmer	$0.74
55 acres, ~~1 horse~~, 2 cows	
Jacob Nitz, farmer	$.99
166 acres, 2 horses, 3 2 cows	
John Nealy, single man, farmer	$0.00
Tobias Painter, farmer	$0.00
150 acres, 2 horses, 1 cow	
Laurence Painter, farmer	$0.83
1 horse, 2 cows, 100 acres	
Jacob ~~Cathrine~~ Christina Painter, farmer	$0.90
100 acres, 1 2 horse, 1 cows	
Samuel Pixler, farmer	$2.33
175 acres, 1 horses, 2 cows	
Adam Peigley, farmer	$0.10
1 horse, 3 2 cows	

85

Abstracts of Westmoreland County, Pennsylvania, Tax Records 1815

Franklin Township Name of Person and Taxable Property	Tax
Henry Patterson, farmer	$0.17
3 horses, 2 cows	
"Left the County"	
Henry Patterson, single man, shoemaker	$0.56
"Left the County"	
William Park, farmer	$1.19
140 acres, 1 ~~2~~ horse, 2 cows	
John Potts, farmer	$1.96
155 acres, 3 ~~2~~ horses, 3 ~~2~~ cows	
Samuel Park, farmer	$2.45
3 horses, 2 cows, 300 acres	
John Purdy, cabinetmaker	$0.95
160 acres, 1 horse, 1 ~~2~~ cow	
Samuel Poth, Senior, farmer ~~shoemaker~~, single man	$0.00
Daniel Poth, single man	$0.00
Michael Potts, single man, farmer ~~weaver~~	$0.00
Jacob Path, single man, "Nater" [?]	$0.00
Robert Reed, carpenter	$0.18
2 horses, 1 cow	
"Left the Township"	
John Rosenberger, farmer	$0.06
1 horse, 1 cow	
Henry Rubright, farmer	$1.63
300 acres, 2 horses, 2 ~~1~~ cows	
Henry Remeleigh, farmer, his executor	$0.25
50 acres, 2 horses, 2 cows	
Michael Rugh, Esquire, farmer	$4.28
340 acres, 1 gristmill, 1 sawmill, 1 horse, 2 ~~1~~ cows	
Christian Remeleigh, single man	$0.56
1 horse	
Robert Riddel, bl [blacksmith]	$0.76
75 acres, 2 ~~1~~ horses, 2 ~~1~~ cows	
Christian Ringer, wagon maker	$1.51
151 acres, 1 ~~2~~ horse, 4 cows	

Abstracts of Westmoreland County, Pennsylvania,
Tax Records 1815

Franklin Township Name of Person and Taxable Property	Tax
Jacob Richards, weaver	$0.08
1 cow	
"Left the township"	
Andrew Row, weaver	$0.13
1 horse, 1 cow	
"Left the Township"	
James Russel, "Jobber"	$0.06
1 cow	
William Ramsay, farmer	$1.03
130 acres, 1 horse, 1 cow	
John Robison, farmer	$2.27
336 acres, 2 horses, 4 cows	
Michael Richard, farmer	$1.68
245 acrews, 1 ~~2~~ horse, 2 cows	
David Rankin, farmer	$0.74
150 acres, ~~3 horses~~, 2 cows	
Michael Remeleigh, bls [blacksmith]	$0.71
100 acres, 1 cow	
John Remeleigh, single man, farmer	$1.64
150 acres, 1 horse, 1 cow	
~~George~~ John Rose, farmer	$0.12
2 ~~1~~ horses, 2 ~~3~~ cows, 100 acres	
Henry Richard, farmer	$0.94
150 acres	
"Left the County"	
Peter Rickard, farmer	$0.00
1 horse, 1 cow	
Peter Roberts, laborer	$0.00
John Robison, single man	$0.00
George Schapper, single man	$0.00
John Sivia, laborer	$0.00
Jacob Shara, weaver	$0.00
1 cow	
William Shield, blacksmith	$0.00
190 acres, ~~1 horse~~, 1 cow	
~~Jacob Silvia, single man~~	~~$0.00~~

Franklin Township Name of Person and Taxable Property	**Tax**
Joseph Steel, farmer	$1.10
156 acres, 2 horses, 1 ~~2~~ cow	
Isaac Sadler, farmer	$0.52
100 acres, 1 ~~2~~ horse, 1 ~~2~~ cow	
John Silveys, blacksmith	~~$1.31~~
190 acres, ~~1 horse~~, 2 ~~1~~ cows	
John Stewart, "Jobber"	$0.06
1 cow	
"Left the Township"	
Leonard Smith, farmer	$0.11
30 acres, 1 horse, 1 cow	
Jacob Silvia, single man	$0.00
~~Philip Smitley, cooper~~	$0.45
~~87 acrews, 1 horse, 1 cow~~	
"Left the Township"	
"and where is the land"	
Jacob Smith, farmer	$0.10
1 horse, 2 cows	
John Schaeffer, farmer	$0.17
1 horses, 2 ~~3~~ cows	
William Silveys, farmer	$1.21
~~113 acres~~, 1 horse, 2 ~~1~~ cows	
"and who is the land taxed to Henry Laupher"	
Thomas Snyder, farmer	$0.08
2 horses, 2 cows, 200 acres	
Leonard Saal, farmer	$0.97
100 acres, 2 ~~1~~ horses, 2 cows	
"who pays for the land to John Borland Jr"	
John Snyder, farmer	$1.31
150 acres, 2 horses, 4 cows	
Abraham Snyder, farmer	$1.51
150 acres, 3 horses, 2 cows	
Henry Smith, shoemaker	$0.08
1 cow	
Simon Smith, farmer	$1.38

Franklin Township Name of Person and Taxable Property	Tax
150 acres, 2 horses, 2 cows, 86 acres	
Jacob Sadler, "Jobber"	$1.43
~~275 acres~~, 1 horse, 1 cow	
"more land run away to James Coo"	
~~Matthew Stanton, auger maker~~	$0.27
~~2 horses, 2 cows~~	
"Left the Township"	
Charles Sampson, farmer	$1.18
150 acres, 1 horse, 1 cow	
James Stafford, miller	$0.08
1 cow	
Jacob Swanger, farmer	$0.13
2 horses 1 cow	
"Lef the Township"	
Peter Swanger, carpenter	$0.06
"Gone"	
Philip Suman, ~~single man, farmer~~	$0.00
William Sadler, single man	$0.00
Abraham Swanger, farmer	$0.00
2 horses, 2 cows	
Philip Stinemeatz, farrier	$0.00
81 acres, 1 horse, 2 cows	
Jacob Shapher, hearpt [?] joiner	$0.00
Michael Taylor	$0.06
1 cow	
Samuel Torrence, joiner	$0.18
2 horses, 1 cow	
"gone"	
Hugh Torrence, Junior, farmer	$0.63
70 acres, 2 horses, 5 cows	
Hugh Torrence, Senior, farmer	$2.18
173 acres, 3 horses, 2 cows	
John Thompson, weaver	$0.10
2 cows	
"Left the Township"	
Frederick Taylor, "Jober"	$0.06

Abstracts of Westmoreland County, Pennsylvania, Tax Records 1815

Franklin Township Name of Person and Taxable Property	Tax
Joseph Turnbleaser, mason	$0.11
1 horse	
William Treece, "Jober"	$0.06
James Vaughan, farmer	$0.17
2 horses, 2 cows	
Conrad Welts, farmer	$1.60
300 acres, ~~1 horse~~, 1 ~~2~~ cow	
Robert Watson, miller	$0.08
1 cow	
"Left the Township"	
Solomon Walts, taylor	$0.06
John Walker, farmer	$0.72
100 acres, 1 horse, 1 ~~2~~ cow	
John Walters, farmer	$0.17
2 horses, 3 cows	
John Wagaman, farmer	$1.02
100 acres, 2 horses, 2 cows	
William Wylie, weaver	$0.76
100 acres, 1 horse, 2 cows	
Barzella Walton, blacksmith	$0.53
50 acres, 1 horse, 2 cows	
Joseph Walton, farmer	$0.28
4 horses, 3 ~~2~~ cows	
Boaz Walton	$0.06
1 cow	
John Waters, single man, "fa" [farmer?]	$0.50
Daniel Waters, single man, weaver	$0.50
John Weigle, "Jobber"	$0.06
1 cow	
David Walter, tanner	$1.33
90 acres 1 ~~2~~ horse, 4 ~~2~~ cows, 1 tanyard	
William Winkler, schoolmaster	$0.06
2 cows	
John Wagaman, single man	$0.00
Joseph Weagly, Esquire ~~Lawyer~~	$0.00
100 acres	

Abstracts of Westmoreland County, Pennsylvania, Tax Records 1815

Franklin Township Name of Person and Taxable Property	Tax
Anthony Walter	$0.00
2 cows	
John Whitlinger, farmer	$0.00
2 cows	
Daniel Williams' heirs	$0.00
200 acres	
"unseated"	

Abstracts of Westmoreland County, Pennsylvania,
Tax Records 1815

Abstracts of Westmoreland County, Pennsylvania, Tax Records 1815

Greensburg Borough Name of Person	Tax
George Armstrong, Esquire, attorney	$4.45
1 house and 2 lots, 2 lots "Wm Jacks," 1 house and lot, 11 acres, 6 acres of Hamilton's, 3 horses, 2 cows	
James Armstrong, taylor	$1.02
1 house and lot, 1 horse, 1 cow	
John B Alexander, Esquire, attorney	$1.08
6 lots, 1 horse, 1 cow	
James Agnew, single man, taylor	$0.67
George Bushfield, saddler	$0.10
1 cow	
Hugh Brady, single man, merchant	$0.75
James Brady, Esquire	$1.33
1.5 house and lot, 1 cow	
John Beerer, butcher	$2.31
1 lot and house, 3.75 acres, 2 horses, 3 cows	
Henry Barton, blacksmith	$0.90
1 lot and house, 1 horse, 1 cow	
Robert Brady, single man, merchant	$0.75
Widow Biggert	$0.25
1 lot and house	
Abraham Baker, weaver	$0.10
1 cow	
Michael Berry	$0.06
1 horse, 1 cow	
William Barnes	$1.17
1 lot and house	
Robert Brown, merchant	$2.52
2.5 lots and house, 2 horses, 1 cow	
Jacob Bowers, single man	$0.50
Arthur Carr	$2.58
1 lot and house, 1 horse	
David Cook, single man	$0.50
Griffith Clark, innkeeper, carpenter	$1.85
1 house and lot, 2 lots of Jack's, 1 horse, 1 cow	
P Michael Casilly, merchant	$5.54

Greensburg Borough Name of Person	Tax
1 house and 2 lots, 2 horses, 2 cows, 1 house and lot	
John Connelly	$0.06
1 cow	
Mas [Mrs?] Christman	$0.00
John Cryder, tanner	$0.90
1 house and lot, 1 horse, 1 cow	
Cust & Jack	$2.33
1 house and lot, 1 cow	
Priscilla Coulter, widow	$2.68
2 houses and lots, 1 cow	
Richard Coulter, Esquire, attorney	$0.75
1 horse	
Eli Coulter, single man, major	$0.50
William Clark, single man	$0.50
Philip Donnelly, blacksmith	$0.52
1 house and lot, 1 horse	
Christian Drum, chair maker	$0.17
1 horse, 1 cow	
Peter Drum, single man, merchant	$0.67
Simon Down, Junior, merchant	$2.35
1 house and lot, 1 horse, 2 cows	
Andrew Dunne	$0.50
1 house and lot	
Cadwallader Evans	$0.10
1 horse, 1 cow	
Peter Fleegar	$0.67
1 house and lot	
Peter Fleegar, single man	$0.50
John Fleegar, blacksmith	$1.28
1 house and lot, 2 cows	
William Friedt, Esquire, single man	$1.25
1 house and lot	
James Fleming, sheriff	$0.27
1 horse, 1 cow	
W. Alexander Foster, attorney	$2.85
1 house and lot, 2 horses, 1 cow	

Abstracts of Westmoreland County, Pennsylvania, Tax Records 1815

Greensburg Borough Name of Person	Tax
Samuel Guthrie, merchant	$2.08
1 house and lot, 1 horse	
George Gibson, innkeeper	$7.67
1 house and 2 lots	
S. William Graham, printer	$1.75
1 house and lot, 1 horse, 1 cow	
Daniel Grant, plasterer	$0.60
3 houses and 1 lot, 1 cow	
Robert Graham, carder	$1.10
1 house and 2 lots, 2 horses, 2 cows	
Joseph Harwick, chair maker	$0.77
1 house and lot, 1 horse, 1 cow	
John Hill, taylor	$1.10
1 house and 3 lots, 1 cow	
John Hornis, single man, shoemaker	$0.58
John Hargrave, weaver	$0.82
1 house and 2 lots, 1 horse	
Richard Hargrave, single man, weaver	$0.58
William Herwich, single man, "Cl"	$1.00
1 lot, 1 horse	
Jacob Hughs, cardmaker	$1.18
1 house and 2 lots, 1 cow	
Joseph Hostater, cardmaker	$1.23
1 house and lot, 1 horse, 1 cow	
John Hettinger, hatter	$0.08
Abraham Horbock, innkeeper	$6.90
1 house and 2 lots, 2 acres, 3 horses, 2 cows, stage and horses	
Thomas Hamilton, Esquire	$0.10
1 lot	
Henry Isell, hatter	$6.12
3 houses and 3 lots, 1 horse, 2 cows	
John Jennings, blacksmith	$0.60
1 house and lot	
George Isterly, cooper	$0.08
Richard Jackson	$0.17
1 lot	

Abstracts of Westmoreland County, Pennsylvania, Tax Records 1815

Greensburg Borough Name of Person	Tax
Alexander Johnston, Esquire	$0.58
2.5 lots	
John Kerns	$3.33
4 houses and 4 lots	
John Kuhns, tanner	$3.68
1 house and 4 lots, 2 horses, 3 cows	
Philip Kuhns, innkeeper	$3.88
2 houses and lots, 3.5 acres, 2 cows	
John Kuhns, single man	$0.50
David Kuhns, single man	$0.50
Joseph Kerns, hatter	$1.33
1 house and lot, 1 horse, 1 cow	
Jacob Kerns, saddler	$2.65
1 house and 2 lots, 1 horse	
Randles McLaughlin, single man	$0.50
Frederick Mecklin, innkeeper	$1.80
1 house and lot, 5 horses, 2 cows	
David McCullough, single man, chair [maker?]	$0.58
Paul Merrew, Esquire	$3.33
1 house and lot	
"formerly Thos Hoges"	
Henry Montgomery, mason	$0.10
1 cow	
Archibald McNeal, blacksmith	$0.58
1 house and lot	
Charles McLaughlin, single man, wagon maker	$0.58
John Melvill, weaver	$0.10
1 cow	
James McCutchen	$0.25
1 house and lot	
James Montgomery, Esquire, "Tegr"	$0.25
1 horse, 1 cow	
John Morrison, Esquire, "Prothy" [probably prothonotary]	$2.95
1 house and lot, 1 horse, 2 cows	
Robert Moore, shoemaker	$0.08
Lewis Mosford, shoemaker	$0.77

Abstracts of Westmoreland County, Pennsylvania, Tax Records 1815

Greensburg Borough Name of Person	Tax
1 house and lot, 1 cow	
Thomas McGuire, Esquire	$2.15
2 houses and lots, 1 horse, 1 cow	
Patrick McGuire	$0.52
2 houses and 3 lots, 1 cow	
David Maclean, single man, printer	$0.67
John McClelland	$1.23
3 houses and 5 lots, 1 horse, 1 cow	
John Morrow, single man, mason	$0.65
1 horse	
Anthony Newhouse, cabinetmaker	$0.13
1 horse, 1 cow	
John Newhouse, single man, cabinetmaker	$0.58
James Postlethwayte, MD	$1.60
1 house and 2 lots, 2 horse, 1 cow	
Benjamin Prater, MD	$1.03
1 house and lot, 1 horse	
George Rohrer	$0.35
1 house and lot, 1 cow	
Henry Ryland, hatter	$0.10
1 cow	
Jacob Rugh	$2.08
1 house and lot, 1 house and lot, 1 house and lot, 1 house and lot	
Ross's heirs	$0.42
2 houses and 2 lots	
John Reed, attorney	$1.80
1 house and 0.5 lot, 1 horse, 1 cow	
Fridirich Rohrer, Esquire	$0.87
1 house and lot, 2 cows	
Tobias Syboth, blue dyer	$0.10
1 cow	
Edward Shillette, barber	$0.08
Samuel Singer, blacksmith	$1.57
1 house and lot	
John Smith, nailor	$1.15
1 house and 2 lots, 1 cow	

Abstracts of Westmoreland County, Pennsylvania, Tax Records 1815

Greensburg Borough Name of Person	Tax
Joseph Smith, single man, nailor	$0.58
John Schaeffer, Esquire, merchant	$2.90
1 house and lot, 5.5 lots, 2 horses, 1 cow	
Daniel Schaeffer, innkeeper	$3.90
1 house and 1.5 lots, 6 horses, 1 cow	
Michael Straw, potter	$0.63
1 house and 2 lots, 1 cow	
Simon Singer, constable	$1.25
1 house and lot, 1 horse, 1 cow	
James Shields's executors	$1.67
2 houses and 2 lots	
Daniel Truxal, taylor	$0.23
1 horses, 1 cow	
Michael Truby, single man, blacksmith	$0.58
Adam Turney, coppersmith	$1.13
1 house and lot, 1 horse, 1 cow	
Jacob Turney, carpenter	$0.10
1 cow	
John Wells, merchant	$3.37
1 house and 2 lots, 1 house and lot, 1.5 [?] acres, 1 horse, 1 cow	
Henry Wise	$0.80
1 house and 0.5 lot,1 horse, 1 cow	
John Wise, single man, silversmith	$0.58
Nathan Williams	$0.06
1 cow	
Robert Williams, Esquire, saddler	$1.83
1 house and lot, 1 horse, 1 cow	
John Williams, single man, founder	$0.58
Robert Williams, Esquire	$1.43
1 house and lot, 1 horse, 1 cow	
Henry Welty, breeches maker	$1.42
carder, 1 house and 4 lots, 2 horses, 2 cows	
Samuel West	$0.18
1 house and lot, 1 cow	
James Waterson	$0.67
1 house and "acre of land"	

Abstracts of Westmoreland County, Pennsylvania,
Tax Records 1815

Greensburg Borough Name of Person	Tax
Yerger & Golloday, merchants	$2.77
2 houses and 1 lot, 1 horse, 1 cow	
John Young, Esquire, judge	$2.38
1 house and 2 lots, 3 horses, 3 cows	
Joseph Young, single man	$0.50

Abstracts of Westmoreland County, Pennsylvania, Tax Records 1815

Abstracts of Westmoreland County, Pennsylvania, Tax Records 1815

Hempfield Township Name of Person	Tax
John Armbrust, weaver	$0.17
1 cow, 10 acres	
Jonas Assyer	$0.30
1 horse, 2 cows	
Henry Assyer	$0.65
100 acres, 2 horses, 5 cows	
Robert Armstrong	$4.12
300 acres, 2 horses, 2 cows	
"the land charged to Do^r Daniel Marchan"	
"gon [*sic*]"	
Mathew Adams, single man, taylor	$0.75
Leonard Assour, carpenter	$0.20
2 lots, 1 cow	
David Altman	$1.10
147 acres, 2 horses, 2 cows	
Widow Altman	$3.48
208 acres, 1 cow, 1 horse	
Henry Aiker, joiner	$0.50
1 house & lot, 10 acres, 1 cow	
"Moved to another Blase and taxt"	
Samuel Armstrong	$0.28
2 horses, 1 stud horse, 2 cows	
"gon [*sic*]"	
Thomas Altman	$0.91
143 acres, 8 acres, 2 horses, 2 cows	
Gasper Altman	$2.17
200 acres, 2 3 horses, 2 3 cows	
Peter Altman, carpenter	$0.18
1 cow	
Isaac Alshouse, taylor	$0.27
1 cow	
Henry Alshouse, Esquire	$1.13
138 acres, 3 horses, 5 cows	
John Alshouse, joiner	$0.30
1 horse	
Samuel Alshouse, single man, joiner	$0.75

Abstracts of Westmoreland County, Pennsylvania, Tax Records 1815

Hempfield Township Name of Person	Tax
Jacob Alshouse, weaver	$0.10
1 cow	
Henry Alshouse, Junior	$0.12
2 horses, 2 cows	
"gon [*sic*]"	
Jacob Alwine	$0.10
2 horses, 2 cows	
William Acklin, single man	$0.84
1 stud horse	
John Altman	$0.20
42 acres, 2 ⊥ horses, 1 cow	
Benjamin Alsworth	$1.90
175 acres, 2 horses, 4 cows	
Thomas Alexander, single man, weaver	$0.58
"gon [*sic*]"	
Andrew Armstrong, carpenter	$0.14
1 horse, 1 cow	
"gon [*sic*]"	
Jacob Altman	$0.06
1 horse, 1 cow	
Major J B Alexander	$0.53
4 acres "of out Lot"	
James Armstrong	$0.67
10 acres "of out Lot"	
George Ashbough	$0.12
2 horses, 2 cows	
Henry Acker	$1.31
150 acres, 1 cow, 1 horse	
Ephraim Blaine's heirs	$1.09
130 acres	
Jacob Becker, single man	$0.50
Mark B. Boyes	$0.06
1 horse, 2 cows	
George Brown	$5.68
200 acres, 1 gristmill, 1 sawmill	
"in the Blase of T^k Rice"	
James Brady, single man	$0.50

Abstracts of Westmoreland County, Pennsylvania, Tax Records 1815

Hempfield Township Name of Person	Tax
Frederick Border	$0.26
30 acres, 2 horses, 2 cows	
William Bets, miller	$0.20
1 cow	
Thomas Bream, carpenter	$0.18
1 cow	
Simon Bell, joiner	$0.41
1 house & lot, 2 cows	
Peter Beaford	$0.06
3 acres, 1 cow	
Henry Boyd, weaver	$1.33
100 acres, 1 horse, 2 cows	
Daniel Beck	$0.06
1 horse, 1 cow	
William Brisbane	$1.87
200 acres, 2 horses, 2 cows, 1 still	
Philip Bush, weaver	$0.12
1 horse	
~~Robert Boyd~~	$5.16
300 acres, 2 stills, 1 horse, 5 cows, 1 tavern	
"this is Charged to Levi Fay in the letter"	
William Brought	$0.73
80 acres, 1 horse, 1 cow	
"the land Charged to Jacob Painter Esq & G Armstrong"	
George Brought, mason	$0.23
1 horse, 1 cow	
"gon [*sic*]"	
Benidict Bartholomew	$0.00
"gon [*sic*]"	
Benedict Bartholomew, Senior	$0.06
1 horse, 1 cow	
"gon [*sic*]"	
James Bodershell	$0.08
1 horse, 2 cows	
"gon [*sic*]"	
Adam Baker	$0.95

Hempfield Township Name of Person	**Tax**
100 acres, 2 horses, 2 cows	
Leonard Beck	$0.80
100 acres, 2 horses, 3 cows	
William Beck, tanner	$1.87
150 acres, 2 horses, 2 cows, 1 tanyard	
John Beck, tanner	$0.18
1 cow	
Jacob Beck, blacksmith	$0.27
1 cow	
Adam Beck, joiner	$0.69
55 acres, 1 horse, 2 cows	
George Baker, single man, joiner	$0.75
Adam Barr	$0.22
4 horses, 3 cows	
David Barr	$2.82
160 acres, 137 acres, ~~1 horse~~, 1 ~~2~~ cow	
Leonard Barr	$0.06
2 cows	
Widow Baum	$1.66
132 acres, 2 horses, 2 cows	
John Baum, single man	$0.50
Peter Baum	$2.06
132 acres, 6 [?] horses, 3 cows	
William Brinkley, plasterer	$0.35
1 cow	
Jacob Black, weaver	$0.13
5 acres	
Lewis Brown	$0.06
1 cow	
John Baughman, carpenter	$0.06
140 acres, 1 horse, 2 cows	
"the Widow Loyd Charged with the land"	
Thomas Brown, cooper	$0.17
James Brady, Esquire	$1.60
1.5 acres, 120 acres	
Abraham Bowman	$1.37
188 acres, 2 horses, 2 cows	

Abstracts of Westmoreland County, Pennsylvania,
Tax Records 1815

Hempfield Township Name of Person	Tax
Daniel Bowman, ~~single man~~	$0.06
1 cow	
George Bughman, Senior	$1.48
130 acres, 2 horses, 1 cow	
Jacob Bughman	$0.12
1 horse, 2 cows	
J. George Bushyager	$0.55
62 acres, 2 cows	
Andrew Boyer	$5.27
152 acres, 1 gristmill, 1 sawmill	
"Peter Kinaman tenant"	
"Charged to Kinaman"	
John Boughman, Senior	$0.08
1 horse, 2 cows	
Daniel Boyer	$0.06
1 cow	
Adam Boughman	$1.43
130 acres, 2 horses, 3 cows	
Jacob Boughman	$1.26
155 acres, 2 horses, 2 cows	
Daniel Bush	$1.84
190 acres, 1 still, 3 horses, 4 cows	
Daniel Bush, ~~single man~~	$0.50
1 cow	
Philip Bricker, shoemaker	$0.22
16 acres, 2 cows	
David Boyer	$0.43
50 acres, 1 cow	
Erasmus Boyer	$0.78
50 acres, 2 horses, 2 cows	
Samuel Bushfield, brickmaker	$1.37
27 acres, 4 acres, 3 horses, 2 cows	
William Barnhart, Senior, joiner	$2.17
270 acres, 2 horses, 2 cows	
Henry Betall	$0.70
7.5 acres, 1 horse, 1 cow	
"Charged to Paul Morrow"	

Abstracts of Westmoreland County, Pennsylvania, Tax Records 1815

Hempfield Township Name of Person	Tax
"gon [*sic*]"	
John Barnhart	$0.12
2 horses, 2 cows	
Abraham Barnhart, single man	$0.50
Frederick Byser, single man, cooper	$0.67
Michael Byerly	$2.22
180 acres, 2 horses, 2 cows	
Captain Joseph Byerly	$1.28
100 acres, 2 horses, 2 cows	
Peter Bush	$0.27
30 acres, 1 horse, 2 cows	
Gasper Byres	$1.01
138 acres, 1 horses, 3 cows	
George Baker	$0.13
40 acres	
Peter Baker	$0.21
30 acres, 1 horse, 1 cow	
Jacob Barr, weaver	$0.10
"gon [*sic*]"	
John Barr, single man	$0.50
Robert Barnett	$0.44
63 acres, ~~1 horse~~, 1 cow	
William Barnhart, Junior	$1.73
160 acres, 2 horses, 2 cows	
John Benninger, shoemaker	$0.16
1 horse, 2 cows	
"gon [*sic*]"	
John Bettinger	$0.06
14 acres "of unseated land"	
Handel Badenhamer, wheelwright	$1.52
0.75 acre, 1 cow	
Daniel Bloos, shoemaker	$0.42
1 cow, 3 acres	
"tenant under Shovey"	
William Best	$8.63
300 acres, 2 horses, 3 cows, 1 gristmill	
George Best	$0.06

Abstracts of Westmoreland County, Pennsylvania, Tax Records 1815

Hempfield Township Name of Person	Tax
1 cow	
Michael Best	$0.06
1 cow	
Henry Borts, single man, shoemaker	$0.58
"gon [*sic*]"	
Michael Borts	$2.74
261 acres, 2 horses, 3 cows	
Isaac Borts, single man	$0.50
Daniel Borts	$3.31
325 acres, 1 horse, 1 cow	
"this is Charged to Michael Frantz"	
Jonathan Bowers	$0.06
2 horses, 1 cow	
Joseph Brady	$0.93
100 acres, 2 ± horses, 2 cows, 30 acres	
James Brovard	$1.80
200 acres, 3 2 horses, 3 cows	
John Bearer, butcher "in Greensburgh"	$0.42
31.75 acres	
Robert Brown	$1.96
10 acres, 135 acres, 1 sawmill	
Widow Biddel	$0.67
4 acres & house	
George Brown	$1.92
160 acres, 3 horses, 3 cows, 1 tavern, 1 stud horse	
"in the Blase of John Drum"	
Adam Brown	$0.06
1 cow	
Marshem Bett, Senior	$0.50
"gon [*sic*]"	
William Brisben, Junior	$0.06
1 horse, 1 cow	
William Cline	$0.15
4 acres, 1 house & lot	
John Cope, single man, cooper	$0.58
Mathias Crawford, mason	$0.23
1 horse, 1 cow	

Abstracts of Westmoreland County, Pennsylvania, Tax Records 1815

Hempfield Township Name of Person	Tax
"gon [*sic*]"	
Joseph Christmore	$0.06
1 cow	
George Cope	$1.91
150 acres, 1 sawmill, 3 horses, 2 cows	
John Clark	$1.12
150 acres, 2 horses, 2 cows	
George Craft, weaver	$0.77
100 acres, 2 horses, 1 cow	
Christopher Cribbs, potter	$2.13
102 acres, 3 horses, 3 cows	
Christian Cline, merchant	$1.16
1 house & 2 lots, 1 cow	
Samuel Craig, blacksmith	$0.25
Widow Cline	$0.06
1.5 acres	
Joseph Cort, Senior	$1.98
160 acres, 2 horses, 2 cows	
Daniel Cort	$1.62
150 acres, 2 horses, 2 cows	
Joseph Cort, Junior	$0.08
1 horse, 2 cows	
Michael Codderman, joiner	$0.51
16 acres, 1 lot in Adamsburgh, 1 cow	
John Cogh, single man	$2.10
88 acres, 2 horses, 3 cows	
Peter Cogh, single man	$2.05
88 acres, 2 horses	
James Chambers	$0.06
100 acres, 1 horse, 1 cow	
John Chrisman, single man	$0.50
Charles Chrisman	$1.01
131 acres, 2 horses, 3 cows	
John Craig	$1.70
150 acres, 1 sawmill, 2 horses, 2 cows	
William Cander, weaver	$0.10
1 cow	

Abstracts of Westmoreland County, Pennsylvania, Tax Records 1815

Hempfield Township Name of Person	Tax
Samuel Craig	$0.06
2 cows	
David Curry, carpenter	$0.93
80 acres, 1 cow	
William Crawford, weaver	$0.22
21 acres	
William Curry	$3.76
245 acres, 2 horses, 2 cows	
Widow Coulter	$0.29
~~4 acres "Meadow Lot"~~, 9 acres "upland"	
P. Michael Cassilly	$1.07
8.25 acres "of an out Lot"	
Arthur Carr	$3.54
160 acres, 50 acres	
George Cline, single man	$0.50
George Doran	$0.18
4 horses, 1 cow	
"gon [*sic*]"	
Thomas Doran	$1.52
100 acres, 1 tavern, 4 horses, 1 cow	
Daniel Dust	$0.52
4 lots, 11 horses	
"gon [*sic*]"	
Widow Dougherty	$0.70
125 acres, 1 horse, 1 cow	
John Dougherty, single man	$0.50
Francis Delong	$0.06
1 horse, 1 cow	
Jacob Dader	$3.18
230 acres, 2 horses, 2 cows	
David Dader	$0.18
1 still, 1 cow	
"gon [*sic*]"	
Patrick Daveling, shoemaker	$0.08
David Davis	$1.62
100 acres, 2 horses, 2 cows	
John Davis	$1.12

Abstracts of Westmoreland County, Pennsylvania, Tax Records 1815

Hempfield Township Name of Person	Tax
100 acres, 2 horses, 2 cows	
John Drum	$1.92
160 acres, 8 horses, 1 cow, 1 tavern	
"Charged to George Brown"	
"I suppose George Brown should be charged in place of John Drum"	
Frederick Dibler	$0.06
1 cow	
George Dormyer, shoemaker	$0.10
1 cow	
Robert Dunlap	$1.02
89 acres, 1 2 horse, 2 3 cows	
Paul Duff	$0.67
100 acres	
Simon Drum, Senior	$2.42
116 acres, 5 acres	
Simon Drum, Junior	$0.75
15 acres	
Harold Daniel's Widow	$6.37
420 acres, 1 horse, 2 cows	
"see in letter H in this & in the Duplicate"	
Christian Erret	$4.25
270 acres, 130 acres, 4 horses, 4 cows	
Michael Einhart	$1.51
125 acres, 2 stills, 2 horses, 3 cows	
John Erret	$1.63
150 acres, 3 2 horses, 3 cows	
George Erret	$0.06
1 horse, 1 cow	
Ephraim Evans	$0.56
1 sawmill, 1 horse, 1 cow	
Jacob Eiker, single man	$0.50
David Eiker, single man	$0.50
Peter Eiker	$2.77
150 acres, 2 horses, 4 cows	
James Eakins	$0.91
130 acres, 1 horse	

Abstracts of Westmoreland County, Pennsylvania, Tax Records 1815

Hempfield Township Name of Person	Tax
Henry Ernest	$1.78
100 acres, 2 horses, 2 cows	
Henry Isett	$1.13
5.75 acres, 4 acres, ~~5.5 acres~~	
"see in letter I"	
Michael Frantz	$3.31
325 acres, 1 horse, 2 cows	
Henry Feidner, weaver	$2.06
190 acres, 1 horse, 2 cows	
John Fulton, weaver	$0.63
95 acres, 1 horse, 2 cows	
Jacob Ferver	$0.06
1 horse, 1 cow	
Peter Fox	$1.45
200 acres, 2 horses, 2 cows	
Peter Fox, single man	$0.50
Philip Fox	$0.12
2 horses, 2 cows	
Jacob Fry, miller	$0.21
1 horse	
Jacob Fisher, single man, shoemaker	$0.58
Adam Fry, miller	$2.59
1 gristmill, 1 horse, 2 cows	
"the Mill Charged to H. P. Klingensmith"	
John Feidner	$0.12
2 horses, 2 cows	
Abraham Feidner	$0.10
2 horses, 1 cow	
David Funk, ~~single man~~, miller	$0.58
Jacob Fox, weaver	$1.13
114 acres, 3 horses, 3 cows	
Philip France	$0.06
1 cow	
David Ferguson, single man, blacksmith	$0.75
"gon [*sic*]"	
Jacob Fissel	$0.20
4 horses, 2 cows	

Abstracts of Westmoreland County, Pennsylvania, Tax Records 1815

Hempfield Township Name of Person	Tax
Widow Fricker	$0.00
1 cow	
John Fluger	$0.13
1 acre "of an out Lot"	
John Finney	$0.06
1 cow	
Nicholas France	$1.08
150 acres, 1 horse, 3 cows	
Jacob Fisher	$0.06
1 cow	
Levi Fay	$5.22
300 acres, 2 stills, 1 horse, 5 cows, 1 tavern	
Isaac Good, shoemaker	$0.14
12 acres, 1 horse, 1 cow	
John Gangaware, weaver	$1.18
100 acres, 3 horses, 3 cows	
Jacob George	$0.16
3 horses, 2 cows	
John Gilchrist, innkeeper	$1.90
30 acres, 1 house & lot, 2 horses, 1 cow	
Jesse Gross	$1.38
150 acres, 2 horses, 3 cows	
Peter Gross, Senior	$2.83
250 acres, 4 horses, 5 cows	
Peter Gross, single man	$0.50
Adam Gross, single man	$0.50
Nathaniel Graham	$1.12
100 acres, 2 horses, 2 cows	
James Gilchrist	$2.42
125 acres, 4 horses, 1 cow	
Thomas Gilchrist	$2.84
125 acres, 4 5 horses, 1 tavern, 3 cows	
Major Andrew Grissinger, joiner	$1.30
123 acres, 2 horses, 4 cows	
Thomas Graham	$2.01
160 acres, 3 horses, 1 cow	
Henry George	$0.55

Abstracts of Westmoreland County, Pennsylvania, Tax Records 1815

Hempfield Township Name of Person	Tax
84 acres, 2 horses, 3 cows	
Peter George	$0.06
1 cow	
John Gourley, Senior	$2.62
250 acres, 2 horses, 2 cows	
Henry Gourley	$0.08
1 horse, 2 cows	
John Gourley, Junior	$0.06
1 horse, 1 cow	
James Gregg, weaver	$0.50
40 acres, 1 cow	
"the land Charged to James McLouglin"	
Henry Guiger	$1.77
100 acres, 2 stills, 4 horses, 1 cow	
Colonel Samuel Guthrie	$3.50
175 acres	
Henry Griffin, potter	$0.21
1 horse, 1 cow	
Peter George	$1.43
130 acres, 2 horses, 3 cows	
Robert Graham	$0.85
17 acres	
James Hays, single man	$0.50
Samuel Hays	$1.18
100 acres, 3 horses, 3 cows, 35 acres	
Daniel Harold, Junior, joiner	$0.45
19 acres, 2 cows	
Jacob Hinebough	$0.06
1 horse, 1 cow	
Daniel Harold, Senior	$7.15
420 acres, ~~2 stills~~, 2 ~~5~~ horses, 2 ~~6~~ cows	
Jacob Harold, single man	$0.50
1 cow	
Samuel Hummel, weaver	$0.12
1 horse, 1 cow	
Peter Hobough, shoemaker	$0.08
Abner Hessam	$1.57

Abstracts of Westmoreland County, Pennsylvania, Tax Records 1815

Hempfield Township Name of Person	Tax
200 acres, 2 horses, 4 cows	
Thomas Hessam, shoemaker	$0.13
10 acres, 2 horses, 2 cows	
William Hurtman	$0.06
1 cow	
"ded"	
Thomas Hissom, Senior	$0.12
2 horses, 2 cows, 100 acres	
"there is 200 acres of John Wyands land and there is but 100 charged to T Hissom how comes that"	
Thomas Hissom, single man	$0.50
"gon [*sic*]"	
Joab Hissom, single man, carpenter	$0.67
"gon [*sic*]"	
Hugh Henderson	$0.57
50 acres, 1 horse, 2 cows	
Alexander Henderson, single man	$1.04
50 acres, 1 horse	
"only the ~~property~~ land"	
Jonathan Hess	$0.10
2 horses, 1 cow	
"gon [*sic*]"	
Frederick Henry	$0.08
1 horse, 2 cows	
Joseph Heasley, single man, gunsmith	$0.67
Peter Huber	$2.97
107 acres, 186 acres, 3 horses, 3 cows	
Frederick Hile	$0.08
1 horse, 2 cows	
"gon [*sic*]"	
Christian Houser	$1.44
125 acres, 3 horses, 3 ~~4~~ cows	
Peter Harold	$2.84
200 acres, 2 stills, 3 horses, 3 cows	
James Hays, Senior	$2.50
200 acres, 2 horses, 5 cows, 35 acres	

Hempfield Township Name of Person	Tax
John Hoofman, single man, weaver	$0.58
John Hoover, blacksmith	$0.80
111 acres, 4 horses, 2 ~~1~~ cows	
Jacob Heasley	$0.08
2 cows, 1 horse	
Henry Heasley, Senior	$3.26
300 acres, 1 still, 3 horses, 4 cows	
Jacob Houk, single man	$0.50
Henry Heasley, Junior, carpenter	$0.10
1 cow	
John Heasley, ~~single man~~	$0.06
1 cow	
Richard Hardin, joiner	$0.17
Conrad Houk now the Widow Houk	$0.08
1 horse, 2 cows	
Anderson Herman, single man, joiner	$0.67
"gon [*sic*]"	
Jacob Houk, Senior	$1.77
130 acres, 1 sawmill, 3 horses, 4 cows	
Peter Hoofman	$0.72
72 acres, 1 ~~2~~ horse, 1 ~~2~~ cow	
John Hanselman	$0.78
100 acres, 2 horses, 2 cows	
Conrad Hoist, shoemaker	$0.13
2 horses, 1 cow	
Peter Hansel	$0.84
111 acres, 6 ~~2~~ horses, 3 ~~1~~ cows	
"there is likely something wrong in Hansel	
peter's return for he was $1.47 tax in 1814 put it	
right M[r] ass[r]"	
William Hill, single man	$0.50
"gon [*sic*]"	
Henry Hawkey, gunsmith	$0.27
1 cow	
"gon [*sic*]"	
Jacob Hawk	$3.44
175 acres, 2 stills, 3 horses, 4 cows	

*Abstracts of Westmoreland County, Pennsylvania,
Tax Records 1815*

Hempfield Township Name of Person	Tax
Frederich Hains, shoemaker	$0.78
60 acres, 1 horse, 2 cows	
John Hill	$0.42
5 acres "of out Lot"	
Thomas Hoge, Esquire	$0.42
5 acres "of out Lot"	
"Charged to Simon Singer"	
Abraham Horbough	$0.43
1.5 acres "of out lot," 6 acres "of out lot," 108 acres	
John Heable, single man	$0.50
Henry Heable	$0.29
35 acres, 1 horse, 1 cow	
Jacob Hains	$1.99
180 acres, 3 horses, 4 cows	
John Hobough	$0.06
1 cow	
Jonathan Hammer	$5.28
100 acres, 1 gristmill, 1 sawmill, 2 horses, 2 cows	
David Hebler, potter	$0.53
1 horse, 1 cow, 61 acres	
Christian Isaman	$1.30
147 acres, 1 horse, 2 cows	
George Isaman	$0.06
1 cow	
Michael Isaman	$1.33
144 acres, 2 horses, 3 cows	
Andrew Isaman	$0.91
100 acres, 1 horse, 2 cows	
Arthur Jervis	$0.15
15 acres, 1 horse, 2 cows	
"the land Charged to Widow Welsh"	
"gon [*sic*]"	
Peter Isaman	$1.45
170 acres, 3 2 horses, 3 2 cows	
Jacob Isehart	$0.08
1 horse, 2 cows	

Abstracts of Westmoreland County, Pennsylvania, Tax Records 1815

Hempfield Township Name of Person	Tax
"gon [*sic*]"	
John Imbel	$0.06
1.5 acres	
Samuel Jones, ~~single man~~, shoemaker	$0.58
William Jack, Esquire	$4.24
100 acres, 70 acres, 1 tanyard, 1 slave, 5 horses, 4 cows	
Mathew Jack, single man, tanner	$0.83
Robert Jones	$0.73
75 acres, ~~2 horses~~, 1 cow	
Alexander Johnston, Esquire	$2.13
16 acres	
"Isett Henry is at the Last of the E's which see"	
Peter Klingensmith "tenant under Deal"	$1.71
165 acres, 1 horse, 1 cow	
Christian Klingensmith	$1.42
260 acres, 2 horses, 2 cows	
George Kleppener	$1.13
150 acres, 2 horses, 3 cows	
Henry Klippiner, single man	$0.50
Adam Kettering, "Sadle tree maker"	$0.18
1 cow	
George Keener	$0.95
127 acres, 2 horses, 1 cow	
"gon [*sic*]"	
John Keppel	$1.41
100 acres, 1 horse, 2 cows	
Peter Keppel, single man	$0.54
1 horse	
Michael Keppel	$2.17
172 acres, 1 sawmill, 1 ~~2~~ horse, 2 cows	
Jacob Keener, weaver	$0.10
1 cow	
"gon [*sic*]"	
Joseph Keller	$0.06
1 cow	
John Kern, hatter	$1.91

Hempfield Township Name of Person	Tax
140 acres, 3 horses, 3 cows	
"the land Charged to J. Tayler"	
"gon [*sic*]"	
Andrew Kimmel	$0.12
3 horses, 2 cows	
John Kimmel, ~~single man, joiner~~, "Single"	$0.50
Benjamin Kirkpatrick	$3.51
292 acres, 1 ~~2~~ horse, 2 cows	
George Kuhn, blacksmith	$0.73
64 acres, 1 horse, 2 cows	
Jacob Knave, single man	$1.80
100 acres, 2 horses, 3 cows	
George Kroushour	$1.81
165 acres, 3 horses, 2 cows	
"the land Charged to P. KlingenSmith tenant	
under Deal"	
"ded [*sic*]"	
Henry Kifir	$1.82
152 acres, 2 horses, 3 cows	
Henry Kifer, single man	$0.54
1 horse	
Peter Kifer, single man	$0.50
George Keck, Senior	$1.56
87 ~~100~~ acres	
David Kemerer, single man	$0.50
Widow Keck	$2.43
213 acres, 1 still, 2 horses, 3 cows	
Adam Kemmerer	$2.26
190 acres, 1 still, 3 horses, 4 cows	
Peter Klingelsmith	$1.12
150 acres, 2 horses, 2 cows	
"the land Charged to Jacob Lander"	
"gon [*sic*]"	
Daniel Klingelsmith, single man	$0.50
"gon [*sic*]"	
Widow Kimmel	$0.12
10 acres, 1 cow	

Abstracts of Westmoreland County, Pennsylvania, Tax Records 1815

Hempfield Township Name of Person	Tax
Peter Klingelsmith	$1.10
148 acres, 2 horses, 2 cows	
"gon [*sic*]"	
John Klingelsmith, Senior	$1.40
150 acres, 2 horses, 4 cows	
Conrad Kroch	$1.65
230 acres, 3 horses, 2 cows	
Philip Klingelsmith	$3.86
270 acres, 70 acres, 1 sawmill, 3 horses, 7 cows, 1 gristmill	
David Klingelsmith, single man	$0.50
1 horse	
John Klingelsmith	$0.06
2 cows	
Peter Klingelsmith, Junior	$0.73
100 acres, 1 horse, 1 cow	
Matthias King, single man	$0.50
William Keys	$1.45
200 acres, 2 horses, 2 cows	
"the land Charged to Peter Small"	
"ded [*sic*]"	
Joseph Kimmel	$1.51
185 acres, 3 horses, 3 cows	
Michael Kimmel, Senior	$1.08
150 acres, 2 horses	
Michael Kimmel, Junior	$0.06
2 cows	
David King, wagon maker	$0.17
John King	$1.32
100 acres, 6 horses, 4 cows	
Peter Kinaman	$0.12
2 horses, 2 cows, 152 acres, 1 gristmill, 1 sawmill	
"tenant under Andrew Boyers"	
George King, single man	$0.50
Philip Krider, single man	$0.50
Jacob Kerns	$0.77
11.5 acres	

Abstracts of Westmoreland County, Pennsylvania, Tax Records 1815

Hempfield Township Name of Person	Tax
Joseph Kerns	$0.93
28 acres	
Andrew Kepler	$1.12
100 acres, 2 horses, 2 cows	
Daniel Kuhns	$0.06
1 horse, 1 cow	
Jonas Kimmel	$0.54
4 acres, 1 horse	
Philip Kuhns	$2.38
162 acres, 4 horses, 3 cows	
Jacob Kimmerer	$0.06
2 cows, 2 horses	
Lewis Kimmerer	$0.06
1 cow	
"gon [*sic*]"	
Adam Kroushour	$0.06
2 horses, 1 cow, 100 acres	
Jacob Kighly, weaver	$0.08
John Kimmerer	$3.55
250 acres, ~~4 horses~~, 3 cows, 1 horse	
Lewis Kimmerer	$3.91
280 acres, 1 horses, 2 cows, ~~2 oxen~~	
Michael Keener, blacksmith	$0.39
9 acres, 1 horse, 1 cow	
Daniel Kimmel	$0.06
1 horse, 1 cow	
Henry Kroushour, shoemaker	$0.56
50 acres, 1 horse, 1 cow	
Peter Kailler, brick maker	$0.08
Jonas Keel, shoemaker	$0.17
10 acres, 1 cow	
"the land Sold"	
Philip Kuhns, Senior	$2.20
250 acres, 2 horses, 2 cows, 30 acres	
John Krock, innkeeper	$1.03
100 acres, 2 horses, 2 cows	
Christian Kuhns, weaver	$0.14

Abstracts of Westmoreland County, Pennsylvania, Tax Records 1815

Hempfield Township Name of Person	Tax
1 horse, 1 cow	
"gon [*sic*]"	
Isaac Keck, taylor	$0.17
"gon [*sic*]"	
Colonel John Kuhns	$4.38
207 acres, 11 acres "out lot"	
Lewis Keppil	$0.96
84 acres, 2 horses, 1 2 cow	
Henry Keppel, joiner	$0.93
84 acres, 1 horse, 1 cow	
Peter Keppel	$0.00
90 acres, 2 cows	
George Keppel	$0.78
80 acres, 2 horses, 2 cows	
Jacob Kiel, shoemaker	$0.65
67 acres, 2 horses, 2 cows	
"gon [*sic*]"	
"Charged to James & La¹ Hays"	
"I don[']t well understand this case"	
Frederich Kiser	$0.06
1 horse, 1 cow	
"gon [*sic*]"	
John Kimmel, single man, joiner	$0.67
Garret Kamp	$2.26
155 acres, 3 horses, 4 cows	
Jacob Kamp	$0.12
2 horses, 2 cows	
"gon [*sic*]"	
Solomon Kamp	$1.02
45 acres, 1 horse, 3 cows	
John Kuhns, single man	$0.50
George Krock, single man	$0.50
Philip Klingensmith	$0.12
2 horses, 1 cow	
Daniel Kean	$1.87
264 acres, 2 horses, 2 cows	
Widow Keck	$0.90

Abstracts of Westmoreland County, Pennsylvania, Tax Records 1815

Hempfield Township Name of Person	Tax
P. Keck	
100 acres, 2 horses, 2 cows	
David Klingensmith	$0.30
40 acres, 2 horses, 1 cow	
Isaiah Lewis	$0.45
57 acres	
Nicholas Long, Senior	$2.93
400 acres, 1 still, 3 horses, 4 cows, 50 acres	
Jacob Long, single man, wagon maker	$0.67
100 acres	
Jacob Lapsley, wagon maker	$0.31
2 horses, 2 cows	
Tobias Long, single man	$0.50
Jacob Long, tenant	~~$2.00~~
264 acres, 5 horses, 2 cows	
"this land Charged to Daniel Kane"	
Adam Long	$0.74
100 acres, 1 horse, 2 cows	
Nicholas Long, cooper	$0.62
70 acres, 2 cows	
Lewis Long, single man	$1.24
100 acres, 1 horse, 2 cows	
Samuel Lippencott	$1.89
150 acres, 2 horses, 4 ~~3~~ cows	
John Lacy, weaver	$0.12
2 cows, ~~6 acres~~	
Samuel Low	$0.06
1 cow, 6 acres	
Michael Leader, wagon maker	$1.47
130 acres, 2 horses, 3 cows	
Thomas Likes	$2.12
200 acres, 2 horses, 2 cows	
John Lambright, single man, cooper	$0.62
1 horse	
Zenas Large, carpenter	$0.17
Conrad Link	$0.06
1 cow	

Abstracts of Westmoreland County, Pennsylvania, Tax Records 1815

Hempfield Township Name of Person	Tax
Daniel Linsenbigler	$0.06
6 acres	
Daniel Loughner, blacksmith	$0.27
1 cow	
"gon [*sic*]"	
Abraham Leasure	$1.37
150 acres, 2 horses, 2 cows	
John Linsenbigler, carpenter	$0.20
2 cows	
John Leighty	$1.12
100 acres, 2 stills, 2 horses, 2 cows	
Rudy Loughtner	$1.45
160 acres, 2 horses, 2 cows	
Jacob Linsenbigler	$0.44
41 acres, 1 horse, 1 cow	
"gon [*sic*]"	
Jonas Loughtner	$2.08
~~250 acres~~, 1 cow	
George Lesley, taylor	$0.08
Robert Larimer	$0.12
2 horses, 2 cows	
Abraham Long, single man, blacksmith	$0.56
Jacob Leeman	$0.40
17 acres, 1 horse, 1 cow	
Widow Loyd	$1.19
140 acres, 1 cow	
Thomas Lewis	$0.06
1 horse, 1 cow	
Jacob Landes	$1.75
150 acres, 23 acres, 41 acres, 4 horses, 3 cows	
Jacob Mecklin, Senior	$1.13
60 acres, 1 tavern, 2 horses, 3 cows	
Philip Mecklin, fuller	$2.45
175 acres, 1 fulling mill, 2 horses, 2 cows	
Henry Miller	$0.87
95 acres, 1 horse, 2 cows	
~~Peter~~ Jacob Miller	$2.45

Abstracts of Westmoreland County, Pennsylvania, Tax Records 1815

Hempfield Township Name of Person	Tax
270 acres, 2 4 horses, 2 cows	
Jacob Moneysmith, potter	$0.61
61 acres, 1 horse, 1 cow	
"the land Charged to David Hebler"	
"gon [*sic*]"	
Michael Mathias	$2.60
250 acres, 2 stills, 3 horses, 3 cows	
Henry Miller	$0.27
30 acres, 1 cow	
Samuel McMullen, single man, weaver	$0.58
"gon [*sic*]"	
Widow Miliron	$2.60
300 acres, 2 horses, 3 cows	
James McFee, joiner	$0.36
23 acres	
Jacob Miller, Junior, blacksmith	$0.27
1 cow	
John Miller, shoemaker	$1.22
150 acres, 2 horses, 3 cows	
Philip Mecklin, mason	$0.90
70 acres, 2 horses, 1 cow	
John McCune	$2.40
136 acres, 3 horses, 3 cows	
Alexander McCartney, shoemaker	$0.12
12 acres	
Israel Musgrove, joiner	$0.18
1 cow	
Hugh McCurdy	$0.10
2 horses, 1 cow	
General David Marchand "MD"	$5.00
192 acres, 236 acres, 1 "Negroe" slave, 4 horses, 6 cows, 2 stills	
David Marchand, weaver	$0.20
2 horses, 2 3 cows	
John Marchand	$0.12
2 horses, 2 cows	
Samuel McCurdy, Junior	$0.10

Abstracts of Westmoreland County, Pennsylvania, Tax Records 1815

Hempfield Township Name of Person	Tax
2 horses, 1 cow	
Widow Marchand	$2.64
250 acres, 1 lot in Adamsburgh, ~~1 cow~~, 4 cows	
Jacob Marchand, single man	$0.58
2 horses	
Philip Miller, shoemaker	$1.38
71 acres, 3 lots & houses, 1 horse, 1 cow	
Adam Miller	$0.30
26 acres, 2 cows	
Peter Martin	$0.06
1 cow	
"gon [sic]"	
Samuel McCurdy, Senior	$2.36
170 acres, 1 horses, 1 cow	
Frederick Macklen	$3.00
300 acres	
John McCurdy, "Girt" weaver	$0.16
2 horses, 2 cows, 60 acres	
David Mitchel	$0.62
60 acres, 2 cows, 2 horses	
Henry Miller, shoemaker	$0.10
1 cow	
Robert Monroe, single man, tanner	$0.67
George Myer's [sic]	$1.66
220 acres, 3 horses, 4 cows	
John Miller, blacksmith	$0.23
1 horse, 1 cow	
John McMurray	$2.08
200 acres, 2 horses, 2 cows	
Alexander McMunay	$0.06
1 cows, 2 horses	
Alexander Mckee	$1.20
130 acres, 2 horses, 2 cows	
Samuel Mecklin	$0.13
2 horses, 3 cows	
"gon [sic]"	
James McGunagle	~~$0.47~~

Abstracts of Westmoreland County, Pennsylvania, Tax Records 1815

Hempfield Township Name of Person	Tax
10 acres, 2 stills, 2 horses	
"this is Jams Mcmanagle Charged in another Blase"	
William Moore	$0.56
100 acres, 1 horse, 1 cow	
Samuel McKissock, single man	$0.50
John McCauley, Senior	$0.80
100 acres, 2 horses, 2 cows	
John McCauley, single man	$0.50
John Mansfield, carpenter	$0.43
36 acres, 1 horses, 2 cows	
Andrew McIlwain, blacksmith	$0.27
1 cow	
"gon [sic]"	
Adam Myers	$0.22
30 acres, 1 cow	
"gon [sic]"	
Samuel McKee, single man	$3.18
133 acres, 2 ~~4~~ cows, ~~1 cow~~	
John McKee, single man	$0.87
2 stills, 1 horse	
John Mecklen	$5.90
200 acres, 40 acres, 4 horses, 3 cows	
John McKee	$0.09
1 horse, 3 cows	
James Marchbanks, weaver	$0.16
1 cow	
James McKelvy	$1.08
100 acres, 1 horse, 2 cows	
Robert McKissock, single man	$3.22
260 acres, 2 horses, 2 cows	
Peter Miller	$1.31
150 acres, 1 horse, 1 cow	
Henry Miller, single man	$0.06
Michael Miller	$0.55
33 acres, ~~1 gristmill~~, 3 cows	
"no Mill"	

Abstracts of Westmoreland County, Pennsylvania, Tax Records 1815

Hempfield Township Name of Person	Tax
Nicholas Miller	$1.17
120 acres, 2 horses, 5 cows	
Jacob Miller, blacksmith	$2.07
200 acres, 2 horses, 4 cows	
David Murich, weaver	$0.23
13 acres, 1 horse, 1 cow	
Alexʳ McKinney, boot maker	$1.57
14 acres, 1 tavern, 1 horse, 2 cows	
Jacob Mecklen	$3.50
192 acres, 6 4 horses, 6 8 cows	
Daniel Myers	$0.06
1 horse, 1 cow	
"gon [sic]"	
John Myers	$0.74
100 acres, 1 horse, 2 cows	
Hugh Mellon	$0.73
100 acres, 1 horse, 1 cow	
Thomas McGuire, Esquire	$0.55
7 acres "of out lot," 1 lot	
David Marchand, doctor	$1.23
5 acres, 5.5 acres	
John McClelland	$1.00
20 acres "of out Lot"	
Milles Moley	~~$0.17~~
1 house & lot	
"Lame"	
Thomas Monroe	$1.21
100 acres, 3 horses, 5 cows	
Joseph Monroe, tanner	$0.60
1 tanyard, 1 horse, 3 cows	
Paul Morrow, Esquire	$0.98
4 acre "out Lot," 7.5 acres "& house"	
"place of Thomas Hoge"	
John Martin, single man	$0.50
"gon [sic]"	
Leonhard Miller	$0.12
2 horses, 3 cows	

Abstracts of Westmoreland County, Pennsylvania, Tax Records 1815

Hempfield Township Name of Person	Tax
Peter Miller	$1.33
120 acres, 2 horses, 2 cows	
James Mcmanigal	$0.43
10 acres, 2 stills, 1 horse, 1 cow	
David Moyer	$0.12
2 horses, 2 cows	
James McGrilles	$0.06
1 cow	
James McLaughlin	$0.89
40 acres, 3 horses, 3 cows, 11 acres	
Jacob Macklen, Junior, single man	$0.50
Daniel Marchand, doctor	$4.01
300 acres	
"in the Blase of Robert Armstrong"	
William Nelson	$1.35
150 acres, 2 horses, 1 cow	
William Nash, wagon maker	$0.17
Jacob Newhouse	$2.62
300 acres, 2 horses, 2 cows	
Samuel Oliver	$1.10
100 acres, 2 horses, 2 cows	
Nicholas Ozenbough, mason	$0.31
1 horse, 1 cow	
"gon [sic]"	
Daniel O'Donald	$0.06
1 cow	
Samuel Pool	$2.43
145 acres, 1 tavern, 6 horses, 4 cows, 32 acres	
Jacob Painter, Esquire	$11.58
600 acres, 1 gristmill, 1 sawmill, 4 horses, 5 cows	
Jacob Pluck, single man, mason	$0.67
Zachariah Pool	$0.54
28 acres, 1 horse, 2 cows	
John Painter	$1.07
146 acres, 2 horses, 1 cow	
George Painter	$1.23
170 acres, 2 ± horses, 3 cows	

Abstracts of Westmoreland County, Pennsylvania, Tax Records 1815

Hempfield Township Name of Person	Tax
"there is an error of 70 acres of land too much in this"	
George Painter	$5.47
270 acres, 1 gristmill, 5 horses, 4 cows	
"the Widow Painter now"	
Christian Potsor	$2.82
270 acres, 2 horses, 2 cows	
George Patty	$1.82
180 acres, 1 cow	
William Philips	$3.05
170 acres, 2 horses, 3 cows	
Michael Painter	$4.28
~~300 acres~~, 6 horses, 2 cows	
"the land Charged to Revd Spoon"	
John Painter, single man	$0.75
6 horses	
Jacob Painter	$0.06
1 cow	
"ded [*sic*]"	
Jacob Perkey	$2.49
139 acres, 1 ~~3~~ horse, 2 ~~3~~ cows	
Daniel Poorman, blacksmith	$0.33
2 horses, 3 cows	
Robert Patterson	$0.06
1 cow	
John Parks	$2.25
108 acres, 2 stills, 2 horses, 2 cows	
"the land Charged to Abram Herbaug"	
"gon [*sic*]"	
James Postlethwaite, doctor	$0.83
25 acres	
Tobias Painter	$1.43
180 acres, 4 horses, 4 cows	
Michael Painter, single man	$0.50
Tobias Painter, single man	$0.50
Jacob Painter, Esquire, and George Armstrong, Esquire	$1.69

Abstracts of Westmoreland County, Pennsylvania, Tax Records 1815

Hempfield Township Name of Person	Tax
200 acres	
Thomas Potter	$2.57
240 acres, 3 horses, 1 cow	
John Riggel	$1.07
150 acres, 1 horses, 2 cows	
John Royer, potter	$0.17
Robert Reed	$2.52
240 acres, 2 horses, 2 cows	
"this Charged to Thomas potter [*sic*]"	
"gon [*sic*]"	
Abrahaim Ritter, Esquire	$0.38
50 acres, 3 cows	
"gon [*sic*]"	
Philip Reesman, miller	$0.20
2 cows	
"gon [*sic*]"	
Jacob Rosensteel, weaver	$0.16
1 horse, 2 cows	
"gon [*sic*]"	
Andrew Rosensteel	$0.33
80 acres, 1 horse, 1 cow	
George Rosensteel, carpenter	$0.35
30 acres, 2 cows	
Edward Ratchford, weaver	$0.10
1 cow	
Adam Richart	$0.07
1 horse, 2 cows	
Peter Rugh	$3.81
194 acres, 4 horses, 5 cows	
Frederick Rice	$5.80
200 acres, 1 gristmill, 1 sawmill, 2 horses, 3 cows	
"land and Mills Charged to George Brown"	
"gon [*sic*]"	
Peter Rice, blacksmith	$0.27
1 cow	
"gon [*sic*]"	
Andrew Rosensteel	$0.06

Abstracts of Westmoreland County, Pennsylvania, Tax Records 1815

Hempfield Township Name of Person	Tax
1 horse, 1 cow	
Elizabeth Royer, widow	$0.26
6 acres, 1 tavern, 1 cow	
Frederick Reims, taylor	$0.25
15 acres, 1 horse, 1 cow	
Frederick Reims, Junior, brick maker	$0.17
"ded [*sic*]"	
Christian Rudebaugh	$1.73
140 acres, 2 horses, 1 cow	
William Richards	$0.06
1 cow	
"gon [*sic*]"	
Henry Reemer	$0.08
1 horse, 2 cows	
Jacob Reemer	$3.49
200 acres, 2 stills, 3 horses, 2 cows	
Christian Rose, shoemaker	$0.74
60 acres, 1 horse, 2 cows	
Jacob Reeger, carpenter	$0.92
80 acres, 2 horses, 2 cows, 30 acres	
James Russel	$0.65
80 acres, 2 horses, 2 cows	
Andrew Row	$2.44
193 acres, 1 still, 2 3 horses, 3 cows	
Jacob Row, single man, mason	$0.67
Christian Row	$2.30
126 acres, 1 gristmill, 1 horse, 2 cows	
George Row, shoemaker	$0.10
1 cow	
George Rimbel	$0.06
1 cow	
"gon [*sic*]"	
Robert Robb	$0.12
2 horses, 2 cows	
Matthew Rowan	$0.98
76 acres, 2 horses, 2 1 cows	
"the land Sold to Al[x] Storry and taxt"	

Abstracts of Westmoreland County, Pennsylvania, Tax Records 1815

Hempfield Township Name of Person	Tax
Joseph Russel	$1.90
119 acres, 2 horses, 2 cows	
Christian Ruffner	$2.54
163 acres, 1 2 horse, 1 cow	
George Ruffner	$0.07
2 horses, 2 cows	
Friderich Rohser, Esquire	$0.50
10 acres "of out Lot"	
Jacob Rugh	$4.25
197 acres, 5 horses, 6 cows	
Daniel Rugh, single man	$0.50
John Rice, single man	$0.50
"gon [sic]"	
Jacob Reed	$1.47
140 acres, 1 horses, 1 cow	
William Rambough	$1.66
107 acres, 1 horse, 2 cows	
Sebastian Swartz	$4.42
170 acres, 1 gristmill, 1 sawmill, 2 horses, 2 cows	
Philip Schaeffer, joiner	$1.34
113 acres, 2 horses, 4 cows	
Adam Schaeffer, joiner	$0.17
Thomas Simpson, Senior	$5.17
300 acres, 3 horses, 3 cows	
Thomas Simpson, Junior	$0.06
1 horse, 1 cow	
Joshua Simpson, Esquire	$0.27
4 horses, 6 cows	
Philip Saynor	$0.86
120 acres, 1 horse, 1 cow	
Joseph Stokely, single man	$1.51
52 acres, 1 horse, 2 cows, 1 tanyard	
Nehimiah Stokely, tanner	$0.31
1 horse, 1 cow	
Daniel Snyder, cooper	$0.14
5 acres, 1 cow	
Benjamin Snyder	$2.02

Abstracts of Westmoreland County, Pennsylvania, Tax Records 1815

Hempfield Township Name of Person	Tax
187 acres, 2 horses, 4 cows	
Jacob Sell, hatter	$0.23
16 acres, 1 horse, 2 cows	
John Steinmetz, single man, miller	$0.75
George Sickafoos, carpenter	$0.20
2 cows	
Jacob Sickapoos, "Cuter"	$0.17
"gon [sic]"	
George Saynor	$3.71
97 acres, 1 tavern, 260 acres, 3 horses, 3 cows	
George Smith	$1.45
200 acres, 2 horses, 2 cows	
Daniel Smith, cooper	$0.08
Friderich Shively	$1.13
100 acres, 2 horses, 3 cows	
George Schetler	$1.06
150 acres, 1 horse, 1 cow	
Jacob Shively, joiner	$0.17
John Singhorse	$0.12
2 horses, 2 cows	
Jacob Snyder, single man	$2.24
190 acres, 3 horses, 2 cows	
"this is Charged to George Wyble"	
"50 Acres of the land Charged to Nicholas Long"	
"ded [sic]"	
Henry Snyder	$1.45
160 acres, 2 horses, 2 cows	
Simon Shoemaker, ~~single man~~	$0.50
1 horse, 1 cow	
William Shoemaker	$0.80
103 acres, 2 horses, 2 cows	
Jacob Saynor, single man	$0.50
Jon Slotterbeck, shoemaker	$1.91
198 acres, 3 horses, 3 cows	
Valentine Staynor	$2.10
250 acres, 1 cow	
John Staynor	$0.13

Abstracts of Westmoreland County, Pennsylvania,
Tax Records 1815

Hempfield Township Name of Person	Tax
2 horses, 3 cows	
John Stough, cooper	$0.22
2 horses, 1 2 cow	
George Shiffler, blacksmith	$0.33
32 acres, 2 cows	
Jacob Spong	$5.48
100 acres, 1 gristmill, 1 brewery, 1 sawmill, 2 horses, 4 cows	
"this is Charged in the last of Ss"	
"He is only charged at the last of S's for what property he has in town and not for what is here"	
Jacob Smith, miller	$0.27
1 cow	
"gon [*sic*]"	
Valentine Schaeffer	$2.89
236 acres, 2 horses, 3 cows	
Jacob Schaeffer, single man	$0.50
Michael Sandel	$0.06
2 cows	
Christopher Snyder	$2.77
200 acres, ~~2 horses~~, 1 cow	
Christian Snyder	$0.06
1 horse, 1 cow	
George Schaeffer, shoemaker	$0.11
3 acres, 1 horse, 1 cow	
John Showberger	$0.10
2 horses, 1 cow	
Jacob Slease	$0.08
1 horse, 2 cows	
Philip Steinmetz	$0.08
1 horse, 2 cows	
"gon [*sic*]"	
Peter Straw	$1.03
50 acres, 2 horses, 2 cows	
Frederick Slife, Senior	$1.95
150 acres, 2 stills, 2 horses, 2 cows	
Frederick Slife, Junior	$0.06

Abstracts of Westmoreland County, Pennsylvania, Tax Records 1815

Hempfield Township Name of Person	Tax
1 cow	
George Schaeffer	$1.12
100 acres, 2 horses, 2 cows	
Frederick Schaeffer, single man	$0.06
George Schaeffer, blacksmith	$0.23
1 horse, 1 cow	
Abraham Sickfried, taylor	$0.28
4 horses, 2 cows	
Peter Shenir, weaver	$0.12
2 cows	
Jacob Swim	$0.06
1 cow	
George Seacrist	$0.16
1 horse, 1 cows, 5 acres	
Widow Shotz	$1.72
200 acres, 1 horse, 1 cow	
Jacob Shull, Senior	$0.06
1 cow	
"gon [sic]"	
John Shull	$1.12
200 acres, 2 horses, 2 cows	
Jacob Smith, Esquire	$1.44
190 acres, 3 horses, 3 cows	
Jacob Smith, Junior	$0.06
1 cow	
Frederick Sparr, mason	$0.18
1 cow	
Jacob Steelsmith, joiner	$1.70
80 acres, 2 horses, 2 cows	
Jacob Sowerwine	$0.10
1 horse, 1 cow	
"gon [sic]"	
Jacob Smelzer, wagon maker	$0.28
2 horses, 2 cows	
Josias Shilling, shoemaker	$0.08
John Sharey	$0.10
2 horses, 1 cow	

Abstracts of Westmoreland County, Pennsylvania, Tax Records 1815

Hempfield Township Name of Person	Tax
"gon [*sic*]"	
Benjamin Swain, mason	$0.25
10 acres, 1 cow	
"gon [*sic*]"	
Widow Sintaff	$0.73
130 acres, 1 horse, 2 cows	
Frederick Steward, single man	$0.50
John Stover	$1.03
92 acres, 2 stills, 3 horses, 1 cow	
Frederick Schaeffer, Senior	$2.85
163 acres, 2 horses, 3 cows	
Frederick Schaeffer, Junior	$0.10
2 horses, 1 cow	
Charles Selsor	$1.12
165 acres, 1 cow	
Conrad Schetler	$1.00
100 acres, 3 horses, 2 cows	
John Shrum, Senior	$0.06
1 cow	
John Shrum, Junior	$1.98
200 acres, 2 horses, 4 cows, 1 still	
Michael Smith	$0.54
82 acres, 1 horse, 1 cow	
Nicholas Shirey	$0.52
50 acres, 2 horses, 1 cow	
Philip Smith	$2.45
200 acres, 2 horses, 2 cows	
Jacob Smith, Junior	$0.95
100 acres, 2 horses, 2 cows	
Michael Sower, shoemaker	$0.12
2 cows	
"gon [*sic*]"	
Benjamin Smith	$3.14
264 acres, 1 horse, 1 cow	
George Sower	$0.06
1 cow	
Michael Saal	$0.27

Abstracts of Westmoreland County, Pennsylvania, Tax Records 1815

Hempfield Township Name of Person	Tax
80 acres, 1 horse, 2 cows	
Martin Starry	$0.10
2 horses, 1 cow	
Philip Swiggert	$1.46
140 acres, 3 horses, ~~1 stud horse~~, 2 cows	
Isaac Silves, blacksmith	$1.00
107 acres, 2 horses, 2 cows	
Patrick Summers, weaver	$0.08
"gon [*sic*]"	
Jacob Smail	$0.20
30 acres	
"Charged in another Blace"	
Henry Shuster, ~~single man~~	$0.06
160 acres, 1 horse, 2 cows	
"land Charged to Isaac Shuster"	
Isaac Shuster	$0.06
1 horse, 1 cow, 160 acres	
George Smith	$0.06
1 cow, 10 acres	
Adam Smith	$0.33
50 acres	
Peter Shellhamer	$2.15
195 acres, 1 sawmill, 3 horses, 4 cows	
Philip Shellhamer, single man	$0.06
Peter Smail	$3.99
112 acres, 200 acres, ~~40 acres~~, ~~125 acres~~, 1 sawmill, 2 stills, 2 horses, 2 cows, 260 acres "these two tracts Charged to others" [referring to the 40 and 125 acres]	
John Smith, mason	$0.18
1 cow, 50 acres, 1 cow	
Captain John Schaeffer	$3.71
1 gristmill, 1 sawmill, 97 acres, 3 horses, 1 horse, 2 cows	
Adam Schaeffer	$1.39
200 acres, 1 horse, 1 cow	
John Schaeffer	$0.06

Hempfield Township Name of Person	Tax
1 horse, 1 cow	
John Suey	$0.06
1 cow	
Conrad Shirey	$3.11
220 acres, 3 horses, 3 cows, 76 acres	
Alexander Storey	$2.40
120 acres, 2 horses, 2 cows, 76 acres	
Jacob Saal, cooper	$0.14
1 horse, 1 cow	
"gon [*sic*]"	
Jacob Smith	$0.60
41 acres, 1 still, 1 horse, 3 cows, 37 acres	
Christian Stump, joiner	$0.95
100 acres, 2 horses, 2 cows	
Robert Storey	$2.12
170 acres, 2 horses, 3 cows	
Jonathan Server, carpenter	$2.15
140 acres, 2 horses, 2 cows	
Robert Storey, single man	$0.50
"gon [*sic*]"	
Esom Scott	$1.00
66 acres, 2 horses, 2 cows	
Reverend Michael Stake	$1.56
95 acres, 2 horses, 3 cows	
William Stephenson, single man	$0.50
"gon [*sic*]"	
Samuel Stephenson, weaver	$1.20
150 acres, 2 horses, 2 cows	
"gon [*sic*]"	
Peter Snyder	$1.24
100 acres, 2 ± horses, 2 cows	
Adam Smith	$2.67
208 acres, 3 horses, 2 cows	
"Charged to Barney Thomas the land only"	
John Schaeffer, Esquire	$1.30
65 acres	
John Snyder, single man	$1.51

Abstracts of Westmoreland County, Pennsylvania, Tax Records 1815

Hempfield Township Name of Person	**Tax**
140 acres, 1 horse, 2 cows	
John Shotz, single man	$0.56
1 horse	
Jacob Spong	$1.46
1 store, 1 house & lot, 2 lots, 1 horse, 2 cows	
Jacob Shull, "S^e"	$0.50
Henry Shaeffer	$0.06
1 horse, 3 cows	
Jacob Smale	$0.59
100 acres, 2 horses	
Reverend William Speers	$4.07
300 acres, 1 horse, 1 cow	
Daniel Shaeffer	$0.06
2 acres	
Simon Singer	$0.42
5 acre "out lot"	
John Totten, ~~single man~~	$0.73
94 acres, 2 horses, 3 2 cows	
"the young man[']s tax is not added on the account of an aged mother"	
John Thompson, single man	$0.50
"gon [*sic*]"	
Barnet Thomas	$6.93
630 acres, 2 stills, 5 horses, 5 cows, 208 acres	
Henry Trout, brewer	$0.12
2 cows	
"gon [*sic*]"	
Jacob Troxal	$0.22
4 horses, 3 cows	
Henry Troxal, single man	$0.50
David Thompson, weaver	$0.53
50 acres, 2 horses, 2 cows	
Robert Thompson, Junior	$0.06
1 cow	
Robert Thompson, Senior	$0.79
100 acres, 2 horses, 2 cows	
Arthur Taylor	$0.34

Hempfield Township Name of Person	Tax
80 acres, 1 horse, 2 cows	
"add the rest of his name Mr ass^r for I cannot make it out"	
John Truby, potter	$0.20
1 acre, 1 cow	
Michael Truby	$0.13
2 horses, 3 cows	
"gon [*sic*]"	
Twiney Philip	$2.25
156 acres, 3 horses, 3 cows	
Daniel Tunney	$2.62
150 acres, 2 horses, 2 cows	
Daniel Tom	$1.43
122 acres, 1 tavern, 5 horses, 1 2 cow	
Adam Turner, wheelwright	$0.37
11 acres, 1 horse, 1 cow	
George Taylor, brickmaker	$0.17
John Tunney	$2.02
190 acres, 2 horses, 2 cows	
William Thompson	$1.65
115 acres, 2 horses, 2 cows	
Adam Truxal	$3.62
300 acres, 2 horses, 2 cows	
Jacob Tom, single man	$0.06
1 cow	
Joseph Torny	$0.06
1 horse, 1 cow	
Jacob Tayler	$1.84
140 acres, 2 horses, 1 cow	
Adam Tarney	$0.12
1 acre "of an out lot"	
Widow Varner	$0.51
99 acres, 1 cow	
Andrew Varner, single man, shoemaker	$0.58
William Vandike, blacksmith	$0.25
20 acres, 1 cow	
Gutherywa Ventzel	$0.06

Abstracts of Westmoreland County, Pennsylvania, Tax Records 1815

Hempfield Township Name of Person	Tax
1 cow	
"gon [*sic*]"	
Adam Ventling, weaver	$0.68
30 acres, 2 cows	
Jonathan Wyrin	$0.70
87 acres, 2 horses, 2 cows	
David Weaver, ~~single man~~	$0.06
1 horse	
John Weaver	$0.95
100 acres, 2 horses, 2 cows	
Widow Welsh	$1.83
257 acres, 2 horses, 2 cows	
Jacob Welker	$0.24
50 acres, 1 horse, 2 cows	
Andrew Waggoner, single man	$0.50
Stephen Wibel	$1.34
190 acres, 1 horse, 2 cows	
Joseph Wibel, single man	$0.75
6 horses	
Widow Waggoner	$1.84
267 acres, ~~1 horse~~, 1 cows	
Hugh Wilson	$0.20
2 horses, 2 cows	
Samuel Wilson, single man	$0.50
John Waggoner	$0.08
1 horse, 2 cows	
Nicholas Weaver, blacksmith	$0.90
145 acres, 1 horse, 1 cow	
"This Charged to his son Abraham"	
Andrew Waggoner	$0.12
2 horses, 2 cows	
Abraham Weaver, single man, weaver	$0.13
1 horse, 145 acres	
Philip Wentzel, wheelwright	$1.73
214 acres, 2 horses, 3 cows	
John Wentzel, wheelwright	$0.25
1 stud horse	

Abstracts of Westmoreland County, Pennsylvania, Tax Records 1815

Hempfield Township Name of Person	Tax
Widow Weimer	$1.02
100 acres, 1 cow	
"Charged to Henry Boyd"	
Daniel Williams	$3.52
184 acres, 2 stills, 2 horses, 2 cows	
George Wibel, innkeeper	$0.89
20 acres, ~~1 horse~~, 2 cows, 140 acres	
Samuel Wibel	$0.25
3 horses	
Reverend William Weaver	$2.15
300 acres, ~~2 horses~~, 2 4 cows	
Andrew Wibel, Senior	$0.84
120 acres, 5 horses, 2 cows	
Thomas Wibel, single man	$0.71
5 horses	
Andrew Wibel, single man	$0.50
John Weaver	$0.06
1 cow	
Abraham Weaver, blacksmith	$0.33
1 house & lot	
Caleb Weyland, taylor	$0.43
16 acres, 1 cow	
John Wibel	$0.45
1 still, 2 horses, 2 cows	
Peter Walter	$0.73
1 tavern, 8 acres, ~~1 horse~~, 1 cow	
Henry Wolgamat	$1.65
112 acres, 2 horses, 2 cows	
George Wybler, comb maker	$0.80
100 acres, 2 horses, 2 cows	
Christian Wilyard	$1.06
100 acres, 1 horse, 1 cow	
"the land Charged to Kroushere"	
Robert Wallace, single man, carpenter	$0.58
Jacob Wingert, Senior	$0.57
74 acres, 1 horse, 2 cows	
Jacob Wingert, Junior	$0.06

Abstracts of Westmoreland County, Pennsylvania, Tax Records 1815

Hempfield Township Name of Person	Tax
1 horse, 1 cow	
John Wingert, blacksmith	$0.30
23 acres, 2 horses, 1 cow, 100 acres	
Frederick Weiser, brewer	$0.91
9.5 acres, 1 brewery, 1 horse, 1 cow	
Widow Wilson	$2.90
275 acres, 2 horses, 4 cows	
Abraham Wagle	$3.84
300 acres, 2 horses, 3 cows	
Abraham Wagle, Junior, ~~single man~~	$0.50
2 horses, 1 cow	
Peter Wanemaker	$1.23
126 acres, 3 horses, 3 cows	
Adam Williams, single man	$0.50
William Whetton, wagon maker	$0.65
1 house & 3 acre lot, 1 acre lot	
John Wyand	$1.33
200 acres	
"the land Charged to Thomas Hissom"	
Thomas Williams	$6.94
300 acres, 194 acres, 65 acres, 2 horses, 3 cows	
George Wallace	$3.16
300 acres, 3 horses, 2 cows	
John Wallace, single man	$0.50
John Wells	$0.70
7 acres "of an out lot"	
Henry Welty	$0.86
10 acres, 9.5 acres	
Joseph Weigley, Esquire	$11.59
300 acres, 58 acres, 4 acres, 2 gristmills, 2 sawmills, 7 horses, 7 cows, 1 slave	
Robert Williams	$0.66
5 acres, 3 acres	
James Waterson	$0.33
8 acres "of meadow land"	
~~George Wybel~~	~~$1.18~~
~~140 acres~~	

Abstracts of Westmoreland County, Pennsylvania, Tax Records 1815

Hempfield Township Name of Person	Tax
Hugh Wallace, single man	$0.50
Widow Welsh	$0.07
15 acres	
Daniel Weaver, single man	$0.50
John Young, Esquire	$2.93
74 acres, 88 acres, 6.25 acres	
William Young	$0.12
2 horses, 2 cows	
David Zuick	$1.27
118 acres, 1 horse, 3 cows	
David Zuick	$1.00
100 acres	
David Zuick	$1.20
120 acres	
"this is Charged to Peter Miller"	
Peter Zimmerman	$1.06
150 acres, 1 horse, 1 cow	
Jacob Zimmerman	$1.05
140 acres, 2 horses, 2 cows	

Hempfield Township Poor Children
Mary Elizabeth and Eleanor Miller, children of Widow Miller
Elizabeth and Mary Eickart, children of Widow Eickart
"these Eickers Children are gon [*sic*]"

Hempfield Township Unseated Land
"James Blaine Ex^r of Ephraim Blaine to be charged with 130 acres unseated land"

Mount Pleasant Township Name of Person	**Tax**
John Albaught	$2.29
300 acres, 1 sawmill, 1 carding machine, 5 horses, 2 cows, trade	
George Aenfrudt	$2.59
380 acres, 3 horses, 3 cows	
Christian Ackerman	$1.83
150 acres, 150 acres, trade, 2 horses, 4 cows	
William Anderson	$0.80
1 improved lot, 1 vacant lot, trade, 1 cow, 1 horse	
Truman Andrews	$1.37
100 acres, 1 still, 1 horse, 3 cows	
John Ackerman, single man	$0.57
1 horse	
Frederick Bauderz	$1.66
250 ~~300~~ acres, 2 cows	
Anthy Boreland, weaver	$0.07
trade	
Peter Bore	$0.65
150 acres, 2 horses, 2 cows	
"John & Christ Lelungine"	
Adam Bare	$5.23
350 acres, 115 acres, 6 horses, 4 cows	
Peter Blystone	$1.44
259 acres, 2 horses, 2 cows	
Michael Burley	$0.77
200 acres, 2 horses, 2 cows	
Adam Byerley	$2.90
380 acres, 7 ~~5~~ horses, 6 cows	
John Bennet "Ca^C"	$3.75
309 acres, 2 horses, 2 cows	
David Boreland	$0.06
1 cow	
Clementz Burleigh	$2.38
50 acres, 460 acres, 2 improved lots, 1 horse	

"there is no Single mans tax charged May be he is

Abstracts of Westmoreland County, Pennsylvania, Tax Records 1815

Mount Pleasant Township Name of Person	Tax
married"	
Jacob Butt	$0.96
75 acres, 1 horse, 2 cows	
"Land to Charles Rigeart"	
Wᵐ Backhenre heirs	$3.73
370 acres, 2 horses, 2 cows	
Andrew Bayer	$1.80
183 acres, 16 acres, 5 horses, 2 cows	
John Bayer	$3.68
183 acres, 153 acres, 4 horses, 2 cows	
David Briere	$1.76
153 acres, 1 still, 1 horse, 3 cows	
Peter Bayers	
"Removed"	
John Brinker	$4.56
277 acres, 5 horses, 4 cows	
John Bierley	$0.60
100 acres, 1 horse, 1 cow	
George Bore	$0.32
4 horses, 3 cows	
George Brinker	$1.38
125 acres, 2 horses, 2 cows	
William Braden, single man	$0.56
1 horse	
John Bare	$0.06
1 cow	
Thomas Byam	$0.73
1 improved lot, 1 horse, 1 cow	
Samuel Blake	$0.35
1 improved lot, trade, 1 cow	
David Barns [illegible word]	$1.71
Joseph McClure	
421 acres, 100 acres, 600 acres, 5 horses, 2 cows	
"See the 18th page of Duplicate"	
Andrew Bystle	$0.95
144 acres, 2 horses, 3 cows, trade	

Abstracts of Westmoreland County, Pennsylvania, Tax Records 1815

Mount Pleasant Township Name of Person	Tax
Many Bursard	$1.87
160 acres	
John Burck, "Casher"	$0.17
1 improved lot	
Amdrew Baleles	$0.42
1 improved lot, trade	
Margerett Baggs	$0.35
1 improved lot, 1 cow	
David Barnhurt	$0.06
1 horse	
John Barney	$0.11
2 horses, 1 cow	
James Conner, single man	$1.22
1 improved lot, 1 horse	
William Chorry	$0.52
1 improved lot, 1 cow	
"Blacksmith at $100"	
William Casklett	$1.12
1 gristmill, 1 horse, 1 cow	
John Cannel, merchant [?]	$2.58
1 store, 1 horse, 1 cow	
Jacob Chrotman	$1.73
112 acres, 2 stills, 3 horses, 4 cows	
James Crackshanks, single man	$0.55
1 horse	
Andrew Clerk	$0.12
2 horses, 1 cow	
Thomas Caley	$0.06
1 cow	
Christian Ceese	$0.10
1 cow, trade	
George Creamer	$0.06
1 cow	
William Davis	$0.22
20 acres, 1 cow	
Jacob Dude	$0.70

Abstracts of Westmoreland County, Pennsylvania, Tax Records 1815

Mount Pleasant Township Name of Person	Tax
80 acres, 1 cow	
John Deeds	$1.62
112 acres, 4 horses, 3 cows	
Adam Days, wagon maker	$0.33
1 improved lot, trade	
Martin Duds, single man	$0.50
William Elderton	$0.06
1 cow	
Hugh Elderton, single man	$0.60
1 cow, trade	
Walter Evans	$0.11
1 horse, 1 cow, trade	
James Etep, deceased	$0.78
1 improved lot, 2 horses, 1 cow, trade	
Joseph Ervine, single man	$0.83
5 horses	
Ezekiel Ervine	$1.41
100 acres, 3 horses, 4 cows	
Abraham Elursale	$0.83
60 acres, 2 horses, 2 cows	
Michael Fetter	$0.06
1 cow	
Paul Frank, blacksmith	$0.25
18 acres, 1 cow	
"is he married"	
Jacob Frank	$0.23
2 horses, 3 cows, 1 cow	
Michael Fry	$1.92
150 acres, 2 horses, 2 cows	
James Fletcher	$0.73
1 lot, 1 horse, 1 cow	
George Fritz	$1.15
150 acres, 3 horses, 3 cows	
William Flinn	$1.12
1 improved lot, 5 vacant lots, 1 horse, 2 cows	
Jacob Fisher	$2.97

Mount Pleasant Township Name of Person	Tax
128 acres, 1 sawmill, 1 card machine, 3 horses, 1 horse, 4 cows	
Adam Fisher	$0.06
78 acres, 2 cows	
William Fisher	$3.12
176 acres, 5 horses, 4 cows	
Catherine Fisher	$1.44
95 acres, 2 horses, 3 cows	
Peter Friend, cabinetmaker	$0.12
1 horse, 2 cows, trade	
Henry Forman	$0.63
77 acres, 2 horses, 1 cow	
Henry Fisher	$1.87
130 acres, 4 horses, 5 cows	
Jacob Fex, cordwinder	$0.06
John Fox	$2.46
194 acres, 3 horses, 3 cows	
Joseph Fox	$0.25
3 horses	
John Felgar	$0.10
1 horse, 2 cows	
David Fletcher	$1.42
190 acres, 2 horses, 3 cows	
John Fletcher	$0.08
1 horse, 2 cows	
Conrad Frantz	$1.12
100 acres, 2 horses, 1 cow	
George Farrel	$0.40
6 horses	
Andrew Farrel, single man	$0.50
John Fox	$0.36
4 horses, 2 cows	
Charles Fullmaad	$0.53
1 improved lot, 1 horse, 1 cow	
Joseph Fraiser	$0.06
1 horse, 1 cow	

Abstracts of Westmoreland County, Pennsylvania, Tax Records 1815

Mount Pleasant Township Name of Person	Tax
Daniel Gotteth, single man 1 horse	$0.53
Mary Grayden 1 improved lot, 1 vacant lot, 1 cow	$0.22
William Gezens, silversmith 1 cow	$0.14
Samuel Gezens 125 acres, 1 cow	$0.32
William Graham, single man	$0.50
William Graham 2 horses, 2 cows	$0.13
Joseph Graham, single man 2 horses	$0.60
John Giffin, single man 2 horses, 1 cow	$0.58
Stephen Geffen 1 horse	$0.06
James Geffen, tenant 157 acres, 1 horse, 1 cow	$1.91
Obizah Griffith, tenant 100 acres	$0.17
John Griffith 1 cow	$0.06
David Gibb, single man 40 acres, 1 horse, 1 cow	$0.95
William Golden 217 acres, 2 stills, 2 horses, 3 cows	$1.71
John Giffin 218 acres, 4 horses, 4 cows	$3.96
Samuel Giles 2 horses, 1 cow	$0.12
James Gallaway 194 acres, 4 horses, 4 cows	$2.53
John Griffin, single man	$0.50
John Gress, "Cordwind" 1 horse, 1 cow	$0.07

Abstracts of Westmoreland County, Pennsylvania, Tax Records 1815

Mount Pleasant Township Name of Person	Tax
John Goode	$0.07
1 horse, 1 cow	
John Galsrest, single man	$0.50
Patrick Griffin	$0.06
1 horse, 1 cow	
John Heaney, single man	$0.50
Adam Hartsel, joiner	$0.40
23 acres, 2 cows	
Capt John Hunter	$1.93
150 acres, 2 horses, 3 cows	
James ~~John~~ Heany, ~~single man~~	$0.06
2 cows	
Michael Hunt	$0.35
1 improved lot, 1 cow	
Gersham Hunt, sadle [saddler?]	$0.67
1 improved lot, 1 horse, 1 cow	
Alexander Hunter	$1.83
128 acres, 4 horses, 4 cows	
William Hunter, chair maker	$0.38
1 improved lot, 1 horse, trade	
Thomas Hurst	$4.52
308 acres, 5 horses, 5 cows	
Nathaniel Hurst	$5.57
329 acres, 200 acres, 5 horses, 4 cows	
Adam Harsel, Senior	$2.02
150 acres, 1 cow	
Jacob Holobaugh, weaver	$0.07
1 horse, 1 cow	
Robert Hillis, single man, weaver	$0.56
John Henderson	$0.20
3 horses, 3 cows	
David Hunter, blacksmith	$1.53
2 improved lots, 4 vacant lots, 1 horse, 1 cow	
Samuel Hunter, joiner	$0.93
2 improved lots, 1 cow, trade	
John Hughges	$3.39

Abstracts of Westmoreland County, Pennsylvania,
Tax Records 1815

Mount Pleasant Township Name of Person	Tax
178 acres, 1 tanyard, 4 horses, 5 cows	
John Hunter	$1.10
100 acres, 2 vacant lots, 2 horses, 2 cows	
John Hoylser, cooper	$0.70
40 acres, 1 horse, 1 cow	
James Hurst, Esquire	$4.34
329 acres, 6 horses, 6 cows	
John Hitchman, single man, carpenter trade	$0.58
William Hyle	$0.06
1 horse, 1 cow	
George Hartsel, taylor	$0.68
50 acres, 1 cow, trade	
David Hunter	$1.08
114 acres, 2 horses, 2 cows	
George Hatfield, tanner	$0.70
1 tanyard, 2 cows	
John Hayny, single man	$0.50
Martin Hiner	$0.06
1 horse	
Jacob Holser	$0.06
1 cow	
James Higgins, weaver	$0.07
1 cow	
Henry Hammond	$2.53
165 acres, 4 horses, 4 cows	
William Hitchman	$0.07
1 horse, 2 cows	
Henry Hook, mason	$0.38
1 improved lot, 1 horse	
Abraham Hammond, single man	$0.50
Martin Heyner	$0.07
1 horse, 1 cow	
John Johnson, single man, cordwinder	$0.56
John Jack	$4.65
360 acres, 5 horses, 7 cows	

Abstracts of Westmoreland County, Pennsylvania, Tax Records 1815

Mount Pleasant Township Name of Person	Tax
Thomas Jack, single man	$0.50
Frances Jarvas, weaver	$0.07
James Jacks	$0.80
1 fulling mill, 1 card machine, 2 horses, 3 cows	
W. John Johnston, cooper	$0.77
2 horses, 2 cows	
John Johnston, tenant	$0.68
200 acres, 1 cow	
Christopher Johnston, weaver	$0.06
1 cow	
William Johnston	$0.30
60 acres	
George Kiser, single man	$0.50
David Kilgore heirs	$3.10
207 acres, 4 horses, 4 cows	
David Kilgore, blacksmith	$0.54
22 acres, 1 horse, 2 cows	
Daniel Kilgore	$1.50
96 acres, 2 horses, 3 cows	
John Kilgore	$0.22
3 horses, 1 cow	
Jacob Kirbaugh	$0.14
300 acres, 1 cow	
Conrad Kasler, taylor	$0.90
1 improved lot, 2 vacant lots, 1 cow, trade	
John Kiser, single man	$0.50
Daniel Kenteigh	$2.23
160 acres, 4 horses, 2 cows	
John Kneff	$1.26
72 acres, 2 stills, 2 horses, 4 cows	
John Kirbey	$0.40
5 horses, 3 cows	
Thomas Kelly	$0.06
1 cow	
Moses Latto, single man	$3.23
175 acres, 5 horses, 4 cows	

Abstracts of Westmoreland County, Pennsylvania, Tax Records 1815

Mount Pleasant Township Name of Person	Tax
John Latto, single man	$0.50
Moses Latto, Senior, single man	$2.95
130 acres, 5 horses, 3 cows	
Henry Laver	$1.95
130 acres, 4 horses, 3 cows	
Christ^r Lobingire	$6.00
295 acres, 45 acres, 5 horses, 5 cows	
John Lobingire	$8.70
272 acres, 175 acres, 100 acres, 300 acres, 1 gristmill, 1 sawmill, 2 stills, 4 horses, 5 cows	
Lobingire & Arnfriedt	$0.33
400 acres	
George Leasure, single man	$0.58
1 horse	
Jacob Long	$1.50
200 acres, 2 horses, 3 cows	
Daniel Leasure	$1.18
56 acres, 3 horses, 4 cows	
James Lipponcott	$0.38
1 improved lot, 1 horse	
Elizabeth Lobingire	$3.81
298 acres, 4 horses, 2 cows	
James Lemmon	$3.93
280 acres, 3 horses	
John Latto, single man	$0.58
1 horse	
Isaiah Lewis	$0.80
100 acres, 2 horses, 2 cows	
John Laughlin	$0.25
17 acres, 1 horse, 2 cows	
"Lives in Unitey township"	
Peggy Lopus	$0.52
100 acres, 1 cow	
Jacob Long	$1.05
166 acres, 4 horses, 3 cows	
Joseph Long	$0.80

Abstracts of Westmoreland County, Pennsylvania, Tax Records 1815

Mount Pleasant Township Name of Person	Tax
150 acres, 1 cow	
Thomas Lewis	$0.06
1 horse, 1 cow	
Elizabeth McGrady	$0.78
2 improved lots, 4 vacant lots, 1 cow	
Mathias Moyer	$2.73
135 acres, 50 acres, 3 horses, 4 cows	
Hugh Marin, Esquire	$3.80
206 acres, 4 horses, 5 cows	
H. Knor Martin, single man	$0.50
Robert Martin, single man	$0.50
William Meeford	$0.27
20 acres	
John McMaster, blacksmith	$0.53
3 acres, 1 improved lot, 1 horse, 1 cow	
Joseph Miller (Say)	$0.67
Peter Nighmeir	
1 improved lot	
"This is set to Neymier in the Duplicate"	
Partrick McGrady	$0.12
1 horse, 1 horse, 1 cow	
William Mackey, miller	$0.18
2 horses, 1 cow, trade	
Robert Morrison	$0.16
2 horses, 1 cow	
John Moyer, smoker	$3.06
208 acres, 4 horses, 7 cows	
Michael Moyer	$2.88
150 acres, 2 horses, 3 cows, 1 tanyard	
Thomas Mitchel	$1.80
132 acres, 4 horses, 4 cows	
John McGinnes	$0.07
1 horse, 1 cow	
Alexander McClerg	$1.67
1 store	
William Milbey	$0.50

Abstracts of Westmoreland County, Pennsylvania, Tax Records 1815

Mount Pleasant Township Name of Person	Tax
Robert Milbey, taylor	$0.58
1 house and lot, 1 cow	
James Milbey, taylor	$0.12
1 lot, trade	
Christine Moyer, widow	$1.60
127 acres, 2 horses, 2 cows	
Chrisp^r Migrance	$1.06
52 acres, 40 acres,	
2 horses, 2 cows	
Robert McCall, mill wright	$0.32
1 horse, 1 cow, trade	
John Moyer, doctor	$1.09
1 improved lot, 2 vacant lots, 1 horse, 1 cow,	
occupation	
Mahlon Moyer	$0.08
1 cow, 1 horse	
~~Michael Mack, single man~~	
"In Feate [sic] County"	
Michael Mack	$0.68
Samuel Tenant	
200 acres, 1 cow	
Margaret McCall, widow	$1.51
148 acres, 1 gristmill, 1 cow	
Mary McMaster, widow	$1.63
100 acres, 1 slave, 2 horses	
Stephen McCall, administrator	$0.20
60 acres	
Thomas McCall, single man	$0.07
150 acres, 1 horse, 1 cow	
Jacob Macklin	$4.18
314 acres	
"if I remember right Mr. Mecklin brought his	
patent into the office to the Comrs and the tract	
contains but 300 acres it was returned formerly	
by the tenant whose name I have forgot"	
Archabald McDonald	$0.06

Abstracts of Westmoreland County, Pennsylvania, Tax Records 1815

Mount Pleasant Township Name of Person	Tax
1 horse, 2 cows	
John Neal, single man	$0.50
John Neal, judge	$0.88
100 acres, 3 horses, 2 cows	
Hugh Neal, single man	$0.50
William Neal	$4.60
200 acres, 1 tanyard, 1 improved lot, 3 vacant lots, 2 stills, 4 horses, 4 cows	
Robert Neal	$0.17
1 horse, 1 horse, 2 cows	
John Neal, single man	$0.50
William Neal, single man, tanner	$0.50
James Neal, single man	$0.50
Richard Newell, single man	$0.50
Stephen Newell	$1.50
350 acres, 2 horses, 3 cows	
John Newel, single man	$1.11
65 acres, 1 horse, 2 cows	
Thomas Newel	$0.64
65 acres, 1 horse, 3 cows	
James Newel	$1.88
150 acres, 2 horses, 2 cows	
George Newel, single man	$0.55
1 horse	
Joseph Noel	$0.27
300 acres, 1 cow	
James Newel, miller	$1.92
26 acres, 120 acres, 1 gristmill, 1 horse, 2 cows	
Andrew Nicholas, single man	$0.59
1 horse	
Gasper Overly	$0.67
100 acres, 2 horses, 4 cows	
Christopher Overly	$0.60
200 ~~300~~ acres, 100 acres, 2 horses, 1 cow	
Michael Oycher	$0.92
75 acres, 2 horses, 2 cows	

Abstracts of Westmoreland County, Pennsylvania, Tax Records 1815

Mount Pleasant Township Name of Person	Tax
Abraham Oycher, ~~single man~~	$0.08
1 cow	
Daniel Oycher, single man	$0.50
Adam Overly, blacksmith	$0.25
1 cow, 1 horse	
Joseph Painter, blacksmith, single man	$0.17
trade	
George Palmer	$1.06
74 acres, 2 horses, 2 cows	
Peter Poorman	$0.67
90 acres, ~~1 horse, 2 cows~~	
James Power, clergyman	$5.15
360 acres, 4 horses, 5 cows	
Connerod Pence, blacksmith	$0.18
1 cow	
William Pollins	$0.07
1 horse, 1 cow	
Jacob Roodman, single man	$0.50
John Roodman	$2.81
300 acres, 4 horses, 7 cows	
William Robinson	$0.10
10 acres	
William Rumbauch, weaver	$0.25
2 horses, 2 cows, trade	
Peter Rumbauch, single man	$0.58
1 horse	
John Rumbauch	$3.42
240 acres, 2 horses, 3 cows	
Augustice Rumbauch, single man	$0.50
Abraham Rumbauch	$1.90
125 acres, 3 horses, 2 cows	
Daniel Rumbauch	$0.07
1 horse, 1 cow	
Henry Rumbauch	$3.38
173 acres, 3 stills, 2 horses, 2 cows	
George Rumbauch	$0.97

Abstracts of Westmoreland County, Pennsylvania, Tax Records 1815

Mount Pleasant Township Name of Person	Tax
125 acres, 2 horses, 2 cows	
Michael Rumbauch, single man	$0.50
Anthony Ruff	$3.47
186 acres, 2 stills, 12 horses, 4 horses, 6 cows	
Martin Rouse, "pompbo^r"	$0.20
1 horse, 1 cow, trade	
Michael Runk	$0.07
1 horse, 1 cow	
William Randles, captain	$5.06
242 acres, 232 acres, 3 horses, 5 cows	
Samuel Rogers, single man	$0.60
trade	
John Roley	$1.97
270 acres, 2 horses, 2 cows	
Charles Robinson	$0.20
10 acres, 1 horse, 2 cows	
Jacob Ruff, cordwinder	$0.32
2 horses, 2 cows, trade	
David Resilon, weaver	$0.07
1 horse, 1 cow	
Frederick Raser	$0.33
100 acres	
Frederick Rimus	$0.17
10 acres, 1 cow	
Elias Stencicum, mason	$0.08
trade	
Henry Swan, tenant	$4.44
359 acres, 5 horses, 4 cows	
Isaac Shoot, single man	$1.23
100 acres, 1 horse	
John Shoop, Senior	$0.17
2 horses	
Samuel Shoop, single man	$2.38
150 acres, 2 horses, 3 cows	
Michael Shoot	
150 acres, 2 horses, 1 cow	

Abstracts of Westmoreland County, Pennsylvania, Tax Records 1815

Mount Pleasant Township Name of Person	Tax
"Removed"	
William Shearer, single man, tanner	$0.72
1 horse	
Hugh Shearer, single man, tanner	$0.73
1 horse	
[illegible], single man	$0.56
trade	
John Shearer, single man	$0.65
3 horses	
Mary Shearer	$2.97
117 acres, 1 tanyard, 1 horse, 3 cows	
Chrisp^r Smeekley, ~~single man~~	~~$0.50~~
"married"	
"See the 26 page of the Duplicate"	
John Shoop	$0.63
375 acres	
"living on the ridge"	
Mathias Stover, weaver	$0.10
2 cows	
Henry Solobarger	$0.51
85 acres, 1 horse, 2 cows	
"to be charged to Geo Thomas"	
John Shoop, "Fayille"	$0.50
300 acres	
"see the 26th page of the Duplicate"	
John Shoup	$0.06
1 cow	
Adam Septer	$0.13
2 horses, 2 cows	
Henry Shoup	$0.72
115 acres, 2 horses, 3 cows	
David Speelman, tenant	$0.18
164 acres, 2 horses	
Levy Swartwood	$0.18
3 horses, 2 cows	
James Scot, weaver	$0.15

Abstracts of Westmoreland County, Pennsylvania, Tax Records 1815

Mount Pleasant Township Name of Person	Tax
200 acres	
Adam Slonecker	$1.69
326 acres, 1 horse, 1 cow	
Jacob Swain, hatter	$0.97
2 improved lots, 1 vacant lot, 1 horse, 1 cow	
Conrod Stam	$6.60
300 acres, 2 improved lots	
Simon Stickle, wagon maker	$0.71
1 improved lot, trade	
John Septer	$0.16
3 horses, 2 cows	
Gasper Smilley	$2.15
190 acres, 3 horses, 3 cows	
James Steel, Junior	$0.07
1 horse, 1 cow	
James Steel, Senior	$2.12
300 acres, 2 horses, 2 cows	
John Steel	$0.06
1 horse	
Jacob Stants	$1.59
108 acres, 2 horses, 3 cows	
Frederick Septer	$0.21
2 horses, 3 cows	
John Segrist	$0.06
1 cow	
John Shibe, cordwinder	$0.40
1 improved lot	
John Stover	$3.00
211 acres, 8 horses, 8 cows	
John Smickley	$0.06
1 cow	
Jacob Smickley	$0.10
1 horse, 2 cows	
Andrew Smull	$1.23
94 acres, 2 horses, 3 cows	
Christopher Sandles	$0.17

Abstracts of Westmoreland County, Pennsylvania, Tax Records 1815

Mount Pleasant Township Name of Person	Tax
10 acres, 1 horse, 1 cow "Removed"	
John Shilling	$0.52
29 acres, 2 horses, 2 cows	
Mary Steel, widow	$0.35
1 house and lot, 1 cow	
Henry Seisler	$0.12
2 horses, 2 cows	
Fredrick Hyel	$0.13
2 horses, 2 cow "I don[']t know what name it is"	
Jacob Stover	$0.66
59 acres, 2 horses, 2 cows	
Christopher Sees	$0.06
1 cow	
William Thompson, tenant	$1.57
300 acres, 1 horse, 1 cow	
John Thompson, tenant	$0.08
2 horses, 1 cow	
Phillip Trout	$3.47
295 acres, 2 mills, 5 horses, 3 cows	
Abraham Traxall	$3.81
263 acres, 3 horses, 3 cows	
Henry Traugher	$1.18
118 acres, 2 stills, 4 horses, 4 cows	
Frederick Thorn	$0.27
40 acres, 1 horse, 1 cow	
Adam Weaver, Senior	$0.06
2 cows	
Adam Weaver, single man	$0.53
3 acres	
Frederick Weaver	$0.96
132 acres, 2 horses, 1 cow "To Bush L Charles"	
Gasper Weaver	$1.37
100 acres, 2 horses, 4 cows	

Abstracts of Westmoreland County, Pennsylvania, Tax Records 1815

Mount Pleasant Township Name of Person	Tax
Abraham Whitmore	$1.23
90 acres, 2 horses, 3 cows	
William Wilson	$0.06
1 horse, 1 cow	
"Removed"	
George Worman	$2.06
159 acres, 2 horses, 4 cows	
Daniel Worman	$1.03
74 acres, 2 horses, 2 cows	
Jacob Waters	$1.18
95 acres, 4 horses, 2 cows	
Henry Walker	$0.06
1 cow	
Nathan Waters, blacksmith	$0.17
Trade	
John Wible	$0.67
20 acres, 1 oil mill, 1 horse, 1 cow	
William Wible, blacksmith	$0.23
1 horse, 1 cow	
Henry Yode	$1.33
100 acres, 2 horses, 3 cows	
Conrad Zleer	$0.76
200 acres, 2 horses, 2 cows	
Philip Zleer, single man	$0.50
John Zleer, single man	$0.50
Henry Pletcher	$0.07
1 horse, 1 cow	
Mary Wallace	$0.06
1 cow	
Abner Patterson	$0.98
128 acres, 2 horses, 2 cows	
Peter Bowman	$0.12
2 horses, 1 cow	
Peter Sadler	$0.27
4 lots, 1 cow	
Henry Tinsman	$0.34

Abstracts of Westmoreland County, Pennsylvania, Tax Records 1815

Mount Pleasant Township Name of Person	Tax
1 improved lot	
Elizabeth McKee	$0.35
1 improved lot, 1 cow	
John Cunning	$1.00
1 tanyard	
John Redember, single man	$1.50
Henry Lare	$2.00
164 acres	
Adam Lang, single man	$0.50
L. Charles Bush	$1.11
132 acres, 1 tanyard, 1 horse, 1 cow	
Jacob Waters, single man	$0.50
Jacob Christman	[not given]
137 acres, 2 horses, 2 cows	
John Micklwane	[not given]
100 acres, 2 horses, 2 cows	
Jacob ~~John~~ Grith, single man	[not given]
1 horse	
John Newell, single man	$0.50
Martin Yentsler	[not given]
2 horses, 2 cows	
Henry Marks, cordwinder	$0.06
Thos Long, cordwinder	$0.16
1 cow	
John Thompson	[not given]
1 sawmill, 13 acres	
Henry Bletcher, tenant	$0.25
50 acres	
Richard Thenderson, single man	$0.50
John Patterson, single man	$0.50
Elias Patterson, single man	$4.00
Danl Huffman	$0.08
1 horse, 2 cows	

Mount Pleasant Township Unseated Lands

Warrantees' Acres	Tax	Called

Abstracts of Westmoreland County, Pennsylvania, Tax Records 1815

Names

Jos[h] Campbell	50	$0.32	Montpelier
James Campbell	50	$0.38	Tenereeff
Ruth Campbell	50	$0.34	Malaga
William Campbell	50	$0.35	Elkton
Margaret Campbell	50	$0.36	Oporto
Jn[o] Campbell	50	$0.32	Lisbon
Rob[t] Campbell	50	$0.35	Richmond
Mary Campbell	50	$0.08	Ulster
Thomas Barclay	50	$0.34	Denmark
Tho[s] Muckhouse	[not given]	[not given]	[not given]

Abstracts of Westmoreland County, Pennsylvania,
Tax Records 1815

Abstracts of Westmoreland County, Pennsylvania, Tax Records 1815

North Huntingdon Township Name of Person	Tax
Robert Aikins	$1.27
130 acres, 2 horses, ~~3 cows~~, 2 horses, 2 cows	
Alberetpeter, taylor	$0.14
1 house, 2 cows, 1 horse	
Henry Arrat, farmer	$1.14
119 acres, 2 horses, ~~4 cows~~, 3 cows	
Georg Ashburgh, farm[er]	$0.07
1 horse, 2 cows	
Wm Ashbaugh, single man	
Samuel Allison, farmer	$0.60
60 acres, 1 house, 1 cow	
Jacob Anderson, farmer	$2.55
114 acres, 2 horses, 2 cows, 1 gristmill, 1 cow	
John ~~James~~ Anderson	$0.06
1 horse, 1 cow	
Martain Ashbough, farm[er]	$2.16
246 acres, 3 horses, 4 cows, 1 cow	
Daniel Ashbough, single man	$0.50
Henry Ashbough	$0.50
100 acres, 1 horse, 2 cows	
"the land to Robert Eaton which see"	
Robert Allen, innkeeper	$0.54
2 ~~3~~ horses, 2 cows, 1 cow	
George Albrigt	$0.90
90 acres	
"For this land See Pluterbech John"	
John Alberson, miller	
2 cows	
~~James Akins "wda"~~	
~~1 cow~~	
William Allison, single man	$0.50
Joseph Brown	$0.07
1 horse, 1 cow	
John Barber," pap^rmkr"	
1 cow	

Abstracts of Westmoreland County, Pennsylvania,
Tax Records 1815

North Huntingdon Township Name of Person	Tax
Ruth Boyd, widow	
1 horse, 1 cow	
Jacob Beygle, single man	
Mayor John Boyed	$3.76
310 acres, 4 horses, 3 cows	
"for this See Wᵐ Robinson"	
William Boyd, single man	$0.50
1 horse	
Moses Blackbourn	$1.76
150 acres, 1 horse	
Thomas Blackbourn, "wheel"	$0.17
2 cows	
Henry Brenamon	$1.59
100 acres, 2 horses, 1 cow, 1 cow, 1 distillery, 50 acres "of Carnahan"	
"one dollar taken off at the appeal"	
Jacob Byerly, Junior	$1.19
98 acres, 1 horse, 1 cow	
Andrew Byerly, Esquire	$2.96
220 acres, ~~4 horses~~, 4 cows, 1 distillery, 3 horses	
Andrew Brown	
1 cow	
John Blackbourn, carpenter	$0.25
~~10 acres~~, 3 cows, 2 horses	
"See Clark George Shomkr"	
Daniel Brenaman, miller	$0.17
1 horse, ~~1 cow~~	
William Blackbourn	$2.02
150 acres, 1 horse, 2 cows	
Robert Brown	$0.13
2 horses, 3 cows	
Arthur Brisbourn	$0.15
2 horses, 2 cows	
"Gone"	
John Brown, ~~single man~~	$0.50
"Gone"	

North Huntingdon Township Name of Person	Tax
Andrew Biggs	$0.90
2 horses, 200 acres, ~~2 cows~~, 1 cow	
Adam Brittin, single man	$0.50
"Gone"	
Thomas Blackbourn	$3.17
188 acres, 100 acres, 2 horses, 3 cows	
"this case must be examined"	
Robert Brown, Junior	$0.06
1 cow	
"Gone"	
Robert Baxter	$1.14
100 acres, 2 horses, ~~2 cows~~, 1 cow	
Benjamon Boyd	$1.29
100 acres, 2 horses, 2 cows	
Benjamin Byerly, single man	$0.50
Andrew Byerly, blacksmith	$0.50
John Bennet	$0.13
1 horse, 1 cow, 135 acres	
Joseph Brush, taylor, single man	$0.50
42 acres, 1 cow	
George Booght	$0.06
1 horse, 1 cow	
"Gone"	
Jacob Brubaker	$0.07
1 horse, 1 cow, 1 cow	
William Boyd	$3.07
227 acres, 3 horses, 2 cows	
"for this land See Alex Robinson"	
Archibald Boyd, single man	$0.50
"Gone"	
William Brisbin	$0.06
1 horse	
"Gone"	
Daniel Beachly	$0.07
2 ⅟ horses, 2 cows	
Peter Boughman	$1.82

North Huntingdon Township Name of Person	Tax
130 acres, 2 horses, 2 cows, 1 horse	
Adam Boughman	$0.14
2 horses, 2 cows, 200 acres, 1 cow	
John Boughman	$1.92
130 acres, 3 horses, 2 cows, 1 cow, 1 horse	
Henry Boughman	$2.33
~~200 acres, 1 horse~~, 1 cow	
"for this see Adam Baughm"	
Conrad Beachly	$1.73
200 acres, 1 ~~2~~ horse, 2 cows	
Barbarah Berry	$0.06
2 cows	
William Beachly	$0.07
1 horse, 1 cow	
"Gone"	
Conrad Buzzerd	
1 cow	
James Brown, Junior	$0.06
1 cow, 1 horse	
John Barns	$2.72
300 acres, 2 horses, 2 cows	
James Brice	$0.82
60 acres, 2 horses, 2 cows	
Patrick Black	$1.92
150 acres, 3 horses, 2 cows	
George Barns	
120 acres, 1 horse, 1 cow	
"for this land See Jo Mehaffe"	
John Boyd "at Wr Swans"	$0.09
1 horse, 2 cows	
George Bughman	$0.10
1 horse, ~~2 cows~~, 1 cow	
Gabriel Blair	$0.77
100 acres, 2 horses, 1 cow	
Atkin Baxter, mason	$0.16
~~17 acres~~, 1 cow, 1 cow	

North Huntingdon Township Name of Person	Tax
"See D Shonn"	
William Brown	$0.07
1 horse, 1 cow	
Henry Brown	
1 cow	
David Bell	$1.83
150 acres, 2 horses, ~~2 cows~~, 2 cows	
James Blackborn, "hat"	$0.09
1 cow	
Jacob Byerly, innkeeper	$2.73
157 acres, 2 horses, 3 cows	
Christian Berger	$1.10
96 acres, 1 ~~2~~ horse, 2 cows	
"for this land"	
"for this land See Fredᵏ Metzker"	
Evins Blair	$0.10
2 horses, 2 cows	
Joseph Beggert	
1 cow	
John Brown	$0.06
1 horse, 1 cow	
Christian Breneman	$3.38
79 acres, 97 acres, 195 acres, 3 horses, 3 cows, 1 distillery, 1 sawmill	
George Beard, Esquire	$0.06
1.75 acres	
Robert Cooper	
rent for distill[ery], 35 acres	
John Clewbine, single man	
Ruth Boyd, widow	
10 acres, 1 horse, 1 cow	
James Caldwell	$3.34
150 acres, 50 acres of hills, 5 horses, 4 cows, 1 gristmill, 1 sawmill, 1 distillery	
Ebanezer Caldwell, miller	$0.25
~~1 horse~~, 2 cows, 1 cow	

Abstracts of Westmoreland County, Pennsylvania, Tax Records 1815

North Huntingdon Township Name of Person	Tax
Grizel Campbell, "notan[?]"	
1 cow	
~~James~~ John Cooper	$4.21
301 acres, ~~4 horses~~, 4 cows, 2 horses	
Robert Cooper, single man	$0.57
1 horse	
Alexr Cooper, single man	$0.57
1 horse	
James Cooper, single man	$0.56
1 horse	
Joseph Cowan	$0.66
30 acres, 2 horses, ~~3 cows~~, 2 cows	
Mathias Cowan	$1.19
100 acres, 3 horses, 3 cows	
George Cowen, single man	$0.50
James Cowan, Senior	
100 acres, 3 horses, 2 cows, 2 cows	
Wm Cooper, single man	
5 horses	
John Cavin, Senior	$2.02
164 acres, 2 horses, 1 ~~2~~ cow	
Bengamen Cavin, single man	$0.50
"Gone"	
John Copeland, "Wagan"	$0.12
1 horse, 1 cow	
Thomas Copeland	$0.06
~~1 horse~~, 1 cow	
William Campbell	~~$3.34~~
170 acres, 150 acres, 2 horses, 4 cows	
"this case to be examined"	
"this 150 acres taken off Campbell and added to A. Biggs at the appeal"	
Joseph Copeland	$1.04
120 acres, 2 horses, 1 cow, 1 cow	
John Campbell	$2.02
160 acres, 3 horses, 4 cows	

North Huntingdon Township Name of Person	Tax
Widow Carr	
1 cow	
"Gone"	
John Carnahan	$2.86
160 acres, ~~200 acres~~, 3 horses, 3 cows, 47 acres of hills	
"for 50 acres of theses hills See F Bac [rest illegible]"	
Samuel Carathers	$2.95
247 acres, 2 horses, 1 cow	
Elizabeth Campbell, "WD"	$1.07
100 acres, ~~1 horse, 2 cows~~, 1 cow	
James Christy, boot maker	$0.18
1 horse, ~~2 cows~~, 1 cow	
~~Sally Carthers, widow~~	
~~1 horse, 1 cow~~	
~~"Gone"~~	
Andrew Christy	$2.08
200 acres, 2 horses, 3 cows	
Daniel Courts	$0.92
30 acres	
Assa Cook, Senior	
150 acres	
"Gone"	
Assa Cook, Junior	$0.06
1 cow	
"Gone"	
William Clark	$0.07
1 horse, 1 cow	
"Gone"	
John Cavit	$5.55
150 acres, 125 acres, 1 gristmill, 1 sawmill, 1 fulling mill, 1 carding machine, 4 horses, 4 cows, 2 cows	
John Cline	$1.09
100 acres, 2 horses, 2 cows	

Abstracts of Westmoreland County, Pennsylvania, Tax Records 1815

North Huntingdon Township Name of Person	Tax
~~John~~ Elizabeth Carlisle, "wd"	$0.88
100 acres, 1 cow, 1 horse	
~~John~~ James Casady	$0.93
100 acres, ~~3 cows~~, 2 horses, 2 cows	
James Chadwick	$2.04
170 acres, 3 horses, ~~12 cows~~, 11 cows	
William Cowan	$2.51
280 acres, 2 horses, 2 cows	
John Cavin, Junior	$2.92
207 acres, 3 horses, 1 cow, 2 horses	
Margaret Campbell	
120 acres, 3 horses, 1 cow, 2 horses	
Andrew Christy, single man	$0.50
George Clark, shoemaker	
10 acres, 1 horse, 1 cow	
"Land to Ruth Boyd at which see"	
Samuel Curry	$0.90
100 acres, 1 ~~2~~ horse, 1 cow	
William Crosby	$2.11
200 acres, 2 horses, 2 cows	
Thomas Campbell	$0.06
~~2 cows~~, 1 cow	
William Coulter	$1.76
150 acres, 1 horse, 1 cow, 1 cow	
Moses Cox	$0.06
1 cow	
John Clark, schoolmaster	$0.06
2 cows, 1 horse	
John Culbertson	
1 horse, 2 cows	
James Collins, tanner	
1 tanyard	
William Cashaday, single man	
Reverend Mungo Dick	$2.06
140 acres, 1 horse, 1 horse, 1 cow	
Mathew Dove, saddler	$0.09

Abstracts of Westmoreland County, Pennsylvania, Tax Records 1815

North Huntingdon Township Name of Person	Tax
1 cow	
Jacob Davison	$1.22
~~102~~ 96 acres, 1 horse, 1 cow, 1 horse, 1 cow	
George Decampe	$1.77
200 acres, 1 horse, 1 cow	
John Dickson, weaver	$0.87
~~57 acres~~, 1 horse, 2 cows	
"for land see Skelly"	
Elijah Dum, fuller	$0.27
2 horses, 1 cow	
John Dunholm	$0.42
60 acres, 2 horses, 1 cow, 1 cow	
John Duff	$1.34
150 acres, 1 horse, 2 cows	
Thomas Duff	$0.29
50 acres, 2 horses, 1 cow	
William Donnel	$0.50
50 acres, 1 horse, 2 cows, 1 horse	
Robert Duff	$1.42
150 acres, 2 horses, 3 cows	
Philip Deal	$3.02
250 acres, 3 horses, 2 cows, 1 cow	
George Deal, single man, married	$0.50
1 cow	
Henry Ditman, deceased	$1.45
156 acres, 2 horses, 3 cows	
"G Kline Jnʳ Delman for land"	
William Dorson	$0.07
1 horse, 2 cows	
John Detman, single man	
Nicholas Develin, weaver	
1 horse, 1 cow	
John Deal, single man	
Henry Dukey	
1 cow	
Nathaniel Ekels, "Cap"	$0.19

North Huntingdon Township Name of Person	Tax
1 horse, 1 cow	
Charles Ekels, Senior	$1.20
95 acres, 2 horses, 2 cows	
John Ekels	$0.96
100 acres, 2 horses, 2 cows	
Charles Ekels	$0.09
2 horses, 2 cows, 1 cow	
William Ewing	$1.33
150 acres, 3 cows, 2 horses	
Robert Eaton	$0.19
3 horses, 100 acres, 2 cows	
John Eyeman	$1.14
80 acres, 2 horses, 2 cows, 2 cows	
Elioth heirs	$2.60
260 acres	
William Fulton, single man	
Amos Fleming, single man	$0.66
"Taxer"	
Michal Fritchman	$9.44
560 acres, 1 gristmill, 1 sawmill, 1 distillery, 2 horses, 1 cow, 2 cows	
Adam Fritchman, single man	$0.50
Christian Funk	$4.00
400 acres	
Christian Funk, Junior	$2.98
220 acres, 2 horses, 3 cows, 1 horse	
Philip Fisher	$1.87
140 acres, 3 4 horses, 3 cows	
Robert Flack, weaver	$0.80
30 acres, 2 horses, 2 cows	
David Frew	$0.06
100 acres, 2 horses, 1 cow	
Adam Frew	$0.64
100 acres, 2 horses, 1 cow, 1 horse	
William Fullerton, store keeper	$3.20
175 acres, 1 still, 3 horses, 4 cows, 10 acres	

North Huntingdon Township Name of Person	**Tax**
Humphry Fullerton	$0.50
1 horse	
Daniel Fleming, Esquire	
225 acres, 3 cows, 4 horses, 1 tanyard	
Robert Fulton	$1.60
108 acres, 3 horses, 3 cows	
John Flemming, mason	
Daniel Funk	
1 horse, 2 cows	
Thomas Greer, saddler	$0.09
1 cow	
Jacob Grenawalt, cooper	$4.08
150 acres, 4 horses, 4 cows, 200 acres "of Browns Place"	
Adam Gold, taylor	
2 cows, 1 horse	
William Gelbreath, single man	$0.56
1 horse	
John Guffy	$3.97
200 ~~250~~ acres, 3 horses, 3 cows, 1 distillery "See 50 acres to James Guffy"	
James Guffy	$0.86
100 acres, ~~100 acres~~, 2 horses, 2 cows	
John Goodlink	$0.06
2 cows	
Christian Grenawalt, plow maker	$0.20
1 horse, 2 cows	
Elizabeth Garret, widow	
1 cow	
Richard Garret, single man	$0.50
John Goodman	$1.16
116.5 acres, 3 horses, 2 cows, 1 cow	
George Greysinger, wagon maker	$0.96
~~90 acres, 1 horse~~, 2 cows	
Samuel Garvin, shoemaker	$0.31
~~10 acres~~	

North Huntingdon Township Name of Person	Tax
John Gongaware	$0.07
1 horse, 2 cows	
James Gray, blacksmith	$0.21
1 horse, ~~1 cow~~	
William Greer	$0.06
1 cow	
"Gone"	
Philip Gongaware	$1.90
130 acres, 2 horses, 2 cows, 1 distillery, 1 cow	
William Gregory	$0.07
2 horses, 1 cow, 2 cows	
George Gray, blacksmith	
1 cow	
"Gone"	
John Green	$1.30
130 acres, 1 cow, 1 horse	
Patrick Greer, wheelwright	$1.07
100 acres, 1 horse, 2 cows, 1 horse	
Abner Gilbert	$4.36
285 acres, 4 horses, 4 cows	
William Guffy, single man	
Horase Garrettg, "papʳmkr"	
William Galt	
1 horse, 1 cow	
William Hare, weaver	$0.33
10 acres, 1 horse, 1 cow	
James Hare, single man	$0.50
"Gone"	
James Holton, single man	$0.50
"Gone"	
James Howard	$0.06
1 cow	
"Gone"	
James Horner, miller	$0.16
1 cow	
Anthony Harres	$0.06

Abstracts of Westmoreland County, Pennsylvania, Tax Records 1815

North Huntingdon Township Name of Person	Tax
2 cows	
"Gone"	
James Howie, blacksmith	$0.14
"Gone"	
James Hamilton	
100 acres, ~~250 acres~~, 2 horses, ~~3 cows~~, 1 cow	
Samuel Hamilton, single man, married	
3 ~~2~~ horses, 3 cows, 1 distillery, 150 acres	
Robert Hannah	$1.30
110 acres, 1 horse, 2 cows	
James Henderson	
1 horse, 2 cows, 1 cow	
Barbara Hyberger	$1.38
107 acres, ~~2 horses~~, 2 cows, 1 horse	
Daniel Hyberger, single man, cooper	$0.64
Andrew Hyberger, single man, nailer	
Edward Henry, Senior	$0.06
1 horse, 1 cow	
Edward Henry	$0.66
100 acres, 2 horses, ~~2 cows~~, 1 cow	
Mary Hendricks	$0.93
100 acres, ~~1 horse~~, 2 cows	
Philip Heck	$2.66
200 acres, ~~6 horses~~, 3 horses, 2 cows	
"170 acres of land of Jas Millers"	
"see Jnº Heck for 270 a land"	
"this need to be explained"	
John Heck, single man, married	~~$0.50~~
270 acres	
"this needs explanation"	
George Hess	$0.06
1 cow	
"Gone"	
William Hindman, innkeeper	
100 acres, 3 horses, 2 cows	
John Holton, single man, taylor	$0.79

*Abstracts of Westmoreland County, Pennsylvania,
Tax Records 1815*

North Huntingdon Township Name of Person	Tax
1 horse, 1 cow, 1 cow	
James Hartford, single man	$3.06
200 acres	
Thomas Harkness, taylor	$0.20
1 horse, ~~2 cows~~, 1 cow	
~~John~~ William Harkness	
50 acres, 1 horse, 1 cow	
Thomas Holmes	$1.41
150 acres, 1 ~~2~~ horse, 2 cows	
John Holmes, single man	$0.50
1 horse	
John Holton, Senior, taylor	$0.12
1 horse, 2 cows	
Joseph Hickman	$0.06
1 cow	
"Gone"	
John Hyberger	$1.34
140 acres, 2 horses, 2 cows	
William Horner	$0.50
Sally Hart, widow	
1 horse, 2 cows	
James Hope	$0.12
70 acres, 2 horses, 2 cows, 1 cow	
George Howie, blacksmith	
1 horse, 1 cow	
"Gone"	
David Henderson	$0.10
2 horses, 1 cow, 1 cow	
Stephen Hendricks, single man, miller	$0.59
"Gone"	
George Hormer	
1 cow	
Philip Heck, single man	
Henry Hess, single man, weaver	
John Hues	
1 cow	

Abstracts of Westmoreland County, Pennsylvania, Tax Records 1815

North Huntingdon Township Name of Person	Tax
Thomas Holmes, Junior	
1 horse, 1 cow	
Michael Isinger	$0.06
1 cow	
"Gone"	
John Ingraham	$2.00
150 acres, 3 horses, 1 cow, 2 cows	
Francis Jamison	$0.07
~~1 horse~~, 2 cows, 1 horse	
Samuel Johnstone	$0.70
90 acres, 1 horse, 2 cows	
David Johnstone, mason	$0.12
1 horse, 1 cow	
James Johnstone, single man, shoemaker	$0.50
"maried"	
Mathew Johnstone	
200 acres, 1 horse, ~~2 cows~~, 1 cow	
Samuel Irwin	$0.06
1 horse, 1 cow	
"Gone"	
Colonel John Irwin, Esquire	$4.74
300 acres, 5 horses, 10 cows, 1 still	
James Irwin, Esquire	$4.74
300 acres, 4 horses, 6 cows, 1 distillery	
Robert Jack	$0.06
1 cow	
John King	$0.06
1 cow, 1 horse	
Henry Izaman	
1 cow	
John Kerns	$0.07
~~1 horse~~, 1 cow	
George Kennedy, weaver	$0.19
1 horse	
~~Thomas Kerr, miller~~	$6.15
300 acres, 1 gristmill, 1 carding machine, 1 cow	

North Huntingdon Township Name of Person	Tax
"To Jacob Walse"	
"Gone"	
George Keefer, single man	$0.50
Gasper Kaffer	$1.22
124.5 acres, 2 horses, 3 cows	
Patrick Kaskadion	$1.99
120 acres, 2 horses, 2 cows	
Daniel Koons, shoemaker	$0.09
1 horse, 2 cows	
Peter Kuns, blacksmith	$0.06
1 cow	
Peter Kunkald	$2.03
150 acres, 1 distillery, 3 horses, 3 cows	
Edward Kerns, single man	$0.50
"mard"	
John Kerns, single man	$0.50
"mard"	
Sebesten Kunkle	$1.21
100 acres, 2 horses, 2 cows	
Daniel Knaus, blacksmith	$0.42
1 stud horse, 2 horses, 3 cows	
"Gone"	
Archibald Kirkwood	$1.23
130 acres, 2 horses, 2 cows	
John Kelly	$0.47
50 acres, 2 horses, 3 cows, 2 cows	
Nicholas Kerns	
1 cow	
Benjamin Keane	
1 cow	
William Long, single man	
Joseph Lash	
200 acres, 2 horses, 3 cows, 2 cows	
David Loutzenhizer	$1.77
180 acres, 2 horses, 2 cows	
Abreham Leasure	$1.77

Abstracts of Westmoreland County, Pennsylvania, Tax Records 1815

North Huntingdon Township Name of Person	Tax
100 acres, 80 acres, 100 acres	
"hempf^d"	
Elizabeth Loutzenhizer	
1 cow, 2 horses	
"Movis to An^{dw} Drumand"	
William Lorimore, innkeeper	$7.02
288 acres, 179 acres, 2 horses, 2 cows	
Robert Lise, wagon maker	$0.20
~~1 horse~~, 1 cow	
Andrew Long, blacksmith	$2.23
160 acres, 2 cows, 2 horses, 1 distillery, 1 horse, 1 cow	
Samuel Long, blacksmith	$0.06
~~1 horse~~	
David Logan	
900 acres, 1 distillery, 1 tanyard, 3 horses, 4 cows, 2 slaves, 1 horse	
Henry Logan, single man	$0.50
"I think Logan [illegible] ought to be returned sm"	
John Lusk, single man	$0.50
"Gone"	
George Lutureh	
1 ~~2~~ horse, 1 cow	
Henry Loutzinhezen	~~$9.06~~
204 acres, 130 acres, 1 gristmill, 1 sawmill, 1 distillery, 3 horses, 3 cows	
"voter"	
David Long	$1.49
100 acres, 80 acres, 2 horses, 2 cows, 1 cow	
~~Thomas Lewis~~ Michael Lesmon	$0.90
100 acres, 2 horses, 2 cows	
Robert Lybe, paper maker	$0.22
1 horse, 2 cows, 1 cow	
Jacob Lutzenhizer	
100 acres, 2 horses, 1 cow	

North Huntingdon Township Name of Person	Tax
"Who pays the tax of the land he lives on"	
berkiax m??er Murphey	
~~William McClurg, single man~~	
Frederick Metzker, saddler maker	
96 acres, 1 horse, 2 cows, 1 sawmill	
A James McGrew	$3.46
240 acres, 3 horses, 4 cows, 1 horse	
"voter"	
John McClain	$1.40
100 acres, 2 horses, 3 cows	
"voter"	
John McClure, cooper	$0.17
1 cow, 1 horse	
Cooper Marsh	$0.21
1 horse, 1 cow, 1 distillery	
William Marsh	$0.06
2 cows, 1 horse	
"voter"	
Nathan McGrew	$0.97
77 acres, 2 horses, 1 cow	
William McDonald, mason	$0.13
1 horse, 1 cow	
John McDonald	$0.99
~~93 acres, 1 horse~~, 1 cow	
Alexander McDonald	$0.12
2 horses, 2 cows, 83 acres	
John McGrail Heirs	$1.10
20 acres, 1 gristmill, 1 horse, 3 cows, 2 cows	
James McGrew, shoemaker	
William McCloy	$1.82
130 acres, 2 horses, 2 cows	
George Miller	$0.31
22 acres, 1 horse, 2 cows	
"voter"	
Frederick Miller, taylor	$0.10
1 horse, 1 cow	

Abstracts of Westmoreland County, Pennsylvania, Tax Records 1815

North Huntingdon Township Name of Person	Tax
"voter"	
John Mays, tanner	$0.10
1 tanyard, 1 cow	
"Gone"	
Samuel Mays	$1.62
150 acres, 2 horses, 2 cows	
Alexander Mays, single man	$0.56
1 horse	
William Mains, cooper	
Jacob McGrew	$3.23
130 acres, 1 gristmill, 1 sawmill, 2 horses, 1 cow, 1 cow	
Dinah McGrew, widow	
2 cows, 1 cow	
Isaac Mains	$0.66
42 acres, 2 horses, 2 cows, 1 cow	
James Miligan, carpenter	$1.60
150 acres, 1 horse, 1 cow	
"Gone"	
"For this land See Jnᵒ Bennet	
Captain Joseph Markle	$4.37
96 acres, 1 gristmill, 2 horses, 2 cows, 1 carding machine, 1 "pap & fatt"	
Aron Macker, paper maker	$0.10
2 cows	
"Gone"	
Markle & Drum	$6.20
180 acres, 1 paper mill, 5 horses, 1 additional "fatt"	
Gasper Markel	$2.53
220 acres	
Samuel Miller, joiner	$0.24
20 acres, 1 horse, 1 cow, 1 cow	
John Miligan, Esquire	$2.97
200 acres, 3 horses, 3 cows, 1 distillery, 1 horse	
James McClurgh	$3.49

North Huntingdon Township Name of Person	Tax
400 acres, 4 horses, 5 4 cows	
Alex^r Miligan	$1.13
76 acres, 1 horse, 1 2 cow, 1 horse	
Joseph McClurgh	$2.18
170 acres, 2 3 horses, 3 2 cows	
James Mains	
60 acres, 3 horses, 3 cows	
Finley Mains	$0.07
1 horse, 2 1 cows, 1 horse	
James McClueas	$0.06
1 cow	
"~~Gone~~"	
"Gone"	
James Morrow, single man	$0.50
James M^cquade, single man	$0.50
"voter"	
Henry Martain	$0.16
2 horses, 3 cows	
"Gone"	
John Martin, single man	$0.50
"Gone"	
Elijah McGrew	$1.24
100 acres, 3 horses, 1 cow	
William McGrew	$0.09
1 horse, 2 cows	
Simon McGrew	$0.33
1 sawmill, 2 horses, 2 cows	
George Maltz	$2.12
174.5 acres, 2 horses, 2 cows	
A Finley McGrew	$1.85
135 acres, 3 horses, 2 cows, 1 cow	
Robert McGuffin, single man	$0.56
1 horse	
Thomas McGown	$0.06
2 horses, 1 cow	
William McCormick	$0.09

Abstracts of Westmoreland County, Pennsylvania, Tax Records 1815

North Huntingdon Township Name of Person	Tax
2 horses, 2 cows	
James Moore, mason	$0.09
1 cow	
John McCoy, shoemaker	$0.12
2 acres, 1 cow, 1 cow	
John McIntyre, auctioneer	$0.06
1 cow	
Robert McKean	$2.10
150 acres, ~~2 horses~~, 2 cows, 1 horse	
Thomas McKean, single man	$0.50
"Gone"	
Widow McCafferty	$0.29
47 acres	
Arthur McMachin	$2.66
300 acres, 1 horse, 2 cows	
"Gon"	
"for this land See Murray Jesp"	
William McGill	$0.06
1 horse, ~~1 cow~~	
Joseph Miller, single man	$1.00
1 carding machine, 1 horse	
Joseph McCormick, single man, carpenter	$0.67
"Gone"	
~~Simon~~ B James McGrew, blacksmith	$2.20
159 acres, 3 horses, 4 ~~2~~ cows	
Finley McGrew, single man, blacksmith	$0.64
1 horse	
Peter Miller	$3.00
200 acres, 2 horses, 4 cows	
George Myer, brush maker	$0.09
1 cow	
"Gone"	
W^m McAluse, single man	$0.06
1 cow	
"Gone"	
William Mitchel	$0.96

North Huntingdon Township Name of Person	Tax
100 acres, 1 horse, 2 cows	
Sally McCormick, widow	$1.82
200 acres, 2 horses, 1 cow, 2 cows, 1 horse	
John McCormick, single man, tanner	~~$0.71~~
1 tanyard	
“not Gone”	
“See Collins, Jos”	
Andrew McCormick, shoemaker	$0.22
1 horse, 1 cow	
David Mains	$0.68
55 acres, 1 horse, 1 horse, 1 cow, 1 cow	
Richard McAnulty	$2.19
138 acres, 2 horses, 3 cows, 1 distillery	
“for 12 acres see Wm Fuller tan”	
Patrick McIntere	
1 cow	
John Mahon	$0.07
1 horse, ~~2 cows~~, 1 cow	
Samuel McGrew, cabinetmaker	$1.37
76 acres, 1 horse, 2 cows	
E James McGrew	$1.09
90 acres, 1 horse, 2 cows,1 horse, 1 cow	
John Moah, single man	$0.50
Andrew Mains	$0.06
1 cow	
William McClurgh, single man	$0.50
Nathan McGrew, Junior	$0.06
~~1 horse~~, 1 cow	
Aaron Martin, shoemaker	
1 horse, 1 cow	
Joseph McClurg, shoemaker	
1 cow	
John Mitcheal, “augr” maker	
Ann McGrew, “wd”	
1 horse, 2 cows	
~~William McKelvey~~	

Abstracts of Westmoreland County, Pennsylvania,
Tax Records 1815

North Huntingdon Township Name of Person	Tax
~~130 acres, 2 horses, 2 cows~~	
"see before"	
James B MᶜGrew	$2.03
140 acres, 3 horses, ~~4 cows~~, 2 cows	
Henry Marsh, Senior	$1.60
100 acres, 2 horses, ~~4 cows~~, 3 cows	
Henry Marsh, Junior	
John Neel, weaver	$0.06
~~1 cow~~, 2 horses	
John Newhouse, paper maker	$0.23
~~1 horse, 3 cows~~, 2 cows	
Simon Newlon	$0.09
1 horse, 2 cows	
Elijah Newlon, blacksmith	$0.06
1 cow	
William Newlon	$2.93
182 acres, 4 horses, 15 cows, 1 distillery	
Elijah Newlon, Senior	$1.77
130 acres, 1 horse, ~~2 cows~~, 1 cow	
Christian Neaff	$0.06
2 horses, 1 cow	
"Gone"	
Frederick Nitz, blacksmith	$0.20
~~1 horse~~, 1 cow	
James Newlon	$0.06
1 cow	
Alexander Osburn	$0.10
2 ~~1~~ horses, 2 cows	
Archibald Osburn	$1.07
80 acres, 2 horses, 3 cows, 1 cow	
Samuel Osburn	$1.90
150 acres, 2 horses, 4 cows	
John Painter	$1.90
150 acres, ~~3 horses~~, 4 cows, 2 horses	
Isaac Painter, single man	$0.50
1 horse	

North Huntingdon Township Name of Person	Tax
William Pinkerton	$1.52
110 acres, 2 horses, 2 cows	
Thomas Peart, blacks[mith]	$0.10
2 cows, 1 cow	
John Patton's executors	$1.94
170 acres	
William Parks	$1.89
136 acres, 50 acres, 3 horses, 4 cows	
"votered [?]"	
James Patterson	$0.07
2 horses, 3 cows	
Joseph Patterson, single man	$0.50
John Patterson	$0.97
100 acres, 2 horses, 2 cows	
James Park	$1.34
150 acres, 1 horse, 2 cows, 1 cow	
Nicholas Peterson	$0.06
1 horse, 2 cows	
Georg Pranale, single man	
Stacey Potts	$1.80
250 acres	
Robert Quail, paper maker	$0.17
2 cows, 1 horse	
Herekia Robins	
4 horses, 16 cows	
Henry Peetal	$2.14
250 acres	
"for Catrine Smith's land"	
Christian Ruffeorn	$0.06
1 cow	
"Gone"	
William Reed	$4.12
300 acres, 4 horses, 2 cows, 1 horse	
William Robison	$0.83
100 acres, 2 horses, 2 cows	
Godfrey Reese, weaver	$0.09

Abstracts of Westmoreland County, Pennsylvania, Tax Records 1815

North Huntingdon Township Name of Person	Tax
1 cow	
Mathew Robison	$2.20
150 acres, 2 ~~3~~ horses, 3 cows	
John Robison	$0.14
~~2 horses~~, 2 cows, 1 horse	
John Rudibaugh	$3.32
275 acres, 2 horses, 1 cow, 1 small still	
Daniel Rudebaugh	$0.07
1 horse, 2 cows, 1 horse	
Henry Robison	$0.06
1 horse, 1 cow, 1 cow	
Brintnel Robbins	$6.37
400 acres, 1 gristmill, 4 horses, 20 cows, 2 cows	
Peter Richer, carpenter	$0.13
1 horse, 1 cow	
Mosses Robins, single man	
1 horse	
Joseph Reed, blacksmith	
1 horse, 2 cows	
Alexander Robison	
227 acres, 3 horses, 3 cows	
Daniel Shenir, blacksmith	$1.75
80 acres, 58 acres, 1 sawmill, 2 ~~3~~ horses, 3 cows	
Philip Swanger	$0.14
2 horses, 2 cows, 1 cow	
Alex^r Sumral, single man	$0.50
1 horse	
"Gone"	
William Skelly, Senior	$2.46
200 acres, ~~2 horses~~, 3 ~~2~~ cows, 1 horse	
Robert Skelly, single man	$0.50
William Skelly, Junior	$0.74
57 acres, 1 horse, 1 cow, 1 horse	
Robert Smith	$1.64
120 acres, 2 horses, 2 cows	
Newton Shannon, single man	$0.50

Abstracts of Westmoreland County, Pennsylvania, Tax Records 1815

North Huntingdon Township Name of Person	Tax
Daniel Shank	$0.06
1 horse	
Alex^r Sumral	$0.06
1 cow	
Henry Shoaff	$1.43
100 acres, 4 horses, ~~4 cows~~, 3 cows	
Joseph Scott, paper maker	$0.37
1 horse, 2 cows	
Christian Saynor	$0.93
100 acres, 1 horse, 1 cow	
Jacob Spencer, shoemaker	$0.12
1 horse, 1 cow	
John Solinger, ~~single man~~, shoemaker	$0.57
1 horse	
Peter Solinger	$0.06
1 horse, 1 horse, 1 cow	
James Sloan, single man, tanner	$2.03
100 acres, 1 tanyard, ~~3 horses~~, 3 cows, 2 horses	
Christian Smith	$0.06
1 horse, 2 cows	
David Shraeder, deceased	$1.04
100 acres, 3 horses, 4 cows	
"see abraham Lasure for this land"	
Catharine Smith, widow	$2.20
250 acres, 1 horse, 2 cows	
"this to Henry Petall"	
John Smith	$0.37
~~6 horses~~, 2 cows, 3 horses	
Jacob Shener	$1.06
100 acres, 1 horse, 1 cow	
"Gone"	
Adam Saam	$2.76
200 acres, 4 horses, 5 cows, 1 distillery	
Frederick Saam	$1.24
89.5 acres, ~~4 horses~~, 3 cows, 2 horses	
Henry Sigler, single man	$0.50

Abstracts of Westmoreland County, Pennsylvania, Tax Records 1815

North Huntingdon Township Name of Person	Tax
"Gone"	
James Stephenson, shoemaker	$0.43
50 acres, 2 horses, 1 cow, 1 horse	
Reverend William Swan	$3.60
220.5 acres, 56 acres, 5 horses, 4 cows, 2 cows	
John Stewart	$1.80
123 acres, 100 acres, 1 stud horse, 1 distillery, 1 horse, 3 horses, 3 cows, 1 cow	
James Sampson	$0.30
50 acres, 1 cow	
George Sampson	$0.06
1 horse, 1 cow	
Joseph Simpson	$1.03
70 acres, 4 horses, 3 horses, 3 4 cows, 1 distillery	
Andrew Simpson, single man	$0.50
Joseph Simpson, single man	$0.50
Joseph Sloan, carpenter	$0.09
1 cow	
John Solinger, "a Jolly weaver"	$0.08
1 horse	
Henry Sloan, carpenter	$1.77
150 acres, 2 horses, 3 cows, 1 horse, 2 cows	
John Sowash	$1.76
150 acres, 3 horses, 1 horse, 4 cows	
John Slutterback	$0.09
1 cow, 90 acres, 2 horses	
Robert Stewart, Esquire, innkeeper	$4.80
140 acres, 142 acres, 12 horses, 4 cows, 1 cow	
Adam Shetler	$2.12
236 acres, 2 horses, 3 cows, 1 cow	
Shenear Sampson, single man	
Frederick Shencer, single man	
Jacob Smele, miller	
1 cow	
David Sheneir, cooper	
1 horse, 1 cow, 17 acres	

193

North Huntingdon Township Name of Person	Tax
Peter Sowash, blacksmith	
1 cow	
Jacob Sowash, single man	
Jacob Saddler	
1 horse, ~~1 cow~~	
John Taylor	$2.59
200 acres, 2 horses, 3 cows, 1 distillery, 1 horse	
Henry Taylor, single man	$0.50
Joseph Thompson	$2.09
200 acres, 2 horses, 2 cows, 1 cow	
William Thompson	$0.07
1 horse, 1 horse, 2 cows	
Henry Tenny, weaver	$0.24
6 acres, 1 cow	
Stacy Thomas, blacksmith	$0.09
~~1 horse~~, 1 cow	
Samuel Thompson	$2.17
180 acres, ~~2 horses~~, 1 horse, 2 cows, 2 cows	
John Temple, weaver	$1.12
100 acres, 2 horses, 2 cows	
John Thompson	$1.40
150 acres, 2 horses, 1 cow	
John Trout	$3.66
300 acres, 5 acres, 3 horses, 3 cows, 1 horse	
Robert Taylor	$2.52
200 acres, ~~4 horses~~, 4 cows, 3 horses	
Micheal Tayney, carpenter	
15 acres, 1 cow	
James Thompson, single man, blacksmith	
1 horse	
Isaac Taylor, single man	
George Wilson	$0.71
50 acres, 3 horses, 2 cows	
Jesse Walton	$0.06
1 cow	
John Woods	$0.07

Abstracts of Westmoreland County, Pennsylvania,
Tax Records 1815

North Huntingdon Township Name of Person	Tax
1 horse, 2 cows, 1 horse	
William Wilson	$1.13
80 acres, 1 sawmill, 2 horses, 3 cows, 1 horse	
James Woods, Senior	$1.39
150 acres, 1 horse, ~~3 cows~~, 2 cows	
"for 27 acres of land Bo^t of his Son James"	
Alexander Woods, single man	$0.50
James Woods, Junior	$0.87
63 acres, 2 horses, 2 cows	
Sampson Wylie, weaver	$0.32
15 acres, ~~2 horses~~, 1 cow, 1 horse	
Charles [W]allace	$0.07
2 horses, 1 cow	
Benjamin Weaver	$0.07
1 horse, 1 cow	
George Waggoner	$0.43
50 acres, 1 horse, ~~2 cows~~, 1 cow	
Solomon Waggoner	$1.00
100 acres, 1 horse, 1 cow	
Valentine Whitehead	$1.90
150 acres, 3 horses, ~~4 cows~~, 2 cows	
Jacob Weaver	$3.20
240 acres, 2 horses, 1 cow, 1 cow	
Jacob Wampler	$1.22
130 acres, 3 horses, 2 cows	
Jacob White	$0.94
100 acres, 1 horse, 2 cows	
Joseph Williamson	$1.37
150 acres, 1 horse, 2 cows	
James Walt	$1.74
200 acres, 1 ~~2~~ cow, 1 horse	
Jemina Walthour, widow	$2.71
203 acres, 2 horses, 1 cow, 1 cow	
Gasper Walthaur, innkeeper	$2.84
140 acres, 2 horses, 3 cows, 1 tanyard	
Dorothy Walthaur, widow	$3.77

Abstracts of Westmoreland County, Pennsylvania, Tax Records 1815

North Huntingdon Township Name of Person	Tax
150 acres, 1 gristmill, ~~1 sawmill~~, 1 horse, 1 cow	
Jacob Walthaur	$2.12
200 acres, 2 horses, 2 cows	
Henry Wilson	$0.12
2 horses, 2 cows	
David Watson	$0.06
1 cow	
Barnabas Wilson	$1.14
84.5 acres, ~~2 horses~~, 4 cows, 1 still, 1 horse	
Christopher Whitehead	$0.07
1 horse, ~~2 cows~~, 1 cow	
John Weaver, teacher	
1 cow	
Jacob Walse	$6.92
380 acres, 1 gristmill, 1 carding machine	
Samuel Waters	$0.06
2 cows	
~~Christopher Walthaur~~	$0.06
2 cows	
George Johnston, fuller	$0.23
1 horse, 2 cows	
~~Wᵐ Means, cooper~~	~~$0.50~~
Archibald Mᶜkenry	$0.16
2 horses, 1 cow	
John Maners, paper maker	$0.16
1 cow	
Wᵐ Mackey	$0.06
2 horses	
Jacob Manersmith, potter	$0.08
1 cow	
Daniel Myers	$0.06
1 horse, 1 cow	
Jerremiah Murry, Esquire	$2.00
300 acres	
Joseph Mehaffe	$0.83
120 acres, 2 horses, 2 cow	

Abstracts of Westmoreland County, Pennsylvania, Tax Records 1815

North Huntingdon Township Name of Person	Tax
Benjamin M{c}Caul	$0.13
2 horses, 1 cow	
William Robinson	$3.80
310 acres, 3 horses, 3 cows	
Daniel Loughner, blacksmith	$0.16
1 cow	
Barnabas Lonch	$0.06
1 cow	

North Huntingdon Township Name	Page
See Jacob Greenaualdt	32
"Trade not followed"	
"200 acres of land Browns Pls only 185"	
See John Taylor	79
"200 acres of land only 134"	
"for Remander [sic] See R Casper agent for Dile"	15
See Thos Pert	65
"Trade not followed"	
See George Guisinger	34
"90 acres of land to Albright"	3
For Henry Detman	26
"See Jno Detman and Caeslan Kline Administrators"	
See Martin Ashbaugh	2
"16 acres of land in adition [sic] to last assessment"	
"for 17 acres of land to Alken Baxter See David Sheneer"	13 78
See Henry Brenaman	6
"for 50 acres of Jno Carnahan hills"	19
See James M{c}Grew, shoemaker	51
"Suporting [sic] his Parents"	
See Abraham Lasure	47
"80 acres of land Tout in hempfield"	
See Thos Blackburn	8
"100 Acres Cald in assessment only 98"	

Abstracts of Westmoreland County, Pennsylvania,
Tax Records 1815

North Huntingdon Township Name	Page
For Elizabeth Lutzetger [?]	47
"See and ᵂ Drumand"	
See Catharine Smith	74
"land to Henry Pelall"	
See Wᵐ Galt	36
"Making improvements"	

North Huntingdon Poor Children
Maryan Pearl – 11 years old
Racheal Pearl – 9 years old
Samuel Fisher – 10 years old
Thomas Fisher – 9 years old
Maria Fisher – 8 years old

Abstracts of Westmoreland County, Pennsylvania,
Tax Records 1815

Rostraver Township Name of Person	Tax
John Arthur, cooper	$0.74
trade, 50 acres, 2 horses, 1 2 cow	
George Anderson	$0.08
2 1 horses, 1 cow	
Robert Armstrong, shoemaker	$0.18
trade, 11.5 acres, 2 cows	
"See Thomas Barige [?]"	
Philip Austro, wagoner	$0.63
trade, 52 acres, 1 2 cow, 2 horses	
William Anderson, single man, cooper	$0.58
trade, 1 horse	
"is he married Mr Ass^r"	
Robert Armstrong, t keeper [probably tavern keeper]	$0.16
4 2 horses, 4 2 cows	
George Armstrong, single man	$0.50
Alexander Anderson, weaver	$0.12
trade, 1 horse, 1 cow	
William Armstrong	$0.06
1 cow	
"gone"	
Joseph Blackburn, smith	$0.19
trade, 2 cows	
"gone"	
Simon Blackburn, single man	$0.57
1 horse	
Nancy Bailey, widow	$0.53
45 acres, 1 horse, 1 cow	
Nathaniel Bailey, single man, cooper	$0.61
trade, 3 horses, 106 acres, 1 cow	
"is he married or no Mr Ass^r"	
Mary Burns, widow	$0.58
50 acres, 1 horse, 1 cow	
John Beazel	$0.18
2 horses, 3 cows	
Nancy Bleaks, widow	$0.08

Abstracts of Westmoreland County, Pennsylvania, Tax Records 1815

Rostraver Township Name of Person	Tax
1 horse, 1 cow	
John Bleaks, carpenter	$0.16
trade, 10 acres, 1 cow	
"see Wᵐ Wight"	
Elizabeth Becket, widow	$0.73
70 acres, 2 cows	
"See Henry Marderty"	
John Berkhamer	$1.22
101 acres, 3 horses, 1 cow	
Joseph Berkhamer, single man	$0.50
1 horse	
Daniel Burgan	$0.24
3 horses, 3 cows	
Abraham Boher	$0.06
1 cow	
William Bigham	$1.04
80 acres, 3 horses, 3 cows	
Daniel Budd	$0.16
1 acre, 1 2 horse, 2 cows	
Joseph Budd, Senior	$5.25
154 acres, 128 acres, 100 acres, 7 5 horses, 10 14 cattle, a 75 gallon still	
Joseph Budd	$0.50
Anthony Blackburn	$0.16
1 2 horse, 3 2 cows	
William Bradshaw, "wv"	$0.06
2 1 cows	
Stephen Boys, single man	$0.50
Joshua Budd, Senior	$11.14
734 acres, 7 horses, 5 4 cows, 1/2 a ferry	
Robert Baldridge	$0.93
10 acres, 1 sawmill	
John Beckett	$1.50
120 acres, 4 2 horses, 1 4 cow	
Matthew Benar	$1.37
180 acres, 2 horses, 2 3 cows	
William Bonar, single man	$0.50

Abstracts of Westmoreland County, Pennsylvania, Tax Records 1815

Rostraver Township Name of Person	Tax
Joseph Budd, Junior	$0.31
4 horses, 3 cows	
"gone"	
William Beazel, Senior	$2.32
150 acres, 4 horses, 2 4 cows	
Matthew Beazel, single man	$0.50
William Beazel, Junior	$1.01
80 acres, 3 horses, 1 cow, 44 acres	
Matthew Bleakley	$0.35
35 acres	
Thomas Bleakley	$0.30
30 acres	
Caleb Brown	$2.77
190 acres, 3 horses, 1 3 cow	
John Bennett	$3.83
50 acres, 1 merchant mill, 2 horses, 3 cows	
Joseph Benom	
3 cows	
Thomas Baldridge	
11.5 acres	
Amaziah Chapin, cabinetmaker	$1.84
trade, 155 acres, 2 horses, 3 2 cows, 156 acres	
Silas Clark	$0.23
1 3 horse, 1 2 cow	
William Campbell	$4.59
107 acres, 2 horses, 2 cows, 125 acres	
Michael Conkle	$0.48
40 acres, 1 horse, 1 cow	
Isaac Call, single man, cooper	$0.63
trade, 1 horse, 1 cow	
Morris Cunin	$0.08
1 horse, 1 cow, 72.5 acres	
Thomas Cloud, Senior	$0.06
1 cow	
Nathaniel Cloud	$0.07
1 horse	
"gone"	

Abstracts of Westmoreland County, Pennsylvania,
Tax Records 1815

Rostraver Township Name of Person	**Tax**
Joseph Cloud, mason	$0.06
Nathaniel Carns	$0.85
70 acres, 1 2 horse, 1 cow	
Joseph Chambers	$0.06
1 cow	
Peter Carns	$0.07
1 horse, 1 cow	
William Carns, single man	$0.07
1 horse	
William Cleaton	$0.08
1 horse, 1 cow	
"Deceased"	
James Carns	$0.13
2 horses	
John Chambers	$0.44
44 acres, 1 2 horse, 2 cows	
"See William Beazel Jun for land"	
Crawford	$0.73
72.5 acres	
"See Morris Cerwin"	
James Cook	$1.67
100 acres	
John Castner	$0.28
30 acres, 1/2 a ferry	
James Cunningham	$3.00
204 acres, 3 horses, 3 cows, 2 old stills 125 gallon	
Robert Cunningham, single man	$0.50
George Campbell	$0.08
1 cow	
Alexander Cunningham, single man	
Michael Darr	$1.24
86 acres, 1 horse, 1 2 cow	
"See George Darr"	
George Darr	$0.16
1 2 horse, 1 2 cow, 86 acres	
Robert Davidson	$0.06
1 cow	

Abstracts of Westmoreland County, Pennsylvania,
Tax Records 1815

Rostraver Township Name of Person	Tax
James Dougherty, shoemaker	$1.10
trade, 60 acres, 1 horse, 2 cows	
John Devitt, taylor	$0.13
trade, 1 horse, ~~1 cow~~	
Abraham Depue	$0.08
~~1 horse~~, 1 cow	
David Davis	$3.39
323 acres, 3 ~~2~~ horses, 3 ~~2~~ cows	
Samuel Davis	$1.11
94 acres, 1 horse, 1/8 of a sawmill, 1 cow	
Benjamin Davis	$1.65
1 slave, 120 acres, 1 ~~2~~ horse, 1 ~~3~~ cow, 1/8 of a sawmill	
Dorsey Davis, single man	$1.44
100 acres, 1/8 of a sawmill	
H. Samuel Daily, single man	$0.50
John Daily	$3.98
335 acres, 6 horses, 4 ~~6~~ cows, 180 gallon of stills	
Jesse Davis	$0.91
76 acres, 1 ~~2~~ horse, 1 cattle	
Wm Davis, single man	
Ephraim Davis	
2 cow	
Danl Essington, blacksmith	$0.18
2 ~~1~~ cows, 1 horse	
Joseph Eckley	$3.06
1 mill, 156 acres, 2 horses, 1 cow	
"See Monym Saul"	
"See Amzi Chapen"	
James Ellis, "W^v"	$0.13
trade, 1 horse, 1 cow	
"gone"	
John Emfield, carpenter	$0.06
trade, 1 cow	
Nathaniel Eberson, cooper	$0.08
1 cow	
Hodge Fisher	$0.07

Rostraver Township Name of Person	Tax
1 horse	
George Fisher	$0.08
1 horse, 1 cow	
"gone"	
Samuel Flack, cooper	$0.88
trade, 100 acres, 2 horses, 2 cows	
William Finley	$2.47
166 acres, 3 horses, 4 cows	
Michael Finley	$2.41
166 acres, 3 horses, 1 cow	
Hannah Finley, widow	$2.35
166 acres, 2 horses, 1 cow	
John Fisher, Junior	$0.07
1 horse	
John Fisher, Senior	$3.69
276 ~~260~~ acres, 4 ~~3~~ horse, 1 ~~2~~ cow	
Joseph Finley, Esquire	$7.84
550 acres, 6 horses, 5 ~~8~~ cows	
John Flemon	$1.21
92 acres, 3 horses, 5 ~~8~~ cows	
James Flemon, single man	$0.50
Reverend Peter Fell	$0.71
55 acres, 2 horses, 3 ~~2~~ cows	
Jesse Fell, single man	$0.66
2 horses, 2 cows	
Benjamin Fell	$2.39
200 acres, 2 ~~3~~ horses, 2 cattle, 1 sawmill	
Joseph Fell, single man	$0.50
John Flemon, Junior, single man	
George Flemon, single man	
William Gardner, carpenter	$0.13
trade, 1 horse, 1 cow	
Andrew Geyr	$0.91
50 acres, 4 ~~3~~ horses, 2 ~~3~~ cows	
George Geyr	$0.91
50 acres, 4 horses, 3 cows	
James Garvin, "Wᵛ"	$0.09

Abstracts of Westmoreland County, Pennsylvania, Tax Records 1815

Rostraver Township Name of Person	Tax
trade, 3 cows	
"gone"	
Charles Gillespie	$1.08
128 acres, 3 horses, 1 2 cow	
"Deceased"	
"See John and Wᵐ Gillespie"	
John Gillespie, single man	$0.50
3 horses, 1 cow, 78.5 acres	
William Gibson, "Wᵛ"	$0.06
trade, 1 cow	
"gone"	
William Gillespie	
50 acres, 1 horse, 1 cow	
John Hanna	$2.85
195 acres, 3 horses, 4 cows	
"gone"	
"see Wᵐ Cambell"	
Job Hastings	$0.09
1 horse, 1 cow	
Valentine Hush, hatter	$0.23
trade, 1 horse	
Peter Hush	$1.15
74 acres, 2 horses, 2 cows	
John Hough	$0.08
1 horse, 1 cow	
Joseph Hill	$1.62
146 acres, 2 horses, 2 cows	
Stephen Hill	$2.16
150 acres, 2 horses, 2 cows	
"gone"	
"See Thomas Robison"	
Laurence Hindland	$2.02
194 acres, 1 horse, 1 cow	
"gone See Wᵐ Mᶜgees"	
Laurence John Higgins, single man	$0.57
1 horse, 2 cows	
"gone"	

Rostraver Township Name of Person	Tax
Henry Hornbeck	$0.08

1 horse, 1 cow
"gone"

Mary Hammond, widow	$0.76

50 acres, 2 horses, 2 cows

Nathaniel Hammond, single man	$0.57

~~1 horse~~

Daniel Hammond, Junior	$2.00

50 acres, 20 acres, 4 ~~5~~ horses, 3 ~~2~~ cows, 1 sawmill

John Hammond, single man	$0.50
Peter Hammond, single man	$0.50
Daniel Hammond, Senior	$1.40

100 acres, 1 horse, 1 cow

James Hammond	$0.66

50 acres, 1 ~~2~~ horse, 2 cows

Samuel Harson, gunsmith	$0.06

trade, 2 cows

Nathaniel Heydon	$1.16

100 acres, 3 ~~2~~ horses, 2 cows, 80 gallon still

Jacob Heydon	$2.87

270 acres, 3 ~~2~~ horses, 3 cows

Frederick Humburt	$3.20

213 acres, ~~2 horses~~

Jacob Housman	$0.84

55 acres, 4 horses, 1 ~~2~~ cow
"Deceased"
"See John Housman"

Christopher Housman, Senior and Junior	$1.63

148 acres, 2 horses, 2 ~~1~~ cows

John Housman, single man	$0.57

1 horse, 1 cow, 55 acres

Daniel Hamilton	$0.17

2 horses, 2 ~~3~~ cows
John Hurh, single man
Henry Hordesty
70 acres

Nathaniel Johnston	$0.08

Abstracts of Westmoreland County, Pennsylvania, Tax Records 1815

Rostraver Township Name of Person	**Tax**
1 horse, 1 cow	
"gone"	
Kinith Joabs, carpenter	$0.06
trade	
"gone"	
John Jay, carpenter	$0.06
trade, 1 cow	
"gone"	
Joseph Johnston	$0.06
1 cow, 1 horse	
Abraham Jacobs	$2.97
217 acres, 1 horse, 2 cows	
Daniel Jacobs, Junior	$0.10
1 horse, 1 2 cows	
Daniel Jacobs, Senior	$0.08
1 horse, 1 cow	
John Johnston	$0.16
2 horses, 2 cows	
Robert Johnston	$8.71
400 acres, 2 3 horses, 3 cows, 1 merchant mill, 1 sawmill, 360 gallon still	
John Kirby	$0.06
1 cow, 1 horse	
Lewis Ketchem, blacksmith	$0.20
trade, 2 horses, 2 1 cows	
John Kirkland	$0.06
1 cow	
"Deceased"	
George Linder, single man	$0.57
1 horse	
"gone"	
Nathaniel Linder	$0.16
2 horses, 1 2 cow	
Lockart Luce	$0.08
1 horse, 2 1 cows	
Benjamin Lucre	$0.15
3 2 horses, 1 cow	

Abstracts of Westmoreland County, Pennsylvania, Tax Records 1815

Rostraver Township Name of Person	Tax
Craig Lucre	$2.09
194 acres, 2 horses, 2 ~~1~~ cows	
Stephen Lowry	$3.03
200 acres, 2 ~~3~~ horses, 5 ~~3~~ cows, 150 gallon still	
John Lane	$0.08
~~1 horse~~, 1 cow	
Jacob Linder	$0.16
2 horses, 2 cows	
"gone"	
Martin Lutz	
91 acres	
A. George Merton	
1 horse	
David Merton	
20 acres	
Jonathan Maclintic	
1 horse, 1 cow	
William Morgan	$4.17
300 acres, 1 ~~2~~ horse, 4 ~~3~~ cows	
Morgan Morgan	$0.91
2 ~~1~~ horses, 2 ~~1~~ cows, 1 sawmill	
Robert Mathers "W.v."	$0.21
trade, 2 horses, 2 cows	
Samuel Morgan	$0.17
26 acres	
Alexander Maclian	$0.16
1 ~~2~~ horse, 2 cows	
John Maclean	$0.25
18 acres, 1 horse	
Peter Marmie	$0.39
56 acres, 1 cow	
Alexander Moorhead	$0.88
72 acres, 2 horses, 2 cows	
William Mathers, saddler	$0.46
trade, 15 acres, 1 ~~2~~ horse, 3 cows	
John McKee	$0.08
1 horse, 1 cow	

Abstracts of Westmoreland County, Pennsylvania, Tax Records 1815

Rostraver Township Name of Person	Tax
Samuel McCord	$0.08
1 horse, 1 cow	
Charles McFall	$0.66
49 acres, 1 ~~2~~ horse, 3 cows	
Samuel Miller	$0.11
1 horse, 1 ~~3~~ cows	
John McGogany	$0.17
2 horses, 3 cows	
"gone"	
Thomas McGavoh, "wv"	$0.12
trade, 6 acres, 1 cow	
James Montgomery	$1.96
145 acres, 1 sawmill, 2 horses, 1 ~~2~~ cow	
Samuel Maxwell	$0.16
2 horses, 2 cows	
William McClure, single man	$0.50
John Moose, fuller, single man	$2.73
50 acres, fulling mill, 1 horse	
Ebenzer Moore, single man	$1.81
124 acres, 2 horses, 2 cows	
George McClure	$3.19
293 acres, 3 ~~2~~ horses, 3 ~~2~~ cows, 118 gallon still	
Archibald McGaughlen "w^v"	$0.20
trade, 2 horses, 1 cow	
"gone"	
Joseph Moorhead, "B. S."	$0.16
trade, ~~1 horse~~, 1 cow	
Joshua Martin	$0.83
102 acres, 2 horses 3 ~~4~~ cows	
David McCleard	
139 acres, 2 horses, 5 cows	
Martin Martezall	
33 acres, 1 cow	
Wm Miligan	
1 horse, 2 cows	
John Morgan, single man	
1 horse	

Abstracts of Westmoreland County, Pennsylvania, Tax Records 1815

Rostraver Township Name of Person	Tax
Robert Mathews, single man	
James Maffet	
1 horse, 1 cow	
Thomas Mathers, single man	
Isaac Morten	
134 acres, 1 cow	
Wᵐ Mᶜgrew	
194 acres, 1 cow	
James Mᶜkeever	
1 horse	
Wᵐ Neely	
trade	
Joshua Nichols	$0.07
1 horse	
"gone"	
Charles Orr	$1.82
150 acres, 4 horses, 4 cows	
Adam Orr, single man	$0.50
John Orr	$3.09
200 acres, 3 4 horses, 5 4 cows, 120 gallon still	
Samuel Orr, single man	
Caleb Porter, cooper	$1.32
trade, 79 acres, 2 horses, 4 cows	
William Peenix	$0.11
1 horse, 2 cows	
"gone"	
David Pollock	$3.63
260 acres, 3 2 horses, 2 cows	
"See Nathaniel Baily and Nicholas Snyder"	
Edward Petty	$0.17
2 horses, 3 cows	
Aaron Power	$0.10
1 horse, 2 cows	
"gone"	
John Patterson, single man	$2.15
150 acres, 185 gallon still, 1 horse, 1 cow	
Thomas Patterson, single man	$0.50

Abstracts of Westmoreland County, Pennsylvania, Tax Records 1815

Rostraver Township Name of Person	Tax
"son of Thos"	
"gone"	
James Patterson, single man	$0.50
"gone"	
William Patterson	$0.08
1 horse, 1 cow	
James Proctor	$0.97
124 acres, 3 2 horses, 2 1 cows	
Robert Patterson	$6.23
440 acres, 3 horses, 2 3 cows, 150 gallon still	
Elijah Patterson, single man	$0.50
Thomas Patterson, single man	$0.50
John Patterson	$0.10
1 horse, 2 cows	
Morgan Paul	$0.88
80 acres, 2 1 horses, 1 cow, 1 gristmill	
David Penny	$0.10
2 1 horses, 2 cows	
Major F. John Power	$3.73
250 acres, 5 horses, 5 cows	
Patrick Power	$1.37
116 acres, 3 horses, 2 1 cows	
Benjamin Pancake	$0.08
1 horse, 1 cow	
"Gone"	
Mathew Patterson	
3 horses	
Samuel Patterson	
1 horse, 1 cow	
Daniel Porter	
80 acres	
George Royal, single man	
Joseph Reed, blacksmith	$0.18
trade, 1 cow	
"gone"	
Peter Reed	$1.43
143 acres, 4 horses, 2 cows	

Rostraver Township Name of Person	Tax
Frederick Rhodorker	$0.66
50 acres, 2 horses, 2 cows	
John Rhodes	$0.16
2 horses, 2 cows	
"gone"	
Thomas Robinson	$1.22
70 acres, 2 ~~1~~ horses, 3 cows, 150 gallon still, 126 acres	
Abner Reeves	$0.83
50 acres, 2 horses, 1 ~~2~~ cow	
Manassa Reeves	$1.21
83 acres, 3 ~~4~~ horses, 3 ~~2~~ cows, 100 gallon still	
John Relan	$3.05
230 acres, 4 ~~3~~ horses, 4 ~~7~~ cows, 1 sawmill, 148 gallon still	
Nicholas Retan, ~~single man~~	$0.50
2 horses, 3 cows	
Stephen Reese	$0.06
1 cow, 1 horse	
John Robinson	$2.79
190 acres, 5 ~~3~~ horses, 3 ~~4~~ cows	
John Roberton's heirs	$1.87
140 acres	
James Ryan, single man	$0.65
2 horses, 1 cow	
"gone"	
Thomas Ryan, single man	$0.50
John Roberts, single man	
John Robb	$1.18
100 acres, 1 horse, 2 ~~1~~ cows	
John Rhea	$0.07
1 horse	
"Gone"	
Andrew Robertson	$6.75
466 acres, 3 ~~6~~ horses, 6 ~~4~~ cows, 100 gallon still	
Colonel David Royal	$3.04
210 acres, 3 horses, 2 ~~3~~ cows	

Abstracts of Westmoreland County, Pennsylvania, Tax Records 1815

Rostraver Township Name of Person	Tax
Major Jesse Reeves	$1.73
150 acres, 3 horses, 3 ~~2~~ cattle, 82 gallon still	
Samuel Reeves	
150 acres, 3 horses, 2 cow	
James Robinson, single man	
Abraham Shela	$0.15
2 horses, 1 cow	
Michael Shilling	$1.10
93.5 acres, 2 horses, 2 cows	
George Shiver, blacksmith	$0.14
trade, 1 cow	
"Deceased"	
Doctor Bela Smith	$6.91
484 acres, 5 ~~6~~ horses, 4 cows	
Gasper Snider	$0.06
1 cow, 1 horse	
Nicholas Snider	$2.04
141 acres, 2 horses, 2 cows, 12 acres	
Staugger & Tinstman	$1.23
123 acres	
"See David Mccleand"	
Henry Seaburn	$0.80
80 acres	
"See Morton Listiz"	
Richard Steel	$2.17
107 acres, 50 acres, 2 ~~3~~ horses, 3 cows	
Adam Steel, ~~single man~~	$2.57
107 acres, 50 acres, 2 horses, 3 ~~1~~ cows	
Isaac Shiplor	$1.35
118 acres, 3 ~~2~~ horses, 2 ~~3~~ cows	
Daniel Springher	$1.95
162 acres, 4 horses, 5 cows	
John Springher, single man	$0.50
Rebekah Smith, widow	$1.69
160 acres, 1 horse, 2 cows	
John Shiplor "Wv"	$2.19
trade, 180 acres, 2 ~~3~~ horses, 3 ~~4~~ cows, 100 gallon	

Rostraver Township Name of Person	**Tax**
still	
~~Mathias Shiplor, single man~~	~~$0.57~~
~~2 horses~~	
Abraham Smock	$0.09
1 horse, 1 ~~2~~ cow	
Philip Shiplor, Senior	$1.64
140 acres, 2 ~~3~~ horses, 2 ~~3~~ cows	
James Stewart, "post[r]"	$0.08
1 horse, 1 cow	
Barnett Smock	$0.16
2 horses, 1 ~~2~~ cow	
George Stump, cooper	$0.13
trade, 1 horse, 1 cow	
Abraham Scott	$2.46
246 acres, ~~2 horses~~	
"land to Tompson heirs"	
Noah Speers	$10.42
166 acres, 678 acres, 5 ~~7~~ horses, 12 ~~14~~ cows, 260 gallon still	
Matthias Shiplor, Senior	$2.81
190 acres, 2 horses, 3 cows, 124 gallon still	
Jacob Shiplor, single man	$0.62
2 horses, 64 gallon still	
Peter Shiplor, Junior	$0.21
2 ~~3~~ horses, 2 ~~1~~ cows, 43.5 acres	
Peter Shiplor, Senior	$2.44
219 acres, 2 ~~3~~ horses, 2 ~~4~~ cows	
Samuel Shiplor	$0.17
1 ~~2~~ horse, 3 cows, 50 acres	
Margaret Sowash, widow	$1.58
134 acres, 2 ~~3~~ cows, 2 ~~3~~ cows	
Daniel Sowash, single man	$0.50
Jacob Sowash, single man	$0.50
John Sutton, carpenter	$0.15
trade, 2 ~~1~~ horses, 2 cows	
William Stewart	$0.08
1 horse, 1 cow	

Abstracts of Westmoreland County, Pennsylvania, Tax Records 1815

Rostraver Township Name of Person	Tax
Archibald Stewart	$3.12
210 acres, 5 ~~4~~ horses, 6 ~~4~~ cows	
John Sampson	$1.04
88 acres, 2 horses, 1 ~~2~~ cows	
Isaac Sowash	$0.16
2 horses, 2 cows	
John Spence "Wᵛ"	$0.28
trade, 4 ~~3~~ horses, 4 ~~2~~ cows	
Joseph Spence, single man	$0.50
[??red]	
Robert Spence, single man	$0.50
Abraham Shiplor	$0.08
1 horse, 1 cow	
Philip Shiplor, Junior	$0.08
1 horse, 1 cow	
"Gone"	
~~James~~ Elizabeth Shields, widow	$1.13
68 acres, 1 horse, 1 cow	
Philip Scheaffer, shoemaker	$0.06
trade, 1 cow	
Dorcas Sampson, widow	$3.08
300 acres, 1 horse, 2 ~~1~~ cows	
Thomas Stephens	$0.15
2 horses, 1 cow	
"Gone"	
John Smith, single man	
1 horse	
Thomas Stewart	
trade	
John Stewart	
trade, 1 cow	
Henry Smock	
1 cow	
Solomon Speers, single man	
1 horse	
Mathias Shiplor, Junior	
1 horse, 1 cow	

Abstracts of Westmoreland County, Pennsylvania, Tax Records 1815

Rostraver Township Name of Person	Tax
John Stewart	
1 horse, 1 cow	
Robert Todd	$1.41
90 acres, 1 tanyard, 2 horses, 3 cows	
Jaby Teale, taylor	$0.18
trade, 5 acres, 1 horse	
James Tippins	$0.07
2 ~~1~~ horses	
Nathaniel Tumbleson	$0.16
2 horses, ~~2 cows~~	
Solomon Tumbleson, single man	$0.50
"gone"	
Thomas Thomas	$0.60
50 acres, 2 ~~1~~ horses, 3 ~~2~~ cows	
"see ~~Daniel Shiplor~~"	
Nathan Turner	$0.08
1 horse, 1 cow	
John Tipton	$0.15
2 horses, 1 cow	
Samuel Thomas	$0.51
50 acres, 1 cow, 6 horses	
"see Sampson Shiplor"	
Benjamin Thomas	$1.01
80 acres, 3 horses, 1 cow	
John Vanmetre, Junior	$0.08
1 horse, 1 cow, 50 acres	
John Vanmetre, Senior	$1.50
50 acres	
"See John Vanmetre Gone"	
Peter Vanostrand	$0.28
12 acres, 2 horses, 3 ~~2~~ cows, 50 acres	
Isaac Vankirk, shoemaker	$0.14
trade, 1 horse, 2 cows	
"Gone"	
Joseph Vankirk	$0.75
34 acres, 1/2 a sawmill	
Jacob Weaver, tanner	$0.06

Abstracts of Westmoreland County, Pennsylvania, Tax Records 1815

Rostraver Township Name of Person	Tax
trade, 1 horse, 1 cow	
~~Ebenzer~~ Mary Walker, widow	$3.24
300 acres, 1 ~~3~~ horses, 3 cows	
David Wilson, "yough"	$0.39
37 acres, 2 cows	
David Wilson	$0.50
50 acres, ~~2 cows~~	
Jacob Wigle, gunsmith	$0.48
trade, 10 acres, 1 sawmill, 1 horse	
William Woolsey	$4.86
335 acres, 4 horses, 7 cows, "an old slave"	
John Wortman	$0.23
3 horses, 2 cows	
"Gone"	
John Wright, Esquire	$2.07
142 acres, 4 ~~2~~ horses, 2 ~~3~~ cows	
Hugh Wright	$1.51
100 acres, 2 horses, 2 ~~3~~ cows	
Philip Wright, Esquire	$1.89
100 acres, 4 ~~3~~ horses, 2 cows	
Richard Wells	$0.06
2 cows	
"Gone"	
Joseph Wortman	$0.23
2 ~~3~~ horses, 2 cows	
John Wortman, single man	$0.50
Lot Wortman, Junior, single man	$0.50
P. Joseph Waddel	$1.53
130 acres, 4 ~~3~~ horses, 3 ~~2~~ cows	
Nancy Wilson, widow	$2.02
186 acres, 2 horses, 2 cow	
Reverend William Wylie	$2.38
165 acres, 2 horses, 5 ~~4~~ cows	
James Widdel, blacksmith	$0.16
1 horse, 1 cow	
Thomas Ward, carpenter	$0.13
trade, 1 horse, 1 cow	

Rostraver Township Name of Person	Tax
"gone"	
John Watkins, single man	$0.50
"Gone"	
Jeremiah Walkins, single man	$0.57
trade, ~~1 horse~~	
Sam¹ Wallace, cooper	$0.06
trade	
"Gone"	
B. Joseph Weddel	$0.72
217 acres	
"See Isaac Morgan Daniel [illegible]"	
Lot Wortmand, Senior	$0.08
1 horse, 1 cow	
Isaac Wilgus	$0.08
2 ± horses, 1 cow	
Thomas Warren	$0.40
30 acres, 1/8 of a sawmill	
Daniel Worley	$0.06
2 cows	
"gone"	

Abstracts of Westmoreland County, Pennsylvania, Tax Records 1815

Salem Township Name of Person	Tax
William Armstrong	$0.76
150 acres, 2 horses, 2 cows	
Thomas Armstrong	$0.50
80 acres, 2 horses, 2 cows	
"one horse less"	
L. John Adair, taylor	$0.40
70 acres, 1 horse, 2cows	
Friderich Amont	$2.51
145 acres, 4 ~~3~~ horses, 5 ~~3~~ cows	
James Armstrong, single man	$2.55
200 acres, 1 horse, 1 cow	
David Anderson	$0.66
185 acres, 1 horse, 1 cow	
Nathaniel Alexander	$1.60
168 acres, 3 horses, 4 cows	
William Alexander	$0.06
1 horse, 1 cow	
Robert Alexander, single man	$0.50
James Armstrong, single man	
2 horses, 2 cows	
John Boyles, taylor	$0.10
1 cow	
John Bush	$1.75
100 acres, 1 horse, 1 cow	
David Brown	$1.32
250 acres, 2 ~~4~~ cows [sic], 1 horse	
Alexander Brown	$0.06
2 cows, ~~1 horse~~	
George Burns	$0.06
2 horses, 1 cow	
William Bittz, weaver	$0.06
1 cow	
John Brown	$0.06
1 cow	
William Brice, single man, tenant	$2.58
250 acres	

Abstracts of Westmoreland County, Pennsylvania, Tax Records 1815

Salem Township Name of Person	Tax
Michael Borts	$0.13
15 acres	
John Barlean	$0.37
100 acres, 2 ~~1~~ horses, 3 ~~2~~ cows	
William Beard	$2.20
173 acres, 3 horses, 3 cows	
Patrick Boyle, single man	$0.56
1 horse	
David Buchanan	$2.17
227 acres, 141 acres, 3 horses, 2 cows	
John Buchanan	$0.07
1 horse, 1 cow	
William Buchanan, single man	$0.50
Thomas Buchanan, single man	$0.50
Ezekiel Brice, single man	$0.60
2 horses, 1 cow, 1 cow	
George Bear, blacksmith	$0.12
1 horse, 1 cow	
Hugh Boyd, taylor	$0.10
1 cow	
George Brown	$0.10
2 horses, 2 cows	
James Borland	$0.06
1 horse	
"gone"	
Thomas ~~Charles~~ Beard	$1.17
200 acres, 1 horse, 1 cow	
John Bovard, Senior	$1.33
200 acres	
John Bovard, Junior	$0.17
3 ~~2~~ horses, 4 cows	
Major Hugh Bigham, store keeper	$1.10
175 acres, 3 horses, 2 cows, 4 lots and houses	
Samuel Bigham, single man	$0.50
1 house and lot, 1 horse	
William Barnet, single man	$0.50
Hugh Bigham	$0.13

Abstracts of Westmoreland County, Pennsylvania, Tax Records 1815

Salem Township Name of Person	Tax
51 acres	
"carried up to the other"	
Daniel Borts	
1 horse, 1 cow	
George Bricker	
1 grist and sawmill, 2 steers, 1 cow	
James Bell, "Tealer"	
1 house and lot, 1 horse, 1 cow	
Robert Barnet	
1 horse, 1 cow	
Jacob Barlin	
1 lot	
Thomas Bigham	
1 lot	
Barnebas Blor	
1 lot	
William Caruthers	$0.28
78 acres, 4 ½ cows	
Philip Cyphert	$0.13
2 horses, 2 cows	
Anthony Cyphert, single man	$0.50
David Cruckshanks	
2 lots	
Samuel Cochran	$1.33
150 acres, 2 ½ horses, 3 cows	
William Cochran, single man	$0.50
"moved"	
James Christy, Junior	$1.15
100 acres, 2 horses, 3 cows	
Jean Campbell, widow	$0.63
160 acres, 2 horses, 2 cows	
William Clark, weaver	$0.10
2 horses, 2 cows	
"gone"	
Robert Culbertson, wheelwright	$1.03
208 acres, 1 horse, 2 cows, 1 horse	
Alexander Campbell	$1.60

Abstracts of Westmoreland County, Pennsylvania, Tax Records 1815

Salem Township Name of Person	Tax
150 acres, 145 acres	
Henry Campbell, single man	$1.28
100 acres, 3 horses, 3 cows	
John Christy, Senior	$2.72
400 acres, 1 horse, 2 cows	
John Christy, Junior	$0.13
2 horses, 1 cow	
Elizabeth Caldwell, widow	$0.08
1 horse, 2 cows, 120 acres	
Henry Clymer	$0.52
206 acres	
James Caldwell	$0.06
1 horse, 1 cow	
George Campbell, single man	$0.50
William Crasgay, single man	$0.50
Samuel Calhoon	$0.68
100 acres, 2 ± horses, 2 ± cows	
James Christy, Senior	$1.67
200 acres, 4 2 horses, 2 cows	
James Christy	$0.06
2 ± horses, 1 cow	
Joseph Christy, single man	$0.50
"is gone"	
Patrick Colgin's heirs	$1.19
238 acres	
Samuel Cooper	$1.68
335 acres	
Gasper Clingelsmith	$0.47
100 acres, 2 horses, 3 2 cows	
Andrew Clingelsmith, single man	$0.50
John Clingelsmith, blacksmith	
John Cochran	$1.51
150 acres, 3 2 horses, 2 cows	
"Soald to Samuel McCutchon"	
Christopher Connor	$1.90
200 acres, 2 horses, 2 cows	
Robert Cowan, weaver	$0.32

Abstracts of Westmoreland County, Pennsylvania, Tax Records 1815

Salem Township Name of Person	Tax
70 acres, 2 horses, 1 cow	
Samuel Campbell, tenant	$2.37
300 acres, 2 horses, 3 cows	
William Cunningham	$0.06
1 cow	
Robert Cunningham	$0.06
1 cow	
Barbara Coffman	$0.52
206 acres	
James Craig, single man	$0.50
Robert Culbertson, cabinetmaker, single man	$0.52
"gone"	
General Alexander Craig	$5.38
500 acres, 3 horses, 5 cows, 2 stills	
"out still on in"	
William Cander	
1 horse, 1 cow	
Joseph Campbell, single man	
James Dobbins, single man	$0.52
1 horse	
Thomas Dickey	$0.78
100 acres, 2 horses, 3 2 cows	
William Dickey	$0.08
2 horses	
"Gone"	
Jacob Dry, joiner	$0.31
50 acres, 1 horse, 1 cow, 1 lot	
David Dickey, single man	$0.90
160 acres, 2 horses, 2 cows	
Patrick Duffey, cooper	$0.23
1 horse, 1 cow	
Samuel Dickson, single man	$0.50
Nicholas Day	$0.17
1 house and lot	
John Dickey	$2.98
240 acres, 4 horses, 3 cows	
George Dickey	$1.58

Salem Township Name of Person	Tax
190 acres, 2 horses	
[167 written above 190]	
John Doyle, shoemaker	$0.06
1 cow	
Johnnathan Deemmer	
1 still, 1 cow	
Jacob Divil	
2 lots	
John Edgar	$0.13
1 still, 1 ө horses, 3 cows	
Robert Faster	$3.48
189 acres, 86 acres, 3 horses, 3 cows, 1 cow	
Alexander Foster	$1.07
200 acres, 1 horse, 2 cows, 1 horse	
Christopher Fennel	$1.56
342 acres, 2 horses, 4 cows	
Michael Fennel, weaver	$0.08
1 horse, 1 cow	
John Fennel	$0.08
1 horse, 1 cow	
Henry Fry	$0.06
1 horse, 2 ɫ cows	
Andrew Fry	$0.07
2 ɫ horses, 2 ɫ cows	
John Fry	$0.57
100 acres, 1 horse, 1 cow	
Michael France	$0.06
1 horse, 1 cow	
"gone"	
Laurence Fry	$0.06
2 horses	
John Fleming, single man	$0.50
"gone"	
Peter George	
William Guthrie	$1.97
200 acres, 4 5 horses, 3 cows, new stone house	
William Graham	$0.06

Abstracts of Westmoreland County, Pennsylvania, Tax Records 1815

Salem Township Name of Person	Tax
1 horse, 1 cow	
[no given name] Gregg	$1.04
200 acres, 2 horses, 1 cow	
"for Robert Smith's land"	
John Hill	$1.73
1 grist and sawmill, 13 acres	
"George Break in Hill's place"	
John Harshey	$1.15
120 acres, 3 horses, 3 cows, 2 stills	
Joseph Harshey, single man	$0.50
"Married"	
Robert Hart, single man	$0.50
John Hart	$2.98
300 acres, 45 acres, 4 horses, 3 cows, 1 negro slave	
William Hart, cabinetmaker	$0.13
1 horse, 1 cow	
John Hartley, tanner	$0.10
1 horse	
"gone"	
Andrew Horn	$1.87
92 acres, 265 acres, 3 2 horses, 3 cows	
Solomon Horn, single man	$0.50
George Horn, single man	$0.50
Joseph Harvey	$0.77
100 acres, 2 horses, 3 cows	
John Hillburn	$0.13
2 horses, 3 4 cows	
Samuel Hillburn, single man	$0.50
Robert Hays	$0.11
3 horses, 2 cows	
Daniel Hawk, tenant	$1.12
150 acres, 2 horses, 3 cows	
"Bought Daniel Hawk William Ramsey"	
"William Ramsey lives on the land"	
Samuel Henry, single man	$0.50
Benjamin Hill	$0.45

Abstracts of Westmoreland County, Pennsylvania, Tax Records 1815

Salem Township Name of Person	Tax
10 acres, 1 tanyard, 2 ~~1~~ horses, 1 ~~2~~ cows	
Adam Hocken, cooper	$1.13
150 acres, 2 horses, 2 cows	
Robert Henry	$1.55
195 acres, 3 horses, 3 cows	
Thomas Henry, cabinetmaker	$1.07
94 acres, 0 acres, 1 ~~2~~ horse 2 cows	
"the 2 [?] acres not his"	
Robert Hunter, Esquire	$3.21
252 acres, 4 horses, 4 cows, 100 acres, 1 lot	
James Hunter	
50 acres, 1 horse, 2 cows	
James Hollidy	
1 lot	
James Irwin	$0.25
5 horses, 5 cows, 140 acres	
"the land to Mr Murphy"	
William Irwin, single man	$0.50
James Irwin, Junior	$0.06
1 cow, 3 acres	
Joseph Irwin	$0.06
1 cow, 3 acres	
William Johnston	$2.30
172 ~~160~~ acres, 3 horses, 5 ~~0~~ cows	
John Johnston, Junior	$0.08
2 horses, 2 cows	
John Johnston, Senior	$1.40
150 acres, 3 horses, 2 cows	
Joseph Johnston	$3.57
350 acres, 2 stills, 4 horses, 3 cows	
Andrew Johnston, single man	$0.50
Matthew Jack, Esquire	$6.63
300 acres, 287 acres, 4 5 [sic] horses, 4 cows	
Samuel Jack, single man	$0.50
Job Johnston	$0.67
100 acres, 2 horses, 2 cows, 380 acres	
William Jams	$0.62

Abstracts of Westmoreland County, Pennsylvania, Tax Records 1815

Salem Township Name of Person	**Tax**
94 acres, 2 ± horses, 2 ± cows	
William Jack, Esquire	$0.50
100 acres	
William Irwin	
2 horses, 1 cow	
Robert Johnston, fuller	
1 cow	
Jacob Keppel, blacksmith	$0.98
90 acres, 2 horses, 3 cows, 55 acres	
Major William Kean	$2.39
120 acres, 33 acres, 1 stud horse, 3 horses, 3 cows	
Paul Kean, single man	$0.50
Jacob Kunkle	$1.25
130 acres, 1 4 horses, 2 cows	
Samuel Kelly	$0.06
2 cows	
Major John Kirkpatrick	$8.68
1 grist and sawmill, 393 acres, 300 acres, 4 3 horses, 4 cows	
David Kerr	$2.42
400 acres, 1 horse, 2 cows	
Jean Kinley, widow	$1.20
200 acres, 2 cows	
Samuel Kinley	$0.54
100 acres, 1 horse	
Charles Kinely, doctor	$0.06
1 cow	
George Kibler	$1.12
200 acres, 2 horses, 3 cows	
Isaac Keck	$1.11
222 acres	
John Kirkpatrick, Junior	$0.08
2 stills, 1 horse	
George Keck	$1.24
237 acres, 2 ± horses, 2 cows, a new barn	
James Kelly, Esquire	$1.03
125 acres, 4 horses, 3 cows	

Abstracts of Westmoreland County, Pennsylvania, Tax Records 1815

Salem Township Name of Person	Tax
Nathaniel Kelly	$1.13
150 acres	
Patrick Kerney	
1 horse, 1 cow	
Adam Loughead, shoemaker	$0.06
1 horse	
Samuel Love, weaver	$0.38
60 acres, 2 horses, 2 cows	
Andrew Love	$0.42
100 acres, 2 horses, 2 cows	
William Love, single man	$0.75
75 acres, 1 horse	
John Leighner, weaver	$0.18
44 acres, 1 horse, 1 cow	
Daniel Lutz, tenant	$0.52
100 acres, 1 cow	
John Lenning, single man	$0.50
"Married"	
Isaac Lenning, tenant	$1.38
150 acres, 4 2 horses, 2 cows	~~$1.33~~
David Lattimore, blacksmith	$0.06
1 horse, 1 cow	
"gone"	
William Leighty, hatter	$0.08
100 acres, 2 cows	
"Mr assessor enquire whether James Todd[']s land ought not to be set down to Leighty"	
Jacob Linseybegler, tavern keeper	
191 acres, 2 horses, 2 cows	
John Linnen	
1 lot	
John McCue	$0.25
50 acres, 1 horse, 2 cows	
"may be not right Spelled"	
Thomas McClure	$0.09
4 acres, 1 horse, 1 cow	
John McKellip	$0.13

Abstracts of Westmoreland County, Pennsylvania,
Tax Records 1815

Salem Township Name of Person	Tax
2 horses, 2 cows	
"gone"	
Daniel McGaw	$0.06
1 cow	
Abraham Mansfield, single man	$0.55
1 horse	
George Michael	$0.29
55 acres, 1 cow, 2 horses	
Thomas Meason	$2.77
198 acres, 3 horses, 2 cows	
Daniel McKnight	$0.06
1 horse, 1 cow	
"gone"	
William Moore, single man	$3.80
308 acres, 3 horses, 3 cows, 2 stills	
Alex^r McBride	$0.12
2 horses, 3 cows	
"gone"	
James McBride	$1.91
179 acres, 200 acres, 2 horses, 3 cows	
the 200 acres was "sold to Stewart W^m"	
Daniel Morrison	$0.97
121 acres, 2 horses, 3 cows	
Stephen McHafffey, single man	$0.06
1 horse	
"gone"	
Samuel Mehaffey	$0.90
250 acres, 1 horse, 2 ₊ cows	
Archibald McLuster, shoemaker	$0.20
2 horses, 2 ₃ cows	
Hannah Moore, widow	$1.10
150 acres, 2 horses, 2 cows	
Adam McCallister, single man	$0.53
1 horse	
"Gone"	
William Moore, waggoner, single man	$0.57
2 horses	

Abstracts of Westmoreland County, Pennsylvania, Tax Records 1815

Salem Township Name of Person	Tax
"gone"	
Agness McConnel	$0.52
100 acres, 1 cow	
John Mirn?n, "Cabinet," single man	
1 lot	
Thomas McGonnigal	$0.06
2 horses, 1 cow	
James McLaughlen	$0.15
2 horses, 3 cows	
"in Hannastown"	
Samuel McCutchen	$1.60
150 ~~100~~ acres, 2 horses, 2 cows	
Barney Mullen, tenant	$0.38
50 acres, 2 horses, 2 cows	
Agness Morrison, widow	$0.53
50 acres, 1 horse, 1 cow	
Jacob Miller, cooper	$1.32
185 acres, 2 horses, 1 cow, 1 cow	
James McKee	$0.28
65 acres, 1 horse, 1 cow, 1 cow	
David McClelland	$0.85
1 grist and sawmill, 1 cow, 1 horse	
William McClelland, blacksmith	$1.02
100 acres, 1 horse, 2 cows	
Samuel McCalley	$0.06
1 horse, 1 cow	
"Gone"	
James Mann, weaver	$0.07
1 cow, 1 horse	
Colonel Thomas McQuead	$2.27
200 acres, 1 ~~2~~ still, 2 horses 2 3 [sic] cows, 1 lot	
Patrick McQuead	$3.50
250 acres, 100 acres	
James McQuilkin, single man	$1.85
150 acres, 2 horses, 2 cows	
"1 horse Less"	
Daniel McQuilkin	$0.92

Salem Township Name of Person	Tax
130 acres, 1 horse, 1 cow	
"1 horse Less"	
John McJunken	$0.08
2 horses, 1 cow	
"gone"	
Matthew McKellep, single man	$1.36
136 acres, 1 horse, 1 ~~2~~ cow	
James McKellep	$0.87
132 acres, 2 horses, 2 cows	
William Martz	$0.23
18 acres, 1 cow	
Robert McIlwain	$1.03
100 acres, 2 horses, 4 ~~3~~ cows	
James McClelland	$1.03
200 acres, 2 cows, 1 horse	
John McClelland	$0.10
2 horses, 2 cows	
George Menium	$1.20
200 acres, 2 stills, 2 ~~1~~ horses, 2 cows	
James McSourley	$0.06
1 horse, 1 cow	
James McKissock, single man	$1.85
168 acres, 2 stills, 2 horses, 4 cows	
"Mkessock Soald to Robert Keany"	
Joseph McKessock, single man	$1.77
168 acres, 3 horses, 3 cows	
"Gone"	
Michael McLaughlen	$0.15
3 horses, 3 cows	
Michael McLaoughlin, single man	
Samuel Moorhead, single man	$2.40
150 acres, 2 horses, 1 ~~3~~ cow	
James Moorhead, single man	$0.50
James Moore, Senior	$3.63
300 acres, 1 still, 1 horse, 2 cows	
James Moore, single man	$0.50
2 horses, 2 cows	

Abstracts of Westmoreland County, Pennsylvania, Tax Records 1815

Salem Township Name of Person	Tax
Michael McGinley, taylor	$0.12
2 cows	
Samuel Miller, weaver	$0.07
2 cows, 2 horses	
Robert McCullough	$0.06
1 cow	
John Moore, single man	$0.50
William Moore, Senior	$2.08
200 acres, 2 horses, 2 ~~1~~ cows	
Benjamin McKee	$0.06
1 cow	
William Moore, Junior	$0.96
100 acres, 3 horses, 3 cows	
James Moore, Junior	$0.75
100 acres, 2 horses, 2 cows	
David McConnel	$1.82
264 acres, 1 horse, 2 cows	
John McCutchen, single man	$1.76
189 acres	
George Moor, single man	$0.50
Niclose Morse	
1 lot	
William ~~Robert~~ Marshal, tanner	$0.50
100 acres, 2 horses, 1 cow, new barn	
Phillip Millear	$0.06
2 cows	
James McKisseck, single man	$0.78
63 acres, 2 horses, 3 cows	
Moses Murfy	$2.35
6 horses, 4 cows, 122 [?] acres, 1 "Mill Scut"	
James Moohead	
1 horse, 1 cow	
Samuel McCullough, stiller, single man	
John Moor, Senior	
2 horses, 1 cow	
Jacob Myers	
2 horses, 2 cows	

Abstracts of Westmoreland County, Pennsylvania, Tax Records 1815

Salem Township Name of Person	Tax
Frederick Myers	
George Nunemaker	$0.46
71 acres, 3 horses, 2 3 cows	
William Neal, weaver	$0.15
44 acres, 1 cow	
Anthony Newhouse	$1.82
200 acres, 2 3 horses, 3 cows	
Henry Newhouse, single man	$0.50
1 horse	
"Marred"	
Henry Nunemaker, blacksmith	$0.06
1 cow, 2 horses	
Henry Neely, shoemaker	$0.15
1 house and lot, 2 cows, 1 lot	
Edward O'Hara, single man	$0.50
"Gone"	
Eve Orey	$0.08
1 house and lot, 1 cow	
Jacob Moor	
1 lot	
John Pifer	$1.05
140 acres, 2 horses, 1 cow, 1 cow, 1 still	
George Pifer	$0.67
100 acres, 1 cow, 2 horses	
Reverend Samuel Porter	$1.53
178 acres, 1 horse	
William Porter	$0.13
2 horses, 4 2 cows	
John Porter	$1.17
220 acres, 1 horse, 1 cow	
John Palmer	$0.06
1 cow	
John Patrick	$0.13
1 house and lot	
John Penner [?]	
1 cow	
William Peppels	

Abstracts of Westmoreland County, Pennsylvania, Tax Records 1815

Salem Township Name of Person	Tax
100 acres, 3 horses, 2 cows, 70 acres the 70 acres "from Hunter" John Rolls	
1 lot Chester Ringer	
1 lot George Ruffner	$0.10
2 horses, 2 cows William Ralston	$1.13
115 acres, 2 ~~1~~ horses, 2 ~~1~~ cows Henry Righard	$0.08
1 ~~2~~ horse, 1 cow James Reed	$0.69
137 acres, 2 horses John ~~James~~ Riddel, wagon maker	$0.06
1 cow John Ralston	$1.56
225 acres, 2 ~~3~~ horses, 2 ~~3~~ cows James Robison, single man	$0.50
184 ~~acres, 1 horse, 1 cow~~ "gone" James Ralston, single man	$0.50
184 acres, 1 horse, 1 cow Robert Ralston, single man	$0.50
William Richey	$0.45
120 acres, 1 horse, 1 cow Michael Ringer	$1.22
130 acres, 3 horses, 3 cows William Riddel	$0.95
170 acres, 3 ~~2~~ horses, 3 ~~2~~ cows Frederich Rinehart	$0.35
100 acres, 1 cow, 1 horse Frederich Rimmel	$0.06
1 horse, 1 cow Abraham Reamer	$0.94
160 acres, 1 ~~2~~ horse, 2 cows Robert Reamey	$2.03

Abstracts of Westmoreland County, Pennsylvania, Tax Records 1815

Salem Township Name of Person	Tax
174 acres	
Robert Roseberry, single man	$0.50
Robert Reaney	
187 acres, 174 acres, 2 stills, 4 horses, 4 cows	
Andrew Reart	
1 cow	
John Stoops	$0.10
2 horses, 2 cows	
Robert Stoops	$0.97
177 acres, 1 horse, 2 cows	
Elizabeth Silveys	$0.70
130 acres, 1 horse, 1 cow	
John Shaw	$1.23
139 acres, 2 ⊥ horses, 2 cows	
David Shaw	$0.90
120 acres, 2 horses, 1 cow	
Alexander Shaw	$1.05
105 acres, 2 horses, 2 cows	
Abraham Shuster	$0.06
2 cows	
Leonard Sourwine	$0.25
50 acres, 2 cows	
John Shryoch	$2.00
183 acres, 2 3 horses, 4 cows	
David Shryock, single man	$0.50
1 lot	
Robert Shields	$2.40
210 acres, 149 acres, 3 horses, 2 cows	
John Snyder	$0.16
26 acres, 2 horses	
Emmanuel Server, blacksmith	$0.55
95 acres, 2 horses, 2 cows	
Joernthan Server	
"the oner [sic] of the Land	
Ludwick Shearer	$0.90
100 acres, 2 horses, 1 cow	
John Shearer, single man	$0.50

Abstracts of Westmoreland County, Pennsylvania, Tax Records 1815

Salem Township Name of Person	Tax
John Shields, Esquire	$2.50
250 acres, 1 horse, 2 cows	
James Shields, Junior	$0.10
2 horses, 3 ~~2~~ cows	
John Shields, blacksmith	$0.10
1 horse, 1 ~~2~~ cow	
~~John Shields, single man~~	$0.50
Samuel Shaw	$0.93
77 acres, 2 horses, 2 ~~3~~ cows	
William Stewart	$0.76
63 acres, 2 horses, 2 cows, 200 acres	
"Six three Soul to Mke??"	
James Stewart	$1.26
87 acres, 2 horses, 2 cows	
James Shearer	$0.06
1 horse, 1 cow, 91 acres	
James Shields, Senior	$1.26
220 acres, 3 horses, 3 cows	
George Shields	$1.20
205 acres, 2 ~~3~~ horses, 2 cows, 1 cow	
Nicholas Sharp, shoemaker	$0.18
3 horses, 4 cows	
John Steel, blacksmith, single man	$1.58
170 acres, 2 horses, 1 cows, 2 cows	
John Sloan	$1.40
175 acres, 4 horses, 5 ~~4~~ cows	
Ralph Spoul	$0.08
2 horses, 2 cows	
Michael Slonaker	$0.17
4 horses, 1 ~~4~~ cow, 149 acres	
George Stewart	$1.67
[22]5 acres, 3 horses, 4 cows	
William Stewart, Junior	$0.06
2 cows	
Thomas Sterret	$0.57
1 horse, 2 cows	
Henry Selves	

Abstracts of Westmoreland County, Pennsylvania, Tax Records 1815

Salem Township Name of Person	**Tax**
2 horses, 1 cow	
Philip Typret	
2 horses, 2 cows	
Antony Typhert, single man	
George Sloaker, single man	
Samuel Shryock, single man	
Mathew Shields, single man	
Jacob Savil	
2 horses, 1 cow	
Mary Shareden, widow	
1 horse, 2 cows	
Philip Shelhamer	
1 lot	
Samuel Shryock	
1 lot	
James Tittle	$1.55
[160] acres, 4 horses, 3 cows	
James Todd, blacksmith	$0.12
1 horse, 1 cow	
James Taylor	$0.63
100 acres, 2 horses, 2 1 cows	
Baltzer Trout	$1.00
172 acres, 3 2 horses, 3 cows	
James Trimble	$0.31
94 acres	
"Soald to James Sherrer"	
John Tom, single man	$0.50
"gone to Stump Creek"	
Samuel Torrance, carpenter	
John Williamson	$1.40
200 acres, 1 horse, 2 cows	
Frederick Williard	$0.55
100 acres, 1 horse, 1 cow, 2 cows	
John Williams	$2.40
240 acres	
Joseph Whitmore	$0.18
1 stud horse, 1 cow	

Abstracts of Westmoreland County, Pennsylvania, Tax Records 1815

Salem Township Name of Person	Tax
"Gone"	
John Woods, Esquire	$4.50
500 acres, 1 distillery, 4 horses, 4 cows	
John Woods, single man	$0.50
James Williamson	$0.06
1 horse, 1 cow	
Robert Wylie	$0.67
94 acres, 4 horses, 2 cows	
"it appears this land is sold charge it right M^r assessor"	
Albert Wylie, single man	$1.12
97 acres, 1 horse, 1 cow	
"the Wills Gone Down the River"	
"gone"	
Hugh Wylie	$0.06
1 horse, 1 cow	
Braglar Waller	$0.06
1 lot	
Philip Walter	$0.96
172 acres, 2 horses, 3 ½ cows	
George Walter	$0.64
115 acres, 2 ½ horses, 2 ½ cows	
Thomas Wilson	$0.87
613 [?] acres, 1 cows, 1 horse, 2 lots	
Peter Waggoner "Wagaman"	$0.20
28 acres, 1 cow	
"Soald"	
Gasper Williard, shoemaker	$0.06
1 horse	
Peter Walter	$1.06
147 acres, 1 horse, 4 cows	
Henry White, single man	$0.57
1 house and lot	
Joseph White	$0.06
1 cow	
George Wilson, joiner	$0.06
1 horse	

Abstracts of Westmoreland County, Pennsylvania, Tax Records 1815

Salem Township Name of Person	Tax
"Gone"	
Joseph Weigley, Esquire	$1.33
100 acres	
"Sold to peoples Says the last Ass"	
Peter Wagaman	
159 acres, 1 horse, 2 cows	
John Young, Senior	$1.32
180 acres, 2 horses, 3 cows	
John Young, single man	$1.15
97 acres	
James Young, single man	$0.50
John Young, Esquire	$0.60
350 acres	
John Young, Junior	$0.88
137 acres, 2 horses, 2 cows	
Thomas Young	$2.67
310 acres, 2 horses, 2 cows	
Mary Young, widow	$1.12
150 acres, 2 horses, 2 cows	
Joseph McCormick, single man	
1 lot	
Adam Reed, single man	
James Reed, single man	
Joseph Reed	
1 lot	
Abraham Varner	$0.08
2 horses, 2 cows	
"Gone"	
Henry McKever	$0.08
1 horse, 1 cow	
Jacob Reachart, weaver	$0.27
28 acres, 2 cows	
George Smith	$0.08
1 horse, 1 cow	
Thomas Willson	$0.06
1 horse, 1 cow	

Abstracts of Westmoreland County, Pennsylvania, Tax Records 1815

Abstracts of Westmoreland County, Pennsylvania, Tax Records 1815

South Huntingdon Township Name of Person	Tax
Ann Armstrong	$0.07
10 acres, 1 cow	
John Aspie	$0.09
1 horse, 2 cows	
Jacob Aspie	$0.84
130 acres, 1 horse, 3 cows	
James Alexander, taylor	$0.46
84 acres, 1 horse, 2 cows, 1 horse	
Jacob Altman	$0.06
2 lots	
James Agnew, single man, taylor [?]	
Samuel Armstrong	
300 acres, 2 horses, 3 cows	
John Beaumont	$0.51
89 acres, 2 horses, 2 cows	
John Beatty	$0.07
1 horse, 2 cows	
"dead"	
John Barr	$3.11
216 acres, "2=4" horses, 2 cows, 100 gallon still, 1 cow	
Abraham Bodle	$0.06
1 cow	
"Runaway"	
Jacob Brenneman	$4.30
293 acres, 2 horses, 2 cows	
William Bell, single man, carpenter	$0.56
Thomas Baldridge, boat builder	$0.06
1 cow, 1 horse	
Robert Baldridge	$1.63
230 acres, 4 horses, 3 cows, 80 acres, 1 gristmill, 1 sawmill	
Charles Bamford, weaver	$0.20
18 acres, 1 horse, 2 cows	
~~John Blair~~	~~$1.22~~

Abstracts of Westmoreland County, Pennsylvania,
Tax Records 1815

South Huntingdon Township Name of Person	Tax
200 acres, 1 horse, 1 cow	
"To J Lillarka & Drum"	
William Baldwin, taylor	$0.14
2 horses, 1 cow	
Phillip Bear	
147 acres, 3 horses, 2 cows	
Doctor James Beatty	$0.87
occupation, 1 lot, ~~1~~ 2 horses, 1 cow	
Gersham Bennet	$2.37
150 acres, 3 horses, 2 cows	
Richard Beaumont	$1.36
200 acres, 3 horses, 3 cows	
Robert Barr, weaver	$0.33
50 acres, 2 horses, 2 cows	
Daniel Black, single man	$0.50
James Baldridge, single man, "blk"	
Walter Bell, joiner	$0.08
1 horse	
Peter Broadswords, single man	$2.33
160 acres, 1 horse	
James Barr, weaver	$0.06
Robert Boyd	$5.11
328 acres, ~~4~~ 5 horses, 5 cows	
Wᵐ Boyd, single man	
John Burton	$0.70
~~100 acres~~, 1 horse, "1=2" cows	
Oliver Brant, single man	$0.50
4 horses	
Jesse Beaumont, single man	$0.50
1 horse	
Philip Beaumont, single man	$0.71
1 horse, 190 gallon still	
Alexander Boyd, blacksmith	
1 horse, 1 cow	
William Clendenning	$0.09
1 horse, 1 cow	

Abstracts of Westmoreland County, Pennsylvania, Tax Records 1815

South Huntingdon Township Name of Person	Tax
John Crise	$0.25
2 acres, 1 sawmill, 2 cows	
John Caruthers, coppersmith	$1.10
66 acres, 67 acres, 2 horse, 2 cows, 1 horse, 1 cow	
John Coffman	$0.06
1 cow	
Andrew Clendenning	$0.46
88 acres, 1 horse, 1 cow	
Elijah Collins	$0.07
1 horse, 1 cow	
Jacob Coter, shoemaker	$0.34
45 acres, 1 horse, 1 cow	
Conrad Coter, Senior	$0.67
100 acres, 1 horse, 2 cows	
Martin Coter	$0.10
1 horse, 2 cows	
Conrad Coter, Junior	$0.24
25 acres, 1 horse, 2 cows	
John Carnahan, Senior	$4.46
300 acres, 2 horses, 2 cows	
John Carnahan, cooper	$0.07
1 horse, 1 cow	
John Cochran [Carnahan crossed out]	$3.02
200 acres, 2 horse, 2 cows, 2 cows	
John Caruthers	$1.91
147 acres, 3 horses, 2 cows	
James Carnahan, tenant	~~$1.40~~
110 acres, 2 horses, 2 cows	
"To Jr Newolls for Land"	
Philip Coter	$1.43
150 acres, 1 sawmill, 2 horses, 2 cows	
John Conkel, tenant	$1.04
80 acres, 2 horses, 2 cows	
"See John C Caruthers for Land"	
John Carlen	$0.07
1 horse, 1 cow	

Abstracts of Westmoreland County, Pennsylvania, Tax Records 1815

South Huntingdon Township Name of Person	Tax
Widow Crice	$0.60
100 acres, 3 horses, 3 cows, 64 gallon still	
Mary Craven, widow	$0.08
20 acres, 1 cow	
Andrew Crice, single man	$0.50
George Crice, ~~single man~~	$0.50
Patrick Cowan	$0.06
1 acre, 1 cow	
Abraham Cope, tenant	$0.55
126 acres, 1 cow	
James Caruthers	$4.44
350 acres, 2 stills, 4 horses, 4 cows, 100 acres	
Ephraim Clark, single man	$0.57
1 horse	
James Calvin, shoemaker	$0.07
1 horse, 1 cow	
George Coter, single man	$0.50
James Carnahan	$0.07
1 horse	
James Cord, single man	$0.50
"Absent"	
William Clark	$1.26
"1=2" horses, 2 cows, 110 acres	
"ad James Thompson Land"	
"Ja^s Hutchesons"	
Benjamin Carnehan, single man	
John Congleton	
1 cow, 1 horse	
John Dunbarr	$0.73
150 acres, 2 horse, ~~1 cow~~	
Robert Donnelly	$0.07
1 horse, 1 cow	
St. Leger De Happart	$3.86
330 acres, 1 horse, 2 cows	
Hugh Darby	$0.61
119 acres, 2 horses, 1 cow	

Abstracts of Westmoreland County, Pennsylvania, Tax Records 1815

South Huntingdon Township Name of Person	Tax
Charles Douglas, weaver	$0.07
1 horse, 2 cows	
John Dillinger, single man	$0.50
1 horse	
Philip Dyel	$0.06
1 cow	
John Dugal, cooper	$0.08
15 acres	
Jacob Dellinger	$0.09
1 horse, 2 cows, 1 horse	
John Dilling	$0.06
1 horse, 1 cow	
[----] Davis	$0.06
1 cow	
"on Bennet[']s place"	
~~M John Eckles~~, single man, joiner	
Charles Douglass, carpenter	
1 house & lot	
Henry Dugal, single man, wheelwright	
William Darby, single man	
John Darby	
1 cow	
M John Eckels, single man, joiner	
John Emberson, single man	
Jacob Fulmer, wagon maker	$0.29
50 acres, 1 horse, 2 cows	
Jacob Fry	$0.10
100 acres, 2 horses, 2 cows, 1 cow	
"on Leppencob place"	
George Frick, ~~single man~~, blacksmith	$0.42
1 horse	
Henry Frick	$0.87
100 acres, 1 cow	
John Frick	$1.74
175 acres, 2 stills (150 gallon), 2 horses, 3 cows	
Henry Fulton, tanner	$0.52

South Huntingdon Township Name of Person	Tax
~~1/2 a tanyard~~, 2 horses, "1=2" cows, 1 tanyard Robert Fulton	$5.53
700 acres, 2 stills (185 gallon), 3 horses, 1 stud horse, 3 cows William Fulton, single man	$0.50
Henry Fulton, tanner, Tobstown	$1.92
9 acres, 5 lots & 1 house, 1 tanyard, 1 horse, 2 cows, 30 acres John Friedt	$1.76
140 acres, 2 horses, 2 cows James Finley, single man, carpenter	$0.52
Henry Funk	$0.89
1 fulling mill, 2 horses, 2 cows Christian Funk, Senior	$6.88
240 acres, 1 gristmill, 1 sawmill, 2 stills (155 gallon), 6 horses, 7 cows Daniel Funk	$0.23
3 horses, 2 cows "In N Huntingdon" Abraham Freidt	
2 cows, 1 horse Robert France, weaver	$0.11
2 horses, 2 cows "In E Huntingdon" Captain John Finley	$0.12
2 horses, 2 cows Andrew Finley, Esquire	$3.81
250 acres, 3 horses, 4 cows John Feathers	$1.30
100 acres, 2 horses, 2 cows John Feathers, ~~single man~~	~~$0.50~~
1 cow Abraham Fulton, single man "Robbtonn" Daniel Fields, single man, "Blk" 1 horse	

246

Abstracts of Westmoreland County, Pennsylvania, Tax Records 1815

South Huntingdon Township Name of Person	Tax
Thomas Forsythe	
1 horse, 1 cow	
Martin Glassburner	$0.12
2 horses, 3 cows, 125 acres	
Daniel Guinn	$0.48
100 acres, 1 horse, 2 cows	
"I suppose Grim Daniel is the wrong name put it right"	
Martin Gaffenney, shoemaker	$0.07
1 horse, 1 cow, 1 cow	
John Gaffenny	$0.06
2 cows	
"no property"	
Edward Gaffenny, tenant	$1.23
~~100 acres~~, 100 acres, 2 horses, 3 cows	
"See James Coruthers for this land"	
William Gibson, ~~single man~~, cooper	$0.52
William Gibson	$1.23
100 acres, 1 horse, 1 cow	
John Gambel	$0.13
1 lot, 1 horse, 2 cows, 1 house, 3 lots, ferry	
George Grim	$1.12
249 acres, 1 horse, 1 cow	
James Gavvin, tenant	$0.93
100 acres, 2 horses	
"on John Leppencotts land"	
"See Jacob Fry for land"	
John Gilbert [?????]master	
1 horse	
John Grimes, single man	
John Griffith, carpenter	
1 cow	
William Gafney, single man	
Jacob George	
144 acres, 2 horses, 2 cows	
James Hite, shoemaker	$0.07

South Huntingdon Township Name of Person	Tax
1 horse, 2 cows, 3 acres	
John Hunter, shoemaker	$0.06
2 cows	
Catharine Hixon	$0.52
100 acres, 1 horse, 1 cow, 1 cow, 1 horse	
Joseph Hixon, single man, carpenter	$0.52
David ~~Hamilton~~ Hall, single man	$0.50
1 horse, 1 cow	
James Hutcheson, single man	$0.50
Daniel Hill	$0.47
95 acres, 1 horse, 1 cow	
William Higgs, miller	$0.43
100 acres	
"add 52 acres"	
Joseph Hough	$3.79
150 acres, 1 grist & sawmill, 2 stills (150 gallon), 2 horses, 3 cows	
Christiana Hamilton	$1.37
100 acres, 2 stills (100 gallon), 2 horses, 1 cow	
William Hunter, weaver	$0.10
1 horse, 1 cow	
William Hunter, Esquire	$1.08
200 acres, 3 horses, 3 cows	
"add 1 cow"	
"Jay 3 Dollars ? acre for Wm Hunters Land"	
"Mr. Hunters land is marked 6 in the column rate per acre in the Original the carried out at the rate of 3"	
Charles Hunter, merchant	$1.56
5 acres, 6 acres, 2 acres, 1 house & lot, 1 horse, 1 cow, 1 ferry, 1 cow	
Jacob Heltebrand	$0.14
2 horses, 2 cows	
Daniel Hepler, potter	$0.16
2 horses, 1 cow	
Daniel Harker	$0.12

Abstracts of Westmoreland County, Pennsylvania, Tax Records 1815

South Huntingdon Township Name of Person	Tax
~~7 acres~~, 1 horse, 1 cow	
Lora Huffman	$0.22
49 acres,1 cow	
Stophel Hepler, shoemaker	$0.18
2 horses, 3 cows, 1 cow	
William Huey	$0.09
1 horse, 2 cows	
Catharine Huey, widow	$1.96
225 acres, 2 cows	
"R & Wᵐ Purgis"	
Robert Hopkins, shoemaker	$0.23
1 cow	
Susanna Hall, widow	$0.23
50 acres, 1 cow	
Moses Hixon, single	$0.50
Thomas Holton, single man	$0.50
James Holton, single man	$0.50
Peter Hough	$1.13
299 acres, 2 stills (168 gallon), 2 horses, "1-2" cows	
Edward Hill	$0.60
100 acres, 2 horses, 2 cows	
George Hill, single man	$0.60
2 stills (140 gallon)	
John Hamilton, single man	$0.50
Joab Hissom, single man	$0.50
William Hutcheson, single man	$0.50
Daniel Hoy, weaver	$0.08
1 horse, 1 cow	
"Dead"	
William Hay, single man, weaver	$0.52
1 horse, 2 cows	
John Hannah	$5.79
300 acres, 150 acres, 3 horses, 3 cows	
"ad 1 cow"	
James Hutcheson	$0.13

South Huntingdon Township Name of Person	Tax
2 horses, 1 cow	
W. John H[-----]	$0.06
2 cows	
David Hunter	$0.60
147 acres	
"See Philip Bear"	
Gaius Hamilton	$0.63
114 acres, 2 horses, 2 cows, 1 horse	
Alexander Hamilton, innkeeper	$1.84
300 acres, "1-2" horses, 1 cow	
Amos Hixon, carpenter	$0.06
1 cow	
John Huey	$0.11
1 still (73 gallon), 1 horse, 1 cow	
John Hunter, innkeeper	$0.59
2 stills (117 gallon), 4 horses, 6 cows	
John Hartman, single man	$0.50
Robert Hartley, single man, tanner	$0.52
John Hannah	$0.06
1 horse, "1-2" cows, 100 acres	
Alice Hamilton, widow	$1.35
214 acres, 1 horse, 2 cows, ~~1 still~~	
Daniel Hutcheson	$0.07
1 horse, 1 cow	
Ebenezer Haydon	$0.16
10 acres, 1 horse, 2 cows	
James Hannah, single man	$0.50
Paul Hough	$0.20
35 acres	
Samuel Howard, single man	
Christopher Herrald	
2 horses, 2 cows	
Mary Hokenshall, widow	
1 horse, 1 cow	
James Huey, blacksmith	
1 horse, 1 cow	

Abstracts of Westmoreland County, Pennsylvania, Tax Records 1815

South Huntingdon Township Name of Person	Tax
Steven Hendricks, single man, miller	
Robert Hunter, shoemaker	
Alexander Henderson, single man	
Thomas Hannah, single man	
Alexander Hannah	
1 cow	
Joab Hirrüm, single man, carpenter	
Alexander Johes, saddler	
Abraham Jewry, blacksmith	$0.13
4 acres, 1 horse, "1=2" cows, 85 acres	
James Johnston, tenant	$1.11
256 acres, 1 cow	
John Irwin	$0.86
200 acres	
Charles Kelly, blacksmith	$0.06
1 horse	
Mathew Kelly, single man	$0.56
1 horse	
George Kelly	$0.44
100 acres, 1 cow	
Adam Kelly	$0.73
150 acres, 1 horse, 1 cow	
Daniel Kelly	$0.67
100 acres, 1 horse, 2 cows, 1 horse	
James Kelly, Senior	$0.96
150 acres, 1 horse, 2 cows	
William Kelly	$0.07
1 horse	
James Kelly, Junior	$0.52
100 acres, 1 horse, 1 cow	
Andrew Kerr	$0.69
80 acres, 1 gristmill, 1 sawmill	
"See Robert Baldridge"	
Adam Kerr	$0.93
100 acres, 1 horse, 1 cow	
Christian Keneagy	$2.40

South Huntingdon Township Name of Person	Tax
150 acres, 3 horses, 2 4 cows	
William Karscadden	$0.59
1 horse, 1 cow	
"ad 1 horse"	
Elizabeth Kean	$0.09
1 house & lot	
"See John Sloan M^{rA}"	
John ~~Adam~~ Kline, single man, wheelwright	$1.00
78 acres, 1 horse, 1 cow	
David Lucar	$0.07
1 house & lot	
Robert Lemmons, single man	$0.57
1 horse, 1 cow	
Michael Lemmons	$0.09
1 horse, 2 cows	
Henry Lake, single man	$0.50
Simon Long, weaver	$0.16
30 acres, 1 cow	
Joseph Longhead	$1.86
150 acres, 2 horses, 2 cows	
William Longhead, single man	$0.50
George Likes, shoemaker	$0.06
1 cow, 1 cow	
Thomas Lindsay	$0.31
40 acres, 1 horse, 1 cow	
"Read Montgomery Samuel for Land"	
Joseph Lloyd, innkeeper	$0.53
2 off 6 horses, 2 cows, 3 cows, still (117 gallon)	
William Laugh[----], single man	$0.58
"Listed in the army"	
"I can[']t make out his name"	
John Latta, single man, merchant	
1 horse	
John Lemmon, single man	
James McWilliams	~~$0.34~~
~~40 acres~~, 3 horses, 3 cows	

Abstracts of Westmoreland County, Pennsylvania, Tax Records 1815

South Huntingdon Township Name of Person	Tax
Henry McClintock	$1.82
150 acres, 1 horse, 2 cows	
Adam Millar, joiner	$0.06
1 cow, 1 cow	
Michael Millar, joiner	$0.06
1 cow	
James Miligan, joiner	$0.66
~~Isaac Morgan~~	
1 house & 2 lots, 1 horse, ~~3 cows~~, 1 cow	
"Read Milligan James Joiner"	
Alexr McClintock, weaver	$0.15
2 horses, 2 cows	
Jean Morrow, widow	$0.21
45 acres, 1 cow	
John Myers	
100 acres, 2 horses, 3 cows, 1 sawmill	
Samuel Mitchel, weaver	$0.70
126 acres, "1=2" horses, "1=2" cows	
Robert McGuffey	$1.00
88 acres, 2 stills (90 gallon), 2 horses, 4 cows, ~~30 acres~~	
"add 11 acres of Land"	
John Martin	$0.17
2 horses, 2 cows	
William Martin	$3.03
200 acres, 2 horses, 2 cows	
David McClelland, blacksmith	$0.12
1 horse, 2 cows	
David Montgomery	$0.43
100 acres	
John McClelland	$0.70
140 acres "1-2" horses, 1 cow	
Samuel Morrow, single man	$0.56
1 horse	
Elizabeth Morrow, widow	$0.32
75 acres	

Abstracts of Westmoreland County, Pennsylvania, Tax Records 1815

South Huntingdon Township Name of Person	Tax
John Morrow, cooper	$0.63
121 acres, 2 horses, 2 cows	
William Morrow, cooper	$0.62
121 acres "1-2" horses, 1 cow	
James Morrow, cooper	$0.18
26 acres, 1 horse, 1 cow	
Jacob Markle, ~~single man~~	
"1=2" horses, 3 cows	
Gasper Markle, Senior	$8.40
352 acres, 1 grist & sawmill, 4 horses, 8 cows	
Philip Mellander	$0.62
100 acres, 1 horse "Stone blind," 2 cows	
Robert McCormick, cooper	$0.11
1 horse, 2 cows	
James McGuffey	$0.15
1 still (102 gallon) 1 horse, 1 cow	
Benjamin Miller, shoemaker	$0.10
1 horse, 2 cows	
Susanna Millar, widow	$0.41
41 acres, 1 horse	
Charles Mitchel	$2.40
150 acres, 3 horses, 3 cows	
Sarah Morrow, widow	$1.99
444 acres, 1 horse, 2 cows	
William McClintock, nailor	$0.42
1 house & lot, 1 out lot, 1 horse, 1 cow	
David Morton, gunsmith	$0.77
1 house & lot, 1 out lot, 1 cow, 1 horse	
Thomas McMullen	$0.63
66 acres, 1 horse, 1 cow, 1 horse, 1 cow	
John Metzker	$0.10
1 horse, "1=2" cows	
Frederick Metzker	$2.45
200 acres, 2 horses, 3 cows	
Adam Metzler	~~$0.77~~
~~125 acres, 1 horse, 1 cow~~	

Abstracts of Westmoreland County, Pennsylvania, Tax Records 1815

South Huntingdon Township Name of Person	Tax
"Read Solomon Suter for Land"	
Peter Mitzler	$0.72
1 cow, 1 horse, 125 acres	
"See Martin Glassburner for the land"	
George Metzler	$0.06
1 cow	
John Markle	$0.17
2 horses, 2 cows, 1 horse, 1 cow	
James McCann	$0.16
2 horses, 3 cows	
Thomas McCann, single man	$0.50
Gilbert McIlwain	$0.13
"1=2" horses, 1 cow, 1 cow	
William McIlwain, single man	$0.50
1 horse	
Hugh McIlwain, single man	$0.50
1 horse	
Daniel McMullen, single man	$0.50
Robert McWilliams, single man	$0.50
John McLaughlin, single man, saddler	$0.52
William Means, cooper	$0.06
Samuel McCormick	$0.06
1 horse, 1 cow	
Thomas Mitchel, single man	$0.50
Neal McNaughtan, single man	$0.50
James McIlwain	$0.50
1 horse	
Thomas McKee, chair maker	
1 house & lot, 1 horse, 1 cow	
Wm Miller, single man, millwright	
Fergus Moorehouse, carpenter	
1 horse, 2 cows, trade	
Robert McCann, single man	
Saml McMicheal	
1 cow	
David McCormick	

South Huntingdon Township Name of Person   Tax

1 cow
Abraham Myers
1 horse, 2 cows
Joseph McCormick, single man
Robert Mahan, single man
"Maried Jene return"
John McCoy, single man, shoemaker
William Mitchel
2 horses, 1 cow
Alexander McClintock, single man
2 cows
~~Robert McCann~~, single man
"I think he is down in the other side"
William McClelland, single man
John McClelland, single man
Isaac Newton $0.06
1 cow
John Nichols, merchant $3.57
80 acres, 2 houses & lots, 3 unimproved lots, 3 horses, 3 cows, 110 acres
Henry Null $1.17
200 acres, 5 horses, 2 cows
Christian Neaff $1.27
77 acres, 2 horses, 2 cows
Robert Nichols, single man $0.57
1 horse
David Neily
1 cow
Samuel Neely, miller
2 cows
Jeremiah Ong, blacksmith   ~~$1.12~~
~~30 acres~~, 1 house & 2 lots, 2 horses, 2 cow
"See Saml Reed for House and 2 Lots"
B. James Oliver, merchant $1.52
1 house & 2 lots, 1 horse, 1 cow, 1 "Hanri" [?]
John Orr, nailor $0.16

Abstracts of Westmoreland County, Pennsylvania, Tax Records 1815

South Huntingdon Township Name of Person	Tax
1 lot & shop, 1 horse	
G Daniel Olos, fuller	
1 cow	
Peter Peper	$0.56
100 acres, 2 horses, 1 cow, 1 cow	
George Plumer, Esquire	$4.54
270 acres, 6 horses, 12 cows, 2 stills (172 gallon)	
Alexander Plumer	$1.39
1 gristmill, 1 house & lot, 1 horse, 1 cows, 1 sawmill	
John Plumer	
1 horse, 3 cows	
Lazarus Plumer, single man	$0.50
Jonathan Plumber, single man	$0.50
Daniel Porter	$0.06
1 horse, 1 cow, 1 cow	
Isaac Pollin	$0.06
1 cow, 1 cow	
James Patterson heirs	$1.44
90 acres, 2 horses, 2 cows	
Samuel Price, carpenter	$0.06
1 cow	
Joseph Patterson, single man, carpenter	$0.52
Aaron Power	$0.56
1 horse	
Robt & Wm Purvis	
225 acres, 4 horses, 2 cows	
John Queery	$0.06
1 horse, 1 cow	
William Rue	$0.06
1 cow	
Andrew Robison, Senior	$0.43
100 acres	
John Ritchey	$4.63
300 acres, 4 horses, 4 cows	
Archibald Ross	$0.09

Abstracts of Westmoreland County, Pennsylvania, Tax Records 1815

South Huntingdon Township Name of Person	Tax
1 horse, 1 cow, 1 cow	
"ad 2 horses"	
James Robison	$0.13
"1=2" horses	
Jonathan Robison	$0.06
1 horse	
William Robison	$4.44
300 acres, 2 horses, 2 cows	
Thomas Robison	$0.17
2 horses, 4 cows	
John Rowan	$2.42
2 houses & lots, 2 vacant lots, 9 acres, 1 horse, 1 cow	
Stephen Rowan, single man	$0.50
Abraham Rhodes, single man, wagon maker	$0.52
Thomas Robison	$2.96
230 acres, 1 horse, 2 cows	
Andrew Robison, Junior	$0.17
2 horses, 2 cows	
James Richey, fuller	
2 cows, 1 horse	
Randles Ross	$2.34
150 acres, 2 horses, 2 4 cows	
John Robison, innkeeper	$4.60
424 acres, 2 horses, 4 cows	
Thomas Read	$0.06
1 cow	
Jacob Reed	$0.19
3 horses, 1 cow	
Henry Rhodes	$0.10
1 horse, 2 cows	
Peter Rhodes	$0.45
43 acres, 1 horse, 1 cow	
Philip Reagan, Esquire	$0.74
130 acres	
George Reader	$0.15

Abstracts of Westmoreland County, Pennsylvania, Tax Records 1815

South Huntingdon Township Name of Person	Tax
15 acres, 1 horse, 1 cow	
George Reader	$0.45
85 acres, 1 horse, 1 cow	
"See Abraham Jewry for the Land"	
Jonas Rider	$0.45
85 acres, 1 horse, 1 cow	
Conrad Rider, shoemaker	$0.10
1 horse, 2 cows	
Joseph Ray, single man	$0.50
John Ross, single man, carpenter	
Henry Rhodes, Senior	$6.02
400 acres, 2 horses, 3 cows, 2 stills (175 gallon)	
William Reynolds	$1.52
90 acres, 3 horses, 4 cows	
Collin Reagan	$0.07
1 horse, 2 cows	
Evan Rickels, potter	$0.06
1 horse	
"don[']t know what his name should be if wrong put it right"	
John Reed, taylor	$0.54
1 house & lot, 2 horses, 1 cow	
C Collen Reagan, potter	
2 cows	
Peter Roadarmer	$4.18
293 acres, 4 horses, 4 cows	
William Rubey, single man, hatter	
Isaac Robb, single man, carpenter	
1 horse	
Abraham Ritter, single man	
Jesse Richey, single man	
Martha Robeson, widow	
1 horse	
Andrew Row, "coverted" weaver	
1 cow	
James Ray	

South Huntingdon Township Name of Person	Tax
1 horse, 2 cows	
"James Ray appears to have been put in the duplicate at the appeal last year in place of John Bennet & the rate is the same this year the numbers of acres I cannot put in here untill [*sic*] I am at the office"	
Ezekiel Sample, Esquire	$0.69
121 acres, 1 horse, 3 cows, 1 cow, 1 horse	
"See John Bennet for the land last year"	
John Sample, single man	$0.56
1 horse, 1 still (70 [gallon])	
Ezekiel Sample, Junior, single man	$0.57
1 horse	
Nathan Smith	$0.84
114 acres, 2 horses, 2 cows, 2 stills (100 gallon)	
John Sterret	$0.56
100 acres, 1 horse, 2 cows, 1 sawmill	
Frederick Smith	$0.73
150 acres, "1=2" horses, 1 cow, 1 still (66 [gallon])	
Robert Smith	$1.47
200 acres, 3 horses, 5 cows, 1 still (54 gallon), 1 still (70 gallon)	
John Smith, single man	$0.50
John Smith, Senior	$1.03
150 acres, 2 horses, "1 off 4" cows	
Alexander Smart, ~~talor~~	$0.32
50 acres, ~~2 horses, 1 cow~~	
Isaac Stimbel	$0.69
100 acres, 2 horses, 2 cows	
Abraham Sowash, carpenter	$0.06
1 cow	
Joseph Stroup	$0.33
50 acres, 2 horses, 2 cows, 1 cow	
Larkin Stincicum	$4.44
1000 acres, 2 horses, 1 cow	
George Sherbandy	$0.22

Abstracts of Westmoreland County, Pennsylvania, Tax Records 1815

South Huntingdon Township Name of Person	Tax
3 horses, 3 cows	
Joseph Smith	$3.77
126 acres, 1 grist & sawmill, 2 horses, 4 cows	
George Swab	$0.86
100 acres, 4 horses, 1 cow	
Samuel Stopplet, taylor	$0.08
1 horse, 1 cow	
Samuel Smith	$0.60
100 acres, 2 horses, 2 cows, 2 stills (100 gallon)	
James Smith, single man	$0.50
Charles Shull	$3.12
100 acres, 1 grist & sawmill, 1 fulling & oil mill, 1 horse, 3 cows, 1 horse, 1 cow	
Henry Sambro, ~~single man~~	$2.33
150 acres, 2 horses, 1 cow	
William Shrader	$2.54
160 acres, 3 horses, 4 cows	
James Smith, saddler	$0.66
1 house & lot, 1 horse, 1 horse, 2 cows	
Alexander Smith, single man	$0.57
1 horse	
Joseph Sumbro	$1.74
150 acres, "1=2" horses, 2 cows, 1 cow	
John Stewart, taylor	$0.06
1 cow	
"Gone away"	
John Smith, single man	$0.93
1/2 a tanyard, 1 horse, 1 cow	
"Gone Away"	
John Stewart, carpenter	$0.09
1 horse, 1 cow	
"Gone away"	
William Stewart, butcher	$0.09
1 horse, 1 cow	
Jackson Stillwell	$0.12
"in Robbstown"	

Abstracts of Westmoreland County, Pennsylvania, Tax Records 1815

South Huntingdon Township Name of Person   Tax

2 horses	
George Swab, Junior	$0.06
1 cow, 1 horse	
Charles Shields	$0.06
1 cow	
"Run away"	
Jacob Swab	
1 horse, 1 cow	
"The rev^d Stouffer	$0.86
200 acres	
John Sloan, merchant	
1 house & lot	
Peter Stirnell, hatter [?]	
Philip Stemnell	
1 cow	
George Stroup, single man	
John Stroup, carpenter	
Jacob Secress	
1 horse	
Jacob Sherbondy, single man	
James Sharp, single man, saddler	
"Married"	
James Smith	
1 horse	
"in frires[?]"	
Samuel Smith, single man, carpenter	
Sollomon Suter	
125 acres	
John Swable, single man	
John Travers, tenant	$1.80
300 acres, 2 horses, 2 cows	
John Thompson "(pines)"	$0.89
200 acres, "1-2" cows, 1 horse	
Robert Thompson, single man	$0.50
Mathew Thompson, single man	$0.50
Brackenridge Thompson, single man	$0.50

Abstracts of Westmoreland County, Pennsylvania, Tax Records 1815

South Huntingdon Township Name of Person	Tax
James Thompson	~~$2.80~~
174 acres, 4 horses, 4 cows	
"land to Wᵐ Clark"	
William Thompson, single man	$0.50
Isabella Turner	$0.13
2 horses, "1-2" cows	
Howel Thomas, single man	
Samuel Tarpenny	
200 acres, 1 horse	
John Trimble	
1 horse, 1 cow	
Abreham Updegraff	$0.07
1 horse, 1 cow	
Joseph Vanhorn	$0.06
1 horse	
Michael Varner	$0.63
100 acres, 2 horses, 2 cows, 2 stills (80 gallon)	
Philip Varner	$0.06
1 cow	
Jacob Varner, single man, wheelwright	$0.50
Philip Varner, single man	$0.50
Isaac Vankirk, shoemaker	
1 house & lot, 1 cow	
Alexander Weaver	$0.06
1 cow, 1 horse	
John Walker, weaver	$0.08
1 horse, 1 cow	
Daniel Waltz	$6.04
500 acres, 3 horses, 3 cows, 2 stills (110 gallon)	
Daniel Wigal, blacksmith	$1.90
150 acres, 2 horses, 3 cows	
Charles Wilson, single man	$0.50
Mary Warren, widow	$0.27
1 house & lot, 1 horse, 1 cow	
Mary Wilson, widow	$2.07
170 acres, 2 horses, 1 cow	

Abstracts of Westmoreland County, Pennsylvania, Tax Records 1815

South Huntingdon Township Name of Person	Tax
Jacob Waltz	$3.23
200 acres, 3 horses, 3 cows, 2 stills (178 gallon), "add 40 acres land" "ad 2 cows" "See Cornelious Carale"	
Hugh Wallace, mason	$0.08
8 acres, 1 cow	
David Weaver	$0.19
32 acres, 1 horse, 1 cow	
Joseph Weaver	$0.21
32 acres, 1 horse, 2 cows	
Christian Walter	$0.76
144 acres, 2 horses, 2 cows "See Jacob George for Land"	
John Weaver	$1.22
250 acres, 1 horse, "2=6" cows, 2 horses	
Samuel Wiseman, innkeeper	$0.16
1 horse, 1 cow	
James Watson, mason	$0.06
1 cow	
Jacob Wible, cooper	$0.06
2 cows "put his name down Mr assessor"	
Martha Weaver, widow	$0.10
20 acres, 1 cow	
William Weaver, single man	$0.56
1 horse	
Peter Weaver, single man	$0.50
James Wright, tenant	$1.27
1 house & lot, 1 lot, 1 out lot, 1 ferry "See John Gamble"	
James Wright, innkeeper	$0.36
1 lot, 3 horses, 1 cow	
Andrew Works, single man	$0.57
1 horse, 1 cow	
James Wilson, single man	$0.50

Abstracts of Westmoreland County, Pennsylvania,
Tax Records 1815

South Huntingdon Township Name of Person	Tax
John Wartz	$2.13

149 acres
"I doubt that is not his name"
Barney Wagoner, hatter
1 horse, 1 cow
Daniel Weaver
1 horse, 1 cow
Thomas Wallace, single man

Names of Poor Children
Hannah Shiry, 11 years old
Nicholas Shiry, 7 years old
Nelly Cravans, 11 years old

Abstracts of Westmoreland County, Pennsylvania, Tax Records 1815

Abstracts of Westmoreland County, Pennsylvania, Tax Records 1815

Unity Township Name of Person	Tax
John Armil, shoemaker	$0.10
1 cow, 21 acres	
William Anderson, weaver	$0.08
4.75 acres, 1 cow	
Captain Andrew Armstrong	$2.00
200 acres	
Daniel Armil	$0.20
2 horses, 2 cows	
Widow Armil	$1.52
100 acres, 100 acres of "ridge land," 1 cow	
John Armil, Senior	$1.43
100 acres, 96 acres of "ridge land," 1 cow	
Robert Anderson	$0.17
2 horses, 2 cows	
Lewis Alshoun, joiner	$0.15
1 horse	
Col. William Anderson	$1.57
88 acres, 1 stud horse, 3 horses, 3 cows	
William Anderson, Senior	$2.13
160 acres	
Philip Aukerman	$2.76
185 acres, 200 acres of "ridge land," 1 horse, 3 cows, 2 stills, 4 horses	
George Aukerman, single man	$1.00
6 horses	
Ludwick Aukerman, "kooper"	$0.29
15 acres, 1 horse, 3 cows	
Jacob Armil	$0.88
110 acres, 1 mill, 1 cow, 1 horse, 2 cows	
Widow Alexander	$1.74
200 acres, 1 horse, 2 cows	
Thomas Arone	$0.57
100 acres, 1 horse, 1 cow	
Joseph Arone	$0.06
1 cow	
David Armor, joiner	$0.25

Abstracts of Westmoreland County, Pennsylvania, Tax Records 1815

Unity Township Name of Person	Tax
1 horse, 1 cow	
John Armor, single man	$0.87
4 horses, 2 cows	
William Armor, innkeeper	$2.10
1 house & 2 lots, 1 house & blacksmith shop, 6 horses, 2 cows	
Ephraim Adams	$3.45
200 acres, 3 horses, 3 cows, 2 stills	
Doctor Irwin Baird	$0.06
1 cow	
William Barns	$0.20
13 acres, 1 horse, 1 cow	
F. Joseph Barns	$1.68
140 acres, 1 horse, 2 cows "Remove"	
John Barns	$0.32
5 horses, 4 cows, 140 acres	
Mark Bois	$0.08
1 horse, 2 cows	
George Brinker	$3.90
280 acres, 2 horses, 2 cows	
Joseph Byers, single man	$0.50
Henry Brinker	$4.50
280 acres, 3 horses, 3 cows	
Henry Brinker, single man	$0.50
Christopher Bore	$0.06
1 cow	
Martin Bash	$2.90
150 acres, 4 horses, 4 cows	
Michael Bash, single man	$0.50
Samuel Buzzard, taylor	$0.67
1 acre & house, 1 cow, 1 house & lot in Youngstown	
Abram Brenninger, carpenter	$0.18
1 cow	
Jacob Barnhart	$0.07
1 horse, 1 cow	

Abstracts of Westmoreland County, Pennsylvania, Tax Records 1815

Unity Township Name of Person	Tax
Gasper Buzzard, taylor	$0.17
John Buzzard	$0.63
38 acres, 2 horses, 2 cows	
Henry Bonebright	$1.87
134 acres, 1 horse, 2 cows	
Daniel Bonebright, store keeper	$0.43
1 horse, 1 cow	
David Brady	$0.06
2.5 acres, 1 cow	
Henery Bonebright [illegible notation]	$0.06
1 horse, 1 cow	
Henry Bare	$0.18
2 stills, 1 cow	
George Brindle	$2.07
140 acres, 3 horses, 3 cows	
Joseph Bulean, wagon maker	$0.17
George Buzzard	$1.13
100 acres, 2 horses, 2 cows, 2 stills	
Jacob Brewer	$0.12
1 horse, 2 cows	
Benjamin Beatty	$3.11
256 acres, 4 horses, 3 cows, 1 stud horse	
Hamilton Beatty, single man	$0.50
James Byers	$1.74
200 acres, 1 horse, 2 cows	
William Barns	$0.95
100 acres, 1 horse, 4 cows	
Peter Bridge	$1.25
150 acres, 2 horses, 2 cows	
"Remove"	
"To the 77 page [sic] of this assessment"	
"the Land belongs to John Montgomery"	
William Barns, Junior	$0.06
1 cow	
John Black	$3.00
180 acres, 5 horses, 6 cows, 2 stills	
John Brewer, single man	$0.50

Abstracts of Westmoreland County, Pennsylvania, Tax Records 1815

Unity Township Name of Person	Tax
Thomas Bevins	$0.14
37 acres, 1 cow	
Joseph Buck, blacksmith	$1.52
109 acres, 3 horses, 3 cows	
Thomas Berry	$0.66
82 acres, 2 horses, 1 cow	
Saml Baldridge, tanner	$1.44
1 tanyard, 2 horses, 2 cows	
"from Joseph Baldridge 18 acres"	
Joseph Baldridge	$5.76
305 acres, 145 acres, 18 acres	
"11 acres transfer to Saml Baldridge"	
"223 transfered [sic] to Jno Baldridge"	
"18 acres transfered [sic] to Samuel Baldridge"	
Jacob Berlian, blacksmith	$0.22
1 horse, 1 cow	
"Remove"	
Widow Baker	$0.17
1 house & lot	
John Baldridge	$0.17
1 horse, 4 cows	
"transfered [sic] from Joseph 228 acres"	
P. William Barclay	$0.06
1 cow	
Christopher Browler	$0.10
1 horse, 2 cows	
John Brindle	$3.02
200 acres, 4 horses, 5 cows	
Benjamin Blythe	$0.06
1 cow	
John Biggert	$2.67
150 acres, 2 horses, 2 cows	
John Buck, single man	$0.50
William Bell, saddle maker	$0.06
1 horse	
Jacob Bonbright	$0.06
1 horse, 1 cow	

Abstracts of Westmoreland County, Pennsylvania,
Tax Records 1815

Unity Township Name of Person	Tax
John Bonbright, single man	$0.50
John Chambers, blacksmith	$2.29
155 acres, 4 horses, 3 cows, 1 stud horse	
William Casada, single man	$0.50
James Carrah	$0.16
14 acres, 1 cow	
Jacob Christman	$1.00
100 acres	
Peter Celer	$0.15
1 horse, 1 cow, 1 house & lot	
Alexander Culbertson	$2.00
121 acres, 2 horses, 2 cows	
Thomas Cain, single man	$0.50
James Crawford	$2.46
279 acres, 3 horses, 2 cows	
John Crawford	$0.06
1 horse, 1 cow	
James Cain	$0.06
1 cow	
George Critzer	$0.06
17 acres, 1 cow	
"Remove"	
Adam Ceil, shoemaker	$0.19
29 acres, 1 cow	
Daniel Ceil, single man	$0.56
1 horse	
Widow Craig	$1.97
127 acres, 1 horse, 1 cow, 1 fulling mill	
"Remove"	
John Craig, single man	$1.96
1 horse, 127 acres, 1 fulling mill	
"add 50 ff"	
Captain William Craig	$0.07
1 horse	
"Remove"	
John Craig	$4.03
105 acres, 90 acres, 40 acres, 2 horses, 3 cows, 1	

Abstracts of Westmoreland County, Pennsylvania, Tax Records 1815

Unity Township Name of Person	Tax
"G" [grist?] mill, 1 sawmill	
"Remove"	
Andrew Craig, single man	$0.50
"Remove"	
Robert Campbell	$0.33
30 acres, 1 horse, 2 cows	
James Clements	$0.06
1 cow	
"Remove"	
Richard Carothers	$2.18
150 acres, 3 horses, 2 cows, 1 cow	
Peter Crossan	$0.07
1 horse, 1 cow	
James Campbell	$0.06
1 cow	
John Currin	$0.23
26 acres, 1 horse, 1 cow	
Jonathan Ceil, shoemaker	
8 acres, 1 cow	
William Campbel, taylor	$0.16
William Dunlap	$1.68
117 acres, 2 horses, 1 cow	
John Dunlap	$2.04
123 acres, 3 horses, 5 cows, 2 stills	
Wᵐ Dougherty, renter	$0.55
90 acres, 2 horses, 1 cow	
John Davis	$0.07
11 acres	
Thomas Dunlap	$6.00
385 acres, 4 horses, 4 cows	
John Dickey, single man	$0.50
Andrew Dum, ~~single man~~	$0.51
1 house & lot, 1 cow	
Robert Duncan	$1.38
100 acres, 2 horses, 1 cow	
Henry Deihl	$0.06
1 cow	

Abstracts of Westmoreland County, Pennsylvania, Tax Records 1815

Unity Township Name of Person	Tax
Francis Davison	$0.13
2 horses, 2 cows	
Wiliam Dinsmore	$0.06
1 horse	
Edward Deleney, single man	$0.50
John Eichard	$2.11
175 acres, 1 horse, 2 cows	
Jacob Eichard	$0.08
1 horse, 2 cows	
"Remove"	
Ferdinand Easley	$0.95
100 acres, 2 cows, 2 horses	
George Elliott	$0.07
1 horse, 1 cow	
Jacob Fries, millwright	$0.06
1 cow	
George Fries	$0.21
8.5 acres, 1 horse, 2 cows	
Alexander Ford	$1.83
149 acres, 2 horses, 3 cows	
Thomas Ferguson	$2.60
296 acres, 2 horses, 2 cows	
"see him again in the 78th page of this assmt"	
"Remove"	
David Fiscus	$0.07
1 horse, 1 cow	
"Remove"	
George Foltz	$0.06
2 cows	
"Remove"	
John Feller, single man	$0.50
"Remove"	
Henry Furry	$2.20
121 acres, 5 horses, 5 cows, 2 stills, ~~25 acres~~	
Walter Ferguson	$0.13
2 horses, 2 cows	
"Remove"	

Abstracts of Westmoreland County, Pennsylvania, Tax Records 1815

Unity Township Name of Person	Tax
William Findley, Esquire	$3.77
250 acres, 40 acres, 4 horses, 6 cows, 25 acres	
William Foster	$0.06
1 horse, 1 cow	
Jacob Foust	$0.15
40 acres, 1 cow	
John Fluke	$0.45
6 horses, 3 cows	
Christopher Feller, single man	$0.50
Abraham Furey, single man	$0.50
Solomon Greenemyer	$0.42
6 horses, 1 cow	
Abraham Gray	$1.00
100 acres	
Alexander Green	$1.06
150 acres, 1 horse, 1 cow	
Moses Gilaspey	$1.00
2 houses & lots	
Christopher Gartner	$1.13
25 acres, 1 mill, 1 horse, 3 cows	
Andrew Gregg, single man	$0.50
"see the last of the G's in the Duplicate"	
Samuel Gardner	$0.13
2 horses, 2 cows	
John Graff	$3.89
150 acres, 300 acres, 5 horses, 3 cows, 1 tanyard, 2 stills	
James Gilchrist	$2.33
200 acres, 3 horses, 3 cows	
Bernard Graham	$1.75
143 acres, 1 horse, 2 cows	
George Gordon	$2.13
176 acres, 1 horse, 2 cows	
"Remove"	
James Gordon	$0.06
1 horse	
"Remove"	

Abstracts of Westmoreland County, Pennsylvania, Tax Records 1815

Unity Township Name of Person	Tax
John Greenawalt, blacksmith	$0.18
1 cow	
Samuel Gordon, single man	$0.50
"Remove"	
Benjamin Geiser	$0.06
1 cow	
George Gibson	$0.32
4 horses, 3 cows	
"Remove"	
James Greer, single man	$4.15
260 acres, 3 horses, 2 cows	
"now the widow"	
"see the last of the G's in the Duplicate"	
Patrick Gaston	$0.75
80 acres, 1 horse, 2 cows	
Major George Gibson	$1.83
80 acres, 300 acres, 1 fulling mill, 1 sawmill, 1 stud horse, 1 horse, 1 cow	
Widow Gallaher	$0.88
71 acres, 1 horse, 1 cow	
Wendel Guiger	$5.00
277 acres, 4 horses, 4 cows	
John Guiger, single man	$0.67
2 stills	
George Guiger, single man	$0.50
2 horses	
John George	$1.19
102 acres, 1 still, 1 horse, 2 cows, 1 horse	
Henery Graff, single man	~~$0.50~~
"see the 34th page in the Duplicate"	
Thomas Gallaher	$1.89
143 acres, 1 horse	
Archibald Gilchrist, single man	$0.50
Henry Hugus	$1.23
72 acres, 1 tanyard, 1 horse, 3 cows	
Paul Hugus	$1.83
100 acres, 2 horses, 2 cows, 1 carding machine	

Abstracts of Westmoreland County, Pennsylvania, Tax Records 1815

Unity Township Name of Person	Tax
Jonathan Hile	$2.13
240 acres, 2 horses, 2 cows	
John Horner	$0.49
41 acres, 1 horse, 2 cows	
Jacob Holser	$0.14
12 acres, 1 cow	
Frederick Holser	$0.90
60 acres, 2 stills, 2 horses, 2 cows	
Daniel Hoffman	$0.08
1 horse, 1 cow	
Joseph Hoffman	$0.50
, single man	
Dennis Handlin, coverlet weaver	$0.25
1 horse, 2 cows	
"Remove"	
Adam Hoffman	$0.08
1 horse, 2 cows	
Peter Hinkle	$0.39
50 acres, 2 horses, 1 cow	
"see the 29th page of this assessment"	
"Remove"	
Jacob Hartzel	$0.17
8 acres, 1 horse, 1 cow, 1 lot	
William Henderson	$0.14
12 acres, 1 horse, 1 cow	
Ralph Hunter	$1.28
85 acres, 2 horses, 1 cow	
James Hunter	$1.35
90 acres, 2 horses, 3 cows	
Samuel Hunter	$2.17
150 acres, 2 horses, 2 cows	
Thomas Hunter	$0.16
1 horse, 1 cow, 1 horse	
Adam Huffman	$0.14
25 acres, 1 cow, 1 horse, 1 cow	
William Huffman	$2.32
168 acres, 1 horse, 2 cows	

Abstracts of Westmoreland County, Pennsylvania, Tax Records 1815

Unity Township Name of Person	Tax
John Henry, Junior	$0.91
66 acres, 2 cows	
David Hossach	$1.86
207 acres, 2 horses, 2 cows	
William Horner	$1.92
150 acres, 2 horses, 4 cows	
Reverend Doctor Peter Helburn, single man	$4.25
250 acres, 5 horses, 5 cows	
James Holland	$5.63
90 acres, 1 horse, 1 cow, 300 acres	
Josiah Harvey	$1.83
50 acres, 2 houses & lots, 1 horse, 1 cow	
"Remove"	
John Hunter, saddler	$0.55
1 house and lot, 1 horse, 1 cow	
William Hughes, carpenter	$0.52
1 house & lot, 1 cow	
"his name is wrote [*sic*] Hugus in both last year[']s and this year[']s Duplicate put it right at the appeal"	
John Henry, Senior	$4.48
200 acres, 100 acres, 2 horses, 3 cows	
John Huffman, single man	$0.53
2 acres	
Michael Huffman	$0.17
40 acres, 2 cows	
Jacob Henry, single man	$0.83
5 horses	
Conrad Henry, single man	$0.77
4 horses	
Retter Hinkle	$0.39
29 acres	
Francis Jamieson	$0.18
1 stud horse, 1 cow	
William Jamieson, joiner	$0.25
1 horse, 2 cows	
Robert Jamieson	$2.53

Unity Township Name of Person	Tax
200 acres, 3 horses, 3 cows	
James Jamieson, single man	$1.63
100 acres, 2 horses, 1 cow, 1 cow	
Robert Jamieson, single man	$0.50
John Jamieson	$3.18
310 acres, 1 horse, 2 cows	
Robert Jamieson, single man	$0.50
Benjamin Jamieson, single man	$0.50
Henry Johnston	$0.13
2 horses, 1 cow, 2 cows	
David Johnston	$1.02
150 acres, 1 cow	
Richard Jackson	$2.13
200 acres, 2 horses, 2 cows	
William Jackson, wagon maker, single man	$0.50
William Jenkeson	$0.43
100 acres, 2 horses, 1 cow	
Alexander Johnston, Esquire	$1.75
1 house & 2 lots, 1 horse, 1 cow	
"Rev^d"	
James Jamieson, single man	$0.50
Philip Kistler	$0.10
1 horse, 1 cow	
Ralph Kells, weaver	$0.13
2 horses, 2 cows	
Gustavus Kells, single man	$0.50
Andrew Kells, wheelwright	$0.17
~~50 acres,~~ 1 horse, 2 cows	
Frederick Kentz	$1.84
32 acres, 94 acres, 4 horses, 3 cows, 1 horse, 1 cow	
Jacob Kuhn	$2.02
187 acres, 2 horses, 2 cows	
Henry Kuhn	$1.85
187 acres, 2 horses, 2 cows	
Henry Kuhn	$0.07
1 horse	

Abstracts of Westmoreland County, Pennsylvania, Tax Records 1815

Unity Township Name of Person	Tax
Daniel Kuhn	$2.65
300 acres, 1 horse, 2 cows, 1 sawmill	
Henry Kuhn, Junior	$0.77
90 acres, 3 horses, 1 cow	
Isaac Kyser, blacksmith	$0.20
2 cows, 1 horse	
Widow Kelly	$0.58
109 acres, 2 cows	
Jacob Kyser	$0.07
1 horse	
James Kinan	$1.82
2 house & 2 lots, 1 out lot, 1 horse, 1 cow	
George Kyser, single man	$0.50
John Kyser	$0.23
4 horses, 2 cows	
Michael Krug, shoemaker	$0.26
2 horses	
Adam Kuhn, single man	$0.50
John Leasure	$2.27
150 acres, 3 horses, 4 cows	
Daniel Leasure	$1.33
100 acres	
Daniel Leasure, Junior	$0.10
1 horse, 2 cows	
"removed"	
Jacob Loos	$0.07
1 horse, 1 cow	
George Loos	$3.88
260 acres, 3 horses, 3 cows, 2 stills	
Henry Loos, blacksmith	$0.20
2 cows	
"Removed"	
John Larimer, single man	$0.50
Jacob Lytick	$0.08
1 horse, 2 cows	
Nicholas Lingle	$1.63
110 acres, 6 cows, 2 horses	

Abstracts of Westmoreland County, Pennsylvania, Tax Records 1815

Unity Township Name of Person	Tax
George Loos, Junior	$2.53
200 acres, 3 horses, 3 cows	
Andrew Larimer	$1.67
150 acres, 2 horses, 4 cows	
David Larimer	$1.58
150 acres, 2 horses, 4 cows	
Levi Lightcap	$0.06
1 cow	
James Lyons, single man	$1.63
130 acres, 1 horse	
"Remove"	
"land sold to M[r] Speer"	
Jacob Lenhart	$0.24
73 acres	
William Lehmer, innkeeper	$2.02
1 house & 3 lots, 6 acres, 1 horse, 1 cow	
James Long	$0.06
1 cow	
John Laughlin	[illegible]
16 acres, 1 horse	
Solomon Lightcap	$0.98
98 acres, 2 horses, 2 cows	
James Leaden	$1.71
200 acres, 1 horse, 1 cow	
James Marshal	$2.65
250 acres, 2 horses, 3 cows	
David Marshal, single man	$0.50
John Millar, Senior	$0.12
1 cow, 1 horse	
Thomas M[c]Clelland	$0.80
1 house & lot, 1 horse, 3 lots [?], 1 stud horse	
John Millar, single man	$0.50
George Millar, single man	$0.50
Peter Millar, single man	$0.50
W[m] M[c]Knight	$1.24
120 acres, 1 horse	
Jacob M[c]Coy	$0.07

Abstracts of Westmoreland County, Pennsylvania, Tax Records 1815

Unity Township Name of Person	Tax
1 horse, 1 cow	
Archibald McCallister	$3.84
269 acres, 3 horses, 3 cows	
John McCall	$2.43
170 acres, 6 horses, 4 cows	
Samuel McCall, single man	$0.50
Arch^d MacDonald	$0.77
100 acres, 2 horses, 1 cow	
James McCutchen	$0.06
2 cows	
Frederick Metzker	$0.47
33 acres, 1 horse, 2 cows	
"Removed"	
William Momyer	$0.68
48 acres, 2 horses, 1 cow	
John Momyer, wagon maker, ~~single man~~	$0.18
1 cow	
James Machesney	$1.00
70 acres, 1 horse, 1 cow	
William Machesney	$2.63
300 acres, 2 horses, 2 cows	
James McFadden	$0.25
4 horses, 3 cows	
James McFadden, single man	$0.50
"see the last of the M's in the Duplicate"	
James Montgomery, Esquire	$2.35
235 acres	
Samuel McCutchen	$0.06
1 cow	
David Maxwill	$0.06
1 cow	
Robert Marshal	$1.19
139 acres, 2 cows	
Samuel Marshal	$0.13
2 horses, 2 cows	
William Marshal	$2.03
190 acres, 2 horses, 2 cows	

Abstracts of Westmoreland County, Pennsylvania, Tax Records 1815

Unity Township Name of Person	Tax
James Marshal, single man	$0.50
Robert Marshal, single man	$0.50
Joseph Marshal	$0.22
10 acres, 1 horse, 1 cow	
James Marshal	$0.19
12 acres, 1 horse, 1 cow	
Armor Melan, weaver	$0.15
16 acres, 1 cow	
William Manwell	$3.50
400 acres, 1 tanyard, 2 horses, 2 cows	
Robert Manwell	$0.95
100 acres, 2 horses, 1 cow	
Joseph McKee	$0.06
1 cow	
William McWhorter	$0.97
100 acres, 2 horses, 2 cows	
Patrick MacAfee	$0.63
65 acres, 1 horse, 2 cows	
John MacDermot	$0.56
65 acres, 1 cow	
Thomas MacFarland	$0.13
~~200 acres,~~ 2 horses, 2 cows	
"Mac Farland widow"	
James MacFarland, single man	$0.50
David MacFarland, single man	$0.50
"Remove"	
William MacFarland, single man	$0.50
"see the 22nd page of the Duplicate"	
John Martin	$0.08
1 horse, 1 cow	
John Markle	$2.08
300 acres, 1 horse, 2 cows	
James MacWilliams	$0.10
2 horses, 1 cow	
Matthew Maclean	$2.88
275 acres, 2 horses, 2 cows	
Hamilton Maclean, single man	$0.58

Abstracts of Westmoreland County, Pennsylvania, Tax Records 1815

Unity Township Name of Person	Tax
1 horse	
Francis Mullen	$0.07
1 horse, 1 cow	
George Millar, "C. weaver"	$0.18
1 cow	
Jacob Mygrants, single man	$0.50
John Macue, cooper, single man	$0.50
Isaac Makissock	$2.20
150 acres, 2 horses, 4 cows	
Andrew Machesney	$0.08
1 horse, 2 cows, 1 horse	
John Machesney, single man	$0.50
Samuel MaGuire, ~~single man~~	$0.06
"see the foot of the page in the Duplicate"	
Samuel Morrison	$1.03
118 acres, 1 horse, 1 cow	
John Morrison	$1.17
118 acres, 3 horses, 3 cows	
James Moore	$0.17
22 acres, 1 horse, 1 horse	
John Macune	$0.06
1 horse	
Samuel MaKee, tanner	$0.18
1 cow	
Zechariah MaCalley, saddler	$0.58
1 house & 2 lots, 1 stud horse, 1 horse, 2 cows, 1 house & lot	
James Macwright	$0.18
1 house & lot, 1 cow	
Wilson MacFarland, fuller [?], single man	$0.50
Daniel MaGuire, single man	$0.50
"Removed"	
Robert MaGoogan	$1.30
100 acres, 2 horses, 2 cows	
Francis Mullen	$0.90
6 horses	
"Remove"	

Abstracts of Westmoreland County, Pennsylvania, Tax Records 1815

Unity Township Name of Person	Tax
Robert Montgomery, Esquire	$0.07
1 horse, 2 cows	
Frederick Myers	$0.33
100 acres "of unseated land"	
Daniel MacGuire, fuller	$0.25
1 horse, 1 cow	
Patrick McBarvere	$0.07
1 horse	
Henry Mycrants, single man	$0.50
William Martin	$0.06
1 horse, 1 cow	
Francis Mullen, single man	$0.50
William Momyer, cooper, single man	$0.50
1 lot	
John Nichols	$2.38
160 acres, 3 horses, 3 cows	
Robert Nichols	$2.13
140 acres, 3 horses, 4 cows	
William Nichols, single man	$2.61
175 acres, 1 horse	
Thomas Neffell	$0.06
2 cows	
"Removed"	
Peter Noel	$1.27
145 acres, 1 horse, 1 cow, 2 horses	
Oliver Nichols	$0.09
4 acres, 1 horse, 1 cow	
Simon Noel	$0.06
4 acres, 1 cow	
Peter Orrans	$0.40
1 2 houses & lots, 1 horse, 1 cow	
Widow OHara	$1.50
120 acres, 1 horse, 2 cows	
Michael Poorman	$1.82
100 acres, 3 horses, 4 cows, 2 stills, 37 acres	
Peter Painter	$1.70
150 acres, 3 horses, 3 cows	

Abstracts of Westmoreland County, Pennsylvania, Tax Records 1815

Unity Township Name of Person	Tax
William Peeples	$2.19
143 acres, 4 horses, 1 cow	
"Removed"	
Jacob Poorman	$5.53
196 acres, 500 acres, 2 horses, 8 cows, 2 stills, 1 stud horse	
John Piles	$0.90
50 acres, 1 horse, 1 cow, 1 horse, 1 cow	
Peter Poorman	$1.23
91 acres, 1 horse, 2 cows	
Adam Pere	$3.62
258 acres, 3 horses, 2 cows	
Adam Palmer	$1.61
88 acres, 150 acres "ridge land," 45 acres, 2 horses, 2 cows, 1 oil mill	
John Polens, carpenter	$0.18
1 cow	
Christian Pershian, weaver	$0.37
40 acres, 2 cows	
Christian Pershian, Junior, weaver	$0.07
1 horse, 1 cow	
Conrad Pershian	$2.98
250 acres, 5 horses, 4 cows, 1 oil mill	
Jacob Pease	$1.82
270 acres, 1 cow	
Benjamin Parker, single man	$1.08
58 acres, 2 horses	
William Pollins, carpenter	$0.19
Christopher Peichtel, miller	$0.18
1 cow	
Michael Penrose	$0.52
1 house & lot, 1 cow	
"Removed"	
Simon Peck, blacksmith, single man	$0.60
1 house & lot	
Robert Patterson	$0.10
15 acres	

Abstracts of Westmoreland County, Pennsylvania, Tax Records 1815

Unity Township Name of Person	Tax
Daniel Piper	$0.06
1 horse, 1 cow	
John Piles	$0.33
5 horses	
Christophel Pershian, single man	$0.50
Michael Penrod	$0.06
1 cow	
George Ruffner, weaver	$1.40
150 acres, 2 horses, 3 cows	
Peter Ruffner, single man	$0.50
Simon Ruffner	$1.26
125 acres, 4 horses, 1 cow	
James Ruffner, single man	$0.50
Peter Ruffner, single man	$0.50
John Richards	$0.85
50 acres, 2 horses, 2 cows, 1 cow, 2 lots	
James Robb	$0.74
68 acres, 1 horse, 2 cows, 1 horse	
Michael Ring	$1.11
71 acres, 2 horses, 2 cows, 2 lots	
William Robinson, weaver	$0.13
2 horses, 1 cow, 1 cow	
John Rodgers	$1.03
200 acres, 2 cows	
Joseph Ross	$1.13
100 acres, 2 horses, 2 cows	
Alexander Ross, ~~single man~~	$0.08
1 horse, 1 cow	
Jacob Rugh	$2.58
300 acres, 1 horse, 2 cows	
Widow Reed	$1.76
134 acres, 3 horses, 3 cows	
Widow Ritter	$0.18
1 house & lot, 1 cow	
Simon Ruffner, constable	$1.01
142 acres, 1 horse, 2 cows	
Charles Richard	$0.16

Abstracts of Westmoreland County, Pennsylvania, Tax Records 1815

Unity Township Name of Person	Tax
2 horses, 2 cows	
Eli Runeor, blacksmith, single man	$0.50
John Ross, single man	$0.56
1 lot	
John Swarts	$1.91
130 acres, 2 horses, 3 cows	
"see the 34th page of the Duplicate for the 7 names that follow"	
Nicholas Snyder	$0.23
8 acres, 2 horses, 1 cow	
"Remove"	
John Schaeffer, wagoner	$0.42
6 horses, 1 cow	
Henry Schaeffer	$0.06
1 cow	
David Showalter	$0.06
1 cow	
Michael Sickfriedt	$1.33
100 acres, 2 horses, 4 cows	
Jonas Speelman	$0.30
4 horses, 2 cows	
"Remove"	
Reverend William Speer	$1.27
2 horses, 3 cows, 130 acres	
"from James Lyons"	
"for the Land"	
Widow Smith	$2.63
187 acres, 2 horses, 2 cows	
"Now John Fetter"	
"See the 35th page in the Duplicate"	
Frederick Stockberger	$0.31
1 horse, 1 cow, 3 horses, 3 cows	
Peter Stockberger, single man	$0.50
Mathias Stockberger	$2.17
158 acres, 1 horse, 1 cow	
John Stockberger	$0.75
100 acres "ridge land," 1 horse, 2 cows, 1 oil mill	

Abstracts of Westmoreland County, Pennsylvania, Tax Records 1815

Unity Township Name of Person	Tax
Adam Snyder	$1.65
130 acres, 2 horses, 2 cows	
"Removed"	
George Snyder	$0.09
2 acres, 1 horse, 1 cow	
"Remove"	
Sebastian Syfret	$3.78
300 acres, 2 horses, 1 cow, 1 sawmill	
Jacob Syfret	$0.12
2 horses, 1 cow	
John Swarts, single man	$0.50
Daniel Shirey	$0.28
4 horses, 1 cow	
Abraham Shirey	$0.35
5 horses, 1 cow	
George Selders	$2.88
400 acres, 3 horses, 4 cows	
Benjamin Selders, single man	$0.50
John Smith	$0.07
10 acres, 1 cow, 1 cow	
Martin Seace	$1.43
100 acres, 3 horses, 4 cows	
David Shirey, single man	$0.50
"Removed"	
John Sloan	$1.13
1 horse, 5 cows, 100 acres	
David Silvius	$3.13
300 acres, 2 horses, 1 cow	
"Remove"	
Edward Steward	$0.06
4 acres, 1 horse	
Thomas Stokeley	$0.83
100 acres	
John S [no other letters for surname]	$1.02
100 acres, 1 cow	
"Removed"	
James Sloan	$2.42

Abstracts of Westmoreland County, Pennsylvania, Tax Records 1815

Unity Township Name of Person	Tax
225 acres, 2 horses, 4 cows, 1 horse	
William Sloan	$2.18
250 acres, 2 horses, 1 cow	
Jacob Sitler	$0.06
1 horse	
Simon Sitler	$0.92
100 acres, 1 horse, 2 cows	
Widow Shoup	$1.35
160 acres, ~~1 cow~~	
George Stump, miller	$0.35
1 horse, 3 cows, 1 horse	
John Schaeffer, merchant	$6.33
100 acres, 1 mill, 1 sawmill	
Robert Shearer	$0.33
40 acres, 1 horse, 1 cow	
Widow Sherrer	$0.32
40 acres, 1 horse	
George Smith, Esquire	$3.49
141 acres, 4 horses, 5 cows, 2 stills, 100 acres	
William Smith, single man	$0.50
Edward Smith, single man	$3.67
228 acres, 2 horses, 2 cows	
Michael Snearly, single man	
David Shirey	$1.25
50 acres, 5 horses	
George Snearley	$0.06
1 cow	
John Steinberger, joiner	$0.17
Jacob Sickfriedt, shoemaker	$0.40
1 house & lot, 1 horse, 1 cow	
Patrick Short, single man	$0.50
Benjamin Swain	$0.87
1 house & lot, 2 horses	
Genl Arthur St. Clair	$4.50
300 acres	
"best charge this land to the tenant"	
"Remove"	

Abstracts of Westmoreland County, Pennsylvania, Tax Records 1815

Unity Township Name of Person	Tax
Philip Shirey	$2.55
150 acres, 20 acres, 8 horses, 4 cows, 1 gristmill, 1 sawmill	
John Simral, single man	$0.50
Christopher Shockey	$1.60
300 acres, 1 horse, 2 cows, 1 horse	
Catharine Smith	$2.07
200 acres, 1 horse, 3 cows	
Widow Smith	$0.06
1 cow	
Henerey Smith	$2.20
130 acres, 3 horses, 3 cows	
Michael Sallentine	$0.06
2 acres, 1 cow	
Jacob Shoulse	$0.06
1 cow	
William Taylor	$0.06
1 cow	
James Taylor, single man	$0.50
Jonathan Teamer, cooper	$0.10
1 cow	
"Remove"	
Peter Teamer	$0.76
75 acres, 2 horses, 2 cows	
Jacob Truxal	$2.07
150 acres, 2 horses, 3 cows, 1 tanyard	
John Thorn	$0.06
1 cow	
"Remove"	
James Thompson	$0.06
1 cow	
William Taylor, Junior	$0.06
1 cow	
Christ^r Traugher	$0.39
26 acres, 1 horse, 2 cows	
Robert Toppins	$0.06
1 horse, 1 cow	

Abstracts of Westmoreland County, Pennsylvania, Tax Records 1815

Unity Township Name of Person	Tax
John Toppper	$0.85
88 acres, 2 horses, 3 cows	
Henry Tectter, blacksmith	$0.48
25 acres, 2 horses, 3 cows	
James Turner, fuller	$0.23
1 horse, 1 cow	
Robert Turner	$0.93
98 acres, 2 horses, 1 cow	
"Remove"	
John Taylor	$3.02
325 acres, 4 horses, 3 cows	
John Taylor, single man	$0.73
2 stills, 1 horse	
Peter Tittle	$1.83
130 acres, 1 horse, 2 cows	
Jonathan Tittle, single man	$0.60
1 horse, 1 cow	
Jeremiah Tittle	$1.12
100 acres, 2 horses, 1 cow, 50 acres	
John Tittle	$1.29
97 acres, 2 horses, 2 cows	
John Taylor	$0.91
1 house & lot, 1 horse, 1 cow	
Mordicy Taylor	$0.20
3 horses, 3 cows	
John Tempele	$0.08
1 horse, 1 cow	
Andrew White, single man	$0.50
James White, Esquire	$2.65
210 acres, 2 horses, 4 cows, 2 horses	
John White	$2.50
182 acres, 6 horses, 4 cows	
Thomas Wible	$1.58
140 acres, 3 horses, 6 cows, 2 stills	
Peter Walter	$0.08
1 horse, 2 cows	
Peter Walter, taylor, single man	$0.50

Abstracts of Westmoreland County, Pennsylvania, Tax Records 1815

Unity Township Name of Person	Tax
George Walter, single man	$3.03
180 acres, 3 horses, 2 cows	
Samuel Weirman, shoemaker	$0.07
1 horse, 1 cow	
Henry Walter, wagon maker, single man	$0.50
John Walter	$2.14
144 acres, 3 horses, 4 cows	
John Walter, single man	$0.50
John Williams	$0.60
1 horse, 1 cow	
Thomas Wilson	$0.42
50 acres	
John Wade	$0.50
100 acres	
George Wade, single man	$0.53
1 horse	
Samuel Workman	$1.32
180 acres, 2 horses, 2 cows	
Jacob Walter	$0.44
100 acres, 3 horses, 2 cows	
Martin West	$2.33
245 acres, 6 horses, 2 cows, 50 acres	
John Williams, Esquire	$1.75
1 house & 2 lots, 1 horse, 1 cow	
Abraham Whetsone	$0.85
15 acres, 1 tanyard, 1 horse, 2 cows, 1 horse	
Robert Wylie	$0.12
20 acres, 1 cow	
Jacob Walters, single man	$0.50
Henerey Walters, blacksmith	$0.16
William Weaver	$0.07
1 horse, 1 cow	
Benjamin Wright	$4.21
105 acres, 90 acres, 40 acres, 5 horses, 3 cows, 1 gristmill, 1 sawmill	
William Yolden	$0.06
1 horse, 1 cow	

Abstracts of Westmoreland County, Pennsylvania, Tax Records 1815

Unity Township Name of Person	Tax
"Remove"	
Alexander Young	$1.92
1 house & lot, 2 acres, 1 horse, 1 cow, 1 tanyard	
David Young	$0.35
5 horses, 1 cow	
Widow Yolden	$0.08
1 cow	
John Yolden, single man	$0.50
Christian Berger	$0.43
33 acres, 3 cows	
Widow Bell	$0.06
1 cow	
Abraham Beever	$0.50
1 house & lot	
Petter Bridge	$1.53
270 acres, 3 horses, 2 cows	
Arron Hill	$2.60
296 acres, 2 horses	
John Shirick	$0.16
3 horses, 4 cows	
"see the 34thpage of the Duplicate"	
Adam Snider	$0.16
2 horses, 3 cows	
Richard Mulin	$0.08
1 horse, 1 cow	
James McCalvey	$0.40
6 horses	
Jacob Walters	$0.06
1 cow	
Thomas Ferguson	$1.60
126 acres, 2 horses, 2 cows	
"See the 9th page of the Duplicate"	
Thomas Ferguson, single man	$0.50
"see the 34th page of the Duplicate"	
Col^n Samuel Gutherey	$3.00
300 acres	
"see the 34 [*sic*] page in the Duplicate"	

*Abstracts of Westmoreland County, Pennsylvania,
Tax Records 1815*

Unity Township Name of Person	Tax
Jamison Beattey, single man	$0.50
Daniel Leader, single man	$0.50

A List of Poor Children

Parent	Child
Robert Patterson	Peggey
Widow Hawkins	James
	Mathew
	Thomas
	David
Widow Kelly	James
	Margret
	Sarah
Michael Solinetine	Christopher Solinetine
	Catherine Solinetine

Abstracts of Westmoreland County, Pennsylvania, Tax Records 1815

Washington Township Name of Person	Tax
Andrew Almos	$0.56
Peter Almos, single man	$0.50
George Alcorn	$0.25
John Alcorn	$0.23
Michael Alcorn	$0.89
Adam Anderson	$0.24
Thomas Anderson	$0.56
Lewis Arb	$0.42
Joseph Alexander	$1.34
Peter Arb	$1.30
Nicholas Andrew	$0.37
John Anderson's "admrs"	$2.13
Andrew Adams, weaver	$0.06
Widow Artman	$2.47
George Anderson	$0.61
James Anderson	$2.17
John Alter	$1.39
Peter Anthony	$0.10
Robert Adams	$0.36
Samuel Alexander, single man	$0.50
John Arb, single man	$0.50
Alexander Ashbaugh	$0.13
Jacob Artman	$0.06
John Bails	$0.59
Samuel Barber	$0.14
Robert Baxter	$0.64
John Brown	$0.76
Robert Boyd	$0.88
James Bailey	$0.67
John Boyd	$0.86
Charles Bovard	$2.54
Thomas Boreland	$0.07
Ludwick Boreland	$0.12
Jacob Bear	$0.88
Andrew Brown	$1.30
Henry Brewer	$0.06

Abstracts of Westmoreland County, Pennsylvania, Tax Records 1815

Washington Township Name of Person	Tax
Adam Bawman	$1.60
John Buzzard	$0.12
L. William Butler	$0.36
Robert Boreland, single man	$0.50
Samuel Boreland, single man	$0.50
Widow Blakely	$0.34
Christian Beaver	$0.06
John Bash	$0.85
John Brown	$0.83
John Barber	$0.47
Laurence Bankard	$0.32
Neal Bayle	$0.25
John Black	$0.74
William Brewer	$0.26
John Bellows	$1.58
John Brown	$0.52
Adam Branthaver	$0.88
James Chambers	$2.30
William Chambers	$0.20
Benjamin Chambers, tanner	$0.28
Magret Chambers	$0.77
Samuel Callen	$0.75
James Carrel	$0.29
John Craig	$0.37
Mary Craig	$1.26
Charles Collins, single man	$0.55
Timothy Collins	$0.41
Jacob Kuhns	$1.51
Michael Kunkle	$2.72
Peter Clawson	$1.11
Barney Cline	$1.33
David Carnahen, Junior	$0.43
David Carnahen, Senior	$0.84
Isaac Clark	$0.06
George Chambers	$0.80
John Clingelsmith	$0.59
Philip Clingelsmith	$0.38

Abstracts of Westmoreland County, Pennsylvania, Tax Records 1815

Washington Township Name of Person	Tax
Jacob Clingelsmith	$1.73
Henry Cline	$0.63
Lewis Kepple	$0.32
James Coyle	$0.08
Joseph Christy	$0.06
George Clingelsmith	$0.56
Widow Crookshanks	$0.35
James Closs	$0.36
George Crawford	$3.32
John Crooks	$1.94
James Crooks	$0.08
Samuel Clingelsmith	$0.08
William Crooks	$0.10
Philip Keppel	$0.46
Thomas Carnahen	$0.41
George Keppel	$0.41
Robert Carnahen, single man	$0.50
Matthew Carnahen, single man	$0.50
Peter Kuhns	$0.06
Michael Claybaugh	$0.65
John Dennis	$0.22
John Dunlap	$0.59
Thomas Dunlap, single man	$0.06
Andrew Dunlap, single man	$0.58
James Dunlap	$0.14
Francis Dougherty	$0.22
Jesse Dougherty, single man	$0.06
Sarah Dougherty	$0.91
John Dougherty	$1.35
John Doughtery, single man	$0.50
Hugh Donley	$0.35
Michael Degraff	$0.06
John Dugan	$2.90
George Dugan, single man	$0.50
William Dunlap	$0.07
James Duff	$0.14
James Dougherty	$0.12

Abstracts of Westmoreland County, Pennsylvania, Tax Records 1815

Washington Township Name of Person	Tax
Alexander Duncan	$0.18
John Erwin	$1.75
Joseph Erwin, single man	$1.15
William Erwin	$0.31
Ephraim Evans	$2.46
Samuel Forman	$3.30
John Floid	$0.09
Daniel France	$1.03
Joseph Freer	$0.44
Peter Frier	$0.06
William Fulton	$0.32
Henry Frich	$1.54
George Fry	$0.06
John Frederick	$0.45
John Graham	$1.18
William Gibson, single man	$0.56
James Guthrie	$0.06
Christian Gumbert, Junior	$0.33
Christian Gumbert, Senior	$1.33
John Guthrie	$0.30
Archibald Gordon	$1.68
Jacob Grim	$0.56
Philip Grim	$0.72
William Guthrie, single man	$0.06
George Gartley	$0.67
John Grass	$2.52
Hugh Grames, single man	$1.25
James Grames	$0.73
Christian George	$0.17
Anthony Goldinger	$0.80
Widow George	$1.07
Thomas Garvey, single man	$2.98
Edward Gallaher	$2.94
Gilbert Grames	$1.32
William Hill	$0.81
William Hill	$0.11
William Hill, Junior, single man	$0.54

Abstracts of Westmoreland County, Pennsylvania, Tax Records 1815

Washington Township Name of Person	Tax
Samuel Hill, single man	$0.50
Robert Henry	$0.42
William Henry	$0.35
George Hawk, single man	$0.50
Daniel Henderson	$0.16
Adam Henderson	$0.77
William Highlands	$1.38
Joseph Huffman	$1.42
Nicholas Hainey	$0.25
Simon Hainey	$2.42
Gasper Hepler	$0.42
Henry Huffman, single man	$0.56
William Huey	$0.10
Frederick Habell	$0.22
Frederick Housholder	$0.72
James Hall, Senior	$0.06
George Hall	$1.36
James Hall, Junior	$1.75
Rowland Hughs	$0.50
David Herey	$0.36
William Herey, single man	$0.56
George Hamilton	$0.06
Samuel Hamilton, single man	$0.50
George Hawk	$1.32
Richard Hockley	$0.07
David Hunnel	$1.55
Philip Hickman	$0.60
Daniel Huey	$0.36
John Hall, single man	$0.50
Solomon Hoover	$0.06
Robert Hamilton	$0.12
Samuel Hindman, single man	$0.50
John Hendrickson	$0.70
Andrew Hindman	$1.45
John Hill	$1.75
Henry Isaman	$0.54
Christ[n] Isaman, single man	$0.50

Abstracts of Westmoreland County, Pennsylvania, Tax Records 1815

Washington Township Name of Person	Tax
Jacob Iman, Senior	$1.05
Jacob Iman, Junior	$0.10
James Jamieson, Junior	$0.50
James Jamieson, Senior	$2.60
John Jamieson	$0.68
John Johnston, Senior	$0.55
John Johnston, Junior	$0.06
Abraham Iman, single man	$0.60
Isaac Jackson, single man	$0.50
Isaac Kip	$0.09
Abraham Kip	$0.06
Widow Kelly	$0.42
David King	$0.38
Charles King	$0.20
William Kinley	$0.87
John Kinley	$0.87
John King	$0.89
James King	$0.06
Thomas Kirkwood	$1.94
James Kirkwood, single man	$0.50
Hugh Kirkwood, single man	$0.50
Michael Kisler	$1.02
John King	$0.06
John Lambright	$0.38
James Lyon	$0.19
William Lyon	$1.30
John Lardner	$0.75
James Livingston	$0.74
John Laffer	$0.39
Ezekiel Linning	$0.06
John Lenning	$0.10
John Lapton	$1.05
William Marshal	$0.34
John McLauglin	$0.35
William McCleod	$0.37
Robert Miller	$1.66
Samuel McLaughlen	$1.25

Abstracts of Westmoreland County, Pennsylvania, Tax Records 1815

Washington Township Name of Person	Tax
William McKee, single man	$0.50
William McLauglen	$0.13
Mathew Miller	$1.41
James McBrier	$1.07
John McDowel	$0.11
Benjamin Montgomery	$0.94
John McGeary	$0.45
William McGeary, Senior	$0.37
James McGeary	$0.06
Captain William McGeary	$0.98
Samuel McCutchen	$2.44
Issey Miller	$1.31
Robert McCown	$1.86
David McCleod, single man	$0.50
Widow McCutchen	$3.31
Samuel McCutchen	$1.05
William McCutchen, single man	$0.50
Robert McCutchen	$0.60
William McLaughlen	$2.20
~~William McLauglen~~	$0.00
James McLauglen, single man	$0.56
Mathew McLaughlen	$0.11
Edward Milligan	$1.22
William McLaughlen	$0.06
William McGeary	$1.20
David McGeary, single man	$0.50
Clement McGeary	$0.38
Thomas McKean	$1.20
William McKean	$1.34
John McKee	$0.84
John Morrison	$1.88
Philip McVey	$1.60
Patrick McVey, single man	$0.50
Hugh McCann	$0.09
Samuel Milligan	$0.80
James McCullough, Senior	$1.94
Samuel McCullough, single man	$0.98

Abstracts of Westmoreland County, Pennsylvania, Tax Records 1815

Washington Township Name of Person	Tax
James McCullough	$0.06
James McLaughlen	$0.40
Prussia Maclean	$1.13
John Maclean	$0.36
Samuel McKee, single man	$0.84
Widow McKee	$1.40
Daniel McCown, single man	$0.60
Christopher Mansfield	$0.34
Nathaniel McBrier	$0.18
David McBrier	$2.10
William Moorhead	$0.60
Hugh McKee	$2.26
Michael Moorhead	$0.36
Widow McDeide	$1.11
Finley McDade, single man	$0.50
Jacob Muffley	$0.08
William Mansfield, Senior	$0.33
John Muffley	$0.60
Widow McLaughlin	$1.56
Patrick Maghan	$0.06
John Maghan	$1.89
William Mansfield	$0.28
Edward McVey, single man	$1.56
Robert McQuilken	$0.56
Isaac Muffley	$0.06
James McKibbens	$0.71
Samuel McLaughlen, single man	$0.50
William Mays, single man	$0.50
William McKee	$1.58
John Marks	$0.70
John McCullough, single man	$0.50
John McVey	$0.50
Samuel McColley	$0.06
Thomas Mays	$0.22
James Mays, single man	$0.56
David Orner	$1.17
Daniel Ollam	$0.75

Abstracts of Westmoreland County, Pennsylvania, Tax Records 1815

Washington Township Name of Person	Tax
Adam Orrey	$0.06
Patrick O'Donald	$2.25
Samuel Paul, Esquire	$2.83
Doran Pennington	$1.31
George Painter	$1.24
William Painter	$0.08
Jacob Painter	$0.65
John Porter	$0.50
Sarah Paul, widow	$2.91
Jacob Philips	$2.27
Henry Philiber	$1.20
Patrick Price	$2.93
John Philips, single man	$0.50
John Quinn, single man	$0.50
John Quinn, Senior	$1.02
Oliver Quinn	$0.40
Robert Quinn, single man	$0.50
James Reed	$0.08
"he stands in the last of the Ys in the assessment"	
John Russel	$0.14
Robert Rochester	$0.15
William Ridenhour	$3.28
George Ridenhour	$0.14
Henry Ridenhour, single man	$0.50
Benjamin Rugh	$2.19
Martin Richard	$0.81
George Richey, single man	$2.04
John Ringle	$2.25
David Ringle	$0.76
Abraham Ringle	$1.08
John Reed	$1.11
Isaac Reed	$0.37
Daniel Ringle	$0.56
Robert Ralston	$0.32
John Rudolph	$0.63
Jacob Rudolph, single man	$0.56
Abraham Rudolph, single man	$0.54

Abstracts of Westmoreland County, Pennsylvania, Tax Records 1815

Washington Township Name of Person	Tax
Mathew Ralston	$0.53
Ditto	$0.67
Asa Rowley, single man	$0.06
Joseph Rowley	$0.56
William Ross, Esquire	$3.22
Daniel Rugh	$0.88
William Richardson	$0.20
William Ross, carpenter	$0.14
James Robison	$1.24
James Reed	$0.62
James Rowan	$0.36
John Rowan	$0.74
Frederick Richard	$1.94
John Ross	$1.20
William Reddick	$0.12
John Stewart	$0.10
John Stewart, Senior	$1.28
Samuel Stewart, single man	$0.88
Alexander Stewart, single man	$0.56
George Sober	$1.60
John Spear	$6.02
Robert Sproul	$1.76
James Sproul	$1.33
Widow Scott	$0.78
James Stanley	$1.58
John Steen	$0.68
Christian Spiker	$0.06
John Shuster	$0.08
William Shilling	$3.60
John Stewart	$1.02
William Stewart	$0.97
Samuel Shilling	$0.50
Robert Steen	$0.06
Robert Smith	$0.48
George Speace	$1.32
John Shear	$0.52
Robert Story	$0.31

Abstracts of Westmoreland County, Pennsylvania, Tax Records 1815

Washington Township Name of Person	Tax
John Swank	$0.08
Jacob Smebzer	$0.38
John Snyder	$0.08
Robison Spear	$0.18
Daniel Suman, single man	$0.50
James Spear	$1.39
Jacob Sluse	$0.18
James Stewart	$0.12
Samuel Stewart, single man	$1.66
William Trip	$0.06
William Thompson	$1.63
James Turk, single man	$0.50
Samuel Thompson	$1.61
Alexander Thompson, single man	$0.50
John Thompson	$0.31
Thomas Taylor	$0.41
Archibald Thompson	$0.41
Archibald Thompson	$0.80
John Townsend	$1.01
Peter Unkafair	$0.71
Thomas Vantine	$0.75
Abraham Varnor	$0.44
Henry Varnor, single man	$0.50
Robert Wylie, single man	$1.52
John Watt	$2.77
William Watt	$0.12
Christian Wolf	$0.15
Jacob Walters	$0.54
John Wylie	$1.63
Jacob Weister	$0.53
Andrew Whitagee	$0.08
John Wolfhart	$1.50
Martin Whitagee	$0.08
Alexander Walker	$0.92
John Walker, single man	$1.17
Samuel Walton	$3.20
Rudolph Weister	$0.56

Abstracts of Westmoreland County, Pennsylvania, Tax Records 1815

Washington Township Name of Person	Tax
John Weister	$0.45
Gasper Williard	$0.45
Jacob Wolfhart	$0.06
~~Jacob~~ William White	$1.01
Jacob Walters	$0.06
Robert Watson	$0.12
Jacob Weister, "Leigns"	$0.06
John Young	$1.28
W John Young, single man	$0.50
Joseph Young	$0.86
Henry Yockey	$0.29
Widow Yockey	$0.39
Christian Yockey "Dutch"	$0.06
Christian Yockey, Senior	$0.70
Christian Yockey, Junior	$0.30
Michael Younkins	$1.22

Washington Township Warrantees Names of Unseated Land	Tax
Thomas Alfrich	$1.30
Jacob Buck	$1.77
Barnabas Buck	$1.66
John and James Beatty	$2.09
John Backhouse	$1.10
Andrew Butler	$2.03
James Beatty	$1.50
Samuel Coats	$1.58
Thomas Cannon	$1.06
William Clark	$0.80
James Cannon	$0.37
Benjamin Davis	$1.89
Joel Evans	$1.91
Ezekiel Edwards	$1.50
Robert Foster	$1.55
John Fox	$1.06
William Fisher	$1.95

Abstracts of Westmoreland County, Pennsylvania,
Tax Records 1815

Washington Township Warrantees Names of Unseated Land

	Tax
Joseph Fox	$1.15
Henry Ferguson	$1.47
Norris Grady	$1.57
George Gray	$1.85
Caleb Graden	$1.57
William Gray	$1.10
George Gray	$0.85
James Hamilton heirs	$0.20
Josiah Hughs	$1.73
Levi or Lewis Hollingsworth	$1.63
James Hunter	$1.31
William Hall	$1.58
David Jamieson	$0.56
Johnston Joab	$1.63
William Jenkins	$1.64
William King	$1.50
William Kinley	$1.45
Mordecai Lewis	$1.57
Doctor Morgan	$1.93
Doctor Morgan	$1.96
John Morton	$1.84
Thomas Moore	$1.60
John Moore, Esquire, heirs	$1.20
William Pitt	$0.70
Sarah Powel	$1.12
Andrew Porter	$1.42
Philip Pancake	$1.61
Sarah Powel	$1.50
George Plenge	$1.76
William Philips	$0.43
John Randles	$1.86
Peter Reeve	$1.42
John Roberts	$1.55
Andrew Robison	$1.75
Wᵐ Stewart & McFarlen	$1.00
John Shaw	$1.11

Abstracts of Westmoreland County, Pennsylvania,
Tax Records 1815

Washington Township Warrantees Names of Unseated Land

	Tax
John Smith	$1.86
John Taylor	$1.30
Henry Woods	$1.50
Charles Wharton	$1.80
Thomas Wharton	$1.50
James Wharton	$1.67
John Evans	$1.50
John Woods, Esquire	$1.50

Appendix

The following is a transcription of the tax law in effect in 1815. The original is available at:
"Smith's Laws," digital images, Legislative Reference Bureau, *Pennsylvania Session Laws* (http://www.palrb.us : accessed 19 May 2014), Vol. 3 (1791–1802), General Laws (1799), p. 392, "An Act to raise and collect county rates and levies."

WHEREAS the several laws of this commonwealth, now in force, for raising county rates and levies, from frequent supplements and references, have become intricate: And whereas it will render the system more intelligible, and its operation more equal, to reduce the whole into one act, with such other provisions as may be necessary: Therefore,

Sect. I. *Be it enacted by the Senate and House of Representatives of the commonwealth of Pennsylvania, in General Assembly met, and it is hereby enacted by the authority of the same*, That the county commissioners and treasurers, and township, ward and district assessors, assistant assessors and collectors, heretofore elected and appointed within this commonwealth, and now holding and exercising their said offices, shall be continued therein, during the time for which they have been elected or appointed respectively.

Sect. II. *And be it further enacted by the authority aforesaid*, That the electors, qualified to vote for members of the state Legislature shall, at their respective general elections, within the city of Philadelphia, and the several counties of this state, annually elect one respectable citizen to be a commissioner of the proper county, to serve for three years next ensuing such election; and when any new county shall be erected, the electors there of shall elect, at their first general election, three citizens to serve as commissioners, of whom the highest in votes shall serve three years, the next highest two years, and the lowest one year, and their places respectively be supplied by the annual election of another citizen, to serve for three years; and if any commissioner shall die, remove from the county, or decline to serve in said office, the remaining commissioner or commissioners and the Court of Common Pleas for such county shall appoint a suitable citizen or citizens, to fill the said office until the next general election.

Sect. III. *And be it further enacted by the authority aforesaid,* That every commissioner, elected or appointed as aforesaid, shall, before he enters on the duties of his office, take and subscribe and oath or affirmation before some Judge of the Court of Common Pleas, Justice of the Peace, or Alderman of the city or county, respectively, for which such commissioner is elected, diligently, faithfully and impartially to perform the several duties enjoined on him by this act, to the best of his ability and judgment, without favour or affection, hatred, malice or ill-will; which oath or affirmation the office before whom the same is taken and subscribed shall certify, under his hand and seal, and deliver the same to the Prothonotary of the proper county, to be filed in his office.

Sect. IV. *And be it further enacted by the authority aforesaid,* That the citizens of every war, township and district, within the city of Philadelphia, and the several counties of this state, shall, on the same day, and at the same time and place, and under the same regulations as Inspectors for the general elections are directed to be chosen, annually elect one citizen, residing within such ward, township or district, to be an assessor for the term of one year; and in the year one thousand eight hundred and one, and every third year following, two other citizens to be assistant assessors for the term of one year, to do and perform the several duties enjoined and required of them by this act; and the constables holding such elections shall make a return thereof, signed by the judges, within ten days, to the commissioners of their proper county, or either of

them, who shall file the same in their office; and if any constable shall neglect to make such a return, he shall forfeit and pay the sum of five dollars for every such neglect.
Sect. V. *And be it further enacted by the authority aforesaid*, That if any person, elected or appointed as an assessor or assistant assessor, shall refuse or neglect to serve in such office for which he has been elected, every such assessor or assistant assessor shall pay a fine of twenty dollars: *Provided always*, That no person shall be obliged to serve as assessor or assistant assessor more than once in ten years. And if the citizens of any ward, township or district, neglect to elect an assessor or assistant assessor, or any citizen, so elected refuse or neglect to serve, or if vacancies happen by death or otherwise, a board of commissioners shall supply the vacancies, by appointing citizens to fill said offices, who shall reside within said township, ward or district, and who shall in all cases have the same powers, be subject to the same penalties, and receive like compensations, as though they had been elected by the citizens within their respective townships, wards or districts.
Sect. VI. *And be it further enacted by the authority aforesaid*, That every assessor, and assistant assessor, before he enters on the duties of his office, shall take and subscribe, before some Judge of the Court of Common Pleas, Alderman of the city, or some Justice of the Peace of the proper county, the same oath or affirmation enjoined on the commissioners by the third section of this act, a certified copy of which oath or affirmation, signed by the officer before whom the same was taken, such assessor or assistant assessor shall produce to the commissioners, within twenty days after his election, who shall file the same in their office.
Sect. VII. *And be if further enacted by the authority aforesaid*, That the commissioners shall annually, within thirty days after the general election, meet together, when each new commissioner shall produce a copy of the certificate, signed by the Prothonotary, proving his election and qualification, according to the provisions contained in this act; and the commissioners shall thereupon proceed to

make an estimate of the probably expense of their counties, respectively, for the ensuing year; and in the year one thousand eight hundred and one, and every third year following, shall within six weeks after the general election, issue their precepts to the respective township assessors, requiring them to make out a just and perfect return, in alphabetical order, or otherwise, as the commissioners may direct, of the names of all the taxable persons within their wards, townships or districts, respectively, and of all the property made taxable by the eighth section of this act, within thirty days after the date of such precept, together with a just valuation of the same, to be made in the manner herein after directed; and on receipt of such return, the said commissioners, or a majority of them, shall proceed to quota the townships, respectively, agreeably to the quantity and quality of land, and other taxable property, and when they have completed and ascertained the quotas for each township, they shall cause accurate transcripts of such assessments to be made out by their clerk, and transmit them to the ward or township assessors or collectors, respectively, on or before the second Monday of April, in each year, with the average rate per cent. in each township, directing such assessor or collector to give notice to each taxable inhabitant, within his ward or township, of the amount of the sum he stands for, and the rate per cent. of such amount, and of the time when, and place where, an appeal will be held, which notice the said assessor or collector shall give in print or writing, at least five days before such day of appeal; at which appeal a board of commissioners shall attend, and hear all persons who may apply for redress, and grant such relief, as to them shall appear just and reasonable; provided that the said commissioners shall not make any allowance or abatement, on account of any real property, in any other year than when a triennial return and assessment is taken and made, agreeably to the directions of this act, excepting where accidents by fire, or otherwise, may destroy buildings or other improvements.

Abstracts of Westmoreland County, Pennsylvania, Tax Records 1815

Sect. VIII. *And be it further enacted by the authority aforesaid*, That the assessors and assistant assessors of the city and county of Philadelphia, and the assessors of the other counties in this states, respectively, on receipt of precepts issued by the commissioners, agreeably to the seventh section of this act, shall preceed to take an account of all the names and surnames, in alphabetically order, or otherwise, as the commissioners may direct, of all taxable inhabitants within their townships, wards or districts, and of the following articles, hereby made taxable, viz. all lands held by patent, warrant, location or improvement; houses and lots of ground and groundrents, all grist-mills, saw-mills, fulling-mills, slitting-mills, rolling-mills, hemp-mills, oil-mills, snuff-mills, paper-mills, and powder-mills; all furnaces, forges, bloomeries, distilleries, sugar-houses, malt-houses, breweries, tan-yards and ferries; all negro and mulatto slaves; all horses, mares, geldings and cattle, above the age of four years; all offices and posts of profit, trades and occupations (ministers of the gospel, of every denomination, and school-masters, only excepted,) and of all single freemen above the age of twenty-one years, who shall not follow any occupation or calling; and when the enumeration shall be made as aforesaid, the assessors shall respectively call together their assistants, who, together with the assessors, shall proceed to value the aforesaid property, to the best of their ability and judgment, for what they think it will *bona fide* sell for in ready money, and rate all offices, professions, occupations and callings of all freemen at their discretion, having due regard to the profits arising from such trades and occupations, as to the amount of taxes to be raised: *Provided*, That not tax in any county shall in one year exceed the rate of one cent in every dollar of the adjusted valuation of the property, and the rate for any trade or occupation, or on any single freeman who follows no occupation, shall at no time exceed then dollars in one year, and shall be lowered in due proportion, as the tax on adjusted property may be lowered below one cent in the dollar.

Abstracts of Westmoreland County, Pennsylvania, Tax Records 1815

Sect. IX. *And be it further enacted by the authority aforesaid*, That the commissioners shall, on or before the first day of April, in ach [*sic*] of the two succeeding years after the triennial return and assessment shall have been made, send a transcript of the last triennial assessment to the respective township, ward and district assessors, within their respective counties, together with their precept, requiring them to take an account of all freemen, and the personal property made taxable by this act, together with a just valuation of the same, and also a valuation of all trades or occupations made taxable by the eighth section of this act, enjoining such assessor to make a just return to them, within thirty days from the date of such precept, noting in such return all alterations in his township, ward or district, occaisioned by transfer or division of real property, and also noting all person who have removed since the last assessment, and all single freemen, who have arrived at the age of twenty-one years since the last triennial assessment, and all others who have since that time came to inhabit in such township, ward or district together with the taxable property such person may possess, and the valuation thereof, agreeably to the provisions of this act; and the assessor or collector shall give like notice of the sum assessed on such person or persons, and of the day of appeal, which appeal the commissioners are hereby empowered to hold, in manner and form aforesaid.

Sect. X. *And be it further enacted by the authority aforesaid*, That the commissioners shall, immediately after the appeals are over, regulate the assessments according to the alterations made, and cause their clerks to make fair duplicated thereof, in alphabetical order, or otherwise, as the commissioners may direct; and it shall be the duty of each assessor, on or before the day of appeals in each year, to return two reputable citizens, who shall be freeholders of his ward or township, to the commissioners, whose duty it shall be to appoint one of them to be the collector; and if any person shall by appointed a collector as aforesaid, and refuse to serve, he shall forfeit and pay a fine of twenty dollars, and

another person shall be appointed in his stead; but any
person having served or paid his fine as a collector shall not
be obliged to serve the said office again, within the term of
ten years.

Sect XI. *And be it further enacted by the authority
aforesaid*, That it shall be the duty of the commissioners
within each county, from and after the passing of this act, to
employ a suitable person for clerk, who shall keep the books
and accounts of the board, and record or file whatsoever
proceedings they may direct and attest all orders and
warrants issued by them, and do and perform every other
act and thing whatsoever, which may pertain to his office as
clerk; and shall receive for his services such sum, as the
commissioners shall at their first meeting in each year, agree
upon.

Sect. XII. *And be it further enacted by the authority
aforesaid*, That the clerks to the boards of commissioners, so
as aforesaid appointed, shall keep fair books, wherein shall
be entered the name of the collector of each ward, township
or district, charging such collector with the amount of the
duplicate delivered him to collect, and crediting him with
allowances made after the appeal; for which purpose, they
shall enter in said books the names of the persons abated or
exonerated, together with the abatements or exonerations,
and the date when made, and shall certify such allowance in
the duplicates of the collectors, to enable the treasurer to
make settlements accordingly; and the said clerks shall,
moreover, keep an account of all orders issued by the board
for the payment of money, and enter the same in numerical
order in their books, and shall send a statement of the
names of the respective collectors, with the sums wherewith
each stands charged, to the county treasurer, as soon as the
duplicates are sent to the said collectors.

Sect. XIII. *And be it further enacted by the authority
aforesaid*, That the treasurers within the respective counties
of this states shall hold their offices during the terms for
which they have been already respectively appointed,* and
the commissioners of the respective counties or any two of

them, at the expiration thereof, and thenceforward annually, shall appoint a reputable citizen, for treasurer, who shall give bond, with sureties, to the satisfaction of the commissioners, conditioned for the faithful execution of the duties of his office, and to account for all monies which may come into his hand in pursuance thereof, and that he will deliver to his successor in office all books of entry, papers, documents and other things, which he may have or hold in right thereof, and pay him the balance of all monies due to the county; and in case of death, removal from the county, or misbehaviour in office of such treasurer, the said commissioners, or any two of them are hereby authorized and required to appoint another citizen to fill said office, whenever circumstances may require the same: *Provided,* That nothing in this act contained shall authorize any commissioners within this commonwealth to appoint any Judge of a court of justice, Clerk or Prothonotary of such courts, or any one of the said commissioners, to be a treasurer in their respective counties.

Sect. XIV. *And be it further enacted by the authority aforesaid,* That it shall be the duty of the treasurer to receive all monies due and accruing to the county, by or in consequence of this act or otherwise, and pay and disburse the same, for the discharge of the debts of the county, or warrants drawn by the board of commissioners; and the treasurer shall keep a just and true account of all monies received and disbursed, and hold and keep the same, at all times, ready for the inspection of the commissioners, and shall, one in three months, or oftener, if required, furnish the said commissioners with a statement thereof, balanced to the day specified by them, shewing all the monies, received and disbursed during the preceding term, and the balance remaining in his hands, together with the names of the collectors in whose hands any arrearages of taxes, and the amount thereof, may be out-standing; and shall, once in every year, settle his accounts, and produce his vouchers, which, being allowed by the commissioners, shall by them be laid before the auditors appointed under the act passed the

thirtieth day of March, one thousand seven hundred and
ninety-one, to settle the account of the commissioners and
treasurers of the respective counties of this state who shall
proceed to the settlement thereof, as by said act is directed;
and the commissioners shall allow the treasurer so much
percent. on all monies received and paid by him as they shall
from time to time deem sufficient for his services, which,
being approved of by the auditors aforesaid, shall be in full
for his services as treasurer.

Sect. XV. *And be it further enacted by the authority
aforesaid*, That the commissioners, or any two of them, shall
form a board in each county, and shall issue there warrants
with duplicates, to the respective collectors therein,
authorizing and requiring them to demand and receive, of
and from every person in such duplicate named, the sum
wherewith such person stand charged; and within six weeks
form the date of such warrant, the said collectors shall pay
all such monies, as they may by that time have received, to
the treasurer, at a certain time and place to be mentioned in
such warrant, at which time and place the treasurer shall
attend; and the board of commissioners shall, at the same
time and place, make abatements or allowances for
mistakes, or indigent persons, after which the collectors
shall proceed to demand and receive the remainders of the
tax; and if any person shall neglect or refuse to make
payment, within thirty days from the time of such demand,
it shall be the duty of the said collectors to levy the said tax,
by distress and sale of the goods and chattels of said
delinquent, giving ten days public notice of such sale, by
written or printed advertisements; and in case goods and
chattels cannot be found sufficient to satisfy the same, with
costs of suit, the said collector shall be authorized to take the
body of such delinquent, and convey him to the gaol of the
proper county, there to remain, until the taxes, with cost, be
paid, or secured to be paid, or he be otherwise discharged by
due course of law.

Sect. XVI. *And be it further enacted by the authority
aforesaid*, That the collectors of the several wards,

townships and districts, as aforesaid, shall within three months after having respectively received the corrected duplicates, subsequent to the appeals, pay into the hands of the respective treasurers, the whole amount of the taxes charged and assessed in such duplicate, without further delay, except such sums as the commissioners, may, in their discretion, exonerate them from, on pain of being answerable for an charged with the whole balance so remaining unpaid; and all the estate, real and personal, of such delinquent collectors shall be bound, as security for the payment of such balance, at and from the expiration of the said three months, a transcript of which balance shall by then entered by the treasurers with the Prothonotaries, whose duty it shall be to file the same, and which shall then operate to all intents and purposes, as if judgment were then entered against them for such balance in a court of record, provided that such balance shall not be a lien on such delinquent's property for a longer term than two years.

Sect. XVII. *And be it further enacted by the authority aforesaid,* That all fines and forfeitures under this act, not otherwise provided for, shall be recoverable before any Justice of the peace, as debts under twenty pounds, at the suit of the county treasurers, respectively, for the use of the respective county; and all inhabitants and taxable of such county shall be lawful witnesses on any trial concerning such fines and forfeitures.

Sect. XVIII. *And be it further enacted by the authority aforesaid,* That no person shall be re-appointed a collectors, who has not finally settled and paid off the whole amount of the balance due former duplicates, or given security for the payment thereof; and if any person who has heretofore been or hereafter shall be a collector of taxes, and shall have neglected or refused, or shall neglect or refuse to pay the treasurer of the respective county within the time limited by law, all the sums of money which shall be due on his duplicate, excepting such sum as may be allowed by the commissioners for unavoidable losses, or for services for collecting, as is herein after mentioned, the treasurer is hereby authorized and required to issue his warrant, under his hand and seal, directed to the Sheriff or Coroner of the proper county, commanding him to take the body and seize and secure all the estate, real and personal, of such delinquent collector, or which, in case of the death of the collector, may come into the hands or possession of his heirs, executors or administrators, and make return thereof to such treasurer, at such time and place as he shall appoint in his said warrant.

Sect. XIX. *And be it further enacted by the authority aforesaid*, That when the said lands and estate are secured as aforesaid, the treasurer of the proper county shall call a meeting of the board of commissioners, who are hereby required to attend, of which meeting he shall, in his said warrant, have notified the said delinquent collector; and if the arrearages are not then immediately discharged, the commissioners shall, and they are hereby empower and required, to issue there warrant to the Sheriff or Coroner of the proper county, empowering and requiring him to sell, at public sale, all such estates, as shall be so seized and secured, or any part thereof, giving ten days previous notice of such sale, by written or printed advertisements, and to bring the money arising from such sale to the commissioners who granted the warrant, at the time and place mentioned therein, in order to satisfy and pay the respective county treasurer the sum or balance that shall be so unpaid, or detained in the hands of the said collectors, or their heirs, executors or administrators, returning the overplus, if any to the owner, after all necessary charges are deducted.

Sect. XX. *And be it further enacted by the authority aforesaid*, That when any sale of lands, tenements or hereditaments shall be made by such Sheriff or Coroner, pursuant to this act, the conveyance thereof shall be by deed, executed and acknowledged in the Court of Common Pleas of the proper county, by the Sheriff or Coroner, or their successors in office, to such person or persons as shall purchase the same, in fee-simple or otherwise, which shall be most absolute and available in law against the said delinquents, their heirs and assigns; and if any delinquent collector has removed or shall remove into any other county within this state, or shall any estate, real or personal, in such other county or counties, and which shall not have been *bona fide*, and for a valuable consideration, disposed of, any process to be issued in pursuance of this act, may be directed to the Sheriff or Coroner of any such other county or counties, and shall be proceeded on as in and by this act is directed in the case before mentioned.

Sect. XXI. *And be it further enacted by the authority aforesaid*, That if any Sheriff or Coroner, who has heretofore received, or hereafter shall receive, any money or monies for taxes, by virtue of their respective offices, and the laws in such cases provided, shall neglect or refuse, within twenty days after demand made by the treasurer of the proper county, to render a just and true account thereof, or to pay the same to such treasurer, a warrant or warrants shall be issued by the commissioners again such delinquent Sheriff or Coroner, in like manner, and such proceedings shall thereon be had to final judgment, execution and sale, as are in and by this act directed respecting delinquent collectors, with this difference only, that if such delinquent officer, at the time or times of the commencement of such proceedings again him or them, continued to be in office, the warrant or warrants to be issued against him or them, in pursuance hereof, shall be directed to the other officer, either Sheriff or Coroner, of the proper county, as the case may be, who shall proceed thereon in like manner, as any Sheriff or Coroner may or can do under this act in like cases; and the property, real and personal of such Sheriff or Coroner shall in such cases be as liable to be seized in such other county or counties, and the like proceedings had on the same, as on the property of delinquent collectors is direct by the nineteen section of this act.

Sect. XXII. *And be it further enacted by the authority aforesaid*, That each of the commissioners shall be allowed, out of the county stock, the sum of one dollar and thirty-three cents, and no more, for every day's attendance on the duties of his office; and each assessor and assistant assessor shall be allowed, out of the county stock, the sum of one dollar, for each and every day's attendance on the duties of their offices respectively; and each collector shall retain, at a final settlement of his duplicate, the sum of five per cent. on all monies by him so collected, which shall be allowed to him by the treasurer, and credited accordingly, and shall be in full compensation for his services as collector.

Sect. XXIII. *And be it further enacted by the authority aforesaid*, That if any of the said commissioners shall neglect or refuse to do his or their duty in office, he or they, so offending, shall, on conviction thereof before the Court of Quarter Sessions of the proper county, be fined for every such offence, in a sum not exceeding one hundred dollars; and if any treasurer appointed by virtue of this act shall neglect or refuse to and perform the duties of his office, he shall, on conviction before the Court of Quarter Sessions of the proper county, be fined in any sum not exceeding two hundred dollars, and be disqualified from holding his office; which fines, by virtue of a writ of *fieri facias*, issuing from such court, and directed to the Sheriff or Coroner where such offender or his estate is, at the time of issuing such write, shall be levied by distress and sale of goods and chattels, lands and tenements, of such person so refusing or neglecting; and if any assessor, assistant assessor or collector, having taken upon themselves to perform the duties of their offices, respectively, according to this act, shall neglect or refuse to comply with their respective order or warrants, issued to them by the commissioners in pursuance of this act, or shall not do and perform the duties hereby enjoined on them, each of them, so neglecting or refusing, shall be fined by the board of commissioners of the proper count in any sum not exceeding forty dollars.

Sect. XXIV. *And be it further enacted by the authority aforesaid*, That when the inhabitants of any county shall be desirous to have a bridge erected or repaired on any public road over any water, they shall apply, by petition, to the Judges of the court of Quarter Sessions of the proper county, stating the place and circumstances of the case, with the probable expense, and the said court shall give said petition in charge to the grand jury, who shall consider of the propriety of erecting or repairing the same; and if the court and jury shall approve thereof, the court shall make and order on the commissioners, requiring them to cause the same to be erected or repaired in the manner prayed for, or in any other manner, to be directed by the said court and jury; and thereupon the said commissioners shall, as soon as conveniently may be done, carry the said order into effect. Sect. XXV. *And be it further enacted by the authority aforesaid*, That the goods and chattels of all tenants occupying any lands or tenements within this state shall be as liable to be distrained for taxes, arising out of such lands and tenements, as though the said tenants were the real owners thereof: *Provided nevertheless*, That the landlord, at the payment of his rents, unless specially agreed upon otherwise by contract or lease; and all unseated lands, held by location, warrant or patent, within this state, shall be valued and assessed in the same manner and form as any other property, but the collection of the taxes by the sale arising from the same shall be stayed by the commissioners of the proper county, until three months [*sic*] notice is given in three of the daily papers of the city of Philadelphia, and in one other newspaper in or nearest the county where such land is situate, that one or more year's tax is due on the unseated land in said county; and the expenses of such publication shall be at the proper cost of the delinquents; [and if any tax due as aforesaid shall, at the expiration of three months remain unpaid, the commissioners shall make a statement of said land, designating the title, as near as may be, with the amount of the tax assessed on each tract, and publish the same three months in the nearest public newspaper, and three times in at least three of the daily newspapers in the city of Philadelphia; and the commissioners shall thereupon, if the tax be not then paid, issue their warrant, under their hands and seals, to the Sheriff or Coroner, directing him to make sale of the whole or any part thereof, as he may find necessarily for the payment of the taxes thereon, with all costs necessarily accruing, and the proceedings therein shall be the same as is herein directed for the sale of the estate of delinquent collectors; and deeds of unseated lands so sold shall be executed in open court, at therein directed.]

Sect. XXVI. *And be it further enacted by the authority aforesaid*, That the commissioners of each county within this commonwealth shall have and use one common seal, for the purpose of sealing their proceedings, and that copies of the same when signed and sealed by the said commissioners and attested by their clerk, shall be good evidence of such proceedings on the trial of any cause in any of the courts within this commonwealth.

Sect. XXVII. *And be it further enacted by the authority aforesaid*, That the commissioners of each and every county shall publish a fair and accurate statement of all receipts and expenditures of the preceding year, for four days at least in one or more of the newspapers printed in their counties respectively, wherein a newspaper is or shall be printed, and where no paper is or shall be printed, then in at least fifty hand bills, to be set up in the most public places in the county, in the month of February, annually, under the penalty of one hundred dollars each, to be recovered by the Prothonotary of the county and paid into the treasury, for the use of the county; and the said statement shall enumerate the respective sums paid by each ward or township within the said city and county, and also designate the various sums expended for the support of the prisons, the pay of each commissioner and their clerks, the repairs of old or erection of new bridges, and the sums paid to individuals, for lands over which roads have been laid out, with such other items, as they may judge will have a tendency to convey general information on the various transactions of the year.

Sect. XXVIII. *And be it further enacted by the authority aforesaid*, That so much of all former laws of this commonwealth, as relates to or any way directs the raising of county rates and levies, are hereby repealed, and declared null and void: *Provided*, That nothing herein contained shall prevent the collection of any tax or taxes laid under any former law or laws. (*p*)

Passed 11th April, 1799—Recorded in Law Book No. VII. page 38.

(*p*) By act of 28th March, 1803, (chap. 2353) no county Treasurer shall serve in said office longer than three years in any term of six years.

A supplement to the act in the text was passed 4th April, 1805, (chap. 2602,) which is repealed and supplied by a further supplement, passed 28th March, 1808, (chap. 2985,) which enacts, that the assessors of the several wards, &c. shall previous to every triennial assessment, meet at the Commissioner's office in the respective counties, on a day by them to be appointed, and a majority of such assessors present shall proceed with said Commissioners to fix upon some uniform standard to ascertain the *bona fide* value of all property made taxable by the act in the text, taking into consideration improvements, proximity to market, and other advantages of situation, so that the same relative value of the aggregate amount of property may be observed as it respects wards, townships, incorporated boroughs and districts in the same county, that is observed in the valuation of property in the same township.

§ 2. The assessors and assistant assessors of the city and county of Philadelphia, and of the other counties, shall proceed according to the standard previously agreed on, and the directions to the act in the text, to ascertain the *bona fide* value of all property made taxable thereby within their respective wards, townships, incorporated boroughs and districts, and after their assessments are completed, the Assessors shall again meet at the Commissioner's office as before directed, to make the returns of their several assessments, when they shall be allowed to point out errors or deviations from said standard, in each other's returns, and the Commissioners shall be authorized upon such appeal to correct any errors or deviations that may be proved to their satisfaction, after which the Commissioners shall apportion the *quotas* of the county tax among the several wards, &c. within their counties respectively, according to the aggregate amount of property in each; and in holding appeals, it shall be the duty of the Assessors to attend said appeal to prevent impositions being practised upon the Commissioners by persons appealing.

§ 3. The supplement of 4th April, 1805, and so much of the act in the text as is hereby altered and supplied, are repealed.

For the mode of selling unseated lands for taxes, see the act of 3d April, 1804, (chap. 2512,) and the act of 4th April, 1809.

County Commissioners and Treasurers prohibited from holding any contract under the board of Commissioners, or superintending any public work, unless in their official capacity. Act of 21st March, 1806, (chap. 2681.)

County Commissioners authorized to administer oaths or affirmations in all cases that relate to the duties of their offices, act of 23d March, 1811.

For various duties enjoined on county Commissioners, and for other matters connected with the subject of county rates and levies, see the General Index, titles "County Commissioners," "County Treasurers," "Auditors," "Taxes," "Accounts."

Abstracts of Westmoreland County, Pennsylvania, Tax Records 1815

Abstracts of Westmoreland County, Pennsylvania,
Tax Records 1815

Index

I included all names in this book in the index exactly as they appear, without consolidating similar names into one entry. This means that there may be multiple entries for people with similar names (John Wilson and John Willson, for example). I also included any references to estate administrators or executors, heirs, military ranks, slaves, tenants, widows, and the word esquire. References to ferries, mills, stills, and farm implements are also included. Horses and cows are not included, but less common types of livestock (mares, oxen, etc.) are.

Abstracts of Westmoreland County, Pennsylvania, Tax Records 1815

Alshouse, Samuel, 101
Alsworth, Benjamin, 102
Alter, John, 295
Altman, David, 101
Altman, Gasper, 101
Altman, Jacob, 102, 241
Altman, John, 69, 102
Altman, Michael, 33
Altman, Peter, 101
Altman, Thomas, 101
Altman, Widow, 101
Alwine, Jacob, 102
Amalong, Catrine, 69
Amalong, Daniel, 69
Amberson, John, 49
Ambrose, Henry, 55
Amond, Anthony, 69
Amond, George, Junior, 69
Amond, George, Senior, 69
Amont, Friderich, 219
Anderson, Adam, 295
Anderson, Agness, 72
Anderson, Alexander, 199
Anderson, David, 19, 28, 219
Anderson, George, 199, 295
Anderson, Jacob, 167
Anderson, James, 69, 70, 167,
   295
Anderson, John, 1, 19, 55, 69,
   167, 295
Anderson, John, Junior, 1
Anderson, John, Senior, 1
Anderson, Joseph, 55
Anderson, Michael, 1
Anderson, Robert, 267
Anderson, Thomas, 1, 55, 295
Anderson, Thomas, Junior, 1
Anderson, William, 69, 145, 199,
   267
Anderson, William, Senior, 267
Andrew, John, 1, 33
Andrew, Joseph, 1
Andrew, Nicholas, 295
Andrews, Truman, 145
Anthony, George, 69
Anthony, John, 69
Anthony, Peter, 295

Anthony, Samuel, 69
Arb, John, 295
Arb, Lewis, 295
Arb, Peter, 295
Armbrust, John, 101
Armil, Daniel, 267
Armil, Jacob, 267
Armil, John, 267
Armil, John, Senior, 267
Armil, Widow, 267
Armor, David, 267
Armor, John, 268
Armor, William, 268
Armstrong, Andrew, 1, 102, 267
Armstrong, Ann, 241
Armstrong, G, 103
Armstrong, George, 93, 129, 199
Armstrong, James, 93, 102, 219
Armstrong, Robert, 101, 128,
   199
Armstrong, Samuel, 101, 241
Armstrong, Thomas, 219
Armstrong, William, 199, 219
Arnfriedt, 154
Arone, Joseph, 267
Arone, Thomas, 267
Arrat, Henry, 167
Arthur, John, 199
Artman, Jacob, 295
Artman, Widow, 295
Ashbaugh, Alexander, 295
Ashbaugh, Martin, 197
Ashbaugh, W^m, 167
Ashbough, Daniel, 167
Ashbough, George, 102
Ashbough, Henry, 167
Ashbough, Martain, 167
Ashburgh, Georg, 167
Aspie, Jacob, 241
Aspie, John, 241
Assour, Leonard, 101
Assyer, Henry, 101
Assyer, Jonas, 101
Atcheson, Thomas, 55
Auble, George, 33
Aukerman, George, 267
Aukerman, Ludwick, 267

Abstracts of Westmoreland County, Pennsylvania, Tax Records 1815

Aukerman, Philip, 267
Austro, Philip, 199
Bac [rest illegible], F, 173
Bachelor, William, 33
Backhenre, W^m, 146
Backhouse, John, 306
Badenhamer, Handel, 106
Baggs, Margerett, 147
Bailey, James, 295
Bailey, Nancy, 199
Bailey, Nathaniel, 199
Bails, John, 295
Baily, Nathaniel, 210
Baird, Charles, 2
Baird, Irwin, 268
Baird, James, Senior, 2
Baird, John, 2
Baird, Joseph, 56
Baird, Robert, 3
Baird, Samuel, 1
Baird, Thomas, 2
Baird, William, Junior, 2
Baird, William, Senior, 1
Baird, Wm, 17
Baker, Abraham, 93
Baker, Adam, 103
Baker, George, 104, 106
Baker, Peter, 106
Baker, Widow, 270
Baldridge, Jno, 270
Baldridge, John, 270
Baldridge, Joseph, 3, 270
Baldridge, Robert, 200, 241, 251
Baldridge, Saml, 270
Baldridge, Samuel, 270
Baldridge, Thomas, 201, 241
Baldwin, William, 242
Baleles, Amdrew, 147
Bamford, Charles, 241
Bankard, Laurence, 296
Barber, John, 167, 296
Barber, Samuel, 70, 295
Barclay, P. William, 270
Barclay, Thomas, 165
Bare, Adam, 145
Bare, Christian, 33
Bare, David, 33

Bare, Henry, 33, 269
Bare, John, 146
Bare, Philip, 34
Barige, Thomas, 199
Barington, 67
Barlean, John, 220
Barlein, Jacob, 4
Barlin, Frederick, 71
Barlin, Jacob, 71, 221
Barlin, Jacob, Senior, 70
Barlin, John, 71
Barnes, William, 93
Barnet, Robert, 221
Barnet, William, 220
Barnett, John, 4
Barnett, Samuel, 4
Barnett, William, 4
Barney, John, 147
Barnhart, Abraham, 106
Barnhart, Jacob, 268
Barnhart, John, 106
Barnhart, William, Junior, 106
Barnhart, William, Senior, 105
Barnhurt, David, 147
Barns, David, 146
Barns, F. Joseph, 268
Barns, George, 170
Barns, John, 170, 268
Barns, Joseph, 2
Barns, William, 56, 268, 269
Barns, William, Junior, 269
Barr, Adam, 104
Barr, David, 104
Barr, Elizabeth, 2
Barr, Jacob, 106
Barr, James, 242
Barr, John, 106, 241
Barr, Leonard, 104
Barr, Robert, 242
Barten, Jacob, 70
Bartholomew, Benedict, Senior, 103
Bartholomew, Benidict, 103
Barton, Henry, 93
Bash, John, 296
Bash, Martin, 268
Bash, Michael, 268

Abstracts of Westmoreland County, Pennsylvania, Tax Records 1815

Bates, Daniel, 3
Bauder, Jacob, 34
Bauderz, Frederick, 145
Baughm, Adam, 170
Baughman, John, 104
Baum, John, 104
Baum, Peter, 104
Baum, Widow, 104
Bawman, Adam, 296
Baxter, Alexander, 70
Baxter, Alken, 197
Baxter, Atkin, 170
Baxter, Robert, 70, 169, 295
Bayer, Andrew, 146
Bayer, John, 146
Bayers, Peter, 146
Bayle, Neal, 296
Beach, John, 55
Beachly, Conrad, 170
Beachly, Daniel, 169
Beachly, William, 170
Beacom, John, Senior, 71
Beacorn, John, Junior, 71
Beacorn, Robert, 71
Beaford, Peter, 103
Beam, Henry, 56
Beamer, John, 71
Bear, George, 220
Bear, Jacob, 295
Bear, Philip, 250
Bear, Phillip, 242
Beard, Charles, 220
Beard, George, 171
Beard, Thomas, 220
Beard, William, 220
Bearer, John, 107
Beattey, Jamison, 294
Beatty, Benjamin, 269
Beatty, David, 2
Beatty, Hamilton, 269
Beatty, James, 242, 306
Beatty, John, 241, 306
Beatty, William, 3
Beaty, Thomas, 4
Beaumont, Jesse, 242
Beaumont, John, 241
Beaumont, Philip, 242

Beaumont, Richard, 242
Beaver, Christian, 296
Beazel, John, 199
Beazel, Matthew, 201
Beazel, William, Jun, 202
Beazel, William, Junior, 201
Beazel, William, Senior, 201
Bechtle, Abraham, 49
Bechtle, Henry, 49
Beck, Adam, 104
Beck, Daniel, 103
Beck, Jacob, 55, 104
Beck, John, 104
Beck, Leonard, 104
Beck, William, 104
Becker, Jacob, 102
Becket, Elizabeth, 200
Beckett, John, 200
Beer, George, 4
Beerer, John, 93
Beever, Abraham, 293
Beggert, Joseph, 171
Bell, Andrew, 3
Bell, David, 171
Bell, James, 1, 221
Bell, John, 2, 3
Bell, John, Junior, 2
Bell, Robert, 2
Bell, Samuel, 2
Bell, Simon, 103
Bell, Walter, 242
Bell, Widow, 293
Bell, William, 2, 241, 270
Bellows, John, 296
Bellows, Peter, 3
Benar, Matthew, 200
Bennet, 245
Bennet, Abraham, 56
Bennet, David, 55
Bennet, Gersham, 242
Bennet, Jn⁰, 185
Bennet, John, 55, 145, 169, 259, 260
Bennet, Nicholas, 55
Bennet, William, Junior, 55
Bennet, William, Senior, 56
Bennett, John, 201

Abstracts of Westmoreland County, Pennsylvania, Tax Records 1815

Benninger, John, 56, 106
Benom, Joseph, 201
Berger, Christian, 171, 293
Berkey, John, 34
Berkhamer, John, 200
Berkhamer, Joseph, 200
Berlian, Jacob, 270
Berry, Barbarah, 170
Berry, John, 3
Berry, Michael, 93
Berry, Thomas, 270
Best, George, 106
Best, Michael, 107
Best, William, 106
Betall, Henry, 105
Bets, William, 103
Bett, Marshem, Senior, 107
Bettinger, John, 106
Beverlin, James, 33
Bevins, Thomas, 270
Beygle, Jacob, 168
Biddel, Widow, 107
Bier, Philip, 55, 67
Bierley, John, 146
Bigelow, Israel, 70
Biggert, John, 270
Biggert, Widow, 93
Biggs, A., 172
Biggs, Andrew, 169
Bigham, Hugh, 220
Bigham, John, 3
Bigham, Samuel, 220
Bigham, Thomas, 221
Bigham, William, 200
Bills, Allanson, 55
Bittz, William, 219
Black, Abraham, 34, 49
Black, Charles, 56
Black, Christian, 33
Black, Daniel, 242
Black, Jacob, 104
Black, James, 55
Black, John, 269, 296
Black, Joshua, 49
Black, Patrick, 170
Black, Robert, 56
Blackborn, James, 171

Blackbourn, John, 168
Blackbourn, Moses, 168
Blackbourn, Thomas, 168, 169
Blackbourn, William, 168
Blackburn, Anthony, 200
Blackburn, Joseph, 199
Blackburn, Simon, 199
Blackburn, Thos, 197
Blackston, Barbara, 52
Blackston, Hanah, 52
Blackston, Susen, 52
Blaine, Ephraim, 102, 144
Blaine, James, 144
Blair, Alexander, 55
Blair, Evins, 171
Blair, Gabriel, 170
Blair, James, 2
Blair, John, 55, 241
Blair, Thomas, 70, 71
Blair, William, 55
Blake, Samuel, 146
Blakely, Widow, 296
Bleakley, Matthew, 201
Bleakley, Thomas, 201
Bleaks, John, 200
Bleaks, Nancy, 199
Bletcher, Henry, 164
Bloos, Daniel, 106
Blor, Barnebas, 221
Bloss, Barnabas, 70
Bloss, George, 70
Blystone, Peter, 145
Blythe, Benjamin, 270
Boch, Christiana, 71
Bodershell, James, 103
Bodle, Abraham, 241
Boher, Abraham, 200
Bois, Mark, 268
Bollman, John, 1
Bonar, William, 200
Bonbright, Jacob, 270
Bonbright, John, 271
Bonebright, Daniel, 269
Bonebright, Henery, 269
Bonebright, Henry, 269
Booght, George, 169
Border, Frederick, 103

Abstracts of Westmoreland County, Pennsylvania, Tax Records 1815

Bore, Christopher, 268
Bore, George, 146
Bore, Peter, 145
Boreland, Anthy, 145
Boreland, David, 145
Boreland, James, 48
Boreland, Ludwick, 295
Boreland, Robert, 296
Boreland, Samuel, 296
Boreland, Thomas, 295
Borland, James, 220
Borland, John, 70
Borland, John, Junior, 88
Borland, Lydia, 70
Borland, Mathew, 71
Borland, Richard, 71
Borts, Daniel, 107, 221
Borts, Henry, 107
Borts, Isaac, 107
Borts, Michael, 107, 220
Boughman, Adam, 105, 170
Boughman, Henry, 170
Boughman, Jacob, 105
Boughman, John, 170
Boughman, John, Senior, 105
Boughman, Peter, 169
Bovard, Charles, 295
Bovard, John, Junior, 220
Bovard, John, Senior, 220
Bovard, Oliver, 34
Bowers, Jacob, 93
Bowers, Jonathan, 107
Bowman, Abraham, 104
Bowman, Daniel, 105
Bowman, Peter, 163
Boyd, Alexander, 242
Boyd, Archibald, 169
Boyd, Benjamon, 169
Boyd, Henry, 103, 142
Boyd, Hugh, 220
Boyd, John, 170, 295
Boyd, Robert, 55, 242, 295
Boyd, Ruth, 168, 171, 174
Boyd, Thomas, 3
Boyd, William, 34, 55, 168, 169
Boyd, Wm, 242
Boyed, John, 168

Boyer, Andrew, 105
Boyer, Daniel, 105
Boyer, David, 105
Boyer, Erasmus, 105
Boyers, Andrew, 119
Boyes, Mark B., 102
Boyle, Patrick, 220
Boyles, John, 219
Boyles, Samuel, 28
Boys, Stephen, 200
Braden, Edward, 3
Braden, John, 3
Braden, William, 4, 146
Bradley, Jeremiah, 56
Bradshaw, William, 200
Brady, 55
Brady, David, 269
Brady, Hugh, 93
Brady, James, 56, 93, 102, 104
Brady, Jane, 55
Brady, John, 55
Brady, Joseph, 107
Brady, Robert, 93
Brake, Philip, 33
Brandon, John, 34
Brant, Abraham, 56
Brant, Oliver, 242
Branthaver, Adam, 296
Brantheiffer, Henry, 71
Breaden, James, 4
Break, George, 225
Bream, Thomas, 103
Brenaman, Daniel, 168
Brenaman, Henry, 197
Brenamon, Henry, 168
Breneman, Christian, 171
Brenison, Michael, 33
Brenneman, David, 33
Brenneman, Jacob, 241
Brenninger, Abram, 268
Brewer, Henry, 295
Brewer, Jacob, 269
Brewer, John, 269
Brewer, William, 296
brewery, 134, 143
Brice, Ezekiel, 220
Brice, James, 170

Abstracts of Westmoreland County, Pennsylvania, Tax Records 1815

Brice, William, 219
Bricker, George, 221
Bricker, Philip, 105
Bridge, Henry, 3
Bridge, Mary, 3
Bridge, Mathias, 3
Bridge, Peter, 269
Bridge, Petter, 293
Briere, David, 146
Brindle, George, 269
Brindle, John, 270
Brine, Daniel, 4
Briney, Michael, 70
Briney, Peter, 70
Brinker, George, 146, 268
Brinker, Henry, 268
Brinker, Jacob, 70, 76
Brinker, John, 146
Brinkley, William, 104
Brisbane, William, 103
Brisben, William, Junior, 107
Brisbin, William, 169
Brisbourn, Arthur, 168
Brittin, Adam, 169
Broadswords, Peter, 242
Brogan, Charles, 2
Brojan, Dennis, 2
Brought, George, 103
Brought, William, 103
Brovard, James, 107
Brow, Peter, 49
Browler, Christopher, 270
Brown, 197
Brown, Adam, 33, 107
Brown, Alexander, 219
Brown, Andrew, 168, 295
Brown, Caleb, 201
Brown, David, 55, 219
Brown, George, 102, 107, 110,
    130, 220
Brown, Henry, 171
Brown, James, 56
Brown, James, Junior, 170
Brown, John, 51, 56, 168, 171,
    219, 295, 296
Brown, Joseph, 167
Brown, Lewis, 104

Brown, Matthew, 55
Brown, Robert, 55, 56, 93, 107,
    168
Brown, Robert, Junior, 169
Brown, Rob$_t$, 38
Brown, Thomas, 104
Brown, William, 55, 56, 171
Brown, William, Senior, 56
Browns, 177
Brubaker, Jacob, 169
Brush, Joseph, 169
Buchanan, David, 220
Buchanan, John, 220
Buchanan, Thomas, 220
Buchanan, William, 220
Buck, Barnabas, 306
Buck, Jacob, 306
Buck, John, 270
Buck, Joseph, 270
Buckholder, Henry, 3
Budd, Daniel, 200
Budd, Joseph, 200
Budd, Joseph, Junior, 201
Budd, Joseph, Senior, 200
Budd, Joshua, Senior, 200
Buel, Benjamin, 71
Bughman, George, 170
Bughman, George, Senior, 105
Bughman, Jacob, 105
Bulean, Joseph, 269
bull, 73
Bunison, Peter, 33
Burck, John, 147
Burgan, Daniel, 200
Burleigh, Clementz, 145
Burley, Michael, 145
Burns, George, 219
Burns, Mary, 199
Burns, Nathaniel, 2
Burris, Daniel, 55
Bursard, Many, 147
Burton, John, 242
Bush, Christian, 70
Bush, Daniel, 105
Bush, John, 219
Bush, L Charles, 162
Bush, L. Charles, 164

Abstracts of Westmoreland County, Pennsylvania, Tax Records 1815

Bush, Peter, 106
Bush, Philip, 103
Bushfield, George, 93
Bushfield, Samuel, 105
Bushyager, J. George, 105
Butler, Andrew, 306
Butler, Jacob, 34
Butler, L. William, 296
Butt, Jacob, 146
Butterfield, Giles, 3
Buzzard, Gasper, 269
Buzzard, George, 269
Buzzard, John, 269, 296
Buzzard, Samuel, 268
Buzzerd, Conrad, 170
Byam, Thomas, 146
Byerley, Adam, 145
Byerly, Andrew, 168, 169
Byerly, Benjamin, 169
Byerly, Jacob, 171
Byerly, Jacob, Junior, 168
Byerly, Joseph, 106
Byerly, Michael, 106
Byers, James, 269
Byers, Joseph, 268
Byres, Gasper, 106
Byser, Frederick, 106
Bystle, Andrew, 146
Cable, Jesse, 7
Cachran, John, 72
Cain, James, 271
Cain, Thomas, 271
Caldwell, Benjamin, 5
Caldwell, Ebanezer, 171
Caldwell, Elizabeth, 222
Caldwell, Henry, 57
Caldwell, James, 5, 171, 222
Caldwell, James, Senior, 5
Caldwell, John, 56
Caldwell, Samuel, 57
Caley, Thomas, 147
Calhoon, Samuel, 222
Call, Isaac, 201
Callen, Samuel, 296
Calvin, James, 244
Cambell, W^m, 205
Cammon, Herman, 57

Campbel, William, 272
Campbell, Alexander, 221
Campbell, Andrew, 4
Campbell, Elizabeth, 173
Campbell, George, 202, 222
Campbell, Grizel, 172
Campbell, Henry, 222
Campbell, James, 6, 165, 272
Campbell, Jean, 221
Campbell, Jno, 165
Campbell, John, 4, 172
Campbell, John, Senior, 4
Campbell, Joseph, 223
Campbell, Jos^h, 165
Campbell, Margaret, 165, 174
Campbell, Mary, 165
Campbell, Robert, 272
Campbell, Robt, 165
Campbell, Ruth, 165
Campbell, Samuel, 223
Campbell, Terrence, 66
Campbell, Thomas, 174
Campbell, William, 57, 72, 165,
    172, 201
Campbelle, Alexander, 48
Camps, Mathias, 51
Camray, Adam, 72
Canaan, Jonathan, 5
Canaan, Richard, 6, 18
Canan, Joseph, 5
Cander, William, 108, 223
Cannel, John, 147
Cannon, Alexander, 7
Cannon, James, 306
Cannon, John, 7
Cannon, Thomas, 306
Captain, 60, 106, 137, 151, 159,
    185, 246, 267, 271, 301
Carale, Cornelious, 264
Carathers, Samuel, 173
card machine, 148, 153
carder, 98
carding machine, 24, 145, 173,
    181, 185, 187, 196, 275
Carlean, Junior, Joseph, 71
Carleen, Joseph, Senior, 72
Carlen, John, 243

Abstracts of Westmoreland County, Pennsylvania, Tax Records 1815

Carlisle, Elizabeth, 174
Carlisle, John, 174
Carlton, 56
Carlton, Edward, 29
Carnahan, 168
Carnahan, James, 243, 244
Carnahan, Jn°, 197
Carnahan, John, 51, 173, 243
Carnahan, John, Senior, 243
Carnahen, David, Junior, 296
Carnahen, David, Senior, 296
Carnahen, Matthew, 297
Carnahen, Robert, 297
Carnahen, Thomas, 297
Carnehan, Benjamin, 244
Carns, James, 202
Carns, Nathaniel, 202
Carns, Peter, 202
Carns, William, 202
Carothers, Richard, 272
Carpenter, John, 73
Carr, Arthur, 93, 109
Carr, Widow, 173
Carrah, James, 271
Carrel, James, 296
Carson, James, 6
Carson, John, Junior, 6
Carson, John, Senior, 6
Carson, Joseph, 6
Carson, Paine, 6
Carson, William, 6
Carthers, Sally, 173
Carty, Daniel, 5
Caruthers, James, 244
Caruthers, John, 243
Caruthers, John C, 243
Caruthers, William, 4, 221
Casada, William, 271
Casady, James, 174
Casady, John, 174
Casally, Cornelius, 8, 27
Case, Joseph, 7
Cashaday, William, 174
Casilly, P Michael, 93
Caskey, John, 29
Caskey, Samuel, 4
Casklett, William, 147

Casper, R, 197
Cassilly, P. Michael, 109
Castner, John, 202
cattle, 200, 203, 204
Cauffield, John, 56
Cavett, John, 4
Cavin, Bengamen, 172
Cavin, John, Junior, 174
Cavin, John, Senior, 172
Cavit, John, 173
Cavode, Jacob, 57
Ceese, Christian, 147
Ceil, Adam, 271
Ceil, Daniel, 271
Ceil, Jonathan, 272
Celer, Peter, 271
Cerwin, Morris, 202
Chadwick, James, 174
Chambers, Benjamin, 296
Chambers, George, 296
Chambers, James, 108, 296
Chambers, John, 202, 271
Chambers, Joseph, 202
Chambers, Magret, 296
Chambers, William, 296
Chapen, Amzi, 203
Chapin, Amaziah, 201
Chapman, Nicholas, 5
Charleton, Robert, 5
Chorry, William, 147
Chrisman, Charles, 108
Chrisman, John, 108
Christman, Jacob, 164, 271
Christman, Mas, 94
Christmore, Joseph, 108
Christy, Andrew, 173, 174
Christy, James, 173, 222
Christy, James, Junior, 221
Christy, James, Senior, 222
Christy, John, Junior, 222
Christy, John, Senior, 222
Christy, Joseph, 222, 297
Christy, William, 71
Chrotman, Jacob, 147
Churn, Michael, 7
Clark, Ephraim, 244
Clark, George, 168, 174

Abstracts of Westmoreland County, Pennsylvania, Tax Records 1815

Clark, Griffith, 93
Clark, Henry, 56
Clark, Isaac, 296
Clark, James, 56, 71
Clark, John, 108, 174
Clark, Moses, 72
Clark, Paul, 56
Clark, Silas, 201
Clark, William, 56, 94, 173, 221, 244, 306
Clark, Wm, 263
Clarke, Wᵐ, 73
Clawson, Cornelius, 56
Clawson, Peter, 296
Claybaugh, Michael, 297
Cleaton, William, 202
Clements, James, 272
Clendenning, Andrew, 243
Clendenning, William, 242
Clerk, Andrew, 147
Clerk, James, 56, 57
Clerk, William, 56
Clever, Henry, 8
Clewbine, John, 171
Clifford, Charles, Junior, 57
Clifford, Charles, Senior, 57
Clifford, Joseph, 57
Clifford, Mary, 56
Clifford, Thomas, 57
Cline, Barnabas, Senior, 5
Cline, Barney, 296
Cline, Barney, Junior, 5
Cline, Christian, 108
Cline, George, 109
Cline, Henry, 297
Cline, Jacob, Senior, 73
Cline, John, 73, 173
Cline, Junior, Jacob, 73
Cline, Michael, 73
Cline, Peter, 5
Cline, Philip, 28
Cline, Widow, 108
Cline, William, 107
Clingelsmith, Andrew, 222
Clingelsmith, Gasper, 222
Clingelsmith, George, 297
Clingelsmith, Jacob, 297

Clingelsmith, John, 222, 296
Clingelsmith, Philip, 296
Clingelsmith, Samuel, 297
Clint, Jacob, 72
Close, Adam, 73
Closs, James, 297
Cloud, Joseph, 202
Cloud, Nathaniel, 201
Cloud, Thomas, Senior, 201
Clymer, Henry, 222
Coats, Samuel, 306
Cochran, James, 6
Cochran, John, 7, 34, 222, 243
Cochran, Robert, 7
Cochran, Samuel, 7, 56, 221
Cochran, William, 7, 221
Codderman, Michael, 108
Coffman, Barbara, 223
Coffman, John, 243
Cogan, Jesse, 7
Cogan, John, 7
Cogh, John, 108
Cogh, Peter, 108
Colgin, Patrick, 222
Coller, Henry, 34
Collin, James, 38
Collins, Charles, 296
Collins, Elijah, 243
Collins, George, 34
Collins, James, 52, 73, 174
Collins, John, 1, 15, 29
Collins, Joˢ, 188
Collins, Joseph, 72
Collins, Timothy, 296
Colonel, 59, 63, 64, 113, 121, 181, 212, 230, 267
Conden, Richard, 6
Congleton, John, 244
Conkel, John, 243
Conkle, Michael, 201
Connelly, John, 94
Conner, James, 147
Connor, Christopher, 222
Connor, Dennes, 7
Connor, John, 8
Connor, Timothy, 7
Conrad, Jacob, 34

Abstracts of Westmoreland County, Pennsylvania, Tax Records 1815

Coo, James, 73, 89
Cook, Asa, 72
Cook, Assa, Junior, 173
Cook, Assa, Senior, 173
Cook, David, 93
Cook, James, 202
Cook, William, 73
Coons, Peter, 71
Cooper, Alexr, 172
Cooper, James, 172
Cooper, John, 172
Cooper, Robert, 5, 171, 172
Cooper, Samuel, 222
Cooper, Wᵐ, 172
Cope, Abraham, 244
Cope, George, 108
Cope, John, 107
Copeland, John, 172
Copeland, Joseph, 172
Copeland, Thomas, 172
Cord, James, 244
Cort, Daniel, 108
Cort, Joseph, Junior, 108
Cort, Joseph, Senior, 108
Coruthers, James, 247
Coter, Conrad, Junior, 243
Coter, Conrad, Senior, 243
Coter, George, 244
Coter, Jacob, 243
Coter, Martin, 243
Coter, Philip, 243
Coughinower, John, 49
Coulter, Eli, 94
Coulter, James, Junior, 7
Coulter, James, Senior, 7
Coulter, Priscilla, 94
Coulter, Richard, 94
Coulter, Robert, 7
Coulter, Widow, 109
Coulter, William, 174
Coup, Michael, 56
Courts, Daniel, 173
Coutler, James, 7
Cowan, James, Senior, 172
Cowan, Joseph, 172
Cowan, Mathias, 172
Cowan, Patrick, 244

Cowan, Robert, 222
Cowan, William, 174
Cowen, George, 172
Cox, Moses, 174
Coy, Dewalt, 72
Coy, John, 72
Coyle, James, 297
Coyle, John, 49
Coyle, Philip, 57
Crackshanks, James, 147
Craft, George, 108
Craig, Alexander, 223
Craig, Andrew, 7, 272
Craig, Elizabeth, 14, 28
Craig, James, 5, 223
Craig, John, 6, 108, 271, 296
Craig, Joseph, 7
Craig, Mary, 296
Craig, Matthews, 6
Craig, Nancy, 6
Craig, Samuel, 108, 109
Craig, Widow, 271
Craig, William, 6, 271
Crasgay, William, 222
Crate, Daniel, 6
Crate, Michael, 4
Cratty, John, 72
Cravans, Nelly, 265
Craven, Mary, 244
Crawford, 202
Crawford, George, 297
Crawford, James, 271
Crawford, John, 271
Crawford, Mathias, 107
Crawford, William, 109
Creamer, George, 147
Cribbs, Christopher, 6, 108
Cribs, Christopher, 25
Crice, Andrew, 244
Crice, George, 244
Crice, Widow, 244
Crise, John, 243
Critzer, George, 271
Crooks, James, 297
Crooks, John, 297
Crooks, William, 297
Crookshank, David, 72

Abstracts of Westmoreland County, Pennsylvania, Tax Records 1815

Crookshanks, Widow, 297
Crosby, William, 174
Cross, John, 56
Crossan, Garret, 6
Crossan, Peter, 272
Crotzy, Michael, 49, 51
Crow, Jane, 5
Crow, Samuel, 5
Crozan, Benjamin, 6
Crozan, John, 29
Crozan, Robert, 29
Cruckshanks, David, 221
Cryder, John, 94
Culbertson, Alexander, 4, 271
Culbertson, Hugh, 5
Culbertson, James, 4, 5
Culbertson, James Samuel, 4
Culbertson, John, 174
Culbertson, Joseph, 4
Culbertson, Robert, 221, 223
Culbertson, Thomas, 8
Cummins, John, 7, 34
Cunin, Morris, 201
Cunning, Elizabeth, 34
Cunning, John, 34, 164
Cunningham, Alexander, 202
Cunningham, James, 202
Cunningham, Moses, 72
Cunningham, Robert, 202, 223
Cunningham, William, 223
Currin, John, 272
Curry, David, 109
Curry, Samuel, 174
Curry, William, 109
Cust, 94
Cyphert, Anthony, 221
Cyphert, Philip, 221
Dader, David, 109
Dader, Jacob, 109
Daily, H. Samuel, 203
Daily, John, 203
Daniel, Harold, 110
Daniel, widow, 110
Darby, Hugh, 244
Darby, John, 245
Darby, William, 245
Darr, George, 202

Darr, Michael, 202
Darragh, John, 73
Darragh, William, Junior, 73
Darragh, William, Senior, 74
Daugherty, Hugh, 33
Daveling, Patrick, 109
David, Wm, 74
Davidson, Robert, 202
Davis, 245
Davis, Benjamin, 203, 306
Davis, Caleb, 57
Davis, David, 109, 203
Davis, Dorsey, 203
Davis, Ephraim, 203
Davis, Isaiah, 57
Davis, Jesse, 203
Davis, John, 74, 109, 272
Davis, Philip, 35
Davis, Samuel, 203
Davis, Sarah, 57
Davis, William, 9, 147
Davis, Wm, 203
Davison, Francis, 273
Davison, Jacob, 175
Day, Nicholas, 8, 223
Days, Adam, 148
De Happart, St. Leger, 244
Deal, 117, 118
Deal, George, 175
Deal, John, 175
Deal, Philip, 175
Decampe, George, 175
Deckart, Daniel, 57
Deckart, Ebenezer, 57
Deckart, Isaac, 57
Deckart, Job, 57
Deckart, John, 57
Deeds, John, 148
Deemer, Frederick, 8
Deemmer, Johnnathan, 224
Degraff, Michael, 297
Deihl, Henry, 272
Deleney, Edward, 273
Delinger, Jacob, 37
Dellinger, Jacob, 245
Delong, Francis, 109
Dennis, John, 297

Abstracts of Westmoreland County, Pennsylvania, Tax Records 1815

Denniston, Samuel, 8
Denniston, William, 9
Depue, Abraham, 203
Detman, Henry, 197
Detman, Jnº, 197
Detman, John, 175
Develin, Nicholas, 175
Dever, Hugh, 57
Devitt, John, 203
Dible, Jacob, 74
Dibler, Frederick, 110
Dibler, Fredrick, 74
Dick, Mungo, 174
Dickey, David, 223
Dickey, George, 223
Dickey, John, 223, 272
Dickey, Thomas, 223
Dickey, William, 223
Dickson, John, 175
Dickson, Samuel, 223
Dile, 197
Dilling, John, 245
Dillinger, John, 245
Dilon, John, 39, 49
Dinsmore, Wiliam, 273
distillery, 3, 4, 5, 9, 10, 11, 14, 17,
    24, 26, 27, 70, 71, 72, 73, 75,
    77, 78, 81, 82, 84, 85, 168,
    171, 176, 177, 178, 179, 181,
    182, 183, 184, 185, 188, 189,
    192, 193, 194, 238, *See also*
    still
Ditman, Henry, 175
Divil, Jacob, 224
Dixen, David, 8
Dixon, Joseph, 9
Dobbins, James, 223
Donald, Francis, 8
Donald, James, 9
Donald, Thomas, 10
Donaldson, James, 57
Donaughy, James, 9
Donley, Hugh, 297
Donnel, William, 175
Donnelly, John, 8
Donnelly, Philip, 94
Donnelly, Robert, 244

Donnelly, Truman, 8
Doran, George, 109
Doran, Thomas, 109
Dormyer, George, 110
Dorson, William, 175
Doty, Israel, 9
Doty, John, 9, 10
Doty, Jonathan, 10
Doty, Jonathan B., 10
Doty, Jonathan, Junior, 9
Doty, Jonathan, Senior, 9
Doty, Levi, 8
Doty, Nathaniel, 8
Doty, Nathaniel, Senior, 9
Doty, Zebulon, 8
Double, Jacob, 74, 81
Dougherty, Andrew, 57
Dougherty, Ephraim, 74
Dougherty, Francis, 297
Dougherty, James, 203, 297
Dougherty, Jesse, 297
Dougherty, John, 109, 297
Dougherty, Sarah, 297
Dougherty, Wm, 272
Dougherty. Widow, 109
Doughtery, John, 297
Douglas, Charles, 245
Douglas, John, 57
Douglass, Charles, 245
Dove, Mathew, 174
Down, Simon, Junior, 94
Doyle, John, 224
Drips, William, 57
Drum, 185, 241
Drum, Christian, 94
Drum, John, 74, 107, 110
Drum, Peter, 94
Drum, Philip, 73
Drum, Simon, 73
Drum, Simon, Junior, 110
Drum, Simon, Senior, 110
Drumand, 198
Drumand, An^{dw}, 183
Drury, Stephen, 8
Dry, Jacob, 223
Dude, Jacob, 147
Duds, Martin, 148

Abstracts of Westmoreland County, Pennsylvania, Tax Records 1815

Duff, Alexander, 73
Duff, James, 73, 297
Duff, John, 175
Duff, John, Junior, 73
Duff, John, Senior, 73
Duff, Paul, 110
Duff, Robert, 74, 175
Duff, Thomas, 175
Duffey, Patrick, 223
Dugal, Henry, 245
Dugal, John, 245
Dugan, George, 297
Dugan, John, 297
Duggin, Widow, 35
Dukey, Henry, 175
Dum, Andrew, 272
Dum, Elijah, 175
Dumars, Christopher, 57
Dunbar, Samuel, 74
Dunbarr, John, 244
Duncan, Alexander, 298
Duncan, James, 9
Duncan, John, 57
Duncan, Robert, 9, 272
Dunholm, John, 175
Dunlap, Andrew, 297
Dunlap, James, 9, 297
Dunlap, John, 9, 272, 297
Dunlap, Robert, 110
Dunlap, Thomas, 9, 272, 297
Dunlap, William, 9, 272, 297
Dunlap, William, Senior, 9
Dunne, Andrew, 94
Durstine, Jacob, 35
Dushane, Andrew, 1, 29, 57
Dushane, Isaac, 57
Dust, Daniel, 109
Dyel, Philip, 245
Eakins, James, 110
Easley, Ferdinand, 273
Eaton, James, 10
Eaton, Robert, 167, 176
Eberson, Nathaniel, 203
Eckels, Joseph, 10
Eckels, M John, 245
Eckels, Samuel, 10
Eckles, M John, 245

Eckley, Joseph, 203
Edgar, John, 224
Edmam, 74
Edwards, Ezekiel, 306
Edwards, Henry, 75
Edwards, William, 75
Edwards, W^m, 71
Eggen, John, 5, 10
Eichard, Jacob, 273
Eichard, John, 273
Eickart, Abraham, 58
Eickart, Elizabeth, 144
Eickart, Mary, 144
Eickart, Widow, 144
Eickleberger, Godfrey, 58
Eiker, David, 110
Eiker, Jacob, 110
Eiker, Peter, 110
Einhart, Michael, 110
Ekels, Charles, 176
Ekels, Charles, Senior, 176
Ekels, John, 176
Ekels, Nathaniel, 175
Elder, Robert, 10
Elder, Samuel, 57
Elder, Thomas, 10
Elder, William, 58
Elderton, Hugh, 148
Elderton, William, 148
Elioth, 176
Elliot, John, 75
Elliott, A Irwin, 58
Elliott, George, 273
Elliott, John, 57
Elliott, John, Senior, 57
Elliott, Thomas, 57
Elliott, William, 57
Ellis, James, 203
Ellison, Andrew, 10
Elliss, Jairas, 75
Ellwood, Robert, 74
Elursale, Abraham, 148
Elwood, George, 74
Elwood, James, 75
Elwood, Thomas, 74
Elwood, William, Junior, 74
Elwood, William, Senior, 74

Abstracts of Westmoreland County, Pennsylvania, Tax Records 1815

Emberson, John, 245
Emfield, John, 203
Enders, Christian, Senior, 74
Enos, James, 58
Enos, Thomas, 58
Ernest, Henry, 111
Erret, Christian, 110
Erret, George, 110
Erret, John, 110
Ervin, John, 75
Ervine, Ezekiel, 148
Ervine, Joseph, 148
Erwin, James, 75
Erwin, John, 298
Erwin, Joseph, 298
Erwin, William, 298
Esquire, 4, 8, 15, 26, 27, 36, 37,
    40, 45, 46, 55, 58, 59, 60, 64,
    67, 77, 82, 84, 86, 90, 93, 94,
    95, 96, 97, 98, 99, 101, 104,
    116, 117, 127, 128, 129, 130,
    132, 135, 138, 143, 144, 152,
    155, 168, 171, 177, 181, 185,
    193, 196, 204, 217, 226, 227,
    236, 238, 239, 246, 248, 257,
    258, 260, 274, 278, 281, 284,
    289, 291, 292, 303, 304, 307,
    308
Essington, Dan¹, 203
Etep, James, 148
Evans, Cadwallader, 94
Evans, Ephraim, 110, 298
Evans, Joel, 306
Evans, John, 308
Evans, Walter, 148
Everheart, Christian, 75
Ewing, William, 176
executor, 61, 79, 86, 98, 190
Eyeman, John, 176
Eykes, John, 10
Falloon, David, 58
Falloon, John, Junior, 58
Falloon, John, Senior, 58
Farrel, Andrew, 149
Farrel, George, 149
Faster, Robert, 224
Fay, Levi, 103, 112

Feathers, John, 246
Feidner, Abraham, 111
Feidner, Henry, 111
Feidner, John, 111
Felgar, John, 149
Felger, Jacob, 35
Fell, Benjamin, 204
Fell, Jesse, 204
Fell, Joseph, 204
Fell, Peter, 204
Feller, Christopher, 274
Feller, John, 273
Fells, Elijah, 10
Fennel, Christopher, 224
Fennel, John, 224
Fennel, Michael, 224
Fenton, John, 10
Ferguson, Albert, 10
Ferguson, David, 111
Ferguson, Henry, 307
Ferguson, James, 11
Ferguson, Margaret, 15, 29
Ferguson, Thomas, 273, 293
Ferguson, Walter, 22, 29, 273
Ferguson, William, 10
ferry, 200, 202, 247, 248
Ferver, Jacob, 111
Fetter, John, 287
Fetter, Michael, 148
Fex, Jacob, 149
Fields, Daniel, 246
Findley, William, 274
Fink, Bastian, 76
Fink, Jacob, 75
Fink, Michael, 75
Finley, Andrew, 246
Finley, Hannah, 204
Finley, James, 246
Finley, John, 58, 246
Finley, Joseph, 204
Finley, Mary, 58
Finley, Michael, 204
Finley, William, 204
Finney, John, 112
Fiscus, David, 273
Fisher, Adam, 149
Fisher, Catherine, 149

Abstracts of Westmoreland County, Pennsylvania, Tax Records 1815

Fisher, George, 204
Fisher, Henry, 149
Fisher, Hodge, 203
Fisher, Jacob, 111, 112, 148
Fisher, John, Junior, 204
Fisher, John, Senior, 204
Fisher, Maria, 198
Fisher, Philip, 176
Fisher, Samuel, 198
Fisher, Thomas, 198
Fisher, William, 149, 306
Fissel, Jacob, 111
Flack, Daniel, 29
Flack, James, 58
Flack, John, 58
Flack, Robert, 176
Flack, Samuel, 204
Flanigan, Charles, 75
Fleegar, John, 94
Fleegar, Peter, 94
Fleming, Amos, 176
Fleming, Daniel, 177
Fleming, James, 10, 94
Fleming, John, 224
Flemming, John, 177
Flemon, George, 204
Flemon, James, 204
Flemon, John, 204
Flemon, John, Junior, 204
Fletcher, David, 149
Fletcher, James, 76, 148
Fletcher, John, 149
Fletcher, William, 76
Flinn, William, 52, 148
Flinn, W^m, 40
Floid, John, 298
Flowers, John, 6, 29
Flowers, Valenitne, 21
Flowers, Valentine, 29
Fluger, John, 112
Fluharty, Joshua, 75
Fluke, John, 274
Foltz, George, 273
Ford, Alexander, 273
forge, 14
Forman, Henry, 149
Forman, Samuel, 298

Forsythe, Thomas, 247
Foster, Alexander, 224
Foster, James, 35
Foster, Robert, 306
Foster, W. Alexander, 94
Foster, William, 274
Foust, Jacob, 274
Fox, Christian, 52
Fox, Henry, 52
Fox, Jacob, 111
Fox, John, 149, 306
Fox, Joseph, 149, 307
Fox, Peter, 111
Fox, Philip, 111
Fox, Samuel M., 67
Fraiser, Joseph, 149
Frame, William, 10
France, Daniel, 298
France, Michael, 224
France, Nicholas, 112
France, Philip, 111
France, Robert, 246
Frances, Samuel, 51
Francis, Robert, 52
Frank, Jacob, 148
Frank, Paul, 148
Frantz, Conrad, 149
Frantz, Michael, 107, 111
Frederick, John, 298
Freer, Joseph, 298
Freidt, Abraham, 246
Frest, John, 35
Frets, Henry, 35
Frew, Adam, 176
Frew, David, 176
Frich, Henry, 298
Frick, George, 245
Frick, Henry, 245
Frick, John, 245
Fricker, Widow, 112
Friedt, Abraham, 75
Friedt, Jacob, 75
Friedt, John, 246
Friedt, William, 94
Friend, Peter, 149
Frier, Joseph, 75
Frier, Peter, 298

Abstracts of Westmoreland County, Pennsylvania, Tax Records 1815

Fries, George, 273
Fries, Jacob, 273
Fritchman, Adam, 176
Fritchman, Michal, 176
Fritz, George, 148
Fruman, George, 58
Frunk, David, 45
Fry, Adam, 111
Fry, Andrew, 224
Fry, George, 298
Fry, Henry, 224
Fry, Jacob, 111, 245, 247
Fry, John, 224
Fry, Joseph, 76
Fry, Laurence, 224
Fry, Martin, 35
Fry, Michael, 148
Fry, Peter, 58
Fuller, W^m, 188
Fullerton, Humphry, 177
Fullerton, William, 176
fulling mill, 21, 79, 123, 153, 173, 209, 246, 261, 271, 275
Fullmaad, Charles, 149
Fulmer, Jacob, 245
Fulton, Abraham, 246
Fulton, Abraham, Senior, 11
Fulton, Cochran, 29
Fulton, Henry, 245, 246
Fulton, James, 10
Fulton, James, Senior, 10
Fulton, John, 29, 111
Fulton, Joseph, 11
Fulton, Robert, 29, 177, 246
Fulton, William, 176, 246, 298
Fultz, Jacob, 35
Funk, Christian, 176
Funk, Christian, Junior, 176
Funk, Christian, Senior, 246
Funk, Daniel, 177, 246
Funk, David, 35, 111
Funk, Henry, 246
Funk, John, 35
Furey, Abraham, 274
Furry, Henry, 273
Gaffenney, Martin, 247
Gaffenny, Edward, 247

Gaffenny, John, 247
Gafney, William, 247
Gageby, James, 58
Gageby, John, 58
Galbreath, James, 58
Gallaher, Edward, 298
Gallaher, John, 11
Gallaher, Thomas, 11, 275
Gallaher, Widow, 275
Gallaway, James, 150
Galloway, John, 36
Galsrest, John, 151
Galt, William, 178
Galt, W^m, 198
Gambel, John, 247
Gamble, Aaron, 11
Gamble, John, 264
Gangaware, John, 112
Gardner, George, 58
Gardner, Jacob, 35
Gardner, John, 51
Gardner, Samuel, 274
Gardner, William, 204
Garland, John, 12
Garner, Nathan, 51
Garret, Elizabeth, 177
Garret, Richard, 177
Garrettg, Horase, 178
Gartley, George, 298
Gartner, Christopher, 274
Garvey, Thomas, 298
Garvin, James, 204
Garvin, Samuel, 177
Gaston, Patrick, 275
Gault, Isaac, 51
Gault, John, 36
Gault, Matthew, 36
Gault, William, 50
Gavvin, James, 247
Geary, John, 12
Geary, Morten, 12
Geffen, James, 150
Geffen, Stephen, 150
Geiser, Benjamin, 275
Gelbreath, William, 177
General, 84, 124, 223
George, Christian, 298

George, Henry, 76, 112
George, Jacob, 112, 247, 264
George, James, 11
George, John, 11, 275
George, Mathew, 11
George, Peter, 113, 224
George, Widow, 298
George, William, 11
Gerby, John, 36
Geyr, Andrew, 204
Geyr, George, 204
Gezens, Samuel, 150
Gezens, William, 150
Gibb, David, 150
Gibb, Robert, 76
Gibson, George, 95, 275
Gibson, James, 12, 76
Gibson, John, 76, 77
Gibson, Widow, 77
Gibson, William, 205, 247, 298
Giffin, John, 150
Giger, John, 76
Giger, Joseph, 76
Gilaspey, Moses, 274
Gilbert, Abner, 178
Gilbert, Jacob, 77
Gilbert, John, 247
Gilchrist, Archibald, 275
Gilchrist, Eleanor, 11
Gilchrist, James, 112, 274
Gilchrist, John, 112
Gilchrist, Thomas, 112
Giles, Samuel, 150
Gillespie, Charles, 205
Gillespie, Christopher, 58
Gillespie, Hugh, 58
Gillespie, John, 205
Gillespie, Moses, 12
Gillespie, William, 76, 205
Gillespie, Wm, 205
Gilmore, James, 58
Gilmore, John, 58
Gilmore, Michael, 36
Gilson, David, 11
Gilson, John, 12
Glassburner, Martin, 247, 255
Gold, Adam, 177

Golden, William, 150
Goldinger, Anthony, 298
Golloday, 99
Gongaware, John, 178
Gongaware, Philip, 178
Good, Isaac, 112
Good, Laurence, 77
Goode, John, 151
Goodlink, John, 177
Goodman, John, 177
Gordon, Archibald, 298
Gordon, George, 274
Gordon, James, 274
Gordon, John, 76, 77
Gordon, Mathew, 77
Gordon, Samuel, 76, 275
Gordon, William, 76
Gotteth, Daniel, 150
Gourley, Henry, 113
Gourley, John, 12
Gourley, John, Junior, 113
Gourley, John, Senior, 113
Gowdy, John, 35
Gowdy, Robert, 50
Graden, Caleb, 307
Grady, Norris, 307
Graff, Henery, 275
Graff, John, 274
Graham, Bernard, 274
Graham, John, 36, 298
Graham, Joseph, 150
Graham, Nathaniel, 112
Graham, Robert, 58, 95, 113
Graham, S. William, 95
Graham, Thomas, 112
Graham, William, 150, 224
Grames, Gilbert, 298
Grames, Hugh, 298
Grames, James, 298
Grant, Daniel, 95
Grass, John, 298
Gray, Abraham, 76, 274
Gray, George, 12, 178, 307
Gray, Israel, 11
Gray, James, 178
Gray, Thomas, 58
Gray, William, 307

Abstracts of Westmoreland County, Pennsylvania, Tax Records 1815

Grayden, Mary, 150
Green, Alexander, 274
Green, John, 178
Greenaualdt, Jacob, 197
Greenawalt, John, 275
Greenemyer, Solomon, 274
Greer, James, 275
Greer, Patrick, 178
Greer, Thomas, 177
Greer, William, 178
Gregg, 225
Gregg, Andrew, 274
Gregg, James, 113
Gregory, William, 178
Grenawalt, Christian, 177
Grenawalt, Jacob, 177
Gress, John, 150
Greysinger, George, 177
Griffin, Henry, 113
Griffin, John, 150
Griffin, Patrick, 151
Griffith, John, 150, 247
Griffith, Obizah, 150
Grim, Daniel, 247
Grim, George, 247
Grim, Jacob, 298
Grim, Philip, 298
Grimes, John, 247
Grissinger, Andrew, 112
gristmill, 3, 7, 8, 14, 15, 17, 21,
    26, 27, 36, 43, 45, 69, 73, 82,
    84, 86, 102, 105, 106, 111,
    116, 119, 126, 128, 129, 130,
    131, 132, 134, 137, 143, 147,
    154, 156, 157, 167, 171, 173,
    176, 181, 183, 184, 185, 191,
    195, 196, 211, 221, 225, 227,
    230, 241, 246, 248, 251, 254,
    257, 261, 290, 292
Grith, Jacob, 164
Grith, John, 164
Gross, Abraham, 36
Gross, Adam, 112
Gross, Jesse, 112
Gross, Peter, 112
Gross, Peter, Senior, 112
Guffy, James, 177

Guffy, John, 177
Guffy, William, 178
Guier, James, 12
Guiger, George, 275
Guiger, Henry, 113
Guiger, John, 275
Guiger, Wendel, 275
Guinn, Daniel, 247
Guinn, John, 11
Guisinger, George, 197
Gumbert, Christian, Junior, 298
Gumbert, Christian, Senior, 298
Gutherey, Samuel, 293
Guthre, 58
Guthrie, James, 11, 298
Guthrie, John, 298
Guthrie, Joseph, 11
Guthrie, Robert, 11
Guthrie, Samuel, 95, 113
Guthrie, William, 224, 298
H[-----], W. John, 250
Habell, Frederick, 299
Hainey, James, 13
Hainey, John, 13
Hainey, Nicholas, 299
Hainey, Simon, 299
Hains, Frederich, 116
Hains, Jacob, 116
Halferty, Edward, 59
Halferty, John, 59
Halferty, Robert, 60
Halferty, William, 59
Hall, David, 248
Hall, George, 299
Hall, James, Junior, 299
Hall, James, Senior, 299
Hall, John, 299
Hall, Susanna, 249
Hall, William, 307
Hamilton, 93
Hamilton, Alexander, 250
Hamilton, Alice, 250
Hamilton, Christiana, 248
Hamilton, Daniel, 206
Hamilton, David, 248
Hamilton, Gaius, 250
Hamilton, George, 299

Abstracts of Westmoreland County, Pennsylvania, Tax Records 1815

Hamilton, James, 59, 179, 307
Hamilton, John, 77, 78, 249
Hamilton, Mathew, 77
Hamilton, Robert, 299
Hamilton, Samuel, 179, 299
Hamilton, Thomas, 77, 95
Hamilton, William, 12
Hammer, Jonathan, 116
Hammil, Hugh, 59
Hammil, Robert, 59
Hammond, Abraham, 152
Hammond, Daniel, Junior, 206
Hammond, Daniel, Senior, 206
Hammond, Henry, 152
Hammond, James, 206
Hammond, John, 206
Hammond, Mary, 206
Hammond, Nathaniel, 206
Hammond, Peter, 206
Handlin, Dennis, 276
Hankey, Daniel, 78
Hanlon, William, 60
Hanna, John, 205
Hannah, Alexander, 251
Hannah, James, 250
Hannah, John, 249, 250
Hannah, Robert, 179
Hannah, Thomas, 251
Hansel, Peter, 115
Hanselman, John, 115
Harbst, Barbary, 49
Hardin, Richard, 115
Hare, James, 178
Hare, John, 13, 59
Hare, William, 178
Hargrave, John, 95
Hargrave, Richard, 95
Harker, Daniel, 248
Harkins, Edward, 12
Harkins, John, 58
Harkins, Neal, 12
Harkness, John, 180
Harkness, Thomas, 180
Harkness, William, 180
Harold, Daniel, Junior, 113
Harold, Daniel, Senior, 113
Harold, Jacob, 113

Harold, Peter, 114
Harps, Andrew, 15, 29
Harres, Anthony, 178
Harsel, Adam, Senior, 151
Harshey, John, 225
Harshey, Joseph, 225
Harshman, George, 13
Harshman, John, 13
Harsman, 13
Harson, Samuel, 206
Hart, John, 225
Hart, Robert, 225
Hart, Sally, 180
Hart, William, 225
Hartford, James, 180
Hartless, Charles, 77
Hartless, Elizabeth, 78
Hartless, Jebus, 78
Hartley, John, 29, 225
Hartley, Robert, 13, 250
Hartman, Jacob, 59, 78
Hartman, John, 250
Hartman, Michael, 58
Hartsel, Adam, 151
Hartsel, George, 152
Hartzel, Jacob, 276
Harvey, Joseph, 225
Harvey, Josiah, 79, 277
Harwick, Joseph, 95
Hashberger, William, 58
Haslet, Andrew, 58
Haslet, Robert, 59
Haslet, William, 59
Hastings, Job, 205
Hatfield, George, 152
Hawk, Andrew, 29
Hawk, Daniel, 225
Hawk, George, 299
Hawk, Jacob, 115
Hawkey, Henry, 115
Hawkins, David, 294
Hawkins, James, 294
Hawkins, Mathew, 294
Hawkins, Thomas, 294
Hawkins, Widow, 294
Hay, Ann, 78
Hay, James, 78

Abstracts of Westmoreland County, Pennsylvania, Tax Records 1815

Hay, Samuel, Senior, 78
Hay, William, 249
Haydon, Ebenezer, 250
Hayley, George, 78
Haymaker, Jacob, 78
Hayny, John, 152
Hays, James, 113, 121
Hays, James, Senior, 114
Hays, La¹, 121
Hays, Robert, 225
Hays, Samuel, 77, 113
Hays, William, 77
Heable, Henry, 116
Heable, John, 116
Heaney, John, 151
Heany, James, 151
Heany, John, 151
Heasley, Henry, 78
Heasley, Henry, Junior, 115
Heasley, Henry, Senior, 115
Heasley, Jacob, 115
Heasley, John, 115
Heasley, Joseph, 114
Heasley, Leonard, 78
Heasley, Michael, 78
Hebler, David, 116, 124
Heck, Jnº, 179
Heck, John, 179
Heck, Philip, 179, 180
Heckman, Philip, 77
Hedinger, John, 79
heirs, 72, 77, 82, 91, 97, 102,
    146, 153, 176, 212, 214, 222,
    257, 307
Heirs, 21, 55, 184
Helburn, Peter, 277
Heltebrand, Jacob, 248
Henderson, Adam, 299
Henderson, Alexander, 59, 114,
    251
Henderson, Andrew, 59
Henderson, Charles, Junior, 59
Henderson, Charles, Senior, 59
Henderson, Daniel, 299
Henderson, David, 180
Henderson, Hugh, 114
Henderson, James, 13, 60, 179

Henderson, John, 59, 78, 151
Henderson, Samuel, 59, 60
Henderson, Samuel, Senior, 59
Henderson, Thomas, 59
Henderson, William, 276
Hendricks, Abraham, 58
Hendricks, Abraham, Junior, 58
Hendricks, Daniel, 60
Hendricks, Daniel, Junior, 59
Hendricks, Daniel, Senior, 59
Hendricks, Jamieson, 59
Hendricks, John, 36
Hendricks, Mary, 179
Hendricks, Stephen, 180
Hendricks, Steven, 251
Hendricks, Thomas, 59
Hendrickson, John, 299
Henen, John, 79
Heney, Catrine, 59
Henon, Anna, 12
Henon, David, 12
Henry, Conrad, 277
Henry, Edward, 179
Henry, Edward, Senior, 179
Henry, Frederick, 114
Henry, Jacob, 277
Henry, James, 12, 36
Henry, John, Junior, 277
Henry, John, Senior, 277
Henry, Robert, 12, 226, 299
Henry, Samuel, 225
Henry, Thomas, 226
Henry, William, 29, 299
Hepler, Daniel, 36, 248
Hepler, Gasper, 299
Hepler, Stophel, 249
Herbaug, Abram, 129
Hercles, Charles, 77
Herey, 299
Herey, William, 299
Herman, Anderson, 115
Herrald, Christopher, 250
Hervy, Josiah, 79
Herwich, William, 95
Hess, George, 179
Hess, Henry, 180
Hess, Jonathan, 114

Hessam, Abner, 113
Hessam, Thomas, 114
Hettick, George, 66
Hettinger, John, 95
Hews, Isaac, 13
Hews, William, Junior, 13
Hews, William, Senior, 13
Heydon, Jacob, 206
Heydon, Nathaniel, 206
Heyner, Martin, 152
Hickman, Joseph, 180
Hickman, Philip, 299
Higgins, James, 152
Higgins, John, 205
Higgins, Laurence, 205
Higgs, William, 248
Highlands, William, 299
Hilborn, John, 29
Hilborn, William, 29
Hile, Frederick, 114
Hile, Jonathan, 276
Hileman, Isaac, 51
Hill, Abraham, 12
Hill, Arron, 293
Hill, Benjamin, 225
Hill, Daniel, 248
Hill, Edward, 13, 249
Hill, Gasper, 58
Hill, George, 59, 249
Hill, Jacob, 77
Hill, James, 60
Hill, John, 60, 78, 95, 116, 225, 299
Hill, Joseph, 12, 24, 205
Hill, Joshua, 12
Hill, Katrine, 77
Hill, Orange, 59
Hill, Peter, 77
Hill, Richard, 12
Hill, Samuel, 299
Hill, Stephen, 205
Hill, William, 115, 298
Hill, William, Junior, 298
Hillburn, John, 225
Hillburn, Samuel, 225
Hillip, John M, 1
Hillis, Robert, 151

Hills, John, 59
Hinckle, Peter, 11, 13
Hindland, Laurence, 205
Hindman, Andrew, 299
Hindman, Samuel, 299
Hindman, William, 179
Hinebough, Jacob, 113
Hiner, Martin, 152
Hinkle, Peter, 276
Hinkle, Retter, 277
Hirrüm, Joab, 251
Hise, Henry, 60
Hissom, Joab, 114, 249
Hissom, Thomas, 114, 143
Hissom, Thomas, Senior, 114
Hitchman, John, 152
Hitchman, William, 152
Hite, James, 247
Hixon, Amos, 250
Hixon, Catharine, 248
Hixon, Joseph, 248
Hixon, Moses, 249
Hobough, John, 116
Hobough, Peter, 113
Hocken, Adam, 226
Hockley, Richard, 299
Hodge, John, 79
Hodge, William, 79
Hoffman, Adam, 276
Hoffman, Daniel, 276
Hoffman, Joseph, 276
Hoge, Thomas, 116, 127
Hoges, Tho[s], 96
Hoist, Conrad, 115
Hokenshall, Mary, 250
Holland, James, 277
Holliday, James, 13
Hollidy, James, 226
Hollingsworth, Levi, 307
Hollingsworth, Lewis, 307
Holmes, John, 180
Holmes, Thomas, 180
Holmes, Thomas, Junior, 181
Holobaugh, Jacob, 151
Holser, Frederick, 276
Holser, Jacob, 152, 276
Holser, John, 79

Abstracts of Westmoreland County, Pennsylvania, Tax Records 1815

Holstein, Samuel, 29
Holston, Mathias, 13
Holton, James, 178, 249
Holton, John, 179
Holton, John, Senior, 180
Holton, Thomas, 249
Hoofman, John, 115
Hoofman, Peter, 115
Hook, Henry, 152
Hooker, William, 78
Hooller, Henry, 60
Hoontsbarger, Peter, 13
Hoover, John, 115
Hoover, Solomon, 299
Hope, James, 180
Hopkins, H. John, 60
Hopkins, Robert, 249
Horbock, Abraham, 95
Horbough, Abraham, 116
Hordesty, Henry, 206
Hormer, George, 180
Horn, Andrew, 225
Horn, George, 225
Horn, Solomon, 225
Hornbeck, Henry, 206
Horner, James, 178
Horner, John, 276
Horner, William, 180, 277
Hornis, John, 95
Horrel, John, 13
Hossach, David, 277
Hostater, Joseph, 95
Hough, John, 205
Hough, Joseph, 248
Hough, Paul, 36, 250
Hough, Peter, 249
Hough, Philip, 51
Hough, Solomon, 37
Houk, Conrad, 115
Houk, Jacob, 115
Houk, Jacob, Senior, 115
Houk, Widow, 115
Houser, Christian, 114
Housholder, Frederick, 299
Housholder, John, 12
Housholder, Jonathan, 13
Housman, Christopher, Junior,
206
Housman, Christopher, Senior,
206
Housman, Jacob, 206
Housman, John, 206
Howard, James, 178
Howard, Peter, 58
Howard, Samuel, 250
Howel, Robert, 59
Howell, Joseph, 59
Howie, George, 180
Howie, James, 179
Hoy, Ann, 79
Hoy, Daniel, 249
Hoy, James, 79
Hoylser, John, 152
Huber, Peter, 114
Hues, John, 180
Huey, Catharine, 249
Huey, Daniel, 299
Huey, James, 250
Huey, John, 250
Huey, William, 249, 299
Huffman, Adam, 276
Huffman, Danl, 164
Huffman, George, 78
Huffman, Henry, 299
Huffman, John, 277
Huffman, Joseph, 299
Huffman, Lora, 249
Huffman, Michael, 277
Huffman, William, 276
Hugh, James, 4
Hugh, Martin, 51
Hughes, William, 277
Hughges, John, 151
Hughs, Jacob, 95
Hughs, Josiah, 307
Hughs, Rowland, 299
Hugus, Henry, 275
Hugus, Paul, 275
Hulen, Joseph, 60
Humbard, Solomon, 60
Humburt, Frederick, 206
Humes, John, 78
Hummel, Samuel, 113
Hunnel, David, 299

Abstracts of Westmoreland County, Pennsylvania, Tax Records 1815

Hunt, Gersham, 151
Hunt, Michael, 151
Hunter, 233
Hunter, Alexander, 151
Hunter, Charles, 248
Hunter, David, 37, 151, 152, 250
Hunter, David, Junior, 37
Hunter, James, 226, 276, 307
Hunter, John, 151, 152, 248,
    250, 277
Hunter, Ralph, 276
Hunter, Robert, 36, 226, 251
Hunter, Samuel, 151, 276
Hunter, Thomas, 276
Hunter, William, 151, 248
Hurh, John, 206
Hurl, Irwin, 59
Hurl, James, 60
Hurst, James, 152
Hurst, Nathaniel, 151
Hurst, Thomas, 151
Hurtman, William, 114
Husband, William, 36
Hush, Peter, 205
Hush, Valentine, 205
Huster, John, 29
Huston, James, 58, 59
Huston, John, 59
Huston, Robert, 59
Hutcheson, Daniel, 250
Hutcheson, James, 79, 248, 249
Hutcheson, James, Senior, 79
Hutcheson, John, 36, 79
Hutcheson, Richard, 79
Hutcheson, William, 249
Hutchesons, Jas, 244
Hyberger, Andrew, 179
Hyberger, Barbara, 179
Hyberger, Daniel, 179
Hyberger, John, 180
Hyel, Fredrick, 162
Hyle, William, 152
Iman, Abraham, 300
Iman, Jacob, Junior, 300
Iman, Jacob, Senior, 300
Imbel, John, 117
Ingles, James, 14

Ingles, James, Senior, 30
Ingles, Joseph, 30
Ingraham, John, 181
Irwin, Ambrose, 37
Irwin, Andrew, 13
Irwin, Boyle, 60
Irwin, Edward, 60
Irwin, Henry, 37
Irwin, Hugh, 14
Irwin, James, 181, 226
Irwin, John, 181, 251
Irwin, Joseph, 226
Irwin, Samuel, 14, 181
Irwin, William, 226, 227
Isaman, Andrew, 116
Isaman, Christian, 116
Isaman, Christn, 299
Isaman, George, 116
Isaman, Henry, 299
Isaman, Michael, 116
Isaman, Peter, 116
Isehart, Jacob, 116
Isell, Henry, 95
Isett, Henry, 111, 117
Isinger, Michael, 181
Isterly, George, 95
Izaman, Henry, 181
Jack, 93, 94
Jack, John, 152
Jack, Mathew, 117
Jack, Matthew, 226
Jack, Robert, 181
Jack, Samuel, 226
Jack, Thomas, 153
Jack, William, 50, 117, 227
Jacks, James, 153
Jacks, W^m, 93
Jackson, Isaac, 300
Jackson, Richard, 95, 278
Jackson, William, 278
Jacob, Bonar, 66
Jacob, Sludebech, 44
Jacobs, Abraham, 207
Jacobs, Daniel, Junior, 207
Jacobs, Daniel, Senior, 207
Jamieson, Benjamin, 278
Jamieson, David, 307

Abstracts of Westmoreland County, Pennsylvania, Tax Records 1815

Jamieson, Francis, 277
Jamieson, James, 278
Jamieson, James, Junior, 300
Jamieson, James, Senior, 300
Jamieson, John, 278, 300
Jamieson, Margret, 60
Jamieson, Robert, 277, 278
Jamieson, Thomas, 60
Jamieson, William, 277
Jamison, Francis, 181
Jams, William, 226
Janes, Timothy, 8
Jarvas, Frances, 153
Jay, John, 207
Jaynes, Timothy, 13
Jellison, Ephraim, 14
Jellison, Robert, Junior, 14
Jellison, Robert, Senior, 13
Jenkeson, William, 278
Jenkins, William, 60, 307
Jennings, John, 95
Jervis, Arthur, 116
Jewry, Abraham, 251, 259
Joab, Johnston, 307
Joabs, Kinith, 207
Johes, Alexander, 251
John Roberton, 212
Johnson, John, 152
Johnston, Alexander, 14, 60, 96, 117, 278
Johnston, Andrew, 226
Johnston, Benjamin, 60
Johnston, Christopher, 153
Johnston, David, 278
Johnston, Ephraim, 14
Johnston, George, 14, 196
Johnston, Henry, 60, 79, 278
Johnston, James, 14, 37, 251
Johnston, Job, 226
Johnston, John, 153, 207
Johnston, John, Junior, 226, 300
Johnston, John, Senior, 226, 300
Johnston, Joseph, 207, 226
Johnston, Nathaniel, 206
Johnston, Robert, 14, 30, 60,

207, 227
Johnston, Samuel, 60
Johnston, W. John, 153
Johnston, William, 14, 153, 226
Johnston, William, Junior, 14
Johnstone, David, 181
Johnstone, James, 181
Johnstone, Mathew, 181
Johnstone, Samuel, 181
Joice, William, 14
Jones, Daniel, 60
Jones, James, 60
Jones, Robert, 117
Jones, Samuel, 117
Jones, Thomas, 14, 79
Jordan, David, 14
Jordan, John, 14
Jordan, Samuel, 14
Jordan, Thomas, 14
Kaffer, Gasper, 182
Kailler, Peter, 120
Kamp, Garret, 121
Kamp, Henry, 50
Kamp, Jacob, 121
Kamp, Matthias, 37
Kamp, Solomon, 121
Kane, Daniel, 122
Karscadden, William, 252
Kaskadion, Patrick, 182
Kasler, Conrad, 153
Kean, Daniel, 121
Kean, Elizabeth, 252
Kean, Paul, 227
Kean, William, 227
Keane, Benjamin, 182
Keany, Robert, 231
Keck, George, 227
Keck, George, Senior, 118
Keck, Isaac, 121, 227
Keck, P., 121
Keck, Widow, 118, 121
Keefer, George, 182
Keel, Jonas, 120
Keely, Daniel, 15
Keely, John, 15
Keener, George, 117
Keener, Jacob, 117

Abstracts of Westmoreland County, Pennsylvania, Tax Records 1815

Keener, Michael, 120
Keister, Jacob, 37
Keller, Joseph, 117
Kells, Andrew, 278
Kells, Gustavus, 278
Kells, Ralph, 278
Kelly, Adam, 251
Kelly, Alexander, 37
Kelly, Charles, 251
Kelly, Daniel, 251
Kelly, George, 251
Kelly, James, 227, 294
Kelly, James, Junior, 251
Kelly, James, Senior, 251
Kelly, John, 182
Kelly, Margret, 294
Kelly, Mathew, 251
Kelly, Nathaniel, 228
Kelly, Samuel, 227
Kelly, Sarah, 294
Kelly, Thomas, 153
Kelly, Widow, 279, 294, 300
Kelly, William, 251
Kemerer, David, 118
Kemmerer, Adam, 118
Keneagy, Christian, 251
Kennedy, George, 181
Kennedy, Samuel, 60
Kenteigh, Daniel, 153
Kentz, Frederick, 278
Kepler, Andrew, 120
Keppel, Andrew, 80
Keppel, Andrew, Junior, 80
Keppel, Christian, 80
Keppel, George, 80, 121, 297
Keppel, Henry, 121
Keppel, Jacob, 227
Keppel, John, 117
Keppel, Michael, 117
Keppel, Peter, 117, 121
Keppel, Philip, 297
Keppil, Lewis, 121
Kepple, Lewis, 297
Kern, John, 117
Kerney, Patrick, 228
Kerns, Barnabas, 79
Kerns, Edward, 182

Kerns, Henry, 15
Kerns, Jacob, 96, 119
Kerns, John, 96, 181, 182
Kerns, Joseph, 96, 120
Kerns, Nicholas, 182
Kerns, William, 60
Kerr, Adam, 251
Kerr, Andrew, 251
Kerr, David, 227
Kerr, James, 38
Kerr, John, 37
Kerr, M, 37
Kerr, Mathew, 80
Kerr, P, 37
Kerr, Thomas, 181
Ketchem, Lewis, 207
Kettering, Adam, 117
Keys, William, 119
Kibler, George, 227
Kiel, Jacob, 121
Kifer, Henry, 118
Kifer, Peter, 118
Kifir, Henry, 118
Kighly, Jacob, 120
Kilday, Francis, 15
Kilgore, Daniel, 153
Kilgore, David, 153
Kilgore, John, 153
Kimmel, Andrew, 118
Kimmel, Daniel, 120
Kimmel, John, 118, 121
Kimmel, Jonas, 120
Kimmel, Joseph, 119
Kimmel, Michael, Junior, 119
Kimmel, Michael, Senior, 119
Kimmel, Widow, 118
Kimmerer, Jacob, 120
Kimmerer, John, 120
Kimmerer, Lewis, 120
Kinaman, Peter, 105, 119
Kinan, James, 279
Kinard, William, 37
Kincaid, Andrew, 15
Kincaid, George, 15
Kincaid, John, 15
Kinely, Charles, 227
King, Charles, 300

King, David, 119, 300
King, George, 119
King, James, 300
King, John, 15, 119, 181, 300
King, Matthias, 119
King, William, 307
Kinley, Jean, 227
Kinley, John, 300
Kinley, Samuel, 227
Kinley, William, 300, 307
Kip, Abraham, 300
Kip, Isaac, 300
Kirbaugh, Jacob, 153
Kirbey, John, 153
Kirby, John, 207
Kirker, Gilbert, 80
Kirkland, John, 207
Kirkpatrick, Benjamin, 118
Kirkpatrick, John, 15, 227
Kirkpatrick, John, Junior, 227
Kirkwood, Archibald, 182
Kirkwood, Hugh, 300
Kirkwood, James, 300
Kirkwood, Nathaniel, 60
Kirkwood, Thomas, 300
Kiser, Frederich, 121
Kiser, George, 153
Kiser, John, 153
Kiskaddin, Arthur, 14
Kiskaddin, James, 15
Kisler, Michael, 300
Kister, Daniel, 80
Kister, John, 80
Kister, Michael, 80
Kister, Philip, 80
Kister, Philip, Junior, 80
Kistler, Philip, 278
Kistler, Samuel, 80
Kleppener, George, 117
Kline, Adam, 252
Kline, Caeslan, 197
Kline, G, Jn^r, 175
Kline, John, 252
Klingelsmith, Daniel, 118
Klingelsmith, David, 119
Klingelsmith, John, 119
Klingelsmith, John, Senior, 119

Klingelsmith, Peter, 118, 119
Klingelsmith, Peter, Junior, 119
Klingelsmith, Philip, 119
Klingensmith, Christian, 117
Klingensmith, David, 122
Klingensmith, H. P., 111
Klingensmith, P., 118
Klingensmith, Peter, 117
Klingensmith, Philip, 121
Klippiner, Henry, 117
Knapinbarger, Philip, 80
Knapinberger, Conrad, 79
Knapinberger, John, 79
Knapinberger, Philip, 80
Knaus, Daniel, 182
Knave, Jacob, 118
Kneff, John, 153
Knight, John, 15, 37
Knott, Wilson, 15
Knox, Robert, 60
Knox, Samuel, 60
Koons, Daniel, 182
Krider, Philip, 119
Kroch, Conrad, 119
Krock, George, 121
Krock, John, 120
Kroushere, 142
Kroushour, Adam, 120
Kroushour, George, 118
Kroushour, Henry, 120
Krug, Michael, 279
Kuhn, Adam, 279
Kuhn, Daniel, 279
Kuhn, George, 118
Kuhn, Henry, 278
Kuhn, Henry, Junior, 279
Kuhn, Jacob, 278
Kuhns, Christian, 120
Kuhns, Daniel, 120
Kuhns, David, 96
Kuhns, Jacob, 60, 296
Kuhns, John, 96, 121
Kuhns, Peter, 297
Kuhns, Philip, 96, 120
Kuhns, Philip, Senior, 120
Kunkald, Peter, 182
Kunkle, Jacob, 227

Abstracts of Westmoreland County, Pennsylvania, Tax Records 1815

Kunkle, Michael, 296
Kunkle, Sebesten, 182
Kuns, Peter, 182
Kyser, George, 279
Kyser, Isaac, 279
Kyser, Jacob, 279
Kyser, John, 279
Lacy, John, 122
Laffer, John, 81, 300
Laird, Francis, 81
Laird, John, 16
Laird, William, 16
Lake, Henry, 252
Lambright, John, 122, 300
Lander, Jacob, 118
Landes, Jacob, 123
Lane, John, 208
Lang, Adam, 164
Lang, Gabriel, Senior, 80
Lang, Henry, 81
Lang, John, 81
Lang, Tobias, 80
Langllen, James, 16
Lapher, Henry, 81
Lapsley, Jacob, 122
Lapton, John, 300
Lardner, John, 300
Lare, Henry, 164
Large, Zenas, 122
Larimer, Andrew, 280
Larimer, David, 280
Larimer, James, 81
Larimer, John, 279
Larimer, Robert, 61, 123
Lash, Joseph, 182
Lasure, Abraham, 192, 197
Latimore, John, 30
Latta, John, 252
Latta, William, 16
Lattimore, David, 228
Lattimore, Robert, 16
Lattimore, William, 16
Latto, John, 154
Latto, Moses, 153
Latto, Moses, Senior, 154
Laugh[----],William, 252
Laughlin, John, 154, 280

Laupher, Henry, 88
Laver, Henry, 154
Lawson, Hugh, 61
Lawson, James, 60, 61
Lawson, Joseph, 61
Leaden, James, 280
Leader, Daniel, 294
Leader, Michael, 122
Leasure, Abraham, 123
Leasure, Abreham, 182
Leasure, Daniel, 154, 279
Leasure, Daniel, Junior, 279
Leasure, George, 154
Leasure, John, 279
Leavely, Philip, 81
Leavly, John, 82
Leavly, Philip, 82
Lee, John, 16
Lee, Robert, 16
Lee, Rob[t], 18
Leedy, Jacob, 38
Leeman, Jacob, 123
Lehmer, William, 280
Leighner, John, 228
Leightley, George, 81
Leighty, John, 123
Leighty, William, 228
Lelungine, Christ, 145
Lelungine, John, 145
Lemmon, Alexander, Junior, 16
Lemmon, Alexander, Senior, 16
Lemmon, James, 16, 61, 154
Lemmon, John, 61, 252
Lemmon, Thomas, 61
Lemmon, William, 15, 60
Lemmons, Michael, 252
Lemmons, Robert, 252
Lenhard, Adam, 15
Lenhart, Jacob, 280
Leninger, Conrad, 81
Lenning, Isaac, 228
Lenning, John, 228, 300
Leppencob, 245
Leppencotts, John, 247
Lesley, George, 123
Lesmon, Michael, 183
Lessley, James, 61

Abstracts of Westmoreland County, Pennsylvania, Tax Records 1815

Lewis, Isaiah, 122, 154
Lewis, Jonathan, 81
Lewis, Joseph, 81
Lewis, Mordecai, 307
Lewis, Thomas, 123, 155, 183
Lightcap, Levi, 280
Lightcap, Samuel, 16
Lightcap, Solomon, 16, 280
Lightly, Marks, 38
Likes, George, 252
Likes, Thomas, 122
Lillarka, J, 241
Lilley, Sarah, 61
Linder, George, 207
Linder, Jacob, 208
Linder, Nathaniel, 207
Lindsay, Thomas, 252
Lingle, Nicholas, 279
Link, Conrad, 122
Linnen, John, 228
Linning, Ezekiel, 300
Linsenbigler, Daniel, 123
Linsenbigler, Jacob, 123
Linsenbigler, John, 123
Linseybegler, Jacob, 228
Lippencott, Samuel, 122
Lipponcott, James, 154
Lise, Robert, 183
Listiz, Morton, 213
Little, James, 15
Little, Jean, 61
Little, John, 16
Little, Sarah, 15
Little, William, 61
Livingood, Henry, 15
Livingston, James, 300
Lloyd, Joseph, 252
Lobingire, 154
Lobingire, Christ^r, 154
Lobingire, Elizabeth, 154
Lobingire, John, 154
Logan, David, 183
Logan, Henry, 183
Lonch, Barnabas, 197
Long, Abraham, 123
Long, Adam, 80, 122
Long, Andrew, 183

Long, David, 183
Long, Jacob, 45, 81, 122, 154
Long, James, 16, 280
Long, John, 16, 61
Long, Joseph, 154
Long, Lewis, 122
Long, Nicholas, 122, 133
Long, Philip, 81
Long, Samuel, 183
Long, Senior, Nicholas, 122
Long, Simon, 252
Long, Thos, 164
Long, Tobias, 122
Long, William, 182
Longeneker, Jacob, 40
Longhead, Joseph, 252
Longhead, William, 252
Loos, George, 279
Loos, George, Junior, 280
Loos, Henry, 279
Loos, Jacob, 279
Lopus, Peggy, 154
Lorimore, William, 183
Loucks, Peter, 38
Loughead, Adam, 228
Loughner, Daniel, 123, 197
Loughtner, Jonas, 123
Loughtner, Rudy, 123
Louther, David, 61
Louther, James, 61
Louther, Jonathan, 61
Loutzenhizer, David, 182
Loutzenhizer, Elizabeth, 183
Loutzinhezen, Henry, 183
Love, Alexander, 61
Love, Andrew, 228
Love, B, 49
Love, Samuel, 228
Love, William, 228
Low, Adam, 50
Low, Conrad, 49, 50
Low, Henry, 38, 50
Low, Samuel, 122
Lowry, Stephen, 208
Loyd, Widow, 104, 123
Lucar, David, 252
Luce, Lockart, 207

Abstracts of Westmoreland County, Pennsylvania, Tax Records 1815

Luch, Robert, 80
Luchins, Abraham, 38
Lucre, Benjamin, 207
Lucre, Craig, 208
Ludwich, Conrad, 81
Ludwich, John, 81
Lules, George, 61
Lup, Jacob, 61
Lusk, John, 183
Lutureh, George, 183
Lutz, Daniel, 228
Lutz, Martin, 208
Lutzenhizer, Jacob, 183
Lutzetger, Elizabeth, 198
Lybe, Robert, 183
Lyon, James, 300
Lyon, William, 300
Lyons, James, 280, 287
Lytick, Jacob, 279
Mabyben, George, 63
MacAfee, Patrick, 282
MaCalley, Zechariah, 283
MacDermot, John, 282
MacDonald, Archd, 281
Macdonald, Samuel, 63
Macfadden, John, 38
MacFarland, David, 282
MacFarland, James, 282
MacFarland, Thomas, 282
MacFarland, William, 282
MacFarland, Wilson, 283
MacGuire, Daniel, 284
Machesney, Andrew, 283
Machesney, James, 281
Machesney, John, 283
Machesney, William, 281
Mack, Michael, 156
Macker, Aron, 185
Mackey, William, 155
Mackey, W^m, 196
Macklen, Frederick, 125
Macklen, Jacob, Junior, 128
Macklin, Jacob, 156
Maclauren, Matthew, 18
MacLauren, W^m, 17
Maclean, Alexander, 19
Maclean, Alexr, 20

Maclean, David, 97
Maclean, Hamilton, 282
Maclean, John, 208, 302
Maclean, Matthew, 282
Maclean, Prussia, 302
Maclian, Alexander, 208
Maclintic, Jonathan, 208
Macue, John, 283
Macune, John, 283
MacWilliams, James, 282
Macwright, James, 283
Maffet, James, 210
Maghan, John, 302
Maghan, Patrick, 302
MaGill, James, 18
MaGoogan, Robert, 283
MaGuire, Daniel, 283
MaGuire, Samuel, 283
Mahan, Robert, 256
Mahon, John, 188
Mains, Andrew, 188
Mains, David, 188
Mains, Finley, 186
Mains, Isaac, 185
Mains, James, 186
Mains, William, 185
Major, 94, 102, 112, 211, 213,
    220, 227, 275
MaKee, Samuel, 283
Makissock, Isaac, 283
malt house, 48, 78
Maltz, George, 186
Maners, John, 196
Manersmith, Jacob, 196
Mann, James, 230
Mansfield, Abraham, 229
Mansfield, Christopher, 302
Mansfield, John, 126
Mansfield, William, 302
Mansfield, William, Senior, 302
Manwell, Robert, 282
Manwell, William, 282
March, Christian, 85
Marchan, Daniel, 101
Marchand, Daniel, 128
Marchand, David, 124, 127
Marchand, Jacob, 125

Abstracts of Westmoreland County, Pennsylvania, Tax Records 1815

Marchand, John, 124
Marchand, Widow, 125
Marchant, David, 62
Marchbanks, James, 126
Marchman, 13
Marderty, Henry, 200
mare, 17, 22
Marhsal, William, 232
Marin, Hugh, 155
Markel, Gasper, 185
Markle, 185
Markle, Gasper, Senior, 254
Markle, Jacob, 46, 254
Markle, John, 255, 282
Markle, Joseph, 185
Marks, Henry, 164
Marks, John, 302
Marmie, Peter, 208
Marsh, Cooper, 184
Marsh, Henry, Junior, 189
Marsh, Henry, Senior, 189
Marsh, William, 184
Marshal, David, 280
Marshal, James, 280, 282
Marshal, Joseph, 282
Marshal, Robert, 19, 232, 281, 282
Marshal, Samuel, 281
Marshal, William, 281, 300
Martain, Henry, 186
Marten, James, 52
Marten, Nancy, 52
Martezall, Martin, 209
Martin, 55
Martin, Aaron, 188
Martin, H. Knor, 155
Martin, Hugh, 38
Martin, James, 39, 50
Martin, John, 63, 127, 186, 253, 282
Martin, Joshua, 209
Martin, Peter, 125
Martin, Robert, 155
Martin, Samuel, 50
Martin, William, 19, 39, 253, 284
Martz, Nicholas, 82

Martz, William, 231
Masters, David, 85
Masters, Isaac, 85
Masters, William, 84
Masters, William, Senior, 82
Mathers, Robert, 208
Mathers, Thomas, 210
Mathers, William, 208
Mathews, Robert, 210
Mathias, Michael, 124
Matson, Samuel, 19
Matson, Uriah, 19
Matthews, Barbara, 62
Matthews, James, 61
Matthews, John, 63
Matthews, William, 61
Mattocks, Daniel, 62
Mawhias, Francis, 39
Maxwell, James, 61
Maxwell, Samuel, 209
Maxwill, David, 281
Mays, Alexander, 185
Mays, James, 302
Mays, John, 185
Mays, Samuel, 185
Mays, Thomas, 302
Mays, William, 302
McAbee, John, 62
McAluse, W^m, 187
McAnulty, Richard, 188
McBarvere, Patrick, 284
McBay, Joseph, 62
McBraem, Andrew, 19
McBride, Alex^r, 229
McBride, James, 229
McBrier, David, 302
McBrier, James, 301
McBrier, Nathaniel, 302
McCafferty, Widow, 187
McCall, David, 83
McCall, John, 83, 281
McCall, Margaret, 156
McCall, Robert, 156
McCall, Samuel, 281
McCall, Stephen, 156
McCall, Thomas, 156
McCalley, Samuel, 230

Abstracts of Westmoreland County, Pennsylvania, Tax Records 1815

McCallister, Adam, 229
McCallister, Archibald, 19, 281
McCalt, Richard, 83
McCalvey, James, 293
McCammont, John, 40
McCann, Hugh, 301
McCann, James, 255
McCann, Robert, 255, 256
McCann, Thomas, 255
McCanoughy, Robert, 11
McCardy, Ephriem, 49
McCartney, Alexander, 124
McCartney, Thomas, 17
McCaul, Benjamin, 197
McCauley, John, 126
McCauley, John, Senior, 126
McClain, John, 184
McClean, David, 82
Mccleand, David, 213
McCleard, David, 209
McClellan, Archibald, 63
McClellan, David, 63
McClellan, William, 63
McClelland, David, 230, 253
McClelland, James, 18, 231
McClelland, John, 97, 127, 231, 253, 256
McClelland, Thomas, 280
McClelland, William, 230, 256
McClelland, Wm, 20
McCleod, David, 301
McCleod, William, 300
McClerg, Alexander, 155
McCletchy, James, 20
McClinahen, Matthew, 38
McClintock, Alexander, 256
McClintock, Alexr, 253
McClintock, Henry, 253
McClintock, William, 254
McCloskey, Manus, 82
McCloskey, Michael, 83
McCloy, William, 184
McClueas, James, 186
McClure, George, 209
McClure, John, 184
McClure, Joseph, 146
McClure, Robert, 16

McClure, Thomas, 228
McClure, William, 209
McClurg, Joseph, 188
McClurg, William, 184
McClurgh, James, 185
McClurgh, Joseph, 186
McClurgh, William, 188
McColley, Samuel, 302
McCommont, Isaac, 50
McConaughy, James, Junior, 62
McConaughy, James, Senior, 63
McConaughy, John, 63
McConaughy, Robert, 17, 63
McConkey, Robert, 62
McConnel, Agness, 230
McConnel, David, 232
McConnel, John, 82, 84
McConnel, Sam], 84
McCord, Samuel, 209
McCormick, Andrew, 188
McCormick, David, 255
McCormick, John, 18, 188
McCormick, Joseph, 187, 239, 256
McCormick, Robert, 254
McCormick, Sally, 188
McCormick, Samuel, 255
McCormick, William, 186
McCown, Daniel, 302
McCown, Robert, 301
McCoy, Daniel, 62
McCoy, Jacob, 280
McCoy, John, 61, 187, 256
McCracken, Richard, 62
McCrea, Robert, 84
McCreary, Charles, 62
McCreary, John, 83
McCreary, Robert, 61
McCreary, William, 62
McCroskey, Wm, 20
McCue, John, 228
McCullen, Daniel, 18
McCullough William, 61
McCullough, David, 96
McCullough, James, 302
McCullough, John, 302
McCullough, Robert, 232

Abstracts of Westmoreland County, Pennsylvania, Tax Records 1815

McCullough, Samuel, 232, 301
McCullough, Senior, James, 301
McCune, John, 124
McCurdy, Andrew, 30
McCurdy, Elizabeth, 62
McCurdy, Hugh, 124
McCurdy, James, 62, 63
McCurdy, James, Senior, 62
McCurdy, John, 62, 63, 125
McCurdy, Robert, 63
McCurdy, Samuel, Junior, 124
McCurdy, Samuel, Senior, 125
McCurdy, William, 62
McCutchen, Alex^r, 82
McCutchen, James, 96, 281
McCutchen, John, 232
McCutchen, Robert, 301
McCutchen, Samuel, 230, 281, 301
McCutchen, Widow, 301
McCutchen, William, 301
McCutchon, Samuel, 222
McDade, Finley, 302
McDeide, Widow, 302
McDonald, Alexander, 184
McDonald, Archabald, 156
McDonald, Edward, 17
McDonald, John, 184
McDonald, William, 184
McDowel, Henry, 62
McDowel, John, 62, 301
McDowel, Robert, 62
McDowel, Robert, Senior, 63
McDowel, Samuel, 62
McDowel, William, 63
McDowel, William, Junior, 61
McElroy, Alexander, 62
McElroy, John, 63
McFadden, Charles, 40
McFadden, James, 281
McFadden, Jane, 52
McFadden, John, 52
McFall, Charles, 209
McFarland, Benjamin, 20
McFarland, William, 20
McFarlen, 307
McFarlen, Thomas, 61

McFee, James, 124
McFeely, Bernard, 61
McGaughey, Archibald, 18
McGaughey, James, 18
McGaughey, John, 19
McGaughey, Samuel, 18
McGaughey, Thomas, Junior, 19
McGaughey, Thomas, Senior, 18
McGaughey, William, 18
McGaughlen, Archibald, 209
McGavoh, Thomas, 209
McGaw, Daniel, 229
McGeary, Clement, 301
McGeary, David, 301
McGeary, James, 301
McGeary, John, 301
McGeary, Senior, William, 301
McGeary, William, 301
McGee, James, 3, 20
Mcgees, W^m, 205
McGenley, Robert, 17
McGill, William, 187
McGinley, David, 19
McGinley, Michael, 232
McGinnes, John, 155
McGlonehy, Neal, 63
McGogany, John, 209
McGonnigal, Thomas, 230
McGown, Thomas, 186
McGrady, Elizabeth, 155
McGrady, Partrick, 155
McGrail, John, 184
McGranahen, James, 82
McGrew, A Finley, 186
McGrew, A James, 184
McGrew, Ann, 188
McGrew, B James, 187
McGrew, Dinah, 185
McGrew, E James, 188
McGrew, Elijah, 186
McGrew, Finley, 187
McGrew, Jacob, 185
McGrew, James, 184, 197
McGrew, James B, 189
McGrew, Nathan, 184
McGrew, Nathan, Junior, 188
McGrew, Samuel, 188

Abstracts of Westmoreland County, Pennsylvania, Tax Records 1815

McGrew, Simon, 186, 187
McGrew, William, 186
Mcgrew, Wᵐ, 210
McGriff, Elizabeth, 61
McGriff, James, 61
McGrilles, James, 128
McGuffey, James, 254
McGuffey, Robert, 253
McGuffin, Robert, 186
McGuire, Barney, 19
McGuire, John, 20
McGuire, John, Senior, 19
McGuire, Mary, 19
McGuire, Patrick, 97
McGuire, Robert, 30
McGuire, Samuel, 83
McGuire, Thomas, 83, 97, 127
McGuire, Wm, 19
McGunagle, James, 125
McHafffey, Stephen, 229
McHenry, Isabella, 40
McHenry, Joshua, 40
McIlvain, Andrew, 84
McIlvain, John, 84
McIlwain, Andrew, 126
McIlwain, Gilbert, 255
McIlwain, Hugh, 255
McIlwain, James, 255
McIlwain, Robert, 231
McIlwain, William, 63, 255
McIntere, Patrick, 188
McIntyre, John, 19, 187
McIntyre, John, Senior, 19
McJunken, John, 231
McJunkins, John, 30
McKeain, Alexander, 83
McKean, James, 39, 50, 82
McKean, Robert, 187
McKean, Thomas, 50, 187, 301
McKean, William, 82, 84, 301
Mckee, Alexander, 125
McKee, Benjamin, 232
McKee, Elizabeth, 164
McKee, Hugh, 302
McKee, James, 230
McKee, John, 126, 208, 301
McKee, Joseph, 282

McKee, Samuel, 20, 126, 302
McKee, Thomas, 19, 255
McKee, Widow, 302
McKee, William, 19, 301, 302
McKeever, Eleanor, 83
Mckeever, James, 210
McKeever, William, 83
McKellep, James, 231
McKellep, John, 30
McKellep, Matthew, 231
McKellip, John, 228
McKelvey, James, 61, 62, 63
McKelvey, John, 62
McKelvey, Lewis, 61
McKelvey, Robert, 62
McKelvey, William, 188
McKelvy, James, 126
Mckenry, Archibald, 196
McKessock, Joseph, 231
McKever, Henry, 239
McKever, Matthew, 83
McKibbens, James, 302
McKinley, George, 63
McKinley, John, 17, 62
McKinley, William, 39
McKinney, Alexʳ, 127
McKisseck, James, 232
McKissock, James, 231
McKissock, Robert, 126
McKissock, Samuel, 126
McKnight, Daniel, 229
McKnight, Wm, 280
McKonkey, William, 63
McLaoughlin, Michael, 231
McLaughlen, James, 230, 302
McLaughlen, Mathew, 301
McLaughlen, Michael, 231
McLaughlen, Samuel, 300, 302
McLaughlen, William, 301
McLaughlin, Charles, 96
McLaughlin, James, 128
McLaughlin, John, 255
McLaughlin, Randles, 96
McLaughlin, Widow, 302
McLauglen, James, 301
McLauglen, William, 301
McLauglin, John, 300

Abstracts of Westmoreland County, Pennsylvania, Tax Records 1815

McLees, Joseph, 83
McLeese, Joseph, 83
McLeese, William, 82
McLouglin, James, 113
McLuster, Archibald, 229
McMachin, Arthur, 187
McMaken, John, 17
Mcmanigal, James, 128
McManus, Joseph, 62
McMaster, Gilbert, 39
McMaster, John, 155
McMaster, Mary, 156
McMaster, William, 19, 50
McMehan, Samuel, 82
McMicheal, Saml, 255
McMullen, Daniel, 255
McMullen, Robert, 18
McMullen, Samuel, 124
McMullen, Smith, 17
McMullen, Thomas, 254
McMullen, William, 17, 18
McMunay, Alexander, 125
McMurray, John, 125
McNair, Robert, 62
McNaughtan, Neal, 255
McNeal, Archibald, 96
McNoher, John, 62
McNutt, Robert, 19
Mcquade, James, 186
McQuaid, Daniel, 85
McQuaid, William, 84
McQuead, Patrick, 82, 230
McQuead, Thomas, 230
McQuilken, Robert, 302
McQuilkin, Daniel, 230
McQuilkin, James, 230
McQuinton, Anna, 17
McQuiston, David, 17
McQuiston, James, Junior, 17
McQuiston, James, Senior, 17
McQuiston, Samuel, 30
McQuiston, William, 17
McQuown, Laurence, 18
McSourley, James, 231
McVey, Edward, 302
McVey, John, 302
McVey, Patrick, 301

McVey, Philip, 301
McWhorter, Jno, 65
McWhorter, William, 282
McWhorter, William, Senior, 62
McWilliams, Andrew, 84
McWilliams, George, 84
McWilliams, James, 82, 84, 252
McWilliams, Robert, 84, 255
McWilliams, William, 84
Meanor, Josias, 82
Means, William, 255
Means, W^m, 196
Mears, David, 20
Mears, John, 20
Mearson, Isaac, 40
Meason, Thomas, 229
Mecklen, Jacob, 127
Mecklen, John, 126
Mecklin, Frederick, 96
Mecklin, Jacob, Senior, 123
Mecklin, Philip, 123, 124
Mecklin, Samuel, 125
Meeford, William, 155
Mehaffe, Jo, 170
Mehaffe, Joseph, 196
Mehaffey, Samuel, 229
Melan, Armor, 282
Mellander, Philip, 254
Mellon, Hugh, 127
Melvill, John, 96
Menium, George, 231
merchant mill, 201, 207
Merrew, Paul, 96
Merton, A. George, 208
Merton, David, 208
Metzker, Frederick, 184, 254, 281
Metzker, Fred^k, 171
Metzker, John, 254
Metzler, Adam, 254
Metzler, George, 255
Michael, George, 229
Micklwane, John, 164
Migrance, Chrisp^r, 156
Milbe, William, 155
Milbey, James, 156
Milbey, Robert, 156

Abstracts of Westmoreland County, Pennsylvania, Tax Records 1815

Miligan, Alex\[r\], 186
Miligan, James, 185, 253
Miligan, John, 185
Miligan, W\[m\], 209
Miliron, Widow, 124
mill, 162, 203, 267, 271, 274, 289
Millar, Adam, 253
Millar, George, 280, 283
Millar, John, 280
Millar, John, Senior, 280
Millar, Michael, 253
Millar, Peter, 280
Millar, Susanna, 254
Millear, Phillip, 232
Miller, Adam, 125
Miller, Alexander, 50
Miller, Benjamin, 254
Miller, Eleanor, 144
Miller, Frederick, 184
Miller, George, 184
Miller, Henry, 38, 123, 124, 125, 126
Miller, Issey, 301
Miller, Jacob, 123, 127, 230
Miller, Jacob, Junior, 124
Miller, James, 53
Miller, John, 30, 53, 124, 125
Miller, Joseph, 40, 155, 187
Miller, Leonhard, 127
Miller, Mary Elizabeth, 144
Miller, Mathew, 301
Miller, Michael, 126
Miller, Nancy, 52, 53
Miller, Nicholas, 20, 127
Miller, Peter, 123, 126, 128, 144, 187
Miller, Philip, 125
Miller, Robert, 300
Miller, Samuel, 185, 209, 232
Miller, Widow, 144
Miller, William, 40
Miller, Wm, 255
Millers, Jas, 179
Milligan, Edward, 301
Milligan, Samuel, 83, 301
Milliron, Philip, 61

Mirn?n, John, 230
Miskelly, Hugh, 82
Miskelly, John, 83
Mitcheal, John, 188
Mitchel, Charles, 254
Mitchel, David, 125
Mitchel, John, 84
Mitchel, Samuel, 253
Mitchel, Thomas, 155, 255
Mitchel, William, 187, 256
Mitzler, Peter, 255
Moah, John, 188
Moley, Milles, 127
Momyer, John, 281
Momyer, William, 281, 284
Moneysmith, Jacob, 124
Monroe, Joseph, 127
Monroe, Robert, 125
Monroe, Thomas, 127
Montgomery, Benjamin, 301
Montgomery, David, 253
Montgomery, Henry, 96
Montgomery, James, 96, 209, 281
Montgomery, John, 20, 269
Montgomery, Robert, 284
Montgomery, Samuel, 39, 252
Montgomery, Thomas, 50
Moohead, James, 232
Moor, George, 232
Moor, Jacob, 233
Moor, John, Senior, 232
Moore, Ebenzer, 209
Moore, Hannah, 229
Moore, Isaac, 83
Moore, James, 187, 231, 283
Moore, James, Junior, 232
Moore, James, Senior, 231
Moore, John, 16, 84, 232, 307
Moore, Martha, 62
Moore, Robert, 96
Moore, Thomas, 18, 307
Moore, William, 126, 229
Moore, William, Junior, 232
Moore, William, Senior, 232
Moorehouse, Fergus, 255
Moorhead, Alexander, 208

Abstracts of Westmoreland County, Pennsylvania, Tax Records 1815

Moorhead, James, 231
Moorhead, John, 18, 20
Moorhead, Joseph, 209
Moorhead, Josiah, 17
Moorhead, Michael, 302
Moorhead, Samuel, 18, 231
Moorhead, William, 302
Moose, John, 209
Moots, Sarah, 82
Morehead, Samuel, 85
Morgan, Doctor, 307
Morgan, Isaac, 218, 253
Morgan, John, 38, 209
Morgan, Morgan, 208
Morgan, Peter, 16
Morgan, Samuel, 208
Morgan, William, 208
Morris, William, 84
Morrison, Agness, 230
Morrison, Daniel, 229
Morrison, John, 96, 283, 301
Morrison, Robert, 155
Morrison, Samuel, 283
Morrow, Elizabeth, 253
Morrow, James, 186, 254
Morrow, Jean, 253
Morrow, John, 71, 85, 97, 254
Morrow, Paul, 105, 127
Morrow, Samuel, 253
Morrow, Sarah, 254
Morrow, William, 254
Morse, Niclose, 232
Morten, Isaac, 210
Morton, David, 254
Morton, John, 307
Mosford, Lewis, 96
Moyer, Christine, 156
Moyer, David, 128
Moyer, Jacob, 38
Moyer, John, 39, 155, 156
Moyer, Mahlon, 156
Moyer, Mathias, 155
Moyer, Michael, 155
Moyers, Abraham, 61
Moyers, Christian, 63
Moyers, Frederick, 63
Muckhouse, Thos, 165

Muffley, Isaac, 302
Muffley, Jacob, 302
Muffley, John, 302
Mulholland, George, 17, 20, 30
Mulholland, James, 17
Mulin, Richard, 293
Mullen, Barney, 230
Mullen, Francis, 283, 284
Mumma, Andrew, 38
Mumma, David, 39
Mumma, George, Junior, 39
Mumma, George, Senior, 39
Murfy, Moses, 232
Murich, David, 127
Murphey, berkiax m??er, 184
Murphy, James, 61
Murphy, John, 62
Murphy, John, Senior, 62
Murphy, M^r, 226
Murphy, Robert, 62
Murphy, William, 62
Murray, Daniel, 17
Murray, James, 84
Murray, Jeremiah, 84
Murray, Jesp, 187
Murray, Squire, 76
Murry, Ja, 75
Murry, Jeremiah, 82
Murry, Jerremiah, 196
Musgrave, Joseph, 17
Musgrove, Israel, 124
Musgrove, Joseph, 63
Mycrants, Henry, 284
Myer, George, 187
Myers, Abraham, 40, 83, 256
Myers, Adam, 126
Myers, Daniel, 127, 196
Myers, David, 40
Myers, Frederick, 233, 284
Myers, George, 125
Myers, Jacob, 232
Myers, John, 127, 253
Mygrants, Jacob, 283
Myler, Thomas, 61
Myler, William, 61
Nash, William, 128
Neaff, Christian, 189, 256

Neal, Hugh, 157
Neal, James, 157
Neal, John, 157
Neal, Robert, 157
Neal, William, 157, 233
Nealy, Frederich, 85
Nealy, Henry, 85
Nealy, John, 85
Nealy, Martin, 85
Nealy, Paul, 85
Nealy, Paul, Junior, 85
Nealy, Philip, 85
Neel, John, 50, 189
Neel, John, Senior, 40
Neel, Samuel, 20, 41
Neely, Henry, 233
Neely, Samuel, 256
Neely, W^m, 210
Neffell, Thomas, 284
Neily, David, 256
Neisbet, Jas, 82
Nelson, Joseph, 63
Nelson, William, 128
Nesbet, John, 63
Nesbet, William, 63
Nesbit, James, 85
Newcomer, Christian, 41
Newcomer, David, 41
Newcomer, Jacob, 40
Newcomer, Peter, 40
Newel, George, 157
Newel, James, 157
Newel, John, 157
Newel, Thomas, 157
Newell, John, 164
Newell, Richard, 157
Newell, Stephen, 157
Newhouse, Anthony, 97, 233
Newhouse, Henry, 233
Newhouse, Jacob, 128
Newhouse, John, 97, 189
Newlon, Elijah, 189
Newlon, Elijah, Senior, 189
Newlon, James, 189
Newlon, Simon, 189
Newlon, William, 189
Newolls, Jr, 243

Newton, Isaac, 256
Nicholas, Andrew, 157
Nichols, John, 256, 284
Nichols, Joshua, 210
Nichols, Oliver, 284
Nichols, Robert, 256, 284
Nichols, William, 284
Nicholson, Robert, 20
Nighmeir, Peter, 155
Nitz, Frederick, 189
Nitz, Jacob, 85
Nixon, Jane, 20
Nixon, Simon, 20
Noel, Joseph, 157
Noel, Peter, 284
Noel, Simon, 284
Norris, Thomas, 41
Null, Henry, 256
Nunemaker, George, 233
Nunemaker, Henry, 233
O'Donald, Daniel, 128
O'Donald, Patrick, 303
O'Hara, Edward, 233
Ogden, James, 63
Ogden, John, 63
Ogden, Joseph, 63
OHara, Widow, 284
oil mill, 38, 163, 261, 285, 287
Oliver, B. James, 256
Oliver, Samuel, 128
Ollam, Daniel, 302
Olos, G Daniel, 257
Ong, Jeremiah, 256
Orey, Eve, 233
Orner, David, 302
Orr, Adam, 210
Orr, Charles, 210
Orr, John, 210, 256
Orr, Samuel, 210
Orrans, Peter, 284
Orrey, Adam, 303
Osburn, Alexander, 189
Osburn, Archibald, 189
Osburn, Michael, 20
Osburn, Samuel, 189
Over, Peter, 63
Overholt, Abraham, 41

Overholt, Christian, 41
Overholt, Jacob, 41
Overholt, Martin, 41
Overly, Adam, 158
Overly, Christopher, 157
Overly, Gasper, 157
oxen, 69, 71, 78, 120
Oycher, Abraham, 158
Oycher, Daniel, 158
Oycher, Michael, 157
Ozenbough, Nicholas, 128
Painter, Cathrine, 85
Painter, Christina, 85
Painter, George, 128, 129, 303
Painter, Isaac, 189
Painter, Jacob, 85, 103, 128,
    129, 303
Painter, John, 128, 129, 189
Painter, Joseph, 158
Painter, Laurence, 85
Painter, Michael, 129
Painter, Peter, 284
Painter, Tobias, 85, 129
Painter, Widow, 129
Painter, William, 303
Palmer, Adam, 285
Palmer, George, 158
Palmer, John, 233
Pancake, Benjamin, 211
Pancake, Philip, 307
paper mill, 185
Park, James, 190
Park, Samuel, 86
Park, William, 86
Parker, Benjamin, 285
Parker, John, 41
Parks, John, 64, 129
Parks, William, 190
Parr, B James, 21
Parr, Benjamin, 21
Parr, Isaac, Junior, 21
Parr, Isaac, Senior, 21
Path, Jacob, 86
Patrick, James, 21
Patrick, John, 233
Patrick, John, Senoir, 22
Patrick, Thomas, 21

Patrick, William, 22
Patterson, Abner, 163
Patterson, Elias, 164
Patterson, Elijah, 211
Patterson, Henry, 86
Patterson, James, 21, 190, 211,
    257
Patterson, James, Senior, 21
Patterson, John, 164, 190, 210,
    211
Patterson, Joseph, 190, 257
Patterson, Mathew, 211
Patterson, Peggey, 294
Patterson, Robert, 21, 129, 211,
    285, 294
Patterson, Samuel, 21, 211
Patterson, Samuel, Junior, 22
Patterson, Thomas, 64, 210, 211
Patterson, Thomas, Junior, 21
Patterson, Thomas, Senior, 21
Patterson, William, 211
Patton, James, 22
Patton, John, 190
Patty, George, 129
Paul, Morgan, 211
Paul, Samuel, 303
Paul, Sarah, 303
Peaghth, Martin, 22
Pearl, Maryan, 198
Pearl, Racheal, 198
Pearson, Robert, 20
Peart, Thomas, 190
Pease, Jacob, 285
Peck, Simon, 285
Peenix, William, 210
Peeples, Samuel, 41
Peeples, William, 285
Peetal, Henry, 190
Pehil, Christianna, 22
Pehil, Martin, 22
Peichtel, Christopher, 285
Peigley, Adam, 85
Pelall, Henry, 198
Pence, Connerod, 158
Penner, John, 233
Pennington, Doran, 303
Penny, David, 211

Abstracts of Westmoreland County, Pennsylvania, Tax Records 1815

Penrod, Michael, 286
Penrose, 67
Penrose, Michael, 285
Peoples, 239
Peoples, Catrine, 64
Peoples, Hugh, 63, 64
Peoples, James, 63
Peoples, John, 55, 64
Peoples, Joseph, 63
Peoples, Robert, 63
Peoples, Samuel, 63
Peper, Peter, 257
Peppels, William, 233
Pere, Adam, 285
Perkey, Jacob, 129
Pershian, Christian, 285
Pershian, Christian, Junior, 285
Pershian, Christophel, 286
Pershian, Conrad, 285
Pershian, Daniel, 22
Pert, Thos, 197
Petall, Henry, 192
Peterson, Nicholas, 190
Peterson's Heirs, 21
Petty, Edward, 210
Philiber, Henry, 303
Philips, Jacob, 303
Philips, John, 303
Philips, William, 129, 307
Phipps, Robert, 64
Phipps, Samuel, 64
Pierce, Isaac, 22
Pifer, George, 233
Pifer, John, 233
Piles, John, 285, 286
Pinkerton, William, 190
Piper, Daniel, 286
Piper, John, 64
Piper, Robert, 64
Piper, William, 64
Pitt, William, 307
Pixler, Samuel, 85
Plenge, George, 307
Pletcher, Henry, 163
Pluck, Jacob, 128
Plumber, Jonathan, 257
Plumer, Alexander, 257

Plumer, George, 257
Plumer, John, 257
Plumer, Lazarus, 257
Pluterbech, John, 167
Polens, John, 285
Pollin, Isaac, 257
Pollins, William, 158, 285
Pollock, David, 210
Pollock, John, 64
Pollock, Thomas, 64
Pool, Peter, 41
Pool, Samuel, 128
Pool, Zachariah, 128
Poorman, Daniel, 129
Poorman, Jacob, 285
Poorman, Michael, 284
Poorman, Peter, 158, 285
Porter, Andrew, 307
Porter, Caleb, 210
Porter, Daniel, 211, 257
Porter, Jacob, 22
Porter, James, 22
Porter, John, 17, 22, 233, 303
Porter, Joseph, 22
Porter, Samuel, 233
Porter, William, 233
Postlethwaite, James, 129
Postlethwayte, James, 97
Poth, Daniel, 86
Poth, Samuel, Senior, 86
Potsor, Christian, 129
Potter, Thomas, 130
Potts, John, 86
Potts, Michael, 86
Potts, Stacey, 190
Pounds, James, 30
Pounds, Joseph, 22
Pounds, Stephen, 21
Powel, Sarah, 307
Power, Aaron, 210, 257
Power, F. John, 211
Power, James, 158
Power, Patrick, 211
Pranale, Georg, 190
Prater, Benjamin, 97
Price, Patrick, 303
Price, Samuel, 257

Abstracts of Westmoreland County, Pennsylvania, Tax Records 1815

Proctor, James, 211
Pumroy, Francis, 22
Pumroy, George, 21
Pumroy, John, 21
Pumroy, Thomas, 21
Purdy, John, 86
Purgis, R, 249
Purgis, Wm, 249
Purnel, Benjamin, 22
Purvis, Robt, 257
Purvis, Wm, 257
Quail, Robert, 190
Queery, John, 257
Quig, Patrick, 64
Quinn, John, 303
Quinn, John, Senior, 303
Quinn, Oliver, 303
Quinn, Robert, 303
Rainey, John, 23
Rainey, Robert, 24
Ralston, James, 234
Ralston, John, 234
Ralston, Mathew, 304
Ralston, Robert, 234, 303
Ralston, William, 234
Rambough, William, 132
Ramsay, John, 64
Ramsay, William, 87
Ramsey, William, 225
Randles, John, 307
Randles, William, 159
Rankin, David, 23, 87
Rankin, Matthew, 24
Ransel, Henry, 24
Raser, Frederick, 159
Ratchford, Edward, 130
Ray, David, 51
Ray, James, 49, 259
Ray, Joseph, 259
Ray, Matthew, 42
Ray, Samuel, 51
Raynold, John, 22
Reachart, Jacob, 239
Read, James, 10
Read, Thomas, 258
Reader, George, 258, 259
Reagan, Alexander, 50

Reagan, C Collen, 259
Reagan, Collin, 42, 259
Reagan, Philip, 42, 258
Reagan, Weldon, 42
Reamer, Abraham, 234
Reamey, Robert, 234
Reaney, Robert, 235
Reart, Andrew, 235
Reasman, Philip, 52
Reddick, William, 304
Redember, John, 164
Reed, Adam, 239
Reed, Isaac, 303
Reed, Jacob, 132, 258
Reed, James, 22, 23, 234, 239, 303, 304
Reed, John, 97, 259, 303
Reed, Joseph, 191, 211, 239
Reed, Peter, 64, 211
Reed, Robert, 40, 64, 86, 130
Reed, Saml, 256
Reed, Samuel, 23
Reed, Widow, 286
Reed, William, 23, 190
Reeger, Jacob, 131
Reemer, Henry, 131
Reemer, Jacob, 131
Reese, Godfrey, 190
Reese, Stephen, 212
Reesman, Philip, 130
Reeve, Peter, 307
Reeves, Abner, 212
Reeves, Jesse, 213
Reeves, Manassa, 212
Reeves, Samuel, 213
Reeves, Thomas, 64
Regee, B., 66
Reiger, Jacob, 64
Reims, Frederick, 131
Reims, Frederick, Junior, 131
Relan, John, 212
Remeleigh, Christian, 86
Remeleigh, Henry, 86
Remeleigh, John, 87
Remeleigh, Michael, 87
Rensel, George, 24
Rensel, Henry, 24

Abstracts of Westmoreland County, Pennsylvania, Tax Records 1815

Resilon, David, 159
Retan, Nicholas, 212
Reynolds, George, 22
Reynolds, John, 23
Reynolds, Robert, 23
Reynolds, Samuel, 23
Reynolds, William, 259
Rhea, John, 212
Rhodes, Abraham, 258
Rhodes, Henry, 258
Rhodes, Henry, Senior, 259
Rhodes, John, 212
Rhodes, Peter, 258
Rhodes, Samuel, 42
Rhodorker, Frederick, 212
Rice, Frederick, 130
Rice, Peter, 130
Rice, T^k, 102
Richard, Charles, 286
Richard, Frederick, 304
Richard, Henry, 24, 87
Richard, Martin, 303
Richard, Michael, 87
Richard, Robert, 24
Richards, Jacob, 87
Richards, John, 286
Richards, William, 131
Richardson, William, 304
Richart, Adam, 130
Richer, Peter, 191
Richeson, George, 64
Richey, George, 303
Richey, James, 258
Richey, James, Junior, 41
Richey, Jesse, 259
Richey, Samuel, 42
Richey, William, 234
Rickard, Peter, 87
Rickels, Evan, 259
Riddel, James, 234
Riddel, John, 234
Riddel, Robert, 86
Riddel, William, 64, 234
Ridenhour, George, 303
Ridenhour, Henry, 303
Ridenhour, William, 303
Rider, Conrad, 259

Rider, Jonas, 259
Rider, William, 23
Rigeart, Charles, 146
Riggel, John, 130
Righard, Henry, 234
Rimbel, George, 131
Rimmel, Frederich, 234
Rimus, Frederick, 159
Rinehart, Frederich, 234
Ring, Michael, 286
Ringer, Chester, 234
Ringer, Christian, 86
Ringer, Michael, 234
Ringle, Abraham, 303
Ringle, Daniel, 303
Ringle, David, 303
Ringle, John, 303
Ritchey, John, 257
Ritter, Abrahaim, 130
Ritter, Abraham, 259
Ritter, Widow, 286
Roadarmer, Peter, 259
Robb, Isaac, 259
Robb, James, 286
Robb, John, 212
Robb, Robert, 131
Robbins, Brintnel, 191
Robenson, George, 51
Robenson, James, 38
Roberts, John, 212, 307
Roberts, Peter, 87
Robertson, Andrew, 212
Robertson, Ephraim, 22
Robertson, John, 23
Robertson, Rebecca, 23
Robeson, Martha, 259
Robins, Herekia, 190
Robins, Mosses, 191
Robinson, Alex, 169
Robinson, Charles, 159
Robinson, James, 213
Robinson, John, 212
Robinson, Thomas, 212
Robinson, William, 158, 197, 286
Robinson, W^m, 168
Robison, Alexander, 191

Robison, Andrew, 307
Robison, Andrew, Junior, 258
Robison, Andrew, Senior, 257
Robison, George, 64
Robison, Henry, 191
Robison, Hugh, 30
Robison, James, 234, 258, 304
Robison, John, 64, 87, 191, 258
Robison, Jonathan, 258
Robison, Mathew, 191
Robison, Thomas, 205, 258
Robison, William, 190, 258
Rochester, Robert, 303
Rodgers, Charles, 64
Rodgers, John, 42, 64, 286
Rogers, Samuel, 159
Rohrer, Fridirich, 97
Rohrer, George, 97
Rohser, Friderich, 132
Roley, John, 159
Rolls, John, 234
Roodman, Jacob, 158
Roodman, John, 158
Roof, Jacob, 24
Rose, Allen, 41
Rose, Christian, 131
Rose, George, 87
Rose, John, 87
Roseberry, Robert, 235
Rosenberger, Henry, 42
Rosenberger, John, 86
Rosenberger, Tilman, 42
Rosensteel, Andrew, 130
Rosensteel, George, 130
Rosensteel, Jacob, 130
Ross, 97
Ross, Alexander, 286
Ross, Archibald, 257
Ross, John, 259, 287, 304
Ross, Joseph, 24, 286
Ross, Randles, 258
Ross, William, 304
Ross, William, carpenter, 304
Roulston, Andrew, 30
Rouse, Martin, 159
Row, Andrew, 87, 131, 259
Row, Christian, 131

Row, George, 131
Row, Jacob, 131
Row, Michael, 64
Rowan, James, 304
Rowan, John, 258, 304
Rowan, Matthew', 131
Rowan, Stephen, 258
Rowley Joseph, 304
Rowley, Asa, 304
Royal, David, 212
Royal, George, 211
Royer, Elizabeth, 131
Royer, John, 130
Rubey, William, 259
Rubright, Henry, 86
Rudebaugh, Christian, 131
Rudebaugh, Daniel, 191
Rudibaugh, John, 191
Rudolph, Abraham, 303
Rudolph, Jacob, 303
Rudolph, John, 303
Rudy, Daniel, 41
Rue, William, 257
Ruff, Anthony, 159
Ruff, Jacob, 159
Ruffeorn, Christian, 190
Ruffner, Christian, 132
Ruffner, George, 132, 234, 286
Ruffner, James, 286
Ruffner, Peter, 286
Ruffner, Simon, 286
Rugh, Benjamin, 303
Rugh, Daniel, 132, 304
Rugh, Jacob, 97, 132, 286
Rugh, Michael, 86
Rugh, Peter, 130
Rumbauch, Abraham, 158
Rumbauch, Augustice, 158
Rumbauch, Daniel, 158
Rumbauch, George, 158
Rumbauch, Henry, 158
Rumbauch, John, 158
Rumbauch, Michael, 159
Rumbauch, Peter, 158
Rumbauch, William, 158
Runeor, Eli, 287
Runk, Michael, 159

Abstracts of Westmoreland County, Pennsylvania, Tax Records 1815

Russel, Agnes, 23
Russel, Caleb, 23
Russel, David, 23
Russel, James, 23, 87, 131
Russel, James, Senior, 23
Russel, John, 23, 303
Russel, Joseph, 132
Russel, William, 64
Ruth, Abraham, 42
Ryan, James, 212
Ryan, Thomas, 212
Ryland, Henry, 97
S, John, 288
Saal, Jacob, 138
Saal, Leonard, 88
Saal, Michael, 136
Saam, Adam, 192
Saam, Frederick, 192
Saddler, Jacob, 194
Sadler, Isaac, 88
Sadler, Jacob, 89
Sadler, Peter, 163
Sadler, William, 89
Sallentine, Michael, 290
Sambro, Henry, 261
Sample, Ezekiel, 260
Sample, Ezekiel, Junior, 260
Sample, John, 260
Sampson, Charles, 89
Sampson, Dorcas, 215
Sampson, George, 193
Sampson, James, 193
Sampson, John, 215
Sampson, Shenear, 193
Sandal, Valentine, 42
Sandals, John, 43
Sandel, Michael, 134
Sandles, Christopher, 161
Saul, Monym, 203
Savil, Jacob, 237
sawmill, 2, 3, 7, 8, 11, 14, 26, 36, 43, 45, 73, 79, 81, 82, 84, 86, 102, 105, 107, 108, 110, 115, 116, 117, 119, 128, 130, 132, 134, 137, 143, 145, 148, 154, 164, 171, 173, 176, 183, 184, 185, 186, 191, 195, 200, 203, 204, 206, 207, 208, 209, 212, 216, 217, 218, 221, 225, 227, 230, 241, 243, 246, 248, 251, 253, 254, 257, 260, 261, 271, 275, 279, 288, 289, 290, 292
Saxman, Christian, Junior, 26
Saxman, Christian, Senior, 26
Saxman, Mathias, 26
Saynor, Christian, 192
Saynor, George, 133
Saynor, Jacob, 133
Saynor, Philip, 132
Schaefer, John, 60
Schaeffer, Adam, 132, 137
Schaeffer, Babara, 64
Schaeffer, Daniel, 98
Schaeffer, Frederick, 25, 135
Schaeffer, Frederick, Junior, 136
Schaeffer, Frederick, Senior, 136
Schaeffer, George, 134, 135
Schaeffer, Henry, 287
Schaeffer, Jacob, 134
Schaeffer, John, 88, 98, 137, 138, 287, 289
Schaeffer, Philip, 132
Schaeffer, Valentine, 134
Schapper, George, 87
Scheaffer, Philip, 215
Schetler, Conrad, 136
Schetler, George, 133
Scot, James, 160
Scott, Abraham, 214
Scott, Esom, 138
Scott, John, 25, 50
Scott, Joseph, 192
Scott, Widow, 304
Scott, William, 30
Seaburd, Joseph, 65
Seaburn, Henry, 213
Seace, Martin, 288
Seacrist, George, 135
Seaton, Alexander, 65
Seaton, George, 65
Seaton, James, 65
Seaton, John, 65
Seaton, Thomas, Senior, 65
Secress, Jacob, 262

Abstracts of Westmoreland County, Pennsylvania, Tax Records 1815

Sees, Christopher, 162
Segrist, John, 161
Seisler, Henry, 162
Selby, John, 45
Selby, Samuel, 50
Selders, Benjamin, 288
Selders, George, 26, 288
Selders, Moore, 65
Sell, Jacob, 133
Selsor, Charles, 136
Selves, Henry, 236
Septer, Adam, 160
Septer, Frederick, 161
Septer, John, 161
Server, Emmanuel, 235
Server, Joernthan, 235
Server, Jonathan, 138
Shaeffer, Daniel, 139
Shaeffer, Henry, 139
Shank, Daniel, 192
Shank, Michael, 65
Shannon, John, 26
Shannon, Newton, 191
Shannon, Robert, 26
Shannon, Samuel, 64
Shapher, Jacob, 89
Shara, Jacob, 87
Shareden, Mary, 237
Sharey, John, 135
Sharg, Joseph, 44
Sharp, James, 262
Sharp, Nicholas, 236
Shaw, Alexander, 235
Shaw, David, 235
Shaw, John, 235, 307
Shear, John, 304
Shearer, Hugh, 160
Shearer, James, 236
Shearer, John, 160, 235
Shearer, Ludwick, 235
Shearer, Mary, 160
Shearer, Robert, 289
Shearer, William, 160
Shela, Abraham, 213
Shelhamer, Philip, 237
Shellhamer, Peter, 137
Shellhamer, Philip, 137

Shencer, Frederick, 193
Sheneer, David, 197
Sheneir, David, 193
Shener, Jacob, 192
Shenir, Daniel, 191
Shenir, Peter, 135
Shepherd, Lennox, 43
Shepherd, Pheobe, 50
Shepherd, Timothy, 45
Shepherd, Widow, 46
Shepperd, Paoly, 49
Sherbandy, George, 51, 260
Sherbandy, John, 46
Sherbandy, Melchar, 45
Sherbondy, Jacob, 262
Sherrer, James, 237
Sherrer, Widow, 289
Shetler, Adam, 193
Shevelar, Henry, 50
Shevler, Widow, 43
Shibe, John, 161
Shield, William, 87
Shields, Charles, 262
Shields, Elizabeth, 215
Shields, George, 236
Shields, Hugh, 65
Shields, James, 98, 215
Shields, James, Junior, 236
Shields, John, 65, 236
Shields, Mathew, 237
Shields, Robert, 235
Shields, Senior, James, 236
Shields, William, 25
Shiffler, George, 134
Shillette, Edward, 97
Shilling, John, 162
Shilling, Josias, 135
Shilling, Michael, 213
Shilling, Samuel, 304
Shilling, William, 304
Shinniman, Isaac, 24
Shiplor, Abraham, 215
Shiplor, Daniel, 216
Shiplor, Isaac, 213
Shiplor, Jacob, 214
Shiplor, John, 213
Shiplor, Mathias, 214

Abstracts of Westmoreland County, Pennsylvania, Tax Records 1815

Shiplor, Mathias, Junior, 215
Shiplor, Matthias, Senior, 214
Shiplor, Peter, Junior, 214
Shiplor, Peter, Senior, 214
Shiplor, Philip, Junior, 215
Shiplor, Philip, Senior, 214
Shiplor, Sampson, 216
Shiplor, Samuel, 214
Shirey, Abraham, 288
Shirey, Conrad, 138
Shirey, Daniel, 288
Shirey, David, 288, 289
Shirey, Nicholas, 136
Shirey, Philip, 290
Shirick, John, 293
Shiry, Hannah, 265
Shiry, Nicholas, 265
Shively, Friderich, 133
Shively, Jacob, 133
Shiver, George, 213
Shoaff, Henry, 192
Shockey, Christopher, 290
Shoemaker, John, 25
Shoemaker, Philip, 25
Shoemaker, Simon, 133
Shoemaker, William, 133
Shonn, D, 170
Shoop, John, 160
Shoop, John, Senior, 159
Shoop, Samuel, 159
Shoot, Isaac, 159
Shoot, Michael, 159
shop, 256, 268
Short, Patrick, 289
Shotz, John, 139
Shotz, Widow, 135
Shoulse, Jacob, 290
Shoup, Henry, 25, 160
Shoup, John, 30, 160
Shoup, Widow, 289
Shovey, 106
Showalter, David, 287
Showalter, Henry, 46
Showalter, Jacob, 43
Showalter, John, 51
Showalter, Joseph, 44
Showalter, Peter, 43

Showberger, John, 134
Shrader, William, 261
Shraeder, David, 192
Shrum, Daniel, 65
Shrum, David, 64
Shrum, George, 64
Shrum, John, Junior, 136
Shrum, John, Senior, 136
Shryoch, John, 235
Shryock, David, 235
Shryock, Samuel, 237
Shull, Charles, 261
Shull, Jacob, 139
Shull, Jacob, Senior, 135
Shull, John, 135
Shull, Michael, 25
Shupe, Jacob, 43
Shupe, John, 45
Shupe, Laurence, 44
Shuster, Abraham, 235
Shuster, Henry, 137
Shuster, Isaac, 137
Shuster, John, 304
Sickafoos, George, 133
Sickapoos, Jacob, 133
Sickesfoos, George, 45
Sickfried, Abraham, 135
Sickfriedt, Jacob, 289
Sickfriedt, Michael, 287
Sigler, Henry, 192
Silves, Isaac, 137
Silveys, Elizabeth, 235
Silveys, John, 88
Silveys, William, 88
Silvia, Jacob, 87, 88
Silvius, David, 288
Simpson, Andrew, 193
Simpson, Joseph, 193
Simpson, Joshua, 132
Simpson, Thomas, Junior, 132
Simpson, Thomas, Senior, 132
Simral, John, 290
Singer, Samuel, 97
Singer, Simon, 98, 116, 139
Singhorse, John, 133
Singley, George, Senior, 24
Singley, Peter, 24

Abstracts of Westmoreland County, Pennsylvania, Tax Records 1815

Sintaff, Widow, 136
Sitler, Jacob, 289
Sitler, Simon, 289
Sivia, John, 87
Skelly, 175
Skelly, Robert, 191
Skelly, William, Junior, 191
Skelly, William, Senior, 191
Skiles, Harman, 26
Skiles, M. Hugh, 65
slave, 9, 39, 117, 124, 143, 156, 183, 203, 217, 225
Slease, Jacob, 134
Slemmons, John, 45
Slemmons, Robert, 44
Slife, Frederick, Junior, 134
Slife, Frederick, Senior, 134
Sloaker, George, 237
Sloan, Henry, 193
Sloan, James, 192, 288
Sloan, John, 26, 236, 252, 262, 288
Sloan, Joseph, 193
Sloan, William, 289
Slonaker, Michael, 236
Slonecker, Adam, 161
Slotterbeck, Jon, 133
Sluse, Jacob, 305
Slutterback, John, 193
Smail, Jacob, 137
Smail, Peter, 137
Smale, Jacob, 139
Small, Peter, 119
Smart, Alexander, 260
Smebzer, Jacob, 305
Smeekley, Chrisp^r, 160
Smele, Jacob, 193
Smelzer, Jacob, 135
Smickley, Jacob, 161
Smickley, John, 161
Smilley, Gasper, 161
Smith, Adam, 137, 138
Smith, Alexander, 261
Smith, Bela, 213
Smith, Benjamin, 136
Smith, Catharine, 192, 198, 290
Smith, Catrine, 190

Smith, Christian, 192
Smith, Church, 25
Smith, Daniel, 133
Smith, Edward, 289
Smith, Frederick, 260
Smith, George, 45, 133, 137, 239, 289
Smith, Henerey, 290
Smith, Henry, 88
Smith, Jacob, 88, 134, 135, 138
Smith, Jacob, Junior, 135, 136
Smith, James, 65, 261, 262
Smith, John, 65, 97, 137, 192, 215, 260, 261, 288, 308
Smith, John, Senior, 260
Smith, Joseph, 25, 98, 261
Smith, Leonard, 88
Smith, Michael, 136
Smith, Nathan, 260
Smith, Peter, 49
Smith, Philip, 136
Smith, Rebekah, 213
Smith, Robert, 65, 191, 225, 260, 304
Smith, Samuel, 261, 262
Smith, Simon, 88
Smith, Thomas, Junior, 65
Smith, Thomas, Senior, 65
Smith, Widow, 287, 290
Smith, William, 26, 43, 50, 289
Smitley, Philip, 88
Smock, Abraham, 214
Smock, Barnett, 214
Smock, Henry, 215
Smull, Andrew, 161
Sndyer, Henry, 50
Snearley, George, 289
Snearly, Michael, 289
Snider, Adam, 293
Snider, Gasper, 213
Snider, Jacob, 26
Snider, John, 24
Snider, Nicholas, 213
Snodgrass, John, 65
Snodgrass, Joseph, 65
Snodgrass, Mary, 65
Snodgrass, Richard, 65

Abstracts of Westmoreland County, Pennsylvania, Tax Records 1815

Snodgrass, William, 24
Snyder, Abraham, 88
Snyder, Adam, 65, 288
Snyder, Benjamin, 132
Snyder, Christena, 49
Snyder, Christian, 134
Snyder, Christopher, 134
Snyder, Daniel, 132
Snyder, George, 288
Snyder, Henry, 133
Snyder, Jacob, 43, 133
Snyder, John, 88, 138, 235, 305
Snyder, John, Junior, 43
Snyder, John, Senior, 44
Snyder, Nicholas, 65, 210
Snyder, Peter, 138
Snyder, Thomas, 83, 88
Sober, George, 304
Soffer, Henry, 45
Solinetine, Catherine, 294
Solinetine, Christopher, 294
Solinetine, Michael, 294
Solinger, John, 192, 193
Solinger, Peter, 192
Solobarger, Henry, 160
Sondels, Christopher, 52
Sourwine, Leonard, 235
Sowash, Abraham, 260
Sowash, Daniel, 214
Sowash, Isaac, 215
Sowash, Jacob, 194, 214
Sowash, John, 193
Sowash, Margaret, 214
Sowash, Peter, 194
Sower, George, 136
Sower, Michael, 136
Sowerwine, Jacob, 135
Sparr, Frederick, 135
Speace, George, 304
Spear, James, 305
Spear, John, 304
Spear, Robison, 305
Speck, Anna, 24
Spedman, David, 11
Speelman, David, 26, 160
Speelman, John, 26
Speelman, Jonas, 287

Speer, Mr, 280
Speer, William, 287
Speers, Noah, 214
Speers, Solomon, 215
Speers, William, 139
Spence, John, 215
Spence, Joseph, 215
Spence, Robert, 215
Spencer, Jacob, 192
Spiker, Christian, 304
Spong, Jacob, 134, 139
Spoon, 129
Spoul, Ralph, 236
Spring, Conrad, 44
Springer, Samuel, 46
Springher, Daniel, 213
Springher, John, 213
Sproul, James, 304
Sproul, Robert, 304
St. Clair, Arthur, 289
St. Clair, John Murray, 65
Stafford, James, 89
stage, 95
Stake, Michael, 138
Stam, Conrod, 161
Stanley, James, 304
Stanton, Matthew, 89
Stants, Jacob, 161
Starry, Martin, 137
States, Mathias, Senior, 65
Staugger, 213
Staut, Jonathan, 3
Staynor, John, 133
Staynor, Valentine, 133
Steefer, Conrad, 25
Steefer, George, 25
Steefer, Jacob, 24
Steel, Adam, 213
Steel, George, 64
Steel, James, 64
Steel, James, Junior, 161
Steel, James, Senior, 161
Steel, John, 161, 236
Steel, Joseph, 88
Steel, Mary, 162
Steel, Richard, 213
Steel, William, 65

Abstracts of Westmoreland County, Pennsylvania, Tax Records 1815

Steelsmith, Jacob, 135
Steen, John, 304
Steen, Robert, 304
steer, 221
Steinberger, John, 289
Steinmetz, John, 133
Steinmetz, Philip, 134
Stem, Conrad, 45
Stem, Jacob, 38
Stemnell, Philip, 262
Stencicum, Elias, 159
Stephen, Randles, 65
Stephens, Thomas, 215
Stephenson, James, 43, 193
Stephenson, Matthew, 24
Stephenson, Samuel, 138
Stephenson, William, 138
Sterret, Andrew, 24
Sterret, John, 260
Sterret, Moses, 43
Sterret, Thomas, 236
Sterrett, Andrew, 26
Steward, Edward, 288
Steward, Frederick, 136
Stewart, Alexander, 64, 304
Stewart, Archibald, 215
Stewart, Charles, 64
Stewart, George, 236
Stewart, Jacob, 65
Stewart, James, 214, 236, 305
Stewart, John, 88, 193, 215, 216,
    261, 304
Stewart, John, Senior, 304
Stewart, Robert, 193
Stewart, Samuel, 304, 305
Stewart, Thomas, 215
Stewart, William, 214, 236, 261,
    304
Stewart, William, Junior, 236
Stewart, Wm, 229, 307
Stickle, Simon, 161
still, 20, 33, 34, 35, 36, 37, 38,
    39, 40, 41, 43, 45, 47, 48,
    103, 105, 112, 113, 114, 115,
    118, 122, 124, 125, 128, 129,
    131, 134, 136, 137, 138, 139,
    142, 145, 146, 147, 150, 153,

154, 157, 158, 159, 162, 176,
181, 191, 196, 200, 202, 203,
206, 207, 208, 209, 210, 211,
212, 213, 214, 223, 224, 225,
226, 227, 229, 230, 231, 233,
235, 241, 242, 244, 245, 246,
248, 249, 250, 252, 253, 254,
257, 259, 260, 261, 263, 264,
267, 268, 269, 272, 273, 274,
275, 276, 279, 284, 285, 289,
291, *See also* distillery
Stillwell, Jackson, 261
Stimbel, Isaac, 260
Stimmel, Peter, 24
Stincicum, Larkin, 260
Stinemeatz, Philip, 89
Stirling, William, 25
Stirnell, Peter, 262
Stockberger, Frederick, 287
Stockberger, John, 287
Stockberger, Mathias, 287
Stockberger, Peter, 287
Stocklager, Peter, 44
Stockslager, Charles, 42
Stokeley, Thomas, 288
Stokely, Joseph, 132
Stokely, Nehimiah, 132
Stoner, Abraham, 44
Stoner, Christian, 45, 51
Stoner, John, 44
Stoops, John, 235
Stoops, Robert, 235
Stopplet, Samuel, 261
store, 139, 147, 155
Storey, Alexander, 138
Storey, Robert, 138
Storry, Al^x, 131
Story, Asher, 42
Story, Robert, 25, 304
Story, William, 65
Stosy, William, 25
Stouffer, 262
Stouffer, Christian, 44
Stouffer, Henry, 43
Stouffer, Jacob, 44
Stough, John, 134
Stout, Abraham, 25

Abstracts of Westmoreland County, Pennsylvania, Tax Records 1815

Taylor, Junior, William, 290
Taylor, Michael, 89
Taylor, Mordicy, 291
Taylor, Robert, 26, 194
Taylor, Thomas, 65, 305
Taylor, William, 290
Tayney, Micheal, 194
Taze, Isaac, 26
Teale, Jaby, 216
Teamer, Jonathan, 290
Teamer, Peter, 290
Tectter, Henry, 291
Tempele, John, 291
Temple, John, 194
tenant, 83, 105, 106, 117, 118,
    119, 122, 150, 153, 156, 159,
    160, 162, 164, 219, 223, 225,
    228, 230, 243, 244, 247, 251,
    262, 264, 289
Tenant, Samuel, 156
Tenny, Henry, 194
Thenderson, Richard, 164
Thomas, Barnet, 139
Thomas, Barney, 138
Thomas, Benjamin, 216
Thomas, Geo, 160
Thomas, Howel, 263
Thomas, Samuel, 216
Thomas, Stacy, 194
Thomas, Thomas, 216
Thompson, Alexander, 305
Thompson, Archibald, 305
Thompson, Brackenridge, 262
Thompson, Daniel, 27, 66
Thompson, David, 139
Thompson, Elizabeth, 27
Thompson, James, 194, 244,
    263, 290
Thompson, John, 27, 47, 89,
    139, 162, 164, 194, 262, 305
Thompson, Joseph, 194
Thompson, Mathew, 262
Thompson, Robert, 26, 27, 262
Thompson, Robert, Junior, 139
Thompson, Robert, Senior, 139
Thompson, Samuel, 194, 305
Thompson, Thomas, 51

Thompson, William, 140, 162,
    194, 263, 305
Thorn, Frederick, 162
Thorn, John, 290
Tinsman, Henry, 163
Tinstman, 213
Tinstman, Abraham, 47
Tinstman, Henry, 46
Tinstman, Jacob, 46
Tinstman, John, 47
Tinstman, Joseph, 42, 47
Tinstman, Matthias, 46
Tippins, James, 216
Tipton, John, 216
Tittle, James, 237
Tittle, Jeremiah, 291
Tittle, John, 291
Tittle, Jonathan, 291
Tittle, Peter, 291
Todd, James, 228, 237
Todd, Robert, 216
Tom, Daniel, 140
Tom, Jacob, 140
Tom, John, 237
Tomen, George, 51
Tompson, 214
Tooman, Jacob, 47
Toppins, Robert, 290
Toppper, John, 291
Torny, Joseph, 140
Torrance, Samuel, 237
Torrence, Hugh, Junior, 89
Torrence, Hugh, Senior, 89
Torrence, Samuel, 89
Totten, John, 139
Townsend, John, 305
Traugher, Christr, 290
Traugher, Henry, 162
Travers, John, 262
Traxall, Abraham, 162
Treece, William, 90
Trimble, Alexander, 27
Trimble, James, 27, 65, 237
Trimble, James, Senior, 27
Trimble, John, 263
Trimble, Joseph, 46
Trimble, Thomas, 65

377

Abstracts of Westmoreland County, Pennsylvania, Tax Records 1815

Trimble, William, 27
Trindle, William, 66
Trinton, Thomas, 49
Trip, William, 305
Trout, Baltzer, 237
Trout, George, 51
Trout, Henry, 139
Trout, John, 194
Trout, Michael, 47
Trout, Phillip, 162
Troxal, Henry, 139
Troxal, Jacob, 139
Troxel, John, 46
Truby, John, 140
Truby, Michael, 98, 140
Truxal, Adam, 140
Truxal, Daniel, 98
Truxal, Jacob, 290
Tub mill, 55, 60
Tumbleson, Nathaniel, 216
Tumbleson, Solomon, 216
Tunney, Daniel, 140
Tunney, John, 140
Turk, James, 305
Turnbleaser, Joseph, 90
Turner, Adam, 140
Turner, Isabella, 263
Turner, James, 291
Turner, Nathan, 216
Turner, Robert, 291
Turney, Adam, 98
Turney, Jacob, 98
Tweedy, John, 26
Twiney, Philip, 140
Typhert, Antony, 237
Typret, Philip, 237
Unkafair, George, 27
Unkafair, Peter, 305
Updegraff, Abreham, 263
Updegraff, Eli, 66
Updegraff, James, 66
Vance, Francis, 47
Vance, John, 47
Vance, William, 47
Vandike, William, 140
Vanhorn, Joseph, 263
Vankirk, Isaac, 216, 263

Vankirk, Joseph, 216
Vanleer, Daniel, 9
Vanlier, Daniel, 27
Vanmetre, John, 216
Vanmetre, John Senior, 216
Vanmetre, John, Junior, 216
Vanostrand, Peter, 216
Vantine, Thomas, 305
Varner, Abraham, 239
Varner, Andrew, 140
Varner, Jacob, 263
Varner, Michael, 263
Varner, Philip, 263
Varner, Widow, 140
Varnor, Abraham, 305
Varnor, Henry, 305
Vaughan, James, 90
Ventling, Adam, 141
Ventzel, Gutherywa, 140
Waddel, James, 28
Waddel, P. Joseph, 217
Wade, George, 292
Wade, John, 292
Wagaman, John, 90
Wagaman, Peter, 239
Waggoner, Andrew, 141
Waggoner, George, 195
Waggoner, John, 27, 141
Waggoner, Peter, 238
Waggoner, Solomon, 195
Waggoner, Widow, 141
Wagle, Abraham, 143
Wagle, Abraham, Junior, 143
Wagoner, Barney, 265
Walker, Alexander, 305
Walker, Anthony, 27
Walker, Ebenzer, 217
Walker, Henry, 163
Walker, Jacob, 66
Walker, John, 90, 263, 305
Walker, Mary, 217
Walker, William, 27
Walkins, Jeremiah, 218
Wallace, Charles, 195
Wallace, Daniel, 66
Wallace, George, 143
Wallace, Hugh, 66, 144, 264

Abstracts of Westmoreland County, Pennsylvania, Tax Records 1815

Wallace, John, 66, 143
Wallace, Mary, 163
Wallace, Peter, 27
Wallace, Robert, 48, 142
Wallace, Sam¹, 218
Wallace, Thomas, 265
Wallace, William, 66
Waller, Braglar, 238
Walse, Jacob, 181, 196
Walt, James, 195
Walter, Anthony, 91
Walter, Christian, 264
Walter, David, 90
Walter, George, 238, 292
Walter, Henry, 292
Walter, Jacob, 292
Walter, John, 48, 292
Walter, Peter, 142, 238, 291
Walter, Philip, 238
Walters, Henerey, 292
Walters, Jacob, 292, 293, 305, 306
Walters, John, 90
Walthaur, Christopher, 196
Walthaur, Dorothy, 195
Walthaur, Gasper, 195
Walthaur, Jacob, 196
Walthour, Jemina, 195
Walton, Barzella, 90
Walton, Boaz, 90
Walton, Jesse, 194
Walton, Joseph, 90
Walton, Samuel, 305
Walts, Solomon, 90
Waltz, Daniel, 263
Waltz, Jacob, 264
Wampler, Jacob, 195
Wanemaker, Peter, 143
Ward, Thomas, 217
Warden, Paul, 51
Warden, Samuel, 48, 51
Warren, Mary, 263
Warren, Thomas, 218
Wartz, John, 265
Waters, Daniel, 90
Waters, Jacob, 163, 164
Waters, John, 90

Waters, Nathan, 163
Waters, Samuel, 196
Waterson, James, 98, 143
Watkins, John, 218
Watson, David, 196
Watson, James, 264
Watson, Robert, 90, 306
Watt, John, 305
Watt, William, 305
Waugh, Michael, 28
Weagly, Joseph, 90
Weaver, Abraham, 141, 142
Weaver, Adam, 162
Weaver, Adam, Senior, 162
Weaver, Alexander, 263
Weaver, Benjamin, 195
Weaver, Daniel, 144, 265
Weaver, David, 141, 264
Weaver, Frederick, 28, 162
Weaver, Gasper, 162
Weaver, Jacob, 195, 216
Weaver, John, 141, 142, 196, 264
Weaver, Joseph, 264
Weaver, Martha, 264
Weaver, Nicholas, 141
Weaver, Peter, 52, 264
Weaver, William, 142, 264, 292
Weddel, B. Joseph, 218
Weigle, John, 90
Weigley, Joseph, 143, 239
Weimer, John, 66
Weimer, Widow, 142
Weirman, Samuel, 292
Weiser, Frederick, 143
Weister, Jacob, 305, 306
Weister, John, 306
Weister, Rudolph, 305
Welker, Jacob, 141
Wells, John, 98, 143
Wells, Richard, 217
Welsh, John, 28
Welsh, Joseph, 27
Welsh, Widow, 116, 141, 144
Welshons, Jacob, 48
Welshunts, Henry, 66
Welshunts, Jacob, 66
Welts, Conrad, 90

379

Welty, Henry, 98, 143
Wenter, Samuel, 48
Wentzel, John, 141
Wentzel, Philip, 141
Wertz, John, Junior, 47
Wertz, John, Senior, 48
West, Martin, 292
West, Samuel, 98
Weyland, Caleb, 142
Whann, John, 48
Wharton, Charles, 308
Wharton, James, 308
Wharton, Thomas, 308
wheelwright manufactory, 8
Whetmore, Joseph, 30
Whetsone, Abraham, 292
Whetton, William, 143
Whitagee, Andrew, 305
Whitagee, Martin, 305
White, Andrew, 291
White, Hannah, 28
White, Henry, 238
White, Jacob, 195, 306
White, James, 28, 48, 66, 291
White, John, 291
White, Joseph, 238
White, Peter, 30
White, Stephen, 51
White, William, 28, 306
Whitehead, Christopher, 196
Whitehead, Valentine, 195
Whitlinger, John, 91
Whitman, John, 28
Whitmore, Abraham, 163
Whitmore, Joseph, 237
Wibel, Andrew, 142
Wibel, Andrew, Senior, 142
Wibel, George, 142
Wibel, John, 142
Wibel, Joseph, 141
Wibel, Samuel, 142
Wibel, Stephen, 141
Wibel, Thomas, 142
Wible, Jacob, 264
Wible, John, 163
Wible, Thomas, 291
Wible, William, 163

Widdel, James, 217
widow, 2, 3, 5, 6, 11, 12, 15, 17,
    19, 20, 22, 23, 24, 28, 29, 35,
    37, 43, 44, 46, 49, 52, 53, 55,
    77, 80, 93, 94, 101, 104, 107,
    108, 109, 110, 112, 115, 116,
    118, 121, 123, 124, 125, 129,
    131, 135, 136, 140, 141, 142,
    143, 144, 156, 162, 168, 171,
    173, 177, 180, 185, 187, 188,
    192, 195, 199, 200, 204, 206,
    213, 214, 215, 217, 221, 222,
    227, 229, 230, 237, 239, 244,
    249, 250, 253, 254, 259, 263,
    264, 267, 270, 271, 275, 279,
    282, 284, 286, 287, 289,
    290, 293, 294, 295, 297, 298,
    300, 301, 302, 303, 304, 306
Wigal, Daniel, 263
Wight, Wm, 200
Wigle, Jacob, 217
Wilgus, Isaac, 218
Wilhifrd, Doc, 27
Williams, Adam, 143
Williams, Daniel, 91, 142
Williams, John, 98, 237, 292
Williams, Joseph, 66
Williams, Nathan, 98
Williams, Peter, 48
Williams, Robert, 66, 98, 143
Williams, Thomas, 143
Williamson, James, 238
Williamson, John, 237
Williamson, Joseph, 195
Williard, Frederick, 237
Williard, Gasper, 238, 306
Willson, Thomas, 239
Willson, William, 47, 52
Wilson, Barnabas, 196
Wilson, Charles, 263
Wilson, David, 217
Wilson, George, 194, 238
Wilson, Henry, 196
Wilson, Hugh, 141
Wilson, James, 66, 264
Wilson, James, Junior, 27, 30
Wilson, James, Senior, 28

Abstracts of Westmoreland County, Pennsylvania, Tax Records 1815

Wilson, John, 66
Wilson, Mary, 263
Wilson, Nancy, 217
Wilson, Samuel, 141
Wilson, Thomas, 66, 238, 292
Wilson, Widow, 143
Wilson, William, 163, 195
Wilyard, Christian, 142
Windland, Michael, 28
Wingert, Jacob, Junior, 142
Wingert, Jacob, Senior, 142
Wingert, John, 143
Winkler, William, 90
Winnings, Hannah, 28
Winter, John, 51
Wise, Henry, 98
Wise, John, 98
Wiseman, Samuel, 264
Wismer, Annanias, 66
Wisner, William, 66
Wolf, Christian, 305
Wolfhart, Jacob, 306
Wolfhart, John, 305
Wolgamat, Henry, 142
Woodruff, Anthony, 28
Woods, Alexander, 195
Woods, Henry, 308
Woods, James, Junior, 195
Woods, James, Senior, 195
Woods, John, 66, 194, 238
Woolsey, William, 217
Workman, Samuel, 292
Works, Andrew, 264
Worley, Daniel, 218
Worman, Daniel, 163
Worman, George, 163
Wortman, John, 217
Wortman, Joseph, 217
Wortman, Lot, Junior, 217
Wortmand, Lot, Senior, 218
Woviel, Isaac, 28
Wright, Benjamin, 31, 292
Wright, Hugh, 217
Wright, James, 264
Wright, John, 217
Wright, Philip, 217
Wyand, John, 143

Wyands, John, 114
Wyandt, Daniel, 51
Wyandt, David, 51
Wyandt, Jacob, 51
Wyandt, John, Senior, 48
Wybel, George, 143
Wyble, George, 133
Wybler, George, 142
Wylie, Albert, 238
Wylie, Hugh, 238
Wylie, James, 66
Wylie, John, 305
Wylie, Robert, 238, 292, 305
Wylie, Sampson, 195
Wylie, William, 66, 90, 217
Wyrin, Jonathan, 141
Yaw, Laurence, 48
Yentsler, Martin, 164
Yerger, 99
Yockey, Christian, 306
Yockey, Christian, Junior, 306
Yockey, Christian, Senior, 306
Yockey, Henry, 306
Yockey, Widow, 306
Yode, Henry, 163
Yolden, John, 293
Yolden, Widow, 293
Yolden, William, 292
Young, Alexander, 293
Young, David, 293
Young, James, 28, 239
Young, John, 67, 99, 144, 239, 306
Young, John, Junior, 239
Young, John, Senior, 239
Young, Joseph, 99, 306
Young, Mary, 239
Young, Thomas, 239
Young, W John, 306
Young, William, 144
Younkins, Michael, 306
Zimmerman, Jacob, 144
Zimmerman, Peter, 144
Zleer, Conrad, 163
Zleer, John, 163
Zleer, Philip, 163
Zuick, David, 144

Abstracts of Westmoreland County, Pennsylvania,
Tax Records 1815